THREE ASPECTS OF POLICY AND POLICYMAKING:
KNOWLEDGE, DATA AND INSTITUTIONS

CARNEGIE – ROCHESTER CONFERENCE SERIES ON PUBLIC POLICY

A supplementary series to the Journal of Monetary Economics

Editors

KARL BRUNNER
ALLAN H. MELTZER

Advisory Committee

CARL CHRIST
JACOB FRENKEL
PIETER KORTEWEG
DAVID LAIDLER
WILLIAM POOLE

Production Editor

KATHLEEN FERRARO

VOLUME 10

NORTH-HOLLAND PUBLISHING COMPANY
AMSTERDAM • NEW YORK • OXFORD

Three Aspects of
POLICY AND POLICYMAKING
Knowledge, Data and Institutions

Editors

KARL BRUNNER

Graduate School of Management
The University of Rochester

ALLAN H. MELTZER

Carnegie-Mellon University

1979

NORTH-HOLLAND PUBLISHING COMPANY
AMSTERDAM • NEW YORK • OXFORD

ISBN: 0 444 85331 6

Publishers:
NORTH-HOLLAND PUBLISHING COMPANY
AMSTERDAM • NEW YORK • OXFORD

Sole distributors for the U.S.A. and Canada:
ELSEVIER NORTH-HOLLAND, INC.
52 VANDERBILT AVENUE,
NEW YORK, N.Y. 10017

Library of Congress Cataloging in Publication Data
Main entry under title:

Three aspects of policy and policymaking.

  (Carnegie-Rochester conference series on public policy ; v. 10)
  "A supplement to the Journal of monetary economics ... [containing] papers presented at the April 1978 conference."
  1. Monetary policy--Congresses. 2. Economic policy--Congresses. 3. Policy sciences--Congresses.
I. Brunner, Karl, 1916-   II. Meltzer, Allan H.
III. Series.
HG221.T46   332.4'6   79-12445
ISBN 0-444-85331-6

PRINTED IN THE NETHERLANDS

Introduction to the Series

The Carnegie-Rochester Conference on Public Policy was initiated several years ago through the efforts of the Center for Research in Government Policy and Business at the University of Rochester and the Center for the Study of Public Policy at Carnegie-Mellon University. This book is the tenth volume in the series which presents the papers prepared for the conferences, plus the comments of discussants and participants.

Policies depend not only on theories and evidence, but on the structure of policymaking bodies and the procedures by which policies are made, implemented, and changed. The conferences direct the attention of economists to major problems of economic policy and institutional arrangements. We hope that the papers and the conferences will encourage further research on policy and on the effects of national agencies and international institutions on the choice of policies.

The Carnegie-Rochester Conference is an open forum. Participants are united by their interest in the issues discussed and by their belief that analysis, evidence, and informed discussion have lasting effects on the public and its institutions.

This tenth volume of the series, offered as a supplement to the *Journal of Monetary Economics*, contains papers presented at the April 1978 conference. Future volumes of the conference proceedings will be mailed to subscribers as a supplement to the journal. The editor of the journal will consider for publication comments on the papers published in the supplement.

Acknowledgement is made of the support of the National Science Foundation for the April 1978 conference and production of this volume. We are pleased to acknowledge the assistance of Jean Morris and Jean Patterson with the conference arrangements. Phyllis McLaughlin typeset the volume.

K. BRUNNER
A.H. MELTZER
Editors

Contents

THREE ASPECTS OF POLICY AND POLICYMAKING:
KNOWLEDGE, DATA AND INSTITUTIONS

Karl BRUNNER
University of Rochester

and

Allan H. MELTZER
Carnegie-Mellon University

Socio-political conditions and cognitive interests subtly mesh in all human actions and decisions. This interaction is most noteworthy in matters bearing on the nature of policy and policymaking where the decisions and the procedures are conditioned by the quality of the information about the environment addressed by the policymaker and by the social arrangements in which the decision process is embedded. The social context shapes the incentive structure affecting the decision-maker's use of information. The socio-political context affects the quality and range of information invested in policymaking.

The six papers presented at the 11th Carnegie-Rochester Conference on Public Policy, held on April 28-29, 1978 at the University of Rochester, dealt with specific aspects of these issues. The first set of papers prepared by Arnold Zellner and G. William Schwert addresses some issues arising in the literature on rational evaluation of policymaking. The second set, authored by Jeffrey M. Perloff and Michael L. Wachter and by Kenneth W. Clarkson and Roger E. Meiners, examines important data problems faced by policymakers. The last set of papers, by Rachel McCulloch and by David I. Meiselman and Paul Craig Roberts, discusses some socio-political institutions and attempts to evaluate their role in the development of policies.

I. Causality

Some years ago new techniques for testing "causal patterns" were derived from the work of Wiener and Granger. These statistical techniques were increasingly applied to test for causality in the relation between money and income, money and prices, between different monetary aggregates, or between monetary aggregates and interest rates, or between selected policy variables and monetary aggregates. The novelty of the procedure assured the studies some acceptance.

The first session of the Conference was devoted to a critical examination and interpretation of the causality tests developed in recent years. In his paper on "Causality and Econometrics," Arnold Zellner surveys a range of conceptual and logical issues associated with recent developments. Zellner juxtaposes the "philosophical definition" of causality developed by philosophers of science with the Wiener-Granger notion. He finds the latter comparatively deficient in operational terms. The contributions made by Basmann, Strotz and Wold, and Simon to the clarification of the causality problem are also probed. Zellner notes that the Basmann definition is almost equivalent to the philosophic definition whereas the Strotz and Wold definition forms a narrow special case of this definition. Herbert Simon's definition does not involve a statement about the world; it is a meta-linguistic statement about the logical structure of theories.

Zellner finds that the Wiener-Granger definition of causality is burdened with restrictions that impair its usefulness in a systematic exploration of causal patterns. With respect to tests of causality, Zellner concludes "that results from these tests are inconclusive. This inconclusiveness reflects in the author's judgment the increasing disposition to sacrifice considerations of subject matter bearing on the formulation of hypotheses for statistical or technical sophistication." The mechanical application of causality tests appears in Zellner's examination "as an extreme form of 'measurement without theory.'"

The paper by G. William Schwert, "Tests of Causality," supplements Zellner's investigation of the concept. Schwert's analysis of the statistical procedures used in the tests leads him to the following conclusions: "First, the distributed lag coefficients between the innovations can be very different in pattern and magnitude from the distributed lag coefficients between the original variables, depending on the form of the ARIMA models for the variables. Second, statistical tests based on residuals from estimated ARIMA models may accept the null hypothesis of series independence too frequently. Third, existing statistical tests based on the sample cross-correlations between residual series may have low power against plausible alternative hypotheses, especially when short measurement intervals, such as a week or a month, are used."

Schwert elaborates, with detailed examples, the inadequate logical basis of the inference procedure associated with the new causality tests. His examination leads him to distinguish "causality" from "incremental predictability." This distinction is particularly important in view of the relevance of properly recognized causal relations as instruments of rational policymaking. Schwert demonstrates that the "causality tests" under consideration are seriously mislabelled. They do not offer any relevant tests bearing on purported causal

2

relations. They offer, instead, useful tests about the "content of incremental predictability." The examples indicate that in systems with intelligent agents, in contrast to engineering systems, "incremental predictive content" is neither a necessary nor a sufficient condition of causality.

Both papers recognize an old issue in recent applications of time series analysis to causality tests. Both find it useful to emphasize that even "sophisticated" manipulation of data offers no relevant information in the absence of a tentatively formulated theory or hypothesis submitted for assessment, or a highly corroborated theory used for interpretation.

II. Measurement

The second set of papers raises issues about the meaning and measurement of widely used data. Measures of the output gap and unemployment hold a central role in the traditional analysis of stabilization policies. These measures also affect the evaluation of evolving states and condition the desired course of monetary and fiscal policy. The large output gap allegedly existing in 1977-78 was used to justify proposals for greater monetary and fiscal expansion. The comparatively high level of measured unemployment was frequently used as evidence of a deficiency in aggregate demand requiring some revision in monetary and fiscal policy.

The heavy burden imposed on measures of the output gap and unemployment justifies a critical examination of these notions. A reexamination of the issues is particularly desirable in view of the massive changes in relative prices associated with a major input (i.e., energy) into the aggregate production process. Jeffrey M. Perloff and Michael L. Wachter investigate the measurement of the output gap in their paper, "A Production Function--Nonaccelerating Inflation Approach to Potential Output.

For many years, Arthur Okun's formulation has dominated professional thinking about the output gap and its relation to unemployment. Okun assumed that the output gap is proportional to the difference between actual unemployment and a fixed rate of unemployment that Okun regarded as "noninflationary unemployment." Other measures of potential output and the output gap had even less relation to economic analysis. They resulted from essentially mechanical fitting along the peaks of the observed time path of output. Perloff and Wachter base their concept of potential output on a production function with capital, labor, and energy as input categories. The labor input required to produce potential output is computed according to the noninflationary level of unemployment determined by a specification of the Phillips curve used for this purpose. This approach produces substantially lower estimates of potential output than most of the existing figures based on exponential fitting or the Okun formula. The difference emerges according to the authors from three reasons:

(a) The noninflationary level of unemployment is not assumed to be at 4 percent but is estimated to be 5.5 percent.

(b) The production function approach produces a measure of potential output occasionally below as well as above actual output. This contrasts with the results of fitting along the peaks of actual output or computations based on some minimal unemployment level.

(c) A translog expression with variable coefficients is used in lieu of a more restrictive production function. The inclusion of energy in the function opens a channel of impact neglected in older procedures.

The paper by Perloff and Wachter raises some additional issues about the influences shaping the noninflationary level of unemployment. It stirs any attentive reader to probe more fundamentally the very notion of a potential output and the relevance of an "output gap."

Kenneth W. Clarkson and Roger E. Meiners address the increasing average level of unemployment observed by Perloff and Wachter and others. Their paper on "Institutional Changes, Reported Unemployment and Induced Institutional Changes" explores the effect on the average level of measured unemployment of policies and new arrangements introduced by government actions. The authors examine, particularly, the impact of the specifications built into the food stamp plan. Beneficiaries under the program must register for work at the employment service. The food stamp plan thus offers an incentive for individuals to be counted among the measured unemployed even in the absence of any relevant intent to enter the labor force and search for or accept work. The authors estimate that these incentives raise the average level of unemployment by one percentage point. Other arrangements raising the unemployment level are noted in their paper.

The authors conclude their investigations with the following passage: "There has been a permanent increase in the number of individuals included in the unemployment statistics. The increase represents individuals excluded from the labor force (the minimum wage law), individuals who find work less attractive (the magnitude and duration of unemployment benefits), and individuals who are not seeking work, but must register for work as a condition for receiving welfare benefits (the work registration requirement). Thus, we find the circle is complete: changes in our institutions (the work registration requirements) have permanently altered official unemployment statistics (a permanent higher reported level), which in turn can be linked to new changes in institutions (public programs to reduce unemployment)."

4

The authors' interpretation of the rising average level of measured unemployment has an important implication for policy and suggests a probing question for policymakers. The implication cautions us that any attempt to execute the mandate of the Humphrey-Hawkins bill with the application of monetary and fiscal policies will produce inflation without lowering average unemployment levels. The most important question addressed to policymakers, and professional economists, involves the nature of institutional changes assuring a better approximation to socially optimal levels of unemployment and the development of relevant measures of actual unemployment.

III. Institutions

Policy proposals and policymaking do not proceed in a social or political vacuum. The socio-political environment conditions the range of questions selected for attention and affects in many ways the answers or "solutions" produced by policy institutions. Some aspects of these issues are addressed by Rachel McCulloch in her paper on "North-South Economic and Political Relations" and in the paper jointly authored by David I. Meiselman and Paul Craig Roberts on "The Political Economy of the Congressional Budget Office."

McCulloch examines the so-called North-South problem in the context of the developments within the United Nations for a "New International Economic Order." In the early years of this decade, the countries of the "Third World" exploited the favorable opportunities encountered in international organizations. These countries advanced, with much political clamor, the demand for a "New International Economic Order" (NIEO) adjusted to the "new political reality" resulting from the substantial Third World presence in the United Nations.

Much of the initial momentum has been lost in recent years in the author's judgment. But she cautions us that the modest record achieved by the Third World still includes some new changes. ". . .[T]hree important developments. . . have come about or at least been pressed forward as a result of protracted negotiations. These concern the perceived requirements for LDC economic progress and even the appropriate ways in which this progress should be gauged, the actual and potential importance of the LDCs as a force in the international economy, and the political role of the LDCs in the major international organizations."

McCulloch's contribution concentrates on three major aspects of the socio-political development. It examines, first, the political evolution of the thrust for a new order. Changing conditions and shifting perceptions, particularly in the "North," eroded the political momentum. "The illusion that real progress for that billion or so living in conditions of absolute poverty was either a primary motivation or a likely outcome of the NIEO" could no longer be supported in the author's view.

The economic issues form the second theme of the paper. The proposal for a NIEO opened with a detailed list of demands addressed to the First World. The ensuing negotiations eventually transformed the endeavor into a "rescue operation for the established social and political order" in the Third World. Any attention to fundamental changes conducive to long-run economic growth was sidetracked. This observation applies to the trade policies of the "North" and particularly to the domestic policies of the "South." The author concludes her investigation with a discussion of the contradictions and conflicts bearing on broad socio-political issues within the North and between "North and South."

The study by Meiselman and Roberts evaluates a new policy institution. The Congressional Budget Office was constituted by the Congressional Budget and Impoundment Control Act of 1974. The authors survey briefly the wide array of problems which attract the C.B.O.'s attention. But the examination concentrates mainly on studies relating to economic stabilization or macro-policy. One section discusses the conception governing the C.B.O.'s view of the world. This view is summarized in a macro-model derived by simplifying a group of large scale econometric models. The resulting "Multipliers Model" reflects, in the authors' judgment, the comparatively "unsophisticated" Keynesianism of the early 1950s. The nominal values determined by the Multipliers Model yield no information about the price-level or real variables.

The C.B.O. supplements the traditional Keynesian cross analysis with a set of price-wage equations. The solution of this set implies that wage movements are dominated by the past evolution of the measured unemployment rate and by changes in wholesale farm and fuel prices. Wage and price movements are not connected to the Basic Multipliers Model. The price-wage process operates independently of the multiplier process, and the multiplier process is not affected by the price-wage process. Real variables, on the other hand, are simultaneously affected by the two independent processes.

The authors note the traditional concentration on short-run responses in the Multipliers Model. The C.B.O.'s explicit attempt at longer run analysis is judged to be a failure. It "has demand without supply, inflation without money, interest rates without capital, outputs without inputs, employment without wage rates and a labor market, and investment without saving or any change in the capital stock." After reviewing the C.B.O.'s most recent fiscal analysis, the authors conclude that the system's responses to fiscal actions conditioned by supply behavior have not been seriously considered so far.

The last section discusses important issues in the political economy of fiscal policymaking including the effect of the C.B.O. on the behavior of Congress. In the authors' judgment, "it is difficult to conclude that the new budget process has changed the incentives that produced the 'over-spending' (deficits) and the perceived lack of expenditure control. . ." They believe that the diverse motivations that encouraged Congress to approve the Budget Control Act of 1974 cannot be satisfied simultaneously by the operation of the budget process. The authors are convinced that the new arrangement "institutionalized Keynesian fiscal policy rather than budget balance as the concept of budget control," so they do not expect balanced budgets to be observed with great frequency.

Each of the three sessions challenged established procedures or notions. They also questioned influential policy institutions. The reader should therefore consult the comments and discussions contributed by a number of participants and the responses of some of the authors. Charles R. Nelson and Christopher A. Sims address the causality issue argued by Zellner and Schwert. A brief reply by Arnold Zellner is also included. Walter Oi commented on the paper by Kenneth W. Clarkson and Roger E. Meiners. The paper by Perloff and Wachter unleashed some very probing contributions by John A. Tatom, Charles I. Plosser and G. William Schwert, and Robert J. Gordon to which Perloff and Wachter replied. Lastly, the Meiselman and Roberts paper created substantial controversy. The reader will find it useful to ponder the critical comments by Frank de Leeuw, Marvin Phaup, and Alice M. Rivlin.

CAUSALITY AND ECONOMETRICS

Arnold ZELLNER*

University of Chicago

I. Introduction

Although the concept of causality has been treated extensively in the philosophical literature and used extensively in interpreting data in many sciences including econometrics, almost all, if not all, textbooks treating the methodology of econometrics, that is, econometric theory and/or principles, exclude terms like *causality* and *cause* from their subject indexes. Indeed these econometrics textbooks also say little, if anything, even about the age-old issue of the relationship between the concepts of correlation and causality.

The glaring failure of econometrics texts to treat the fundamental concept of causality could be excused if this concept were irrelevant to or unimportant for economics and econometrics. That such is not the case is easily established by taking note of the following observations:

1.   On the opening page of Stigler's (1949, p. 3) influential textbook on price theory, he writes, "The important purpose of a scientific law is to permit prediction, and prediction is in turn sought because it permits control over phenomena. That control requires prediction is self-evident, for unless one knows what 'causes' a particular phenomenon, one cannot effect or prevent its occurrence." Although the word *causes* in this quotation is central, it is not defined, perhaps because its meaning is thought to be self-evident or, more likely, because its meaning is rather controversial, hence the use of quotation marks. Be that as it may, causation is clearly a central concept in Stigler's discussion of the purpose of scientific laws that appear in price theory and econometrics.

2.   Cowles Commission Monograph 14, *Studies in Econometric Method*, edited by T.C. Koopmans and W.C. Hood, a key contribution to the development of econometrics, includes a paper by H. Simon (1953) on the nature of causal orderings.

3.   In the 1950s and 1960s, controversies regarding the causal interpretation of econometric models involving H.A.O. Wold, R.L. Basmann, R.H. Strotz, and others raged in the literature, giving evidence of much concern and no little confusion regarding the causal interpretation of fully recursive and interdependent or simultaneous econometric models. Given confusion about the

* Research financed in part by National Science Foundation Grant 77-15662 and by income from the H.G.B. Alexander Endowment Fund, Graduate School of Business, University of Chicago.

9

causal interpretation of econometric models, there was also confusion regarding the relation of these models to the scientific laws that they were supposed to represent.

4.   The more recent economic and econometric literature abounds with papers in which the Wiener-Granger concept of causality appears. In addition, various tests of causality have been formulated and applied, sometimes with startling results.

The few observations listed above, and many more that could be added, testify to the importance of the concept of causality in economics and econometrics. The fact that many textbooks have little or nothing to say about causality is thus considered to be an important omission, one that may be in large part responsible for the difficulties that some have in understanding the results of recent analyses that purport to be tests of causality.

Further difficulties in understanding recent analyses of causality are produced by statements like that of T. Sargent (1977, p. 216):

> It is true that Granger's definition of a causal relation does *not*, in general, coincide with the economist's usual definition of one: namely, a relation that is invariant with respect to interventions in the form of imposed changes in the processes governing the causing variables.

The statement is accompanied by the following footnote:

> Sims suggests to me that it is not really so clear that economists' use of the word cause typically coincides with "invariance under an intervention" rather than "a one-sided relation with a strictly exogenous variable on the right-hand side." Certainly in the mathematics and engineering literature the concept of a causal relation coincides with the latter one.

From these statements, it seems apparent that the man in the street may not be the only one who is at a loss to understand the nature of causality and causal relations.

Further, in his Report on the NBER-NSF Seminar on Time Series (1977), C.F. Ansley states:

Granger said that he wanted to clarify the notion of causality. Causality is defined as a reduction in forecasting variance with respect to a given information set; this idea dated back to Wiener. The various tests that had been proposed were equivalent only in the population, not in the sample. Given a stationary series, one should use postsample forecasting as a test. Cross-correlation methods are tests of identification [in the time series analysts' sense] only. (p.20)

While Ansley's statement may provide clarification for some, it is pertinent to note that Granger and Newbold (1977) write:

It is doubtful that philosophers would completely accept this definition [their definition of causality], and possibly *cause* is too strong a term, or one too emotionally laden, to be used. A better term might be *temporally related*, but since cause is such a simple term we shall continue to use it. (p.225)

While the five letter word *cause* is indeed a simple word, Granger and Newbold's remarks attest to the fact, long appreciated by philosophers, that cause is a rather subtle and difficult concept, which is not completely synonymous with *temporally related* or with *a reduction in forecasting variance with respect to a given information set.*

The discussion presented above reveals that concepts of causation, causality, cause, causal relations, etc. have been important in economics and econometrics. Indeed Simon (1953) writes, "The most orthodox of empiricists and antideterminists can use the term 'cause,' as we shall define it, with a clear conscience" (p.51). As this statement implies, a satisfactory definition of cause is relevant for many. However, as is clear from the above discussion, many different definitions of cause, causation, causal relation, etc. have appeared in the literature, some of them inconsistent with each other and inconsistent with definitions provided by philosophers. There is thus a need to reconsider these definitions and try to arrive at a better understanding of the issues involved and how they relate to current econometric practice.

In what follows, I will attempt to arrive at a better understanding of causation and associated concepts. I will begin by reviewing a philosophical definition of causation and its implications in Section II. In Section III, the discussion in Section II will be brought to bear on some major definitions of causation that have appeared in the econometric literature. In Section IV, the

11

implications of the preceding sections for tests of causality will be explored. Finally, in Section V, a summary of findings and some concluding remarks will be presented.

II. Review of a Philosophical Definition of Causality and Its Implications

At the end of the last section, we recognized a need for a clear-cut definition of causation. Fortunately, a sophisticatedly simple and deep definition of causation is available in a paper by H. Feigl (1953), which "was written with the purpose of summarizing succinctly some results of the logical and methodological analyses of the concept of causation" (n., p. 408). According to Feigl:

> The clarified (purified) concept of causation is defined in terms of *predictability according to a law* (or more adequately, according to a set of laws). (p. 408)

This deceptively simple definition is noteworthy both for what it includes and what it excludes. Most importantly it links causation *not just to predictability* but to *predictability according to a law or set of laws*. According to this philosophical definition, predictability without a law or set of laws, or as econometricians might put it, without theory, is *not* causation. As will be seen, linking predictability to a law or set of laws is critical in appraising various tests of causality that have appeared in the econometric literature. This view also coincides with that of Jeffreys (1967), who remarks that the most important part of our knowledge "consists of making inferences from past experience to predict future experience. This part may be called generalization or induction" (p. 1). Jeffreys emphasizes the important role of laws, such as Newton's or Einstein's laws, in efforts to predict future experience or as yet unobserved outcomes. With respect to causality, Jeffreys (1957) writes, "If we can say with high probability that a set of circumstances would be followed by another set, that is enough for our purposes" (p. 190). Since, for Jeffreys, the process of prediction is identified with generalization, his concept of causality is very close to that presented above. Note, however, that Jeffreys mentions "a high probability," while Feigl does not similarly qualify his use of the term *predictability*. Consideration will be given to this point below.

In his definition of causation, Feigl speaks of the "clarified (purified) concept of causation." By *clarified* or *purified*, he means a concept of causation that is purged of "metaphysical, i.e. in principle unconfirmable, connotations that had traditionally obscured, if not eclipsed, the only meaning of causation that is logically tenable and methodologically adequate and fruitful" (p. 408).

12

What are some of these so-called unconfirmable connotations? First, there is the teleological conception (final cause or causes, considered by Aristotle and others). According to Feigl, final cause is eliminated from the modern concept of causation. In this connection, it is interesting to consider J.M. Keynes's (1921) analysis of the issue of final causes. Keynes writes:

> The discussion of *final* causes and of the argument from design has suffered confusion from its supposed connection with theology. But the logical problem is plain and can be determined upon formal and abstract considerations. The argument is in all cases simply this--an event has occurred and has been observed which would be very improbable *a priori* if we did not know that it had actually happened; on the other hand, the event is of such a character that it might have been not unreasonably predicted if we had assumed the existence of a conscious agent whose motives are of a certain kind and whose powers are sufficient. (p. 297)

Keynes then provides the following analysis of the problem:

> Let h be our original *data*, a the occurrence of the event, b the existence of the supposed conscious agent. Then a/h [the probability of a given h] is assumed very small in comparison with a/bh [the probability of a given b and h]; and we require b/ah [the probability of b given a and h], the probability, that is to say, of b after a is known. The inverse principle of probability [Bayes's theorem]. . .shows that $b/ah = a/bh \cdot \dfrac{b/h}{a/h}$, and b/ah is therefore not determinate in terms of a/bh and a/h alone. Thus we cannot measure the probability of the conscious agent's existence *after* the event, unless we can measure its probability *before* the event. . . .The argument tells us that the existence of the hypothetical agent is more likely after the event than before it; but, . . .unless there is an appreciable probability first, there cannot be an appreciable probability afterwards. No conclusion, therefore which is worth having, can be based on the argument from design *alone*; like induction, this type of argument can only strengthen the probability of conclusions, for which there is something to be said on *other* grounds. (p. 298)

Keynes has thus shown that the hypothesis of final causes can be subjected to scientific logical analysis and that the critical result that emerges is one of degree of confirmation; that is, if the initial or prior probability (*b/h* in Keynes's notation) is very small, the posterior probability (*b/ah*) will also be very small under Keynes's conditions. This does not lead to a "conclusion worth having." This analysis has relevance for those who argue that an unusual event, for example, World War I or the Great Depression of the 1930s, is the result of some final cause or grand design. Unless there are other grounds or evidence leading to enhancing the value of our prior probability, the result of Keynes's analysis will be an inconclusive result regarding the hypothesis that the supposed conscious agent or grand design exists.

In closing this discussion of final causes or grand design, it is important to point out that Keynes's analysis indicates that these concepts are not to be ruled out a priori. The concepts, according to Keynes, are amenable to scientific deductive and inductive analysis. This important finding is in accord with one of Jeffreys's rules governing any theory of scientific learning or induction, namely, Jeffreys's (1967) Rule 5, which states, "The theory must not deny any empirical proposition *a priori*; any precisely stated empirical proposition must be formally capable of being accepted. . .given a moderate amount of relevant evidence" (p. 9).

A second conception of causation that Feigl has purged from his modern definition is the animistic conception. He explains that the animistic conception of causation implies that:

> there is an internal (but unconfirmable) compulsion (conceived anthropomorphically in analogy to coercion as experienced on the human level when forced against our own impulses), which supposedly accounts for the invariable connection of causes with their effects. One fallacious inference from this conception is the doctrine of *fatalism*. (p. 408)

Taking a cue from Keynes's treatment of final causes, I think it may be possible to sharpen and explicate the animistic concept to render it in the form of a clear-cut empirical proposition. If this were done, it seems that an analysis similar to Keynes's analysis of final causes would apply. In this case, however, the hypothesis of the existence of an internal compulsion would replace the hypothesis of the existence of a final cause. The proposition would then become susceptible to empirical investigation in accord with Jeffreys's theory of scientific induction, and the application of Keynes's analysis would lead to a conclusion similar to that reached in the case of his analysis of final causes. Since the animistic concept of causation is sometimes encountered in the economic and historical literature in the guise of "A is the inevitable consequence of B by the very nature of the circumstances," having an explicit analysis of the nature of such statements is valuable.

The third concept of causation eliminated by Feigl is "the *rationalistic* conception which identifies (I should say, confuses) the causal relation with the logical relation of implication (or entailment)" (p. 408). Feigl says that this conception of causation was repudiated by Hume and that attempts by Kant and others to revive a conception of causation based on conceptions of logical identity, entailment, or necessity "may be said to have failed (for diverse reasons such as mistaken conceptions of logical identity or necessity, . . .)" (p. 408).

The rationalistic conception of causality is rejected, because it conflicts with basic principles of scientific methodology that distinguish the rules of induction and deduction in scientific work. As Jeffreys (1967) puts it:

> Traditional or deductive logic admits only three attitudes to
> any proposition: definite proof, disproof, or blank ignorance.
> But no number of previous instances of a rule [or law] will
> provide a deductive proof that the rule [or law] will hold in
> a new instance. There is always the formal possibility of an
> exception. (pp. 1-2)

This statement embodies the negative findings of Hume's analysis of the nature of causality, namely that there is no logically necessary relationship connecting cause and effect. Jeffreys (1967) comments further that in much writing on scientific method there is a "tendency to claim that scientific method can be reduced in some way to deductive logic, which is the most fundamental fallacy of all: it can be done only by rejecting its chief feature, induction" (p. 2). Jeffreys (1957) also states, ". . .inference from past observations to future ones is not deductive. The observations not yet made may concern events either in the future or simply at places not yet inspected. It is technically called induction. . . .There is an element of uncertainty in all inferences of the kind considered" (p. 13).

The unavoidable uncertainty involved in making inferences from past data to as yet unobserved data is a basic reason for rejecting the rationalistic conception of causality, which involves the concept of deductive logical necessity, or entailment. Thus, using deduction to prove that, according to economic theory,

15

event *A* must produce or cause event *B* obviously does not imply that there is a logical necessity that event *B* will actually be observed given the occurrence of *A*. What is needed in such a case is an application of inductive logic that would produce a statement like "Given the occurrence of *A*, *B* will *probably* occur." Most important, there is no element of deductive logical necessity in this last statement. The appropriate concept of probability to be utilized in such a statement yielded by inductive logic and the quantification of the phrase *will probably occur* are issues treated at length by Jeffreys (1957, 1967) in his development of a theory of scientific induction. He states, ". . .*the essence of the present theory* is that no probability. . .is simply a frequency. The fundamental idea is that of a reasonable degree of belief, which satisfies certain rules of consistency and can in consequence of these rules be formally expressed by numbers. . ." (1967, p. 401).

Thus, Jeffreys, along with Hume, provides compelling arguments against the rationalistic conception of causality. Further, while perhaps more controversial, Jeffreys's theory of scientific induction requires a particular concept of probability, and in his work he provides many applied analyses illustrating how his concept of probability can be employed to obtain numerical probabilities associated with alternative laws, models, or hypotheses, many of which are frequently encountered in econometrics. In summary, the deductive, rationalistic conception of causality is considered inappropriate and can be replaced by one grounded in inductive rather than deductive logic.

Returning to Feigl's definition of causality, we see that it involves the concept of "laws." It is relevant to consider the types and forms of laws and the domains and levels of their application. Feigl (1953) presents the following list of characteristics:

A. *Types of Laws*

    1. Deterministic
    2. Statistical

B. *Forms of Laws*
    1. Qualitative
    2. Semi-quantitative (topological)
    3. Fully quantitative (metrical)

C. *Domains of Laws*

    1. Temporal (sequential)
    2. Coexistential (simultaneous)

D. Levels of Laws

1. Macro
2. Micro

In addition, he recognizes that certain laws may have combinations of these characteristics.

Although the above list may not be all inclusive, it does contain many of the characteristics of laws. A brief discussion of these characteristics is worth undertaking. With respect to deterministic laws and determinism, Feigl writes:

> The principle of determinism [i.e., ideally complete and precise predictability, given the momentary conditions, the pertinent laws, and the required mathematical techniques] may therefore be interpreted as a--to be sure, very bold and hence extremely problematic--hypothesis concerning the order of nature. (p. 412)

He goes on to say that most of the younger-generation physicists have definitely abandoned determinism. Jeffreys (1967) also writes, "We must also reject what is variously called the principle of causality, determinism, or the uniformity of nature, in any such form as 'Precisely similar antecedents lead to precisely similar consequences'" (p. 11). He explains that no two sets of antecedents are ever identical. He even rejects a looser form of determinism such as "In precisely the same circumstances very similar things can be observed, or very similar things can usually be observed," with the observations that "If 'precisely the same' is intended to be a matter of absolute truth, we cannot achieve it" (pp. 11-12). He also states:

> The most that can be done is to make those conditions the same that we believe to be relevant--"the same" can never in practice mean more than "the same as far as we know", and usually means a great deal less. The question then arises, How do we know that the neglected variables are irrelevant? Only by actually allowing them to vary and verifying that there is no associated variation in the result; but this requires the use of significance tests, a theory of which must therefore be given before there is any application of the principle, and when it is given it is found that the principle is no longer needed. . .(p. 12)

17

While the existence of quantum theory, a probabilistic theory, is often cited as evidence against determinism, Jeffreys's critique of determinism goes much deeper and relates to the operational uses of systems, not just their deductive logical structure. Thus, Burks's (1977) observations that "John von Neumann argues that quantum mechanical systems are inherently probabilistic and cannot be embedded in deterministic systems" (p. 589), and that "Einstein believed that when a complete theory of quantum phenomena is developed, it will be deterministic" (p. 590), while interesting, do not have much bearing on the issues raised by Jeffreys's critique of determinism. It is thus concluded that laws to which Feigl's definition of causality relates are in the main, if not exclusively, nondeterministic, statistical or probabilistic laws.

Next, we take up the forms of laws. There does not appear to be any compelling reason to limit the concept of causality to laws that are "fully quantitative (metrical)." Qualitative laws that yield predictions about the presence or absence of qualities or characteristics and semi-quantitative laws involving, as Feigl puts it, "only the relations of 'equal' or 'greater than'" (p. 409) are just as relevant as fully quantitative laws in defining causality.

As regards the forms of mathematical functions appearing in laws, it is sometimes convenient to assume them, and perhaps their first and second derivatives, to be continuous. However, other representations are not precluded. In fact at various stages of the development of a subject, two alternative formulations may coexist. For example, Jeffreys (1967) remarks that:

> The quantum theory and the continuous emission theory both accounted for one set of facts, but each, in its existing form, was inconsistent with the facts explained by the other. The proper conclusion was that both explanations were wrong and that. . .some new explanation must be sought. . . . But meanwhile, physicists based their predictions on the laws; in types of phenomena that had been found predictable by quantum methods, they made their predictions by quantum methods; in phenomena of interference they made predictions by assuming continuous wave trains. (pp. 411-12)

Another point about forms of laws is that they be capable of yielding verifiable predictions about as yet unobserved data. This requirement does not place overly severe restrictions on the forms of laws or of mathematical functions appearing in them. However, many including G.E.P. Box, R.A. Fisher,

M. Friedman, H. Jeffreys, the present writer, and a number of others do emphasize the virtues of simplicity in formulating laws. Some exhibit a preference for simplicity by appealing to Ockham's Razor, the Principle of Parsimony, or the Jeffreys-Wrinch Simplicity Postulate. With respect to the Simplicity Postulate, Jeffreys (1967) states that contrary to the widespread belief that the choice of the simplest law is merely a convention, "...the simplest law is chosen because it is the most likely to give correct predictions; that the choice is based on a reasonable degree of belief. . ." (pp. 4-5). Further Jeffreys (1967) writes:

> Precise statement of the prior probabilities of the laws in accordance with the condition of convergence requires that they should actually be put in an order of decreasing prior probability. . .All we have to say is that the simpler laws have the greater prior probabilities. This is what Wrinch and I called the *Simplicity Postulate*. (p. 47)

He goes on to suggest a tentative numerical rule for assessing the complexity of laws expressible by differential equations. Jeffreys (1957) also presents an analysis of developments in the history of science that provides support for the Simplicity Postulate. Thus, if the Simplicity Postulate is accepted as probably valid, it involves a most important ordering of causal laws.

We now consider several aspects of the domains of laws involved in Feigl's definition of causation. The domains of many laws are temporal or temporal-spatial. In regard to the temporal-spatial aspects of laws, Feigl (1953) writes:

> This principle [the homogeneity and isotropy of space, and homogeneity of time], clearly formulated by Maxwell, states the irrelevance of absolute space or time co-ordinates, and in this sense the purely relational character of space and time as seen already by Leibniz and re-emphasized in Einstein's theory of relativity. The place and the time at which events occur do not by themselves have any modifying effect on these events. (p. 412)

He goes on to say, "Differences in effects must always be accounted for in terms of differences in the *conditions*, not in terms of purely spatio-temporal location" (p. 412). These considerations and considerations of the reversibility (symmetry) of the cause-effect relation in molecular processes that is assumed in the work of Gibbs and Boltzmann and empirically observed in the case of Brownian motion lead Feigl to state:

> Since the basic laws of classical mechanics and electro-dynamics as well as those of modern quantum mechanics are temporally symmetrical, it would seem that the direction of causality may indeed be reducible to Boltzmann's explana-tion [the probabilities for a transition from a more highly ordered state to one of lower order (greater disorder) are always higher than those for the process in the opposite direction]. Once this is assumed, such statements as "earlier actions can influence later events but not vice versa" are recognized as sheer tautologies... (p. 414)

These considerations of time and space as they relate to physical laws indicate an important probabilistic reversibility of laws in time. As regards laws in the social sciences, it has been customary to think in terms of chrono-logical time and to require that laws be such that causes precede their effects in chronological time. From what has been presented above, it is clear that such a requirement is at odds with important physical laws. In addition, if Allais's (1966) concept of psychological time is considered, then there is no assurance that laws stated in a psychological time frame will necessarily meet the requirement that cause precede effect in chronological time.

Another issue regarding the temporal domain of laws is whether laws relate to continuous or discrete time. There does not seem to be any compelling reason to favor either continuous or discrete time formulations of laws, and, in fact, mixed difference-differential equation formulations of laws are not only possible but have been employed.

Finally with respect to temporal matters, there is the problem of laws that involve "simultaneity" or "instantaneous causality." As Feigl notes, "...an equally well established usage [of the crude concepts of cause and effect] seems to prevail even if the two events (factors, processes) are contemporaneous" (p. 417). In terms of the discussion of temporal ordering presented above, it seems clear that simultaneous or instantaneous formulations of laws cannot be ruled out, provided that these laws are capable of yielding predictions about as yet unobserved data. If they can, then such laws are causal laws according to Feigl's definition.

As regards the levels, macro or micro, to which laws relate, it is of course possible to have laws relating specifically to macro phenomena, specifically to micro phenomena, or to combined micro and macro phenomena. While there is a natural desire to have a consistent law applicable to both micro and macro phenomena, the fact that in some areas such a law does not exist does not preclude the use of laws relating to one level until an improved, more general law is formulated.

In the above discussion of some characteristics of a philosopher's definition of causation, namely, "predictability according to a law" (or, more adequately, "according to a set of laws"), not much has been said about the deductive, logical nature of causal laws; rather, more emphasis has been placed on the inductive logical nature of causation, since this aspect seems very relevant to the tasks of working scientists. Also, it must be mentioned that the calculus of inductive logic plays a central role in comparing and testing alternative laws' predictions. Jeffreys (1967, ch. 5-6) and Burks (1977, pp. 65-91) describe the theory and some applications of this use of inductive logic that involves Bayes's theorem to compute probabilities associated with alternative laws or hypotheses. This inductive logical analysis is needed to provide information about the quality of the predictability of various laws.

In the next section attention is directed to reviewing and discussing several works dealing with causation that have appeared in the econometric literature.

III. Review of Selected Discussions of Causation in the Econometric Literature

The objectives of this review are to establish the extent to which concepts of causation in the econometric literature coincide with or differ from those considered in Section II and to provide a basis for approaching the tests of causality to be considered in the next section. Because not all discussions of causality that have appeared in the econometric literature can be covered, I have selected several leading works that appear important and relevant for assessing the meaningfulness of tests of causality.

A. Simon's "Causal Ordering and Identifiability"

H. Simon's essay "Causal Ordering and Identifiability" (1953) was published as chapter III in one of the most influential monographs on econometric methodology. For this reason and because some recent work by Sims (1977) builds on Simon's contribution, it is worthwhile to review Simon's analysis.

Simon agrees with Feigl that the concept of causation is in need of purification and clarification. In fact, Simon mentions ". . .objectionable ontological and epistemological overtones that have attached themselves to the causal concept. . ." (p. 49). He also notes:

> In view of the generally unsavory epistemological status of the notion of causality, it is somewhat surprising to find the term in rather common use in scientific writing (when the scientist is writing about his science, not about its methodology). Moreover, it is not easy to explain this usage as metaphorical, or even as a carry-over of outmoded language. (p. 50)

Thus Simon is in agreement with the view, expressed above, that the notion of causality is in widespread use in science.

In view of the impure connotations associated with the term *causation* and of "Hume's critique that necessary connections among events cannot be perceived (and hence can have no empirical basis)," (p. 49), Simon opts for a narrower concept of causality. Simon's narrower notion of causality is "that causal orderings are simply properties of the scientist's model, properties that are subject to change as the model is altered to fit new observations. . ." (p. 50). He rightly points out that such a notion of causality can be applied to probabilistic as well as deterministic models. Applicability to probabilistic models is important, since Simon believes that ". . .the viewpoint is becoming more and more prevalent that the appropriate model of the world is not a deterministic model but a probabilistic one" (p. 50).

Whether this last statement is true or not, it is evident that Simon's notion of causality is a deductive logical concept relating to models' characteristics, not to empirical features of the world that require statements of inductive logic. Indeed, Simon (p. 51) states, "It is the aim of this chapter. . .to provide a clear and rigorous basis for determining when a causal ordering can be said to hold between two variables or groups of variables in a model [and not the 'real' world]," and ". . .the concepts to be defined all refer to a model--a system of equations--and not to the "real" world the model purports to describe." Thus, Simon's narrower notion of causality or causation is radically different from Feigl's concept of causation, i.e., predictability according to a law or set of laws. For Feigl predictability means predictability of empirically observable outcomes, certainly not just a deductive logical property of a model or of a law. While Simon's notion of causality can be used to describe logically the laws that Feigl mentions, it involves no necessary relation to the prediction of "real" world outcomes. Obviously a law that is causal in Simon's sense need not be causal in Feigl's; that is, the law may be incapable of predicting "real-world" outcomes. Such a law would not be termed causal in an inductive, empirical sense.

In addition to this important distinction between Simon's and Feigl's concepts of causation, it is relevant to note that even within his narrower concept of causality Simon explains that:

> . . .we might say that if *A* and *B* are functionally related and if *A* precedes *B* in time, then *A* causes *B*. There is no logical obstacle to this procedure. Nevertheless, we shall not adopt it. We shall argue that time sequence does, indeed, sometimes provide a basis for asymmetry between *A* and *B*, but that asymmetry is the important thing, not the sequence. By putting asymmetry, without necessarily implying a time sequence, at the basis of our definition we shall admit causal orderings where no time sequence appears (and sometimes exclude them even where there is a time sequence). By so doing we shall find ourselves in closer accord with actual usage, and with a better understanding of the meaning of the concept than if we had adopted the other, and easier, course. We shall discover that causation (as we shall define it) does not imply time sequence, nor does time sequence imply causation. (p. 51)

Thus, Simon is in agreement with the discussion in the previous section regarding the non-necessity of a chronological time ordering between cause and effect. While Simon agrees with this position in the early part of his essay, in his concluding section he remarks,

> There is no necessary connection between the asymmetry of this relation [among certain variables] and asymmetry in time, although an analysis of the causal structure of dynamical systems in econometrics and physics will show that lagged relations can generally be interpreted as causal relations. (pp. 73-74)

Since it is not clear to what specific lagged relations Simon is referring, it is difficult to evaluate this last remark. Suffice it to say that there are many examples of empirically fitted dynamical systems in econometrics in which a lagged relation cannot be regarded as causal in Feigl's sense.

To illustrate the nature of Simon's analysis of causal orderings, we will review the simplest example presented in his paper. In this example, he considers the following three-equation, linear, deterministic system (p. 58):

$$a_{11}x_1 = a_{10}, \tag{1}$$

$$a_{21}x_1 + a_{22}x_2 = a_{20}, \tag{2}$$

$$a_{32}x_2 + a_{33}x_3 = a_{30}, \tag{3}$$

where x_1 is an index measuring the favorableness of weather for growing wheat; x_2 is the size of the wheat crop; x_3 is the price of wheat; and the a's are parameters. Simon writes, "We suppose the weather to depend only on a parameter; the wheat crop, upon the weather (we ignore a possible dependence of supply on price); and the price of wheat, on the wheat crop. . ." (p. 58).

Since the value of x_1 can be determined from (1) alone, it is possible to substitute this value in equations (2) and (3) to get a reduced system involving x_2 and x_3. The substitution from (1) into (2) yields a relation determining the value of x_2, which when substituted in (3) along with the value of x_1 from (1), determines the value of x_3. This ordering of the algebraic solution of the system in (1)-(3) results in Simon's writing:

$$(1) \longrightarrow (2) \longrightarrow (3),$$

which Simon interprets as "(1) has direct precedence over (2), and (2) over (3)," (p. 58) and

$$x_1 \longrightarrow x_2 \longrightarrow x_3,$$

which he interprets as "x_1 is the direct cause of x_2, and x_2 of x_3" (p. 58).

24

While Simon analyzes systems more complicated than that shown above, this simple system reveals well the nature of his notions of causality and causal orderings, which are, as he emphasizes, just logical properties of the model considered. He leaves the inductive relevance of the model aside, probably on purpose; yet, it is the inductive aspect of this and other models that is critical for appraising the degree to which the model is causal.[1] In discussing a concept of causality close to Simon's, Jeffreys (1967) expresses a similar point of view:

> Causality, as used in applied mathematics, has a more general form, such as: "Physical laws are expressible by mathematical equations, possibly connecting continuous variables, such that in any case, given a finite number of parameters, some variable or set of variables that appears in the equations is uniquely determined in terms of the others.". . .The equations, which we call laws, are inferred from previous instances and then applied to instances where the relevant quantities are different. This form permits astronomical prediction. But it still leaves the questions "How do we know that no other parameters than those stated are needed?" "How do we know that we need consider no variables as relevant other than those mentioned explicitly in the laws?" and "Why do we believe the laws themselves?" It is only after these questions have been answered that we can make any actual application of the principle, and the principle is useless until we have attended to the epistemological problems. (p. 12)

B. The Basmann-Strotz-Wold Discussion of Causality

In three papers, published together as "a triptych on causal chain systems," R.H. Strotz and H.O.A. Wold (1960), R.H. Strotz (1960) and H.O.A. Wold (1960), bring together and extend earlier work of Wold (See references in Strotz and Wold, 1960) attempting to clarify the causal nature and properties of econometric models, including entire models and particular equations and parameters appearing in models. In a paper dealing with the Strotz-Wold papers, Basmann (1963) writes:

---

[1] In a letter, dated May 2, 1978, to the author, Simon emphasizes that while in earlier work he ". . .neglected to emphasize the correspondence principle that connects the syntactic with the semantic dimensions of any theory," in more recent work he does recognize this important link.

. . .Wold and Strotz have not stated from what specific definition of causality they argue to the conclusion that only *triangular* recursive systems are causal. Their own view lacks several essential features of the classical notion of causality; the classical notion. . .is not mentioned by them as a possible alternative to their own. It is the purpose of this note to show constructively, by an example, that, contrary to the Wold-Strotz assertion, the hypothethical structural equations which underlie "interdependent," i.e., non-triangular, systems can be validly given a straightforward causal interpretation, at least in the classical sense. . . (pp. 441-42)[2]

As the quotation reveals, two of the basic issues in this discussion are (*a*) the definitions of causality employed by the participants in this discussion and (*b*) the relationship between concepts of causality and the forms of econometric models. These two aspects of the Strotz-Wold and Basmann discussion are considered below.

With respect to the definition, or definitions, of causality, Strotz and Wold (1960) are rather eclectic. They write, "No one has monopoly rights in defining 'causality.' The term is in common parlance and the only meaningful challenge is that of providing an explication of it. No explication need be unique, and some may prefer never to use the word at all" (p. 418). Also, Wold (1960) states that ". . .in the treatment of the models at issue, problems come up for which the natural sciences give no guidance, an unusual situation in the social sciences. This is in particular so with regard to the causal interpretation of econometric models" (p. 461). These comments raise the issue of whether a single definition of causality, such as Feigl's, is adequate for work in both the natural and social sciences. While it is recognized that improvements in a definition of causality are possible, it would have to be shown that entertaining different concepts of causality in the natural and social sciences is necessary and empirically fruitful. Since this has not been done, as far as the present writer is aware, the proposition that different concepts of causality are required is purely speculative. It is also noteworthy that Strotz and Wold adopt a definition of causality that they believe is in agreement with "common scientific and statistical-inference usage." Strotz and Wold write,

---

[2]References cited in original have been omitted.

For us, however, the word [*causality*] in common scientific and statistical-inference usage has the following general meaning. z is a cause of y if, by hypothesis, it is or "would be" possible by *controlling z* indirectly to control y, at least stochastically. But it may or may not be possible by controlling y indirectly to control z. A causal relation is therefore in essence asymmetric, in that in any instance of its realization it is asymmetric. Only in special cases may it be reversible and symmetric in a causal sense. These are the cases in which sometimes a controlled change in z may cause a change in y and at other times a controlled change in y may cause a change in z, but y and z cannot both be subjected to simultaneous controlled changes independently of one another without the causal relationship between them being violated. (p. 418)

The Strotz-Wold definition, presented above, differs from Feigl's most markedly by bringing in the concept of controlled changes in variables. Feigl's definition of causality or causation can be fruitfully applied to areas of science in which no variables are under control. In addition, the Feigl definition can also apply in cases in which laws or models contain one or more variables that can actually be controlled. Note too that Strotz and Wold say, ". . .it is or 'would be' possible by *controlling z* . . ." What do they mean by *would be*? If they mean that z cannot actually be controlled but that they are considering a hypothetical controlled variation of z, then they appear to be admitting impossible experiments into their definition of causality. Whether impossible experiments are admissible in an operational theory of scientific induction incorporating a consistent definition of causality is a controversial issue. Jeffreys (1967), for example, takes the position that "the existence of a thing [e.g., causality] or the estimate of a quantity must not involve an impossible experiment" (p. 8). While the issue of the admissibility of impossible experiments may be relevant to the Strotz-Wold definition, it is still the case that their definition is subsumed under Feigl's more general definition of causation and causal laws.

In his comment on the Strotz-Wold papers, Basmann (1963) presents the following definition of causality:

The classical scientific notion of causality to which we shall appeal, can be expressed satisfactorily as follows: *Assume that* [the] *mechanism under investigation can be isolated*

27

from all systematic, i.e., non-random external influences;
assume that the mechanism can be started over repeatedly
from any definite initial condition. If, every time the
mechanism is started up from approximately the same
initial condition, it tends to run through approximately the
same sequence of events, then the mechanism is said to be
causal. (p.442, references omitted).

Also, directly following his definition, Basmann writes,

Any model that (1) represents a mechanism in *isolation*
from non-random external influences and (2) asserts that,
when started up from approximately the same initial conditions the mechanism always tends to run through
approximately the same sequence of states, is a causal model
expressing a causal hypothesis about the mechanism under
investigation. (p. 442)

In a footnote to this last sentence, he remarks, "It is not necessary that such
experiments be feasible; it is sufficient that they are not ruled out in principle"
(p. 442).

If we equate Feigl's concept of "law or set of laws" with Basmann's
concept of a "model that represents a mechanism," and Feigl's concept of
"predictability" with Basmann's requirement that a model assert that "when
started up from approximately the same initial conditions the mechanism
always tends to run through approximately the same sequence of states. . . ,"
we see that Feigl's and Basmann's concepts of causality or causation and causal
laws or models are similar from a logical point of view. There may, however,
be some question as to whether Feigl's concept of predictability is precisely the
same as Basmann's, a point considered below.

Feigl does not rule out the concept of causation; i.e., predictability
according to a law or set of laws, in cases in which, as is common in mainly
nonexperimental sciences, a single realization of a process is the rule rather than
the exception. Indeed, Feigl (1953) writes,

In the case of unrepeatable (unique) events, as described in
the historical disciplines (as in the history of the inorganic,
organic, mental, social, cultural or individual-biographical
occurrences), the assertion of causal relations (as in statements

regarding who or what influenced events to what degree and in which direction) is often methodologically precarious, i.e., only very weakly confirmable. But it is not meaningless. (p. 410)

Similarly Jeffreys (1967), who has applied his causal concept to much nonexperimental data from astronomy and geophysics, remarks,

There must be a uniform standard of validity for all hypotheses, irrespective of the subject. Different laws may hold in different subjects, but they must be tested by the same criteria; otherwise we have no guarantee that our decisions will be those warranted by the data and not merely the result of inadequate analysis or of believing what we want to believe. (p. 7)

Thus, predictability and confirmation of predictability are relevant in situations in which repetition of outcomes is impossible. Thus, Basmann's requirement that the experiment mentioned in his definition "not be ruled out in principle" appears to be superfluous. Of course, however, repetition of experiments, when possible, is usually highly desirable, since it provides a greater degree of confirmation, or lack thereof, for a particular model.

On the issue of the forms of econometric models or laws and causality, it is apparent that Feigl's, Jeffreys's, and Basmann's definitions of causality apply to complete econometric models, whether the models are formulated in fully recursive, triangular, or interdependent forms. Models in any of these forms can embody economic laws and are capable of providing predictions about as yet unobserved phenomena. Thus, they are all causal in a logical, deductive sense. Whether particular parts or single equations of such models are capable of yielding predictions and thus can, in isolation, be interpreted causally is a separate issue that can be decided by a careful examination of the structures of particular models as, for example, carried through by Simon (1953) and Basmann (1963). That models be built so as to have *each* equation capable of a causal interpretation in the above sense is an a priori restriction on the forms of models that cannot be justified methodologically. This requirement could be justified if it were found empirically that models so constructed performed better in prediction than models not so constructed. Since this empirical issue has not been settled, or perhaps cannot be settled in view of Basmann's (1965) demonstration of the observational equivalence of fully recursive and interdependent models, it is inappropriate to require that econometric models necessarily be of one form or another simply on a priori grounds.

A similar conclusion applies to the Strotz-Wold view, expressed in Strotz (1960):

> If a causal interpretation of an interdependent system is possible it is to be provided in terms of a recursive system. The interdependent system is then either an approximation to the recursive system or a description of its equilibrium state. This was the conclusion of the preceding paper, written jointly with Professor Wold.[3] (p. 428)

This statement is an a priori view about the forms of causal laws and, as indicated above, it is methodologically unsound to rule out, on a priori grounds alone, logically consistent laws that assume particular forms. Aside from the observational equivalence of fully recursive and interdependent systems, discrimination among different laws is an inductive issue involving empirical confirmation procedures. Thus, the Strotz-Wold position that interdependent systems are in some sense approximations to "true" underlying recursive systems and that the former systems involve, as Strotz puts it, ". . .some form of specification error. . ." (p. 428) is unacceptable as a general proposition.

C. The Wiener-Granger Concept of Causality

Granger (1969) considers a theory of causality that he views as an alternative to those of Simon, Strotz, Wold, and Basmann reviewed above. Granger writes,

> In the alternative theory to be discussed here, the stochastic nature of the variables and the direction of the flow of time will be central features. The theory is, in fact, not relevant for nonstochastic variables and will rely entirely on the assumption that the future cannot cause the past. This theory will not, of course, be contradictory to previous work but there appears to be little common ground. Its origins may be found in a suggestion by Wiener. . . (p. 428)

Contrary to what Granger says, it is apparent that his theory is contradictory to previous work on causality in at least two important respects.

---

[3] Footnote included in original has been omitted.

First, in the previous work of Feigl, Jeffreys, Simon, Strotz, Wold, Basmann, and others, *both* stochastic and nonstochastic variables are considered. The analysis is not limited to stochastic variables, and such limitation is certainly not warranted on either methodological or subject matter considerations. Second, Granger, in contrast to Feigl, Simon and Basmann, embeds the notion of temporal asymmetry in his theory of causality. Feigl and Simon, as explicitly pointed out above, do not identify causal asymmetry with succession of "cause" and "effect" in chronological time. These requirements of the Granger concept of causality that appear contrary to previous concepts of causality are stated explicitly in Granger and Newbold (1977) as follows: "(i) The future cannot cause the past. Strict causality can occur only with the past causing the present or future." "(ii) It is sensible to discuss causality only for a group of stochastic processes. It is not possible to detect causality between two deterministic processes" (pp. 224-25). As stated above, these restrictions, which do not appear in other concepts of causality, definitely restrict the range of applicability of the Granger concept. If an inductive case could be made that such restrictions are required, then they would be acceptable. Because, as far as the present writer is aware, no such convincing case has been made, it is questionable that the restrictions are required for a fruitful definition of causality. In fact, Granger's restrictions appear to rule out economic laws which state that *nonstochastic* variation in one variable causes variation in a second variable or that a nonstochastic trend in one variable causes a nonstochastic trend in a second variable. As discussed above, such a priori restrictions on the forms of economic laws have to be justified on inductive grounds.

Despite the restrictiveness of his theory of causality, Granger (1969) regards his definition of causality as ". . .very general in nature" (p. 428). In developing this definition, Granger considers a stationary stochastic process, A_t. He lets $\bar{A}_t$ represent the set of *past* values of A_t, and $\bar{\bar{A}}_t$ the set of *past and present* values of A_t. Further, he lets $\bar{A}(k)$ represent the set $\{A_{t-j}, j = k, k + 1, \ldots, \infty\}$. He also denotes the optimum, unbiased least squares predictor of A_t using the set of values B_t by $P_t(A|B)$, the predictive error series by $\epsilon_t(A|B) = A_t - P_t(A|B)$, and the variance of $\epsilon_t(A|B)$ by $\sigma^2(A|B)$. Then Granger (1969) writes,

> Let U_t be all the information in the universe accumulated since time t-1 and let $U_t - Y_t$ denote all this information *apart* from the specified series Y_t. We then have the following definitions.

31

Definition 1: *Causality*. If $\sigma^2(X|U) < \sigma^2(X|\overline{U\text{-}Y})$, we say that Y is causing X, denoted by $Y_t \Rightarrow X_t$. We say that Y_t is causing X_t if we are better able to predict X_t using all available information than if the information apart from Y_t had been used.

Definition 2: *Feedback*. If

$$\sigma^2(X|\overline{U}) < \sigma^2(X|\overline{U\text{-}Y}) \,,$$

$$\sigma^2(Y|\overline{U}) < \sigma^2(Y|\overline{U\text{-}X}) \,,$$

We say that feedback is occurring, which is denoted $Y_t \Leftrightarrow X_t$, i.e., feedback is said to occur when X_t is causing Y_t and also Y_t is causing X_t.

Definition 3: *Instantaneous Causality*. If $\sigma^2(X|\overline{U},\overline{\overline{Y}})$ $< \sigma^2(X|\overline{U})$, we say that instantaneous causality $Y_t \Leftrightarrow X_t$ is occurring. In other words, the current value of X_t is better "predicted" if the present value of Y_t is included in the "prediction" than if it is not.

Definition 4: *Causality Lag*. If $Y_t \Rightarrow X_t$, we define the (integer) causality lag m to be the least value of k such that $\sigma^2(X|U\text{-}Y(k)) < \sigma^2(X|U\text{-}Y(k+1))$. Thus, knowing the values of $Y_{t\text{-}j}$, $j = 0,1, \ldots ,m\text{-}1$, will be of no help in improving the prediction of X_t. (pp. 428-29)

Granger's definition of causality, his definition 1 above, states that if the variance of the forecast error of an unbiased least squares predictor of a stationary stochastic variable X_t, based on all the information in the universe accumulated since time t-1, is smaller than the variance of the forecast error of an unbiased least squares predictor of X_t, based on all the information in the universe since time t-1 except for the past values of Y_t, then "Y is causing X." Several important characteristics of this definition follow. First, as recognized by Granger (1969), "The one completely unreal aspect of the above definitions is the use of the series U_t, representing *all* available information" (p. 429). In fact, this requirement makes the Granger definition nonoperational and in violation of one of Jeffreys's (1967) rules for theories of scientific induction, namely, "Any rule given must be applicable in practice. A definition is useless unless the thing defined can be recognized in terms of the definition when it occurs. The existence of a thing or the estimate of a quantity must not involve an impossible experiment" (p. 8). In dealing with this problem, Granger suggests replacing "all the information in the universe" with the concept of "all relevant information" (p. 429). While this modification is a step in the direction of making his definition operational, Granger does not explicitly mention the important role of economic laws in defining the set of "all relevant information." By not mentioning the role of economic laws or theory, Granger gives the impression that purely statistical criteria can be employed in defining causality.

Second, Granger's definition of causality is unusual in that embedded in it is a particular confirmatory criterion, the variance of the forecast error of an unbiased least squares predictor. This confirmatory criterion is not applicable to processes that do not possess finite moments. Also, for most processes, even just stationary processes, which involve parameters whose values must be estimated from finite sets of data, an unbiased least squares "optimum" predictor is often not available. Recognizing some of these difficulties, Granger (1969) writes,

> In practice it will not usually be possible to use completely optimum predictors, unless all sets of series are assumed to be normally distributed, since such optimum predictors may be nonlinear in complicated ways. It seems natural to use only linear predictors and the above definitions may again be used under this assumption of linearity. (p. 429)

Even in the case of linear systems with parameters that must be estimated from finite sets of data, an "optimum" (in finite samples) linear unbiased predictor will not always be available. In fact, the restriction that a predictor be linear and unbiased can result in an inadmissible predictor relative to a quadratic loss function even in linear normal models, given the results of Stein. Thus, it is not clear that the confirmatory procedures embedded in the Granger definition of causality are entirely satisfactory.

Third, as regards the implied quadratic criterion involved in the use of unbiased predictors and variance of forecast or prediction errors, Granger (1969) writes:

> It can be argued that the variance is not the proper criterion to use to measure the closeness of a predictor P_t to the true

value X_t. Certainly if some other criteria were used it may be possible to reach different conclusions about whether one series is causing another. The variance does seem to be a natural criterion to use in connection with linear predictors as it is mathematically easy to handle and simple to interpret. If one uses this criterion, a better name might be "causality in mean." (p. 430)

Thus linking the confirmatory procedure to comparisons of variances is viewed as a matter of convenience. However, as Granger notes, it is not applicable in general. Further, Granger's confirmation procedures depart from those based on posterior probabilities associated with laws that are adopted by Jeffreys (1967), Burks (1977), and others. The posterior probability concept of confirmation is much more general than Granger's; however, it must be recognized that not all technical problems of applying it to a number of cases encountered in practice have been solved.

Fourth, in commenting on the general concept of causality, Granger and Newbold (1977) write,

The definition as it stands is far too general to be testable. It is possible to reach a testable definition only by imposing considerable simplification and particularization to this definition. It must be recognized that, in so doing, the definition will become less intuitively acceptable and more error-prone. (p. 225)

Some of the simplifications and particularizations have been mentioned above. Most important, though, is the failure of Granger and Newbold to recognize explicitly the role of economic laws or theories in defining causality. They, perhaps inadvertently, give the impression that the concept of causality can be defined entirely in terms of statistical considerations, a point of view that is contrary to those of Feigl, Jeffreys, Basmann, and others. The simplifications and particularizations that Granger and Newbold discuss appear to be statistical in nature and not of the kind involved in the Jeffreys-Wrinch Simplicity Postulate that deals with the forms of laws.

Fifth, Granger's definitions 2-4 are also subject to the criticisms brought up in connection with his definition 1. In addition, since the two processes X and Y are not considered within the context of particular economic laws, it is hard to determine whether the modified, operational Granger concepts are indeed applicable and lead to unambiguous results. On this latter point, Granger (1969) himself points out, "Even for stochastic series, the definitions introduced above may give apparently silly answers" (p. 430). After analyzing a case illustrating this point, he goes on to say, "It will often be found that constructed examples which seem to produce results contrary to common sense can be resolved by widening the set of data within which causality is defined" (p. 431). Perhaps a more satisfactory position would be to define causality, as Feigl and others have, in terms of predictability according to well-thought-out economic laws.

Last, while Granger (1969) does not completely rule out the concept of instantaneous causality, he does remark that in some cases,

> . . .although there is no real instantaneous causality, the definitions will appear to suggest that such causality is occurring. This is because certain relevant information, the missing readings in the data, have not been used. Due to this effect, one might suggest that in many economic situations an apparent instantaneous causality would disappear if the economic variables were recorded at more frequent time intervals. (p. 430)

This statement and what has been presented above reveal that Granger generally adopts a temporal asymmetrical view of cause and effect. As mentioned earlier, such a view is not compatible with certain physical science considerations and is not a necessary component of a definition of causality.

In summary, Granger's definition of causality, his definition 1 above, is a nonoperational definition involving consideration of predictability in a very special confirmatory setting. The definition does not involve mention of laws, economic or otherwise. In fact, the conditions surrounding the definition and the suggestions for making the definition operational have important implications for the forms of laws. For example, nonstochastic variables are excluded, and forms of laws for which least squares unbiased predictors are not at least approximately optimal are not covered. Perhaps in principle such variables could be covered if definition 1 were broadened. However, if definition 1 is so broadened, it appears to the present writer that it may as well be broadened to coincide with Feigl's definition of causality, namely predictability according to a law or set of laws. Given careful attention to the formulation of such laws, confirmatory procedures that are appropriate for them can be applied. Indeed, this last approach seems very similar to that employed traditionally in econometrics.

IV. Empirical Tests of Causality

In this section several empirical studies involving issues discussed in the preceding sections will be analyzed. First, consideration will be given to studies that employ what has been referred to above as the "traditional econometric approach." Then recent studies employing the Granger-Wiener concept of causality will be reviewed. In the discussion, it will be assumed that readers are familiar with standard econometric terminology.

Haavelmo's (1947) early paper, reprinted in Cowles Commission Monograph 14, involves an econometric formulation and estimation of a simple Keynesian macroeconomic model that appeared and appears in many introductory economics textbooks. The simple model that Haavelmo considered is given by:

$$c_t = \beta + a y_t + u_t \tag{4}$$

$$t = 1, 2, \ldots, T$$

$$y_t = c_t + z_t . \tag{5}$$

Equation (4) is a consumption function relating two endogenous variables, (a) consumption in period t, c_t and (b) income in period t, y_t. β and a are parameters with unknown values, and u_t is an unobservable random disturbance. In Haavelmo's empirical work, he employs U.S. Department of Commerce data on consumers' expenditures in constant dollars per capita to measure c_t, and disposable income in constant dollars per capita, to measure y_t. No attention will be given here to the adequacy of these empirical measures. If they are adopted, then equation (5) is an identity satisfied by the data with z_t equal to "investment expenditures, in constant dollars," the difference between disposable income and consumers' expenditure, which Haavelmo points out is equal to private net investment minus corporate savings plus government deficits. While much more could be said about the interpretation of (5) in terms of an equilibrium condition involving aggregate demand and supply with special assumptions regarding aggregate supply, this matter will not be pursued. Haavelmo then completes his model by assuming (a) that the u_t's have zero means, constant common variance, and are serially uncorrelated and (b) that the time series z_t is autonomous in relation to u_t and y_t, a condition that is fulfilled if the sequence z_t is a sequence of given numbers, or if each z_t is a random variable which is stochastically independent of u_t. Further, he assumes that sample variance of the z_t's converges, either mathematically in the case of nonstochastic z_t's or in a weak probability sense in the case of stochastic z_t's, to a positive, finite constant. In a deductive logical sense, Haavelmo's model is a causal model, since it allows us to obtain predictions of future values of c_t and y_t given parameter estimates and future values of z_t. In an inductive sense, the model may not yield good predictions if it is difficult to obtain (in the case of nonstochastic z_t's) future values of the z_t's or to predict (in the case of stochastic z_t's) the future z_t's very well. Also, the model may not predict very well if there are errors in specifying the consumption function's form or the disturbance term's properties, or if it is assumed that z_t is autonomous. Thus, the autonomous or exogenous assumption regarding z_t is just one of several possible reasons for the model's possible poor performance in actual prediction.

In his paper, Haavelmo gives special attention to the assumption that z_t is autonomous or exogenous. His approach involves elaborating his simple model to provide two alternative models in which z_t is no longer autonomous. His third model involves the following equations:

$$c_t = \beta + a y_t + u_t \qquad , \tag{6}$$

$$r_t = v + \mu(c_t + x_t) + w_t \quad , \tag{7}$$

$$y_t = c_t + x_t - r_t \qquad , \tag{8}$$

$$x_t = \text{an autonomous variable} \tag{9}$$

in which c_t, y_t, and r_t are endogenous variables, (7) is a business saving equation, and u_t and w_t are disturbance terms, not necessarily uncorrelated but with zero means, constant covariance matrix, and serially uncorrelated. Note from (5) and (8) that $z_t = x_t - r_t$ so that if r_t is endogenous, z_t will be also. Given future values of x_t and parameter estimates, it is clear that the expanded model in (6)-(9) can be employed to generate predictions of corresponding future values of c_t, y_t, and r_t.

In his analysis of Haavelmo's expanded model, (6)-(9), Chetty (1966, 1968) points out that if the parameter μ in (7) has a zero value and if the covariance between the disturbance terms u_t and w_t is zero, then the expanded model collapses to become the original model shown in (4)-(5) with z_t autonomous or exogenous. Thus a test of the joint hypothesis $\mu = 0$ and $cov(u_t, w_t) = 0$ is a test of the hypothesis that z_t is autonomous or exogenous and that the original model (4)-(5) may be adequate if it is not defective in other respects.

The review of Haavelmo's models provides some elements of what might be called the traditional econometric approach to building causal econometric models. In this approach, one uses economic theory and other outside information to formulate a tentative model. If the Simplicity Postulate is taken seriously, the initial formulation will be sophisticatedly simple. Such simplicity does not necessarily stand in a one-to-one relationship with the size (number of equations) of a model. Clearly, it is possible to have complicated single-equation models. Given the initially entertained model, it is subjected to a number of diagnostic and prediction checks. In this connection, economic considerations, as in Haavelmo's case, may suggest certain broader formulations. After diagnostic and prediction checks have been performed, the model may have to be reformulated. Then the reformulated version is subjected to diagnostic and prediction checks, and so on. Various aspects of this approach to model-building have been discussed both in the econometric and in the statistical literature. For present purposes, it is most important to emphasize the central role of economic considerations, including economic theory, in developing causal economic models. To state this point more generally, subject matter considerations, including theory, play an important role in developing causal models in science. While some may regard this point as obvious, as several empirical tests of causality considered below will show, adequate account is not taken of this "obvious" point.

Since it is impossible to consider all reported tests of causality that employ the Granger concept of causality, attention will be given to just three leading examples, namely Sims (1972), Feige and Pearce (1976), and Pierce (1977). Sims (1972) writes, "The main empirical finding is that the hypothesis that causality is unidirectional from money to income agrees with the postwar U.S. data, whereas the hypothesis that causality is unidirectional from income to money is rejected" (p. 540). On the other hand, Pierce (1977), who analyzed similar data for the U.S., concludes, "Results of this type [independence or lack of causal relations between important economic variables] have also been obtained in several other studies. Using a similar methodology, Feige and

38

Pearce. . .have found little or no association between the money supply (or the monetary base) and gross national product, using quarterly data" (p. 19). Thus, it appears that the findings of Sims (1972), on the one hand, and of Feige and Pearce (1976) and Pierce (1977), on the other hand, are diametrically opposite. This and other features of these tests of causality are considered in what follows.

First, on the issue of whether the three empirical tests of causality cited above embody anything resembling what Feigl would call a law or set of laws, Pierce (1977) is most explicit when he writes, "The present study centers around an empirical specification of relations between economic time series. The data themselves are permitted, insofar as feasible, to suggest, at least in general terms, the patterns of interrelationships that do or do not exist" (p. 11). Thus, Pierce's approach is described quite frankly as one that involves "measurement without [economic] theory." The phrase *measurement without theory* is not used to condemn Pierce's approach as useless; his approach may be capable of generating important empirical results that can then, perhaps, be explained by old or new economic theories. Until this latter task is accomplished, however, by not incorporating economic law or laws, his analysis is not causal according to Feigl's definition, presented in Section II. Similarly, Sims (1972) and Feige and Pearce (1976), while not as explicit about the omission of theory as Pierce (1977), do not develop the relationships that they examine in the context of a detailed specification of economic laws or theories. As is well-known, if relevant economic theory is not considered, incorrect forms of variables, e.g., nominal variables rather than real variables, may be included, or relevant economic variables may be excluded. Failure to include more than two variables in these analyses has been recognized as a serious problem by Pierce (1977, p. 18) and by Sims (1977, p. 40). In a conversation with the author, Newbold[4] described the problem as simply analogous to the problem of left-out variables in regression models. Because they do not pay attention to subject matter theory, the studies considered offer little assurance that, in each case, the two variables examined are appropriate and/or the only two relevant for the analyses performed. Thus, the attempt to establish causality without use of economic theory or economic laws is a departure from investigation of causal laws in the sense of Feigl. Sims (1972) appears to realize this fact when he writes, "The method of identifying causal direction employed here does rest on a sophisticated version of the *post hoc ergo propter hoc* principle" (p. 543). Whether the version is "sophisticated" or just "obscure" will not be argued here.

Second, in order to make Granger's definition of causality operational, all three studies introduce specific statistical operations and assumptions that

---

[4]Newbold (1978), Personal communication.

have implications for the forms of economic laws and, probably, for the particular results of these and similar studies. Sims (1972) states some of these assumptions quite cryptically, "We will give content to Granger's definitions by assuming all time-series to be jointly covariance-stationary, by considering only linear predictors, and by taking expected squared forecast error as our criterion for predictive accuracy" (p. 544). Some implications of these assumptions have already been discussed in Section III. Here it is relevant to emphasize that most economic time series are nonstationary, not, as Sims assumes, covariance-stationary. Sims may mean that he will consider filtered series that are stationary. In fact, he mentions that

> all variables used in [his] regressions were measured as natural *logs* and prefiltered using the filter $1 - 1.5L + 0.5625L^2$ [where L is the lag operator] . . . .This filter approximately flattens the spectral density of most economic time-series, and the hope was that regression residuals would be very nearly white noise with this prefiltering. (p. 545)

It is very questionable that this specific filter does what Sims claims (or should do what he claims in terms of producing flat spectra). Further, if his regression error terms were generated by a particular AR(2) process, $u_t - 1.5u_{t-1} + 0.5625 u_{t-2} = \epsilon_t$, where ϵ_t is white noise, his procedure would produce white noise errors. The results of his empirical tests for disturbance autocorrelation throw considerable doubt on the adequacy of his filtering procedure. However, there may be some filter or filters that, when applied to highly nonstationary variables, render them stationary. Feige and Pearce (1976) and Pierce (1977), following Box and Jenkins, employ differencing to render series approximately stationary; that is, their filters are $(1-L)^a$, where a assumes an integer value, usually 1 or 2, and need not be the same for different variables. Then relationships to be studied are formulated in terms of the transformed or filtered variables, certainly an important restriction on the forms of economic laws. It might be asked, "Why filter?" and "What are the possible effects of filtering?"

On the question "Why filter?" it appears that forms of laws are being thereby restricted so that stationary, *statistical* theory can be applied. In terms of stationary variables, one can employ autocorrelation functions, cross-correlation functions, etc. However, if it makes economic sense to formulate a law or model in terms of nonstationary variables, e.g., nonstochastic variables or trending stochastic variables, it is not necessary to filter variables in order to estimate parameters' values and to predict from such estimated models.

Thus, it can be seen that the filtering of variables to produce variables that are covariance-stationary is not necessary in general and is inapplicable to nonstochastic variables. This is not to say, however, that use of prefiltered, stationary variables is never appropriate. Rather, it is to say that subject matter considerations are very relevant in this regard. An excellent example illustrating some of these considerations is provided by Hendry (1977, p. 196). In addition, in terms of analyses using a money variable, it is obvious that controlled non-stochastic changes in the rate of growth of money can produce a series that is difficult, if not impossible, to be made covariance stationary by filtering.

On the question "What are the possible effects of filtering?" it must be remarked that the effects of filtering, whether by differencing or by use of more general filters, can be drastic enough in some circumstances to justify Friedman's phrase[5] "*throwing the baby out with the bath.*" Also, Friedman's remarks in his letter regarding an earlier draft of the Pierce (1977) paper led me to formulate the following example to dramatize the effects of filtering on tests of causality of the type carried through in the papers under consideration. Consider the nonstationary processes $\ln C_t$ and $\ln Y_t$, where C_t and Y_t are measured real consumption and income, respectively. Assume that

$$\ln C_t = \ln C_t^p + u_t \ ,$$

$$\ln Y_t = \ln Y_t^p + v_t \ ,$$

where C_t^p and Y_t^p are real permanent consumption and real permanent income, respectively. Further, assume that $\ln C_t$ and $\ln Y_t$ are each filtered (if $C_t^p = kY_t^p$, with k assumed constant, the same filter can be employed) to produce the stationary innovations, u_t and v_t. If u_t and v_t are cross-correlated or subjected to the Sims regression techniques and found to be totally uncorrelated, what is being obtained is a confirmation of one form of Friedman's theory of the consumption function; the conclusion that filtered $\ln C_t$ and filtered $\ln Y_t$ are uncorrelated or independent says nothing about the causal relation between C_t^p and Y_t^p and/or the causal relation between C_t and Y_t. The nature of the underlying economic theory is critical in interpreting results based on pre-filtering. In addition, measurement considerations are relevant, since u_t and v_t

---

[5] Friedman (1975), Personal communication.

41

contain errors in measuring consumption and income. It is also the case that filtering is not required in a "nonstationary" version of the Granger (1969, p. 429) definition of causality. This consumption-income example illustrates how important economic laws are in defining causality. While Pierce (1977) recognizes in a special case that ". . .the deterministic detrending/deseasonalization procedure possibly took too much out of the series" (p. 19), he does not link up this possibility with any economic theory. Thus, it is difficult to interpret what is "too much" or "too little."

In general then, it has to be recognized that filtering economic time series is not usually a mechanical, neutral procedure that necessarily produces satisfactory results. The issues of whether to filter and what kinds of filters to employ, e.g., seasonal filtering (Sims, 1972, uses seasonally adjusted data), are most fruitfully resolved in relation to specific economic laws or theories and other serious subject matter considerations.

In terms of analyses involving money and either GNP or the rate of inflation, there is the issue of monetary policy and its possible impact on the results of tests of causality. Sims (1972) and Pierce (1977) mention this complication, but Feige and Pearce (1976) do not seem to appreciate it adequately. Pierce (1977) writes, "Thus if the money supply grows by exactly 5 percent over the sample period, it will show up as unrelated to anything else, despite what its actual relationship to interest rates, reserves, income, etc., might be" (p. 18). He also explains:

> The data may be even worse than happenstance [in terms of experimental design considerations] insofar as closed-loop control has probably been operative over the sample period for many macroeconomic series, including such instruments as money, interest rates and government spending and such targets as inflation, unemployment and income. If in the context of the dynamic regression model. . . ,suppose x [the input variable] has been adjusted to keep y [the output or dependent variable] on a desired path according to a control strategy $x_t = C(B)y_t$ [where $C(B)$ is a polynomial in the backshift or lag operator B]. Then it can be shown that not only is the lag distribution [$V(B)$ in $y_t = V(B)x_t + u_t$] unidentifiable, but that identical residuals and model forecasts can result from

42

i.   a model with $V(B)$ chosen so that the disturbances [the u_t's] will be white noise;

ii. a "model" with $V(B) = 0$ so that y is formally related only to its own past;

iii. an infinite number of intermediate models.

Perhaps this is not surprising; if x is determined from present and past y then, knowing y, knowing x in addition tells us nothing new. Certainly control strategies over the past 30 years have been imprecise in the short run and shifting in the long run; but certainly they have existed. (p. 20)[6]

Pierce's thoughtful and insightful remarks regarding the possible effects of monetary control policies on the results of causality tests highlight the importance of serious study of what monetary policies have been pursued in the particular sample period being analyzed. Without such study, as Pierce's remarks indicate, the results of mechanical tests of causality cannot be unambiguously interpreted. Irritating as it may be to those who seek purely statistical panaceas, the nature of policy control requires detailed consideration in formulating causal economic laws and testing their performance in prediction, a problem appreciated, if not completely solved, in the traditional econometric approach.

To return to some other aspects of how "operationalizing" Granger's nonoperational definition of causality leads to restrictions, some of them severe, on the nature of economic laws and some specific test results, consider Sims's (1972) analysis of money, X_t, and income, Y_t, variables. Since these variables are nonstationary, as mentioned above, Sims prefilters the natural logarithms of these variables to obtain x_t and y_t, assumed stationary. He then considers the following linear autoregressive representation of the assumed stationary variables x_t and y_t:

$$\begin{bmatrix} b_{11}(L) & b_{12}(L) \\ b_{21}(L) & b_{22}(L) \end{bmatrix} \begin{pmatrix} x_t \\ y_t \end{pmatrix} = \begin{pmatrix} u_t \\ v_t \end{pmatrix}, \tag{10}$$

where $b_{ij}(L)$ is a polynomial in the lag operator L, $i, j = 1, 2$, and u_t and v_t are mutually uncorrelated white noise errors.

---

[6] References cited in original have been omitted.

As Sims (1972, p. 544) mentions, Granger has shown that if there is an autoregressive representation as given in (10), then the *absence* of causality, in the Granger sense, running from y_t to x_t is equivalent to the condition that $b_{12}(L) \equiv 0$. Given this condition, (10) reduces to

$$b_{11}(L)x_t = u_t, \tag{11a}$$

$$b_{22}(L)y_t + b_{21}(L)x_t = v_t. \tag{11b}$$

Since u_t and v_t are mutually uncorrelated and non-serially correlated disturbance terms, (11) is an extreme form of a fully recursive model, extreme since no lagged values of y_t appear in (11a), *an added restriction* to the usual definition of a fully recursive model. From (11b), it is possible to write the dynamic regression for y_t as

$$y_t = -\frac{b_{21}(L)}{b_{22}(L)} x_t + \frac{1}{b_{22}(L)} v_t, \tag{12}$$

$$= V(L)x_t + \frac{1}{b_{22}(L)} v_t,$$

with $V(L) \equiv -b_{21}(L)/b_{22}(L)$. As can be seen from (12), the disturbance term is in the form of an infinite moving average, $b_{22}^{-1}(L)v_t$, and hence will in general be autocorrelated. Under the special assumption that $b_{22}(L)$ is of degree zero in L, the disturbance term will not be autocorrelated. On the other hand, if nonstationary variables Y_t and X_t are related by $Y_t = V(L)X_t + w_t$, and a common filter, $C(L)$, is applied to both sides, $C(L)Y_t = V(L)C(L)X_t + C(L)w_t$, or $y_t = V(L)x_t + C(L)w_t$. Then *if* $w_t = v_t/C(L)$, $y_t = V(L)x_t + v_t$. The disturbance term, v_t, in this last equation differs from that in (12), namely, $b_{22}^{-1}(L)v_t$. Thus, in terms of the system (11) with $x_t = C(L)Y_t$ and $y_t = C(L)Y_t$, the result in (12) indicates that disturbance terms will generally be autocorrelated. If the relationship $Y_t = V(L)X_t + w_t$ is viewed as a starting point, it is clearly not derived from (11), and on filtering both sides using $C(L)$, it will generally have autocorrelated disturbances, except in very special cases. Indeed, Sims

(1972) reports results of tests for serial correlation of disturbance terms in (11) and concludes, "The conclusion from this list of approximate or inconclusive tests can only be that there is room for doubt about the accuracy of the F-tests on regression coefficients" (p. 549). Also, Quenouille (1957, pp. 43-44) has pointed out explicitly that serial correlation in the error terms in (10) can be produced by the omission of relevant variables.

For the empirical implementation of (12), it is necessary to make assumptions regarding the form of $V(L)x_t$, an *infinite* distributed lag. Sims (1972) chooses to approximate this infinite distributed lag term by a finite distributed lag term and explains ". . .the length of the estimated lag distributions was kept generous" (p. 545). Keeping the length "generous" is understandable in terms of avoiding a misspecification of the lag pattern. However, this approach does involve a finite truncation of the lag and introduction of many lag parameters, an important consideration when only 78 degrees of freedom are available in his data. A basic result of this approach is evident from the reported standard errors associated with the estimates of the distributed lag coefficients in Sims's Table 4 (p. 547). In his regression of quarterly filtered GNP on eight past, current and four future quarterly values of filtered monetary base, his largest standard error is 0.338, while his smallest is 0.276. The absolute values of his coefficient estimates for the four future values of the monetary base range from 0.088 to 0.65. In the case of GNP on M1, his coefficient standard errors range from 0.294 to 0.318, while the future coefficient estimates range from 0.105 to 0.300 in absolute value. These results indicate that the precision of estimation is quite low even when possible autocorrelation of disturbance terms is overlooked. The same can be said of his other two-sided regressions. This lack of precision in estimation is noted as a statistical caveat by Sims (1972) in about the middle of his paper:

> Though the estimated distribution looks like what we expect from a one-sided true distribution, the standard errors on the future coefficients are relatively high. These results are just what a unidirectional causality believer would expect, but they are not such as to necessarily force a believer in bidirectional causality to change his mind. (p. 547)

In other words, Sims is saying that his analyses, viewed from an estimation point of view, *have yielded inconclusive results*. The results would be even more inconclusive if one were to do a detailed analysis of the validity and power of the *F*-tests employed in the paper. In view of these considerations, it must be stated that Sims's strong conclusions about the exogeneity of money, stated at the opening and end of his paper, are not convincingly supported by his empirical analyses. As pointed out above, his estimates are imprecise and his tests are not very powerful, even when no consideration is given to autocorrelated errors, seasonal complications, effects of filtering, left-out variables, and forms of monetary policies. When these latter points are considered, Sims's conclusion becomes even more uncertain.

Unlike Sims, Feige and Pearce (1976) and Pierce (1977) do not directly estimate a dynamic regression. Instead, they (a) use differencing to make their variables stationary, (b) construct autoregressive-moving average (ARMA) models for their differenced variables, and (c) then compute contemporaneous and lagged cross-correlations from the estimated innovations of their ARMA schemes for the pairs of variables under consideration and test their significance. Enough has been said above about the possible important effects of differencing or other filtering techniques on results of analyses as well as complications associated with policy control, errors of measurement, etc. As regards step (b) of the process, there is often some difficulty in determining the forms of ARMA schemes from data. Any errors in this operation would be carried over to affect the operation in (c). Finally, in step (c), a large sample χ^2 test is employed to test the hypothesis that population cross-correlations are all zero. As lucidly explained by Pierce (1977, p. 15), step (c) is closely related to, but not exactly the same as, analyzing a dynamic regression directly, as Sims (1972) does.

In the one explicitly reported example in Pierce's (1977, p. 15) paper, he investigates the relationship between weekly retail sales and currency in circulation. After completing steps (a)-(c) above, he obtains a sample test statistics' value, $\sum_{k=-10}^{k=10} n \hat{r}_k^2 = 39.1 > \chi_{0.01}^2 (21) = 38.1$. Thus, at the 1 percent level of significance, his large sample χ^2 test, using the estimated cross-correlations of the innovations, the $\hat{r}_k$'s, yields a "significant" result. Pierce comments,

> One could tentatively conclude that there is unidirectional causality from retail sales to currency (although the situation concerning feedback is somewhat unclear): evidently a rise in retail sales results in a somewhat greater demand for currency. . .The explanatory power of this relationship is quite small, however, as the cross correlations are not large. (p. 16)

These remarks are quite confusing to the uninitiated reader. Pierce's statistical test yields "significant" results at the 1 percent level of significance; yet, he has doubts about the results of the test. A similar methodological statement is made by Sims (1972):

> In applying the F-tests for causal direction suggested in the preceding section, one should bear in mind that the absolute size of the coefficients is important regardless of the F value. It is a truism too often ignored that coefficients which are "large" from the economic point of view should not be casually set to zero no matter how statistically "insignificant" they are. (p. 545)

Apparently, Pierce and Sims are pointing to a defect of mechanical significance tests. The information in the testing procedures does not reflect all the relevant information. Nowhere is what Sims suggests is reasonable done by Pierce or by Feige and Pearce; that is, Pierce and Feige and Pearce do not look at the absolute sizes of the individual dynamic regression coefficients and/or their sum. In a simple regression of y on x, the regression coefficient is $\beta = \sigma_{xy}/\sigma_x^2$, while the correlation coefficient is $\rho = \sigma_{xy}/\sigma_x\sigma_y = (\sigma_x/\sigma_y)\beta$. Clearly, a small ρ need not necessarily imply a small β. Similar considerations carry over to apply to cross-correlations and dynamic regression coefficients. Thus, there is an element of uncertainty regarding an analysis of causality that relies only on the estimated cross-correlations and standard significance tests, as employed by Pierce and Feige and Pearce, without adequate concern for the power of these tests relative to precisely specified alternative hypotheses. This point was raised by the author in connection with the Feige-Pearce analysis several years ago in a meeting of the University of Chicago Money Workshop.

From this review of three papers in which tests of causality have been applied, it is concluded that for a variety of reasons the tests' results are inconclusive with respect to the basic issues considered. The inconclusive nature of the results may, in part, be due to technical problems discussed quite extensively by the authors, particularly Pierce and Sims. However, the problem goes deeper than just "technical issues." The fundamental lack of subject matter considerations and theory exhibited in these studies is probably at the heart of the inconclusive nature of the results. Instead of formulating sophisticated models, which take account of subject matter considerations and relevant economic theory, the authors attempted to operationalize a nonoperational definition of causality. This operation led to consideration of an extreme form

47

of a fully recursive model as the null hypothesis with little or no attention paid to economically motivated, *specific* alternatives. The very special null hypothesis appears to have been tested against a very wide range of loosely specified, from an economic point of view, alternatives. Given such a broad range of alternatives, it is no wonder that results are as inconclusive as they are. Further, with little in the way of economic laws and other subject matter considerations involved in the testing, it is questionable that the analyses are properly termed "tests of causality," according to Feigl's definition.

It is indeed surprising that, of the authors considered, only the statistician Pierce appears sensitive to the important role of economic laws or theory mentioned in the previous paragraph. Pierce (1977) writes in his concluding paragraph,

> Considering all of these problems, it is perhaps small wonder that incompatible propositions can often be "confirmed" by the same data, including in particular the proposition that a variable is not related to any of a number of other variables. If future research bears out this type of result, we might justifiably conclude that econometric [i.e., statistical] analysis is of rather limited use in ascertaining certain economic relationships. Economic theory is in such situations all the more important: since we cannot assume that the mathematical relationships contained within this theory can be established as valid statistical relationships-- that is, as more valid than statistical "relationships" where a variable is related only to its own past--it is imperative that prior information be available concerning these relationships. (p. 21)

Recognizing the failure of "measurement without theory" and the failure of "theory without measurement," Pierce offers the hope that intelligent use of sophisticated economic theory and relevant statistical techniques may be successful. This approach is in line with Feigl's definition of causation and with what has been preached, if not always practiced, in the traditional econometric approach.

V. Summary and Conclusions

In the preceding sections, a philosophical definition of causation, which reflects philosophers' thinking and clarification of the concept of causation, has been reviewed and compared with several definitions of causation that have been published in the econometric literature. In addition, consideration was given to several applications of "causality tests" that have appeared in the literature. From this review and comparison of definitions of causation and analysis of causality tests, the following major conclusions have been reached:

1.   The philosophical definition of causality, reviewed above, is adequate for work in econometrics and other areas of science, a conclusion considered to be fortunate, given the importance that the present writer attaches to the "unity of science" principle.

2.   The philosophical definition of causality, reviewed above, is an operational definition in contrast to the Wiener-Granger "population" definition of causality, a fact that would lead some to dismiss the latter definition on methodological grounds alone.

3.   Basmann's definition of causality is very close to the philosophical definition provided by Feigl. The former differs from the latter slightly in certain respects in cases in which only data relating to a single realization of a process are available.

4.   The Strotz-Wold definition of causality is subsumed in Feigl's and is rather narrow. Insofar as Strotz and Wold require that the world be "truly" recursive, they are placing an a priori restriction on the forms of economic models and laws that cannot be justified on purely *deductive* methodological grounds and is not required by Feigl's, Jeffreys's, Basmann's and Simon's definitions of causality.

5.   Simon's definition of causality is a formal, deductive property of models, not an inductive property involving the quality of models' predictability, a consideration embedded in Feigl's, Jeffreys's and others' definitions. By narrowing the concept of causality, Simon and others have omitted a fundamental part of what is meant by causation or causality, namely the quality of predictions. Thus, a model can be causal in Simon's sense and yet yield worthless predictions.

6.   Simon's definition of causality does not require temporal asymmetry between cause and effect in chronological time. Simon's definition is in agreement with Feigl's point of view, but in conflict with the "true recursive model" view of Strotz and Wold and with views expressed by Granger.

7. The Wiener-Granger definition of causality is unusual in that in it is embedded a particular confirmatory criterion that is not very general and is inapplicable in a variety of circumstances. In contrast, Fiegl's definition does not mention any particular confirmatory procedure.

8. The Wiener-Granger definition involves a special form of predictability but no mention of economic laws. In this regard it is devoid of subject matter considerations, including subject matter theory, and thus is in conflict with others' definitions, including Feigl's, that do mention both predictability and laws.

9. In "operationalizing" the Wiener-Granger definition of causality, various a priori restrictions are imposed on the class of economic laws covered by the definition. It is concluded that it is preferable to employ a more general definition of causality, such as Feigl's, which imposes only the restriction of predictability on forms of economic laws.

10. From the review of applied "causality tests," it is concluded that results of these tests are inconclusive. The specific reasons for this conclusion can perhaps be summarized by saying that there was inadequate attention to subject matter considerations, or to put it slightly differently, the studies represent examples of measurement without much economic theory and other subject matter considerations. Where subject matter considerations were brought to bear, they were not satisfactorily integrated with the statistical analyses.

11. In the tests of causality involving linear stationary processes, a particularly extreme form of a fully recursive model is regarded as defining the condition under which "one variable causes another" in the Wiener-Granger sense. This extreme restriction on the form of models is not required by a broader definition of a causal model linking the two variables.

12. Sims's use of "forward and backward" regressions and Feige, Pearce, and Pierce's use of cross-correlations of estimated innovations involve consideration of forms of stationary single-equation models involving many, many parameters. This is in violation of the Principle of Parsimony and the Simplicity Postulate. Practically, the result of such a violation in the present instance is consideration of regressions with many free parameters, which when analyzed with limited data resulted in rather imprecise estimates and tests with low power relative to alternative hypotheses involving serious departures from independence.

13. Mechanical filtering of series can exert a substantial influence on causality tests of the kind considered above.

In summary, it can be said that an adequate definition of causality is available. Departures from this definition have produced problems, while offering little in the way of dependable and convincing results. The mechanical application of causality tests is an extreme form of "measurement without theory," perhaps motivated by the hope that application of statistical techniques without the delicate and difficult work of integrating statistical techniques and subject matter considerations will be able to produce useful and dependable results. That this hope is generally naive and misguided has been recognized by econometricians for a long time and is a reason that reference is made to laws in Feigl's definition of causation. In establishing and using these laws in econometrics, there seems to be little doubt but that economic theory, data, and other subject matter considerations as well as econometric techniques, including modern time series analysis, will all play a role. "Theory without measurement" and "measurement without theory" are extremes to be avoided.

References

Allais, M. (1966), "A Restatement of the Quantity Theory of Money," *American Economic Review*, **56**: 1123-57.

Ansley, C.F. (1977), "Report on the NBER-NSF Seminar on Time Series," Graduate School of Business, University of Chicago. Mimeographed.

Basmann, R.L. (1963), "The Causal Interpretation of Non-Triangular Systems of Economic Relations," *Econometrica*, **31**: 439-48.

_____(1965), "A Note on the Statistical Testability of 'Explicit Causal Chains' against the Class of 'Interdependent' Models," *Journal of the American Statistical Association*, **60**: 1080-93.

Burks, A.W. (1977). *Chance, Cause, Reason: An Inquiry into the Nature of Scientific Evidence*. Chicago: University of Chicago Press.

Chetty, V.K. (1966), "Bayesian Analysis of Some Simultaneous Econometric Models." Ph.D. dissertation, Department of Economics, University of Wisconsin at Madison.

_____(1968), "Bayesian Analysis of Haavelmo's Models," *Econometrica*, **36**: 582-602, reprinted in *Studies in Bayesian Econometrics and Statistics in Honor of Leonard J. Savage*, eds. S.E. Fienberg and A. Zellner. Amsterdam: North-Holland, 1975.

Feige, E.L., and Pearce, D.K. (1976), "Economically Rational Expectations: Are Innovations in the Rate of Inflation Independent of Innovations in Measures of Monetary and Fiscal Policy?" *Journal of Political Economy*, **84**: 499-552.

Feigl, H. (1953), "Notes on Causality," *Readings in the Philosophy of Science*, eds. H. Feigl and M. Brodbeck. New York: Appleton-Century-Crofts, Inc.

Friedman, M. (1975), Personal communication.

Granger, C.W.J. (1969), "Investigating Causal Relations by Econometric Models and Cross-spectral Methods," *Econometrica*, 37: 424-38.

Granger, C.W.J., and Newbold, P. (1977). *Forecasting Economic Time Series.* New York: Academic Press.

Haavelmo, T. (1947), "Methods of Measuring the Marginal Propensity to Consume," *Journal of the American Statistical Association,* 42: 105-22, reprinted in *Studies in Econometric Method*, Cowles Commission Monograph No. 14, eds. W.C. Hood and T.C. Koopmans. New York: John Wiley & Sons, Inc., 1953.

Hendry, D.F. (1977), "Comments on Granger-Newbold's 'Time Series Approach to Econometric Model Building' and Sargent-Sims' 'Business Cycle Modeling Without Pretending to Have Too Much *A Priori* Economic Theory,'" *New Methods in Business Cycle Research: Proceedings from a Conference*, ed. C.A. Sims. Minneapolis: Federal Reserve Bank of Minneapolis.

Jeffreys, H. (1957). *Scientific Inference.* 2nd ed. Cambridge: University Press.

_____(1967). *Theory of Probability.* 3rd rev. ed. London: Oxford University Press.

Keynes, J.M. (1921). *A Treatise on Probability.* London: Macmillan and Co., Ltd.

Newbold, P. (1978), Personal communication.

Pierce, D.A. (1977), "Relationships--and the Lack Thereof--Between Economic Time Series, with Special Reference to Money and Interest Rates," *Journal of the American Statistical Association*, 72: 11-21.

Quenouille, M.H. (1957). *The Analysis of Multiple Time Series.* New York: Hafner Publishing Company.

Sargent, T.J. (1977), "Response to Gordon and Ando," *New Methods in Business Cycle Research: Proceedings from a Conference*, ed. C.A. Sims. Minneapolis: Federal Reserve Bank of Minneapolis.

Simon, H. (1953), "Causal Ordering and Identifiability," *Studies in Econometric Method*, Cowles Commission Monograph No. 14, eds. W.C. Hood and T.C. Koopmans. New York: John Wiley & Sons, Inc.

_____(1978), Personal communication.

Sims, C.A. (1972), "Money, Income and Causality," *American Economic Review*, 62: 540-52.

_____(1977), "Exogeneity and Causal Ordering in Macroeconomic Models," *New Methods in Business Cycle Research: Proceedings from a Conference*, ed. C.A. Sims. Minneapolis: Federal Reserve Bank of Minneapolis.

Stigler, G.J. (1949). *The Theory of Price*. New York: Macmillan Company.

Strotz, R.H. (1960), "Interdependence as a Specification Error," *Econometrica*, 28: 428-42.

Strotz, R.H., and Wold, H.O.A. (1960), "Recursive vs. Nonrecursive Systems: An Attempt at Synthesis," *Econometrica*, 28: 417-27.

Wold, H.O.A. (1960), "A Generalization of Causal Chain Models," *Econometrica*, 28: 443-63.

TESTS OF CAUSALITY
The Message in the Innovations

G. William SCHWERT*
University of Rochester

I. Introduction

Recently, several authors have used new time series techniques to analyze the pairwise relationships between such macroeconomic variables as the rate of growth of the money supply (defined several ways) and the rate of inflation (Feige and Pearce, 1976), or the rate of growth of demand deposits and the treasury bill rate (Pierce, 1977a). No statistically significant relationship could be found between these variables. Because such findings are in conflict with most previous empirical work using similar data, they raise questions about the validity of the previous methodologies, the new time series techniques, or both.

This paper describes the new time series techniques and illustrates the advantages and disadvantages of these techniques relative to more traditional methods. Autoregressive-integrated-moving average (ARIMA) time series models are used to construct predictions of the variable based on the past history of the series. The residuals or prediction errors from the ARIMA model are estimates of the "innovations" of the series, the part of each observation which could not be predicted using past data. The innovations from one series are correlated with the innovations from another series at several leads and lags to determine the relationship between the variables. Several special cases are worked out to illustrate the advantages and shortcomings of this technique. I conclude that it is important to consider the *power* of this procedure before putting much faith in empirical results which seem to find a "lack of relationship" between macroeconomic time series variables.

II. A Definition of Causality

Suppose that there are time series observations available on two economic variables, $\{y_t\}$ and $\{x_t\}$, and there is a question about whether "y causes x," or "x causes y." For example, suppose that one questions whether the money supply "causes" nominal income, or vice versa.

*The Center for Research in Government Policy and Business provided support for this research. The comments of Truman Clark, Eugene Fama, Martin Geisel, John Geweke, Michael Jensen, Charles Nelson, David Pierce, Charles Plosser, Harry Roberts, Clifford Smith, Jerold Warner, and William Wecker are gratefully acknowledged.

Granger (1969) suggests a definition of "causality" which is testable using regression or correlation techniques. Granger defines *simple causality* such that "x causes y" if knowledge of past x reduces the variance of the errors in forecasting y_t beyond the variance of the errors which would be made from knowledge of past y alone:

$$\sigma^2 (y_t | y_{t-1}, \ldots, x_{t-1}, x_{t-2}, \ldots) < \sigma^2 (y_t | y_{t-1}, \ldots) .$$

Granger also defines *instantaneous causality*, where current as well as past values of x are used to predict y_t.[1] If y is related to current or lagged x, but not future x, x is *exogenous* relative to y. (This parallels the concept of statistical exogeneity which is assumed when least squares techniques are used to estimate distributed lag or linear regression models.)[2] If x causes y and y causes x, then there is *feedback* between the variables. If y does not cause x and x does not cause y (even instantaneously), the two series are *unrelated*.

Appendix A provides a more formal definition of causality in the context of a system of linear stochastic difference equations. For the purpose of this paper, consider the distributed lag model between current y and both current and past x,

$$y_t = a + \sum_{i=0}^{\infty} \beta_i x_{t-i} + \eta_t$$

$$= a + \beta(L) x_t + \eta_t , \tag{1}$$

where $\beta(L)$ is a polynomial in the lag operator L, which is defined such that $L^k x_t \equiv x_{t-k}$. Sims (1972) proves that the disturbance η_t in (1) is uncorrelated with past, current, and future x if and only if "y does not cause x." If all of the coefficients of $\beta(L)$ are equal to zero, "x does not cause y."

Before considering time series methods of testing for causal relationships, it is worthwhile to consider the relationship of Granger causality to other

---

[1] Pierce and Haugh (1977) prove that it is impossible to determine a unique direction of causality if instantaneous causality exists.

[2] However, this definition of exogeneity does not rule out the possibility of feedback between the variables, since instantaneous causality could exist. Nelson (1978) illustrates this possibility and argues that exogeneity, in the sense of being determined outside the system, cannot be tested using nonexperimental data.

concepts of causality. Wold (1954) advocates the notion of *causal chains* between variables in order to specify a recursive structure for a system of simultaneous equations. However, Basmann (1965) shows that it is impossible to identify a unique direction of causality when the relationship between the variables is strictly contemporaneous. In contrast, the Granger concept of causality based on temporal ordering or predictability can be tested by determining whether y_t is related to past, current, or future values of x in addition to past values of y.

In a physical system, the principle of *post hoc ergo propter hoc* can be readily related to "causation." For example, if it rains and then the pond fills up, it is easy to believe that the rain caused the pond to fill up. However, in economic systems it is less clear that temporal ordering and causality should be synonymous. Economic agents make decisions based on expectations of what state of the world will occur in the future, and the process of forming expectations about the future can change the interpretation of Granger causality. The concept of *rational expectations* (Muth, 1961) or *efficient markets* (Fama, 1970) suggests that this problem will occur whenever one deals with a market where arbitrage profits could be made if actual prices deviate from expected prices in a systematic way.

For example, Fama (1975) has analyzed the relationship between the monthly Consumer Price Index (CPI) inflation rate and the nominal return on a one-month treasury bill, which is known at the beginning of the month. He finds that the treasury bill rate predicts the subsequently observed inflation rate. Subsequent work by Nelson and Schwert (1977) indicates that the treasury bill rate *causes* the rate of inflation in the Granger sense, since the treasury bill rate adds significant information beyond that contained in past inflation rates for predicting inflation. However, this interpretation of the relationship between interest rates and inflation is misleading. An alternative interpretation of these empirical results is that the treasury bill rate contains an efficient assessment of the expected inflation rate, so that interest rates adjust to different levels of *expected* inflation over time. In this scenario, predictable movements of inflation *cause* movements in the interest rate in the usual sense of the word.

Thus, the Granger concept of causality based on temporal ordering will not lead to sensible conclusions about directions of causation in many instances. Zellner (1977, 1979) provides a valuable discussion of this and other problems with temporal ordering as a definition of causality. Nevertheless, this definition of causality provides a focus for empirical work designed to determine the relationships between economic time series variables. For example, if there is feedback between y and x, usual regression techniques applied to one-way distributed lag models would often yield inconsistent parameter estimates.[3] Thus, tests of Granger causality can be an important part of the analysis of the specification of econometric models between time series variables.

III. Some Examples

Sims (1972) uses seasonally adjusted quarterly data from 1947-69 to test for unidirectional causality (exogeneity) in the relationships between gross national product (GNP) and the nominal money supply defined in two ways: (*a*) the monetary base (MB), which is currency plus reserves adjusted for changes in reserve requirements, and (*b*) M1, which is currency plus demand deposits. Sims estimates two-sided distributed lag equations:

$$y_t = a + \sum_{i=-4}^{8} \beta_i x_{t-i} + \gamma \underline{z}_t' + \epsilon_t ,$$

where y_t and x_t are transformed values of GNP, MB, or M1 (regressions of both GNP on money, and money on GNP are estimated), and $\underline{z}_t$ represents a vector of seasonal dummy variables and a time trend variable. Sims then uses F-tests to determine the joint significance of the lead coefficients ($\beta_{-4}, \ldots, \beta_{-1}$) and the lag coefficients ($\beta_0, \beta_1, \ldots, \beta_8$) from each of the regressions. Because Sims recognizes the importance of having serially uncorrelated disturbances in his regression, he uses the natural logarithms of all of his variables, and he uses the autoregressive filter $(1-0.75L)^2 = (1-1.5L + 0.5625L^2)$ to transform each of the variables. For example,

---

[3] If $\{x_t\}$ is autocorrelated and the true relationship between y and x is a two-sided distributed lag,

$$y_t = a + \sum_{i=-k}^{m} \beta_i x_{t-i} + \epsilon_t ,$$

then least squares estimators of the regression coefficients for the one-sided distributed lag,

$$y_t = a + \sum_{i=0}^{m} \beta_i x_{t-i} + \eta_t ,$$

are biased and inconsistent because the disturbance, $\eta_t = \sum_{i=-k}^{-1} \beta_i x_{t-i} + \epsilon_t$, is correlated with the regressors.

$$y_t \equiv \ln \text{GNP}_t - 1.5 \ln \text{GNP}_{t-1} + 0.5625 \ln \text{GNP}_{t-2}$$

is the transformed value of GNP.

On the basis of F-tests, Sims (1972) concludes that although GNP is not exogenous to money, there is "no evidence that appears to contradict the common assumption that money can be treated as exogenous in a regression of GNP on current and past money" (p. 550). However, as a result of several types of tests on the regression residuals, Sims notes that "there is room for doubt about the accuracy of the F-tests on regression coefficients" (p. 549).

Indeed, Feige and Pearce (1974) reexamine Sims's tests using different types of prefilters and note that Sims's results do not hold up under some choices of transformations of the variables. In particular, when they analyze estimates of the innovations of money and income, which are the residuals from univariate ARIMA models for each of the variables, they cannot reject the hypothesis that there is no relationship between money and income at usual significance levels.

Williams, Goodhart, and Gowland (1976) use similar data from the United Kingdom for the 1958-71 period to test for causal relationships between money and income. Using different transformations, including first differencing, they find no strong noncontemporaneous relationships between money and income in the U.K. In fact, the regression relationships between transformed money and transformed income are so weak that Williams, Goodhart, and Gowland cannot reject the hypothesis that all of the regression coefficients are zero at usual significance levels. Thus, they cannot reject the null hypothesis that nominal income is unrelated to the money supply.

Rutner (1975) analyzes the relationships between the monetary base and M1 using spectral analysis and finds little relationship between these time series after they have been transformed or filtered. He estimates a high order autoregression for each variable and then takes the residuals from that regression as his "detrended" series. Rutner finds no significant contemporaneous relationship between the transformed money supply (M1 or M2) and the transformed monetary base (adjusted or unadjusted for changes in reserve requirements). However, spectral analysis of the transformed series indicates a statistically significant long-run (low frequency) relationship between the transformed series, with some indication that the base leads the money supply in the long run.

Feige and Pearce (1976) examine the relationship between several definitions of the money supply (M1, M2, or MB) and the price level as measured by the Consumer Price Index (CPI) or the Wholesale Price Index (WPI) during the

1953-71 period. They estimate ARIMA models for monthly and quarterly versions of the variables and use the residuals from these models as estimates of the innovations for the respective series. They perform two tests to determine causal relationships based on the cross-correlations between the residuals from the monetary variables and the residuals from the price variables. First, they compute the correlation coefficients between the residuals from a price series, a_{yt}, and the residuals from a monetary series, a_{xt},

$$r_{a_y a_x}(i) = \operatorname{corr}(a_{yt}, a_{xt-i}).$$

They compare each individual cross-correlation estimate with its asymptotic standard error (which is $T^{-1/2}$ under the null hypothesis of zero cross-correlations), and they look for estimates which are more than two standard errors different from zero for $i = 12, \ldots, 0, \ldots, -12$. Second, they use a joint test developed by Haugh (1972) to test whether all of the cross-correlations are zero.[4] On the basis of these test procedures, Feige and Pearce "could not reject the hypothesis that the rate of inflation is causally independent of the monetary aggregates. . .which appears to be in direct conflict with both popular doctrine and a substantial body of published econometric literature" (p. 519).

Pierce (1977a) examines the causal relationships between a variety of economic time series variables using weekly data from September, 1968 through April, 1974. For example, using tests based on Haugh's S-statistic, he cannot reject the hypothesis that demand deposits (DD) are unrelated to the 90-day treasury bill rate (TB) at all leads and lags.

These examples, which highlight existing applications of time series techniques to questions of causal relationships between economic variables, indicate some of the puzzling and conflicting results which have been derived using different methodologies. Since the procedure of analyzing the innovations of different series has surprisingly failed to detect any substantial relationship between economic variables such as the money supply and nominal income or the price level, the remainder of the paper investigates the properties of the new time series methodologies.

---

[4] The statistic

$$S = T \sum_{i=-M}^{M} [r_{a_y a_x}(i)]^2$$

has an asymptotic χ^2 distribution with $2M+1$ degrees of freedom under the null hypothesis that all $2M+1$ cross-correlations are zero. Note that S can be defined over any range of the cross-correlation function; it does not have to be symmetric around lag zero. Appendix B discusses these test procedures further.

IV. Time Series Methods for Analyzing Causality

On the basis of work by Haugh (1972, 1976) and Haugh and Box (1977), Pierce and Haugh (1977) suggest a two-step procedure for implementing tests of causality. First, each variable is transformed to have a constant unconditional mean and variance over the sample period (possibly by using logarithmic and/or differencing transformations of the raw data). For example, the rates of change of many economic time series, the first differences of the natural logarithms, are stationary in this sense. Then, univariate autoregressive-moving average (ARMA) models are estimated for the transformed variables[5]

$$\phi_y(L)y_t = a_1' + \theta_y(L)a_{yt},$$

$$\phi_x(L)x_t = a_2' + \theta_x(L)a_{xt}, \tag{2}$$

where $\phi_y(L)$ and $\phi_x(L)$ are finite autoregressive polynomials in the lag operator; $\theta_y(L)$ and $\theta_x(L)$ are finite moving average polynomials in the lag operator; and a_{yt} and a_{xt} are each serially uncorrelated. Based on the univariate models for y and x in (2), the unexpected part of y which could not be predicted on the basis of its past history is a_{yt}. Similarly, a_{xt} is the part of x_t which could not be predicted on the basis of its past history. The disturbances a_{yt} and a_{xt} are referred to in the time series literature as the "innovations" of the ARMA processes in (2).

Note that the current value of a stationary ARMA process can always be represented as a weighted sum of the current and past innovations

$$y_t = \sum_{i=0}^{\infty} \Psi_i a_{yt-i}, \qquad \Psi_0 = 1,$$

where the Ψ_i weights are functions of the autoregressive and moving average parameters. The "systematic" or predictable part of the ARMA process is also a weighted sum of the past innovations

---

[5] Box and Jenkins (1976) and Nelson (1973) discuss procedures for specifying and estimating univariate ARMA models.

$$\hat{y}_t = y_t - a_{yt} = \sum_{i=1}^{\infty} \Psi_i a_{yt-i}.$$

Thus, analyzing the innovations of the time series does not eliminate or throw away the systematic part of the variable.

The second step in the Pierce-Haugh causality test is to examine the cross-correlations between a_{yt} and past, current, and future values of a_x, which is referred to as the cross-correlation function between a_y and a_x (as a function of lag i). Pierce and Haugh (1977) prove that the innovations, a_y and a_x, yield conclusions about causality identical to those about the transformed variables, y and x, in (2). For example, if "a_x causes a_y (but not instantaneously)" and "a_y does not cause a_x," then "x causes y (but not instantaneously)" and "y does not cause x." Nevertheless, the distributed lag model between the innovations series, $\{a_{yt}\}$ and $\{a_{xt}\}$, can be substantially different from the distributed lag model between the original variables, $\{y_t\}$ and $\{x_t\}$.

For example, consider the distributed lag model in (1) where y does not cause x, but x causes y,

$$y_t = a + \beta(L)x_t + \eta_t,$$

where
$$\beta(L) = \beta_0 + \beta_1 L + \beta_2 L^2 + \dots$$

is a polynomial in the lag operator, and η_t is a stationary disturbance which may be autocorrelated. Assume that η_t follows an ARMA process,

$$\phi_N(L)\eta_t = \theta_N(L)\epsilon_t,$$

where $\{\epsilon_t\}$ is "white noise," serially independent, identically distributed variables with mean zero and constant variance, σ_ϵ^2. The univariate ARMA representation of x_t in (2) can be substituted into (1) to yield

$$y_t = a' + \beta(L) \frac{\theta_x(L)}{\phi_x(L)} a_{xt} + \frac{\theta_N(L)}{\phi_N(L)} \epsilon_t .$$

Further substitution of the ARMA representation of y_t from (2) yields

$$\frac{\theta_y(L)}{\phi_y(L)} a_{yt} = \beta(L) \frac{\theta_x(L)}{\phi_x(L)} a_{xt} + \frac{\theta_N(L)}{\phi_N(L)} \epsilon_t$$

or

$$a_{yt} = \beta(L) \frac{\phi_y(L)}{\theta_y(L)} \frac{\theta_x(L)}{\phi_x(L)} a_{xt} + \frac{\phi_y(L)}{\theta_y(L)} \frac{\theta_N(L)}{\phi_N(L)} \epsilon_t , \qquad (3)$$

which is simply a distributed lag model for a_{yt} in terms of current and lagged values of a_x with ARMA disturbances,

$$a_{yt} = v(L) a_{xt} + \omega(L) \epsilon_t . \qquad (4)$$

Thus, if there is a one-sided distributed lag model between y and x such as (1), there is a corresponding one-sided distributed lag model between the innovations for the univariate ARMA models, a_y and a_x. We can test for "causal" relationships between time series variables using either the original variables or the innovations.

However, the distributed lag model between the innovations in (3) can be substantially different from the distributed lag model between the original variables in (1). The coefficients between y and x, $\beta(L)$, are generally different from the coefficients between a_y and a_x, $v(L)$. The contemporaneous coefficient is the same ($\beta_0 = v_0$), but it is necessary to consider the form of the ARMA models for y and x in order to determine the relationship between the lagged coefficients in $\beta(L)$ and $v(L)$.

The autocorrelation properties of the disturbances in (3) are also generally different from the autocorrelations of the disturbances of the original model (1). The ARMA models for y and x make a_y and a_x serially uncorrelated. Given the usual assumption that a_x and ϵ are independent, the distributed lag polynomial, $v(L) = \beta(L) \dfrac{\phi_y(L)}{\theta_y(L)} \dfrac{\theta_x(L)}{\phi_x(L)}$, places restrictions on the ARMA model

for the disturbances in (4), $\omega(L) = \dfrac{\phi_y(L)}{\theta_y(L)} \dfrac{\theta_N(L)}{\phi_N(L)}$. This is easy to see since

a_{yt} is just the sum of two independent ARMA processes which must cancel each other to produce a serially uncorrelated series. For example, suppose that v_0 and v_1 are nonzero, but all other v_i are equal to zero,

$$a_{yt} = v_0 a_{xt} + v_1 a_{xt-1} + N_t .$$

Since a_{yt} and a_{xt} are serially uncorrelated by construction, N_t must follow a first order moving average process

$$N_t = \epsilon_t - \theta_1 \epsilon_{t-1} .$$

The magnitude of θ_1 depends on the ratio v_1/v_0 and the relative variances of a_{xt} and ϵ_t.[6]

A few special cases should illustrate the differences between the distributed lag model for the original variables in (1) and the distributed lag model for the innovations in (3).

Case 1: Suppose that y and x have exactly the same ARMA representations, $\phi_y(L) = \phi_x(L)$ and $\theta_y(L) = \theta_x(L)$. In this special case, the distributed lag model between the innovations is exactly the same as the distributed lag model between the original variables,

$$v(L) = \beta(L) \dfrac{\phi_y(L)}{\theta_y(L)} \dfrac{\theta_x(L)}{\phi_x(L)} = \beta(L) .$$

---

[6] Box and Jenkins (1976, pp. 121-25) and Haugh and Box (1977, p. 126) discuss the relationships between $v(L)$ and $\omega(L)$ which are implied by the fact that a_{yt}, a_{xt}, and ϵ_t are all serially uncorrelated in (4).

However, the autocorrelation structure of the disturbances of the innovations model,

$$\frac{\phi_y(L)}{\theta_y(L)} \; \frac{\theta_N(L)}{\phi_N(L)} \; \epsilon_t \; ,$$

is generally different from the autocorrelation structure of the disturbances of the original model.

Case 2: Suppose there is a strictly *contemporaneous* relationship between y_t and x_t in (1), $\beta_0 \neq 0$ and $\beta_i = 0$ for $i = 1, 2, \ldots$. In general, the distributed lag coefficients between the innovations are nonzero at all lags, unless the ARMA models for y and x are identical. For example, suppose that y_t follows the first-order AR process with $\phi_y(L) = (1 - 0.9L)$ and $\theta_y(L) = 1$, and x_t is serially uncorrelated, so $\phi_x(L) = \theta_x(L) = 1$. Then

$$v(L) = \beta_0 \phi_y(L) \; . \tag{5}$$

By matching coefficients on both sides of equation (5), we can solve for the coefficients of $v(L)$:

$$v_0 = \beta_0 \; ,$$

$$v_1 = -0.9\beta_0 \; ,$$

$$v_j = 0 \; , \qquad\qquad j > 1 \; .$$

Note that if either $\theta_y(L)$ or $\phi_x(L)$ had been a polynomial of order greater than zero, the coefficients of $v(L)$ would generally be nonzero at all lags. Also, note that the *steady-state gain* (total multiplier)[7] between x and y is $\sum_{i=0}^{\infty} \beta_i = \beta_0$, while the gain between a_x and a_y is only one tenth as large,

$$\sum_{i=0}^{\infty} v_i = \beta_0 - 0.9\beta_0 = 0.1\beta_0 .$$

In this case, the relationship between y_t and x_t is only contemporaneous, so there is no easy way to identify a unique direction of causality based on equation (1). Nevertheless, there is evidence that x causes y from the relationship between a_y and a_x, since v_1 is nonzero.

The disturbance term in the model for the original variables must follow an ARMA process, since y is serially correlated, while x is not. The disturbance in the model for the innovations must follow a first order moving average process.

Case 3: Suppose there is a Koyck distributed lag relationship between y and x,

$$y_t = a + \frac{\beta_0}{1 - \delta L} x_t + \eta_t ,$$

where $\dfrac{\beta_0}{1 - \delta L} = \beta_0 (1 + \delta L + \delta^2 L^2 + \delta^3 L^3 + \ldots)$, so the distributed lag coefficients between x and y decay at the geometric rate: $\beta_i = \beta_0 \delta^i$. For example, suppose $\delta = 0.9$ and $\beta_0 = 0.1$, so that the steady-state gain between y and x is 1.0. As in Case 2, suppose that y_t follows the first order AR process with $\phi_y(L) = (1 - 0.9L)$ and $\theta_y(L) = 1$, and x_t is serially uncorrelated, so $\phi_x(L) = \theta_x(L) = 1$. In this case, the relationship between a_y and a_x is strictly contemporaneous:

$$v(L) = \beta(L)\phi_y(L) = \frac{\beta_0}{(1 - 0.9L)} (1 - 0.9L) = \beta_0 .$$

---

[7] The steady-state gain can be thought of as the long-run change in the level of y if x is set equal to one in all future periods. It represents the cumulative effect on all future values of y of the current value of x_t.

66

Thus, even though it appears that x causes y based on the one-sided distributed lag model between y and x, the relationship between a_y and a_x is strictly contemporaneous, so there is only instantaneous causality between y and x in this case. As in Case 2, the gain between a_x and a_y is only one-tenth as large as the gain between x and y.

These three cases highlight the differences between the distributed lag models for the original variables in (1) and for the innovations in (3). Case 1, where the ARMA models for y and x are identical, represents the only case where the distributed lag coefficients are the same at all lags for the two models. The last two cases illustrate the difficulty of determining anything about *simple causality* from the distributed lag model for the original variables. In Case 2, there is only a contemporaneous relationship between y and x, but there is a lagged causal relationship between the innovations, current a_y and past a_x. On the other hand, Case 3 involves a distributed lag of y on x, but only a contemporaneous relationship between a_y and a_x, so there is no evidence of simple causality (since lagged values of x or a_x *alone* cannot reduce the variance of the error in predicting y_t).[8]

Since the innovations $\{a_{x\,t}\}$ are serially uncorrelated, the distributed lag coefficients between a_y and a_x are proportional to the cross-correlation coefficients between $a_{y\,t}$ and $a_{x\,t-i}$. These illustrations indicate that the size and pattern of the cross-correlations between the innovations should be considered in relation to the implied values of the distributed lag coefficients for the relationship between the original variables. In the next section, two examples are provided to illustrate the importance of analyzing the implied coefficients of $\beta(L)$ in (1) as an integral part of the analysis of the innovations series.

V. Lack of Relationships?

A. *Inflation and the Money Supply*

As mentioned in Section III, Feige and Pearce (1976) analyze the relationships between monetary growth rates and inflation using the time series techniques described in the previous section and cannot reject the hypothesis that these variables are unrelated. Such a finding, if true, could have profound implications for the study of monetary economics. However, the inability to reject the null hypothesis does not confirm the hypothesis that the inflation

---

[8]Pierce (1975, pp. 355-56); Nelson (1975a, p. 342); and Pierce and Haugh (1977, pp. 274-75) note that this result occurs whenever $\beta(L) \cdot x_t$ has the same stochastic structure as the disturbance η_t in (1).

rate is unrelated to the growth rate of the money supply. It is necessary to consider the *power* of the test, the probability that the null hypothesis is rejected when it is false, before concluding that there is no relationship between inflation and monetary growth.

In order to analyze the Feige-Pearce results, monthly data from July, 1953-June, 1971 are used to estimate ARIMA models for the CPI inflation rate (not seasonally adjusted),

$$(1 - L^4)(1 - L)\rho_t = 0.30 \times 10^{-6} + (1 - 0.94L^4)(1 - 0.88L)a_{yt}$$
$$(1.80 \times 10^{-6}) \qquad (0.01) \qquad (0.03) \tag{6}$$

$$S(a_y) = 0.00194 \qquad Q^{a_y}(10) = 13.1 ,$$

and for the rate of growth of the monetary base (not seasonally adjusted or adjusted for changes in reserve requirements),

$$(1 - L^{12})m_t = 0.37 \times 10^{-3} + (1 - 0.89L^{12})a_{xt}$$
$$(0.07 \times 10^{-3}) \qquad (0.02) \tag{7}$$

$$S(a_x) = 0.00448 \qquad Q^{a_x}(11) = 16.7 ,$$

where standard errors are in parentheses, $S(a)$ is the standard deviation of the residuals, and $Q^a(K)$ is the Box-Pierce (1970) statistic for 12 lags of the residual autocorrelation function which has a χ_K^2 distribution in large samples under the hypothesis that all residual autocorrelations are zero. These ARIMA models are of the same form as the models used by Feige and Pearce, although the parameter estimates are somewhat different.[9] For the purposes of this illustration, the important thing to note is that the residuals, a_y and a_x, are not serially correlated.

Table 1 presents estimates of the cross-correlations between the price residuals, a_{yt}, and the monetary base residuals, a_{xt-i}, for $i = -12, \ldots, 0, \ldots, 12$. None of the estimated cross-correlations is more than two standard errors from zero, and there is no obvious pattern in the cross-correlation function.

---

[9] The differences may be attributable to several things. The estimates in (6) and (7) are obtained from an unconditional maximum likelihood procedure (see Box and Jenkins, 1976, pp. 212-20), whereas the Feige-Pearce estimates may be conditional on the initial conditions of the ARIMA process (see Box and Jenkins, 1976, pp. 209-12). Also, Feige and Pearce use monetary base data from the *Federal Reserve Bulletin*, while the data used in this paper are from the Federal Reserve Bank of St. Louis.

Table 2 presents Haugh's S-statistic for various combinations of leads and lags of the cross-correlation function.[10] None of these test statistics would reject the hypothesis that the monetary base and the CPI are unrelated at usual significance levels. In fact, all of the S-statistics are near their mean values under the null hypothesis of no relationship.

Although the cross-correlations between residuals in Table 1 are somewhat different from the estimates plotted by Feige and Pearce (1976, p. 513), the test results in Tables 1 and 2 lead to the same disturbing conclusion reached by Feige and Pearce: the CPI inflation rate, ρ, seems to be unrelated to the growth rate of the monetary base, m. However, the distributed lag model between ρ and m which is implied by the cross-correlations of the residuals in Table 1 gives a different impression of the relationship between the monetary base and the CPI.

Column (2) of Table 3 presents estimates of the distributed lag coefficients, v_i, between the innovations, a_{yt} and $a_{x\,t-i}$, which are proportionately smaller than the cross-correlations in Table 1. Column (3) of Table 3 contains the coefficients of the distributed lag model between ρ and m,

$$ \rho_t = \sum_{i=0}^{12} \beta_i m_{t-i} + \eta_t , $$

which are implied by the ARIMA models for ρ and m and the estimates of v_i in column (2). The footnotes to Table 3 and Appendix C describe the details of the calculations.

Taken at face value, the numbers in column (3) say that a 1 percent increase in the growth rate of the monetary base has a negligible effect on the current inflation rate, but the current growth rate of the monetary base increases the inflation rate in succeeding months by about 0.04 percent per month. Thus, a 1 percent increase in m leads to a 0.52 percent increase in ρ after one year. Such a finding is quite consistent with accepted beliefs about the time lag between a change in the growth rate of the money supply and a subsequent change in the inflation rate. However, when one realizes that most of the coefficients in column (2) have standard errors which are larger than the estimates, it is apparent that the set of implied values of β_i in column (3) is fortuitously in conformance with previous findings. In fact, a very wide range of patterns of β_i is consistent with the cross-correlations of the innovations in Table 1. Thus, even if knowledge of past monetary growth rates does not

---

[10]Note that the asymptotic distribution of S is χ^2 only in the case where *all* cross-correlations are zero, whether they are included in the computation of S or not. Pierce (1977a, p. 15), Sims (1977b, p. 24), Pierce (1977b, p. 25), and Pierce and Haugh (1977, p. 284) all discuss this problem.

TABLE 1

Cross-Correlations between the Residuals for the
Consumer Price Index and the Monetary Base

Lag, i	Corr(a_{yt}, a_{xt-i})	Lag, i	Corr(a_{yt}, a_{xt-i})
12	0.06	-1	0.07
11	0.06	-2	-0.11
10	0.02	-3	0.00
9	0.03	-4	0.01
8	0.00	-5	0.13
7	-0.03	-6	-0.08
6	-0.01	-7	-0.03
5	0.11	-8	-0.11
4	0.13	-9	0.03
3	0.08	-10	0.07
2	0.07	-11	-0.07
1	0.09	-12	0.03
0	0.00		

Note: Based on data from July, 1953 to June, 1971. The large sample standard error for each estimate is 0.07, under the null hypothesis that the series are unrelated.

TABLE 2

Tests of the Lack of Relationship
between Monetary Growth and the Inflation Rate

$$S = T \cdot \sum_{i=L}^{M} [r_{a_y a_x}(i)]^2$$

	L	M	Degrees of Freedom	S
Feedback				
	-24	24	49	46.7
	-12	12	25	26.4
x causes y				
	1	24	24	27.5
	1	12	12	13.9
y causes x				
	-24	-1	24	19.2
	-12	-1	12	12.6

Note: Tests based on the cross-correlations between the residuals from the ARIMA model for the growth rate of the monetary base, a_x, and the residuals from the ARIMA model for the inflation rate of the CPI, a_y.

70

TABLE 3

Distributed Lag Model between the CPI and the Monetary Base
Implied by Cross-Correlations of the Innovations

Lag i	Estimates of Distributed* Lag Coefficients for Innovations, $\hat{v}_i$	Implied Distributed† Lag Coefficients for Original Variables, β_i	Cumulative Sum of β_i, $\sum_{k=0}^{i} \beta_k$
(1)	(2)	(3)	(4)
0	0.001	0.001	0.001
1	0.041	0.041	0.041
2	0.028	0.033	0.074
3	0.033	0.041	0.115
4	0.058	0.070	0.186
5	0.047	0.069	0.255
6	- 0.006	0.022	0.277
7	- 0.012	0.015	0.292
8	0.001	0.029	0.320
9	0.011	0.041	0.362
10	0.009	0.037	0.399
11	0.026	0.056	0.455
12	0.026	0.060	0.515

*$\hat{v}_i = r_{a_y a_x}(i) \cdot S(a_y)/S(a_x)$, where $S(a_y)$ and $S(a_x)$ are the estimates of the standard deviations of a_y and a_x from equations (6) and (7).

†Implied values of β_i are computed from the estimates of v_i using the relationship

$$\beta(L) = v(L) \frac{\theta_y(L)}{\phi_y(L)} \frac{\phi_x(L)}{\theta_x(L)} .$$

Based on the time series models for the CPI and the monetary base in equations (6) and (7),

$$\beta(L) = v(L) \left\{ \frac{(1 - 0.88L)(1 - 0.94L^4)}{(1 - L)(1 - L^4)} \right\} \left\{ \frac{(1 - L^{12})}{(1 - 0.89L^{12})} \right\} .$$

The β_i coefficients can be obtained by matching coefficients of the polynomials on each side of the equation. Appendix C contains some representative calculations.

provide a substantial improvement in predictions of future inflation rates, it is not appropriate to assume that the series are literally unrelated. Perhaps more conventional regression techniques applied to the analysis of the original data, ρ and m, can provide more powerful tests of specific hypotheses of interest to monetary economists.[11]

B. Demand Deposits and the Treasury Bill Rate

As mentioned in Section III, Pierce (1977a) cannot reject the hypothesis that demand deposits, DD, are unrelated to the 90-day treasury bill rate, TB, at all leads and lags using the time series techniques described in Section IV. Pierce does not report the cross-correlations between the innovations of these series, but he does report the ARIMA models used to construct the innovations series. Table 4 presents three hypothetical sets of coefficients relating demand deposits to current and lagged values of the treasury bill rate on a weekly basis,

$$DD_t = a + \sum_{i=0}^{9} \beta_i TB_{t-i} + \eta_t ,$$

along with the coefficients of the distributed lag models between the innovations of DD and TB,

$$a_{yt} = \sum_{i=0}^{9} v_i a_{xt-i} + N_t , \tag{8}$$

which are implied by the ARIMA models Pierce reports. Even when the relationship between DD and TB is strictly contemporaneous in column (1) of Table 4, the distributed lag coefficients between the innovations are small, erratic, and spread over time. The cumulative effects through ten lags for the innovations are less than half of the steady-state gain between TB and DD. The steady-state gain between a_x and a_y is only one-third of the gain between the original variables.[12]

---

[11]Plosser (1976, pp. 106-11) uses similar data, including the growth rate of industrial production as an additional regressor, and finds a more significant distributed lag model between ρ and m which has coefficients similar to those in column (3) of Table 3.

[12]The steady-state gain between a_x and a_y can be determined by evaluating the formula

$$v(L) = \beta(L) \; \frac{\phi_y(L) \; \theta_x(L)}{\theta_y(L) \; \phi_x(L)}$$

with $L = 1$.

TABLE 4

Distributed Lag Coefficients between Demand Deposits and the Treasury Bill Rate

Lag i	β_i^*	$v_i\dagger$	β_i^*	$v_i\dagger$	β_i^*	$v_i\dagger$
	(1)		(2)		(3)	
0	1.0	1.0	0.50	0.50	0.10	0.10
1	0.0	- 0.53	0.30	0.04	0.10	0.05
2	0.0	0.12	0.20	0.10	0.10	0.06
3	0.0	- 0.21	0.0	- 0.17	0.10	0.04
4	0.0	- 0.04	0.0	- 0.06	0.10	0.03
5	0.0	- 0.34	0.0	- 0.22	0.10	0.00
6	0.0	0.51	0.0	0.15	0.10	0.05
7	0.0	- 0.18	0.0	- 0.01	0.10	0.03
8	0.0	0.19	0.0	0.14	0.10	0.05
9	0.0	- 0.09	0.0	- 0.02	0.10	0.04
Sum of the Coefficients	1.0	0.44	1.0	0.45	1.0	0.46

Note: Pierce (1977a) uses weekly data from September, 1968 through April, 1974 to estimate the ARIMA model,

$$(1 - L)\, TB_t = (1 - 0.30L - 0.10L^5 + 0.12L^6)a_{xt}$$

for the 90-day treasury bill rate, and the ARIMA model,

$$(1 - L)\, DD_t = (1 + 0.23L + 0.18L^3 + 0.18L^4 + 0.32L^5 - 0.13L^6 + 0.16L^{16}$$
$$- 0.32L^{22} + 0.17L^{34} + 0.16L^{38} + 0.18L^{45})a_{yt}$$

for demand deposits. A periodic seasonal mean is subtracted out of each variable prior to estimating the ARIMA models.

*Coefficients for the hypothethical distributed lag model for the original variables,

$$DD_t = a + \sum_{i=0}^{9} \beta_i\, TB_{t-i} + \eta_t.$$

†Coefficients for the distributed lag model for the innovations,

$$a_{yt} = \sum_{i=0}^{9} v_i\, a_{xt-i} + N_t,$$

implied by the ARIMA models for TB_t and DD_t and the assumed values of $\beta_0, \beta_1, \cdots, \beta_9$.

Columns (2) and (3) in Table 4 show distributed lag models between DD and TB which are spread over 3 and 10 weeks with the same total impact. It is not difficult to believe that a change in the treasury bill rate would lead to changes in demand deposits for several subsequent weeks, so columns (2) and (3) probably present a more realistic set of assumptions about $\beta(L)$ than column (1). The implied coefficients of (8), the distributed lag model for the innovations, contained in columns (2) and (3) are small and erratic with no discernible pattern, and the cross-correlations of the innovations would be proportional to the v_i coefficients.

These calculations are presented to illustrate the difficulty of detecting relationships between DD and TB based on the cross-correlations between the innovations of these series. As with the Feige and Pearce (1976) example, the illustrative calculations in Table 4 show that quite reasonable relationships between the original variables can be difficult to detect from the cross-correlations of the innovations. Thus, failure to reject the hypothesis that the innovations series are unrelated at conventional significance levels should not be the end of the analysis. The power of such procedures against plausible alternative hypotheses should also be investigated.

VI. An Application of Alternative Test Procedures: Interest Rates and Inflation

As a final illustration of the weakness of the Pierce-Haugh tests against specific economic hypotheses, the time series techniques of Section IV are applied to Fama's (1975) model of short-term interest rates as predictors of inflation. Irving Fisher (1930) noted that the nominal interest rate, R_t, can always be viewed as the sum of the expected inflation rate, $E(\rho_t)$, and the expected real rate of interest, $E(r_t)$. The nominal interest rate on a default-free bond is known at the beginning of the period, but the inflation rate and real interest rate are not realized until the end of the period. Fama hypothesizes that the expected real interest rate on short-term U.S. treasury bills was constant over the 1953-71 period, so the expected inflation rate is the nominal interest rate minus the constant expected real rate,

$$E(\rho_t) = R_t - E(r) . \tag{9}$$

Fama tests his model using the regression model

$$\rho_t = a + \beta R_t + \epsilon_t \,, \tag{10}$$

where (9) implies that $\beta = 1$ and $a = -E(r)$ in (10). Using monthly data on one-month treasury bill yields and the CPI inflation rate for the January, 1953-July, 1971 period, $\hat{\beta} = 0.98$ with a standard error of 0.10, and the residuals are not substantially autocorrelated. Therefore, Fama concludes that the data support his model as expressed in (9).

A. Pierce-Haugh Tests

In order to carry out the Pierce-Haugh tests, it is necessary to construct ARIMA models for the inflation rate and the interest rate. Following the procedures of Box and Jenkins (1976), the CPI inflation rate from February, 1954 to July, 1971 is modeled as a multiplicative seasonal ARIMA process,

$$(1-L)(1-L^{12})\rho_t = (1 - 0.87L)(1 - 0.92L^{12})a_{yt} \,,$$
$$\phantom{(1-L)(1-L^{12})\rho_t = (1 - }(0.03)(0.02) \tag{11}$$

$$S(a_y) = 0.0019 \qquad Q^{ay}(10) = 13.9 \,,$$

where standard errors are in parentheses under the estimates of the ordinary and seasonal moving average parameters. The Box-Pierce (1970) statistic for 12 lags of the residual autocorrelation function indicates no model inadequacies.

The ARIMA model for the one-month treasury bill rate is of similar form,

$$(1-L)(1-L^{12})R_t = (1 - 0.27L + 0.20L^2)(1 - 0.90L^{12})a_{xt} \,,$$
$$\phantom{(1-L)(1-L^{12})R_t = (1}(0.07)(0.07)(0.02) \tag{12}$$

$$S(a_x) = 0.0003 \qquad Q^{ax}(9) = 20.1 \,.$$

Although the Box-Pierce statistic for the residual autocorrelations of (12) is large, the large autocorrelations occur at lags which are difficult to believe are

75

TABLE 5

Relationships between Interest Rates and Inflation, and Their Innovations

Lag i (1)	Cross-Correlations* of Innovations, $r_{a_y a_x}(i)$ (2)	Estimates of Distributed† Lag Coefficients for Innovations, $\hat{v}_i$ (3)	Implied Distributed‡ Lag Coefficients for Original Variables, β_i (4)	Sum of the Coefficients, $\sum_{k=0}^{i} \beta_k$ (5)	Cross-Correlations§ of Innovations Implied by Fama's Model, $\beta_0 = 1$ (6)
0	0.05	0.32	0.32	0.32	0.16
1	0.09	0.52	0.33	0.65	0.09
2	0.05	0.31	-0.12	0.53	0.11
3	-0.03	-0.15	-0.52	0.01	0.10
4	0.10	0.61	0.62	0.63	0.09
5	0.10	0.59	0.33	0.96	0.08
6	0.00	0.02	-0.53	0.43	0.07
7	0.11	0.64	0.41	0.84	0.06
8	0.00	-0.01	-0.35	0.49	0.05
9	0.13	0.77	0.60	1.09	0.04
10	0.11	0.65	0.21	1.30	0.04
11	0.00	0.02	-0.61	0.69	0.03
12	0.02	0.14	-0.09	0.60	0.03

*The large sample standard error for each of these estimates is 0.07 under the hypothesis that the series are unrelated.

†$\hat{v}_i = r_{a_y a_x}(i) \dfrac{S(a_y)}{S(a_x)}$, where $S(a_y)$ and $S(a_x)$ are the standard deviations of a_y and a_x from equations (11) and (12), respectively.

‡β_i coefficients determined by solving the equation

$$\beta(L) = v(L) \left\{ \frac{(1 - 0.87L)(1 - 0.92L^{12})}{(1 - 0.27L + 0.20L^2)(1 - 0.90L^{12})} \right\}$$

using the estimates of v_i in column (3).

§The cross-correlations of the innovations implied by the ARIMA models in equations (11) and (12) and Fama's model that $\beta_0 = 1$ and $\beta_i = 0$, for $i \neq 0$.

important, so (12) is accepted as an adequate univariate time series model for the interest rate.[13]

Column (2) of Table 5 contains the cross-correlations of a_{yt} with $a_{x\,t-i}$, for $i = 0, 1, \ldots, 12$, where a_y and a_x are the residuals from (11) and (12) respectively. None of these cross-correlation estimates is more than 2 standard errors different from zero, and Haugh's S-statistic for these 13 lags is 15.3, which is just slightly larger than the expected value of the statistic under the hypothesis that the series are unrelated. Thus, the cross-correlations of the innovations suggest that the inflation rate is unrelated to the interest rate.

Column (4) of Table 5 contains the values of the distributed lag coefficients, β_i, between the inflation rate and current and lagged interest rates. These coefficients are derived from the estimates of v_i in column (3) and the relationship

$$\beta(L) = v(L) \left\{ \frac{(1 - 0.87L)(1 - 0.92L^{12})}{(1 - 0.27L + 0.20L^2)(1 - 0.90L^{12})} \right\}.$$

Although the implied contemporaneous coefficient, β_0, is only 0.32, the cumulative sum of the coefficients in column (5) is close to 1. This implies that a 1 percent increase in the treasury bill rate is associated with a 1 percent increase in the inflation rate within a few months.

As an indication that the cross-correlations of the innovations in column (2) of Table 5 are not strong evidence against Fama's hypothesis, the cross-correlations of the innovations which are implied by Fama's model are listed in column (6). First, the relationship

$$v(L) = \beta_0 \frac{(1 - 0.27L + 0.20L^2)(1 - 0.90L^{12})}{(1 - 0.87L)(1 - 0.92L^{12})},$$

where $\beta_0 = 1$, is used to solve for the implied distributed lag coefficients between the innovations, v_i. Then, the relationship

$$r_{a_y a_x}(i) = v_i \frac{S(a_x)}{S(a_y)}$$

---

[13]The time series models in (11) and (12) are the same ones selected by Plosser (1976) after considering a wide variety of model forms. Alternative models yielded similar results in the Pierce-Haugh tests of relationships between interest rates and inflation.

is used to solve for the implied cross-correlations of the innovations. Because the cross-correlations implied by Fama's model in column (6) are small and close to the actual estimates in column (2), the Pierce-Haugh tests do not provide strong evidence against Fama's hypothesis.

B. Parametric Tests of Causality

As mentioned in Section II, Nelson and Schwert (1977) take a more direct approach to testing whether the interest rate contains predictive information about inflation beyond that contained in past inflation rates. Nelson and Schwert embed the interest rate as an additional variable in the time series model for inflation and find that the interest rate does contain significant incremental information. For example, the model

$$(1-L^{12})(1-L)\rho_t = 0.67(1-L^{12})(1-L)R_t + (1-0.68L^{12})(1-0.74L)\epsilon_t$$
$$(0.33) \qquad\qquad (0.05) \qquad (0.05) \quad (13)$$

is a generalization of both Fama's model (10) and the ARIMA model for inflation (11). If the coefficient of $(1-L^{12})(1-L)R_t$ is zero, (13) specializes to the ARIMA model, and the interest rate does not "cause" inflation in Granger's sense. On the other hand, if both the ordinary and seasonal moving average parameters are equal to one, (13) specializes to Fama's model where all of the information about inflation contained in past inflation is subsumed by the interest rate.[14] Both extreme cases are rejected by the data at usual significance levels. Thus, the test against the specific alternative hypothesis implied by Fama's model can reject the null hypothesis that the variables are unrelated. The test in (13) is more powerful than the Pierce-Haugh test against Fama's alternative hypothesis. All of the diagnostic checks recommended by Box and Jenkins (1976, ch. 11) indicate that (13) is an adequate representation of the relationship between inflation and interest rates.

---

[14]Note that a conventional *t*-test of the hypothesis that a moving average parameter equals one cannot be based on the Student-*t* distribution since such a parameter is on the boundary of the admissible parameter space (i.e., the moving average process is not invertible when the MA parameter equals one). Plosser and Schwert (1977) report sampling experiments which can be used as a basis for this test.

VII. Summary and Conclusions

A. Advantages of the Time Series Techniques

The primary motivation for adopting the Pierce-Haugh method is that application of conventional regression techniques to untransformed economic time series variables can often result in "spurious regressions." If both $\{y_t\}$ and $\{x_t\}$ are serially correlated or nonstationary through time, which is often the case with aggregate economic data, regression equations which are estimated using least squares can often yield spuriously "significant" results because of autocorrelated disturbances. Yule (1926) and Granger and Newbold (1974) illustrate the seriousness of this problem. In order to test causality hypotheses using conventional regression procedures, it is important that the disturbances of the regression equation be serially independent, identically distributed random variables. This is often an inappropriate assumption when dealing with the levels of macroeconomic time series variables. Plosser and Schwert (1978) discuss this argument in detail and provide some examples.

A secondary motivation for using the Pierce-Haugh procedure is that estimates of the regression coefficients v_i are unbiased even if some significant lagged values of a_x are omitted from the estimated regression equation. Unbiased regression coefficients result from the fact that the sequence $\{a_{x\,t}\}$ is serially uncorrelated by construction. On the other hand, omitted lagged values of the original regressor x generally cause the estimates of the regression coefficients β_i to be biased, because x_t is correlated with the omitted lagged values, x_{t-k}. Thus, the problem of specifying the length or form of the distributed lag model is less serious when using the serially uncorrelated innovations.

In summary, the Pierce-Haugh technique is relatively simple to apply in situations where the relationship between two time series variables is not well specified a priori. The Pierce-Haugh methodology reduces the problems of model specification required to perform tests of causality hypotheses. However, the increased flexibility does not come without sacrifices in other dimensions; in particular, the power of the Pierce-Haugh tests is likely to be low, relative to other test procedures, against specific alternative hypotheses.

B. Disadvantages of the Time Series Techniques

Even if one wishes to analyze the relationship between the innovations of two variables, the cross-correlation tests advocated by Pierce and Haugh (1977) may be less accurate than comparable statistics derived from the multiple regression

$$a_{yt} = \sum_{i=0}^{M} v_i a_{xt-i} + N_t . \qquad (14)$$

For example, the F-statistic which tests the significance of the regression (14) is proportional to Haugh's S-statistic divided by $(1 - R^2)$, where R^2 is the coefficient of determination from (14). $(M+1) \cdot F$ and S have identical asymptotic χ^2 distributions under the null hypothesis that all of the distributed lag coefficients v_i are zero. However, because $(M+1) \cdot F$ is always greater than or equal to S, the critical regions for these tests are not identical when asymptotic results are used. Thus, the null hypothesis of no relationship will be rejected by the F-test but not by the S-statistic. It is not clear which of these tests has the correct significance level in finite samples. Appendix B derives the algebraic relationship between the cross-correlation tests and regression tests in detail.

Of course, if the distributed lag model between a_y and a_x can be specialized, reducing the number of parameters to be estimated, more powerful tests can be constructed. For example, if $v(L)$ can be modeled as a Koyck distributed lag,

$$v(L) = \frac{v_0}{1 - \delta L} ,$$

it is only necessary to estimate two parameters, v_0 and δ, in order to specify all of the v_i coefficients. Each v_i does not have to be estimated as a separate coefficient in the multiple regression (14), as it does when the Koyck restriction is not imposed on the coefficients.

All of the preceding discussion assumes that the innovations a_{yt} and a_{xt} are directly observable (or, equivalently, that we know the form and parameter values of the ARIMA models for y_t and x_t a priori). In practice, it is necessary to identify (specify) the form of the ARIMA model for each variable based on sample autocorrelations and partial autocorrelations (cf. Box and Jenkins, 1976), and then to estimate the parameters of the ARIMA models using the same sample of data. Thus, the residuals from the ARIMA models, $\hat{a}_{yt}$ and $\hat{a}_{xt}$, are estimates of the unobservable innovations, a_{yt} and a_{xt}. Haugh (1972) proves that $\hat{a}_{yt}$ and $\hat{a}_{xt}$ are consistent estimates of the innovations, so the S-statistic has the same asymptotic distribution under the hypothesis that the series are unrelated when the residuals are used in place of the true innovations. Nevertheless, Pierce (1977a) recognizes that the use of residuals to estimate the coefficients of (14) is analogous to the "errors-in-variables" problem:

It is well known that measurement error biases estimated regression coefficients toward zero when it occurs in the independent variable and inflates their standard errors when it occurs in the dependent variables. These influences would be expected to exert a like effect on the sample residual cross correlations as well. (p. 20)

Thus, tests of the hypothesis that innovations series are uncorrelated with each other at all leads and lags are more likely to accept the null hypothesis of no correlation in finite samples when residuals are used in place of the unobservable innovations.

If the original variables, y_t and x_t, are measured with error, the measurement errors will generally have a different influence on the estimators of the relationship between the innovations than on the estimators of the relationship between the original variables. Although it is impossible to say a priori, in some plausible cases the least squares estimators of the coefficients of $v(L)$ will be biased towards zero more than the least squares estimators of the coefficients of $\beta(L)$ (see Plosser and Schwert, 1978, for some examples). Thus, if the original variables are measured with random errors, causality tests based on the estimated innovations series could fail to detect relationships that would be detected using the untransformed data.

Finally, the relative power of the Pierce-Haugh test in comparison with other tests that two variables are unrelated, such as Sims's (1972) test based on the regression of y_t on past and future x, is unknown in general. It is very important that the regression disturbances are serially uncorrelated for Sims's test to be valid, but Hsiao (1977) argues that Sims's test, as well as some other tests, are likely to be more powerful than the Pierce-Haugh test if this condition is satisfied.

C. Summary

The merits of any statistical procedure must be considered in the context of the model and data which are available. In situations where there is no well-formed model to test, a general procedure which is not highly susceptible to specification errors, such as the Pierce-Haugh methodology, may be the best alternative. On the other hand, if one has a model about the relationship between two variables, such as the rate of inflation and the rate of growth in the money supply, the structure of the model will suggest a more powerful test of his hypothesis.

This paper has described and illustrated the new time series methodology for analyzing relationships between economic variables. Several important facts should be considered before adopting this new methodology to test for "causal" relationships between variables. First, the distributed lag coefficients between the innovations can be very different in pattern and magnitude from the distributed lag coefficients between the original variables, depending on the form of the ARIMA models for the variables. Second, statistical tests based on residuals from estimated ARIMA models may accept the null hypothesis of series independence too frequently. Third, existing statistical tests based on the sample cross-correlations between residual series may have low power against plausible alternative hypotheses, especially when short measurement intervals, such as a week or a month, are used.

Given these qualifications, Feige and Pearce's (1976) inability to reject the hypothesis that the rate of inflation is independent of the rate of growth of monetary aggregates or Pierce's (1977a) inability to reject the hypothesis that demand deposits are unrelated to the treasury bill rate should not be alarming. This paper does suggest that future analyses using the Pierce-Haugh methodology concentrate more on the relationship between the model for the innovations and the model for the original variables.

Finally, the semantic distinction between "causality" and "incremental predictability" should be emphasized. Economists are clearly interested in cause-effect relationships for the purpose of policy formulation; the *effect* on the inflation rate *caused* by a change in the rate of monetary growth is an example. On the other hand, forecasters, such as Pierce (1977a), have a legitimate interest in finding the best predictive model for economic variables. All of the variety of tests of Granger causality are clearly applicable in the latter context, but they may be misleading in the former context, because economic agents make decisions based on expectations about future events. Therefore, in the interests of clarity, future tests of Granger causality ought to be called tests of "incremental predictive content."

Representations of Causality

Suppose that $\{y_t\}$ and $\{x_t\}$ follow a covariance-stationary bivariate linear stochastic process,

$$
\begin{bmatrix} y_t \\ x_t \end{bmatrix} = \begin{bmatrix} \mu_y \\ \mu_x \end{bmatrix} + \begin{bmatrix} b_{11}(L) & b_{12}(L) \\ b_{21}(L) & b_{22}(L) \end{bmatrix} \begin{bmatrix} u_{1t} \\ u_{2t} \end{bmatrix} , \tag{15}
$$

where μ_y and μ_x are the unconditional means of y and x, and $b_{11}(L)$, $b_{12}(L)$, $b_{21}(L)$, and $b_{22}(L)$ are all polynomials in the lag operator L, which is defined such that: $L^k x_t \equiv x_{t-k}$. The disturbances, $\underline{u}_t' = [u_{1t} \ u_{2t}]$, have mean zero, $E(\underline{u}_t) = \underline{0}$, variances equal to one, and contemporaneous covariance equal to zero, $E(\underline{u}_t \underline{u}_t') = \underline{I}$, and they are serially uncorrelated within and between series, $E(\underline{u}_t \underline{u}_{t+s}') = \underline{0}$ for $s \neq 0$.[15] Equation (15) is a moving average (MA) representation of the relationship between y and x. Sims (1972) proved that "x does not cause y" if and only if either $b_{11}(L)$ or $b_{12}(L)$ is zero or $b_{11}(L)$ is proportional to $b_{12}(L)$ in equation (15).

Granger's (1969) proof was expressed in terms of the autoregressive (AR) form of the bivariate process,[16]

$$
\begin{bmatrix} c_{11}(L) & c_{12}(L) \\ c_{21}(L) & c_{22}(L) \end{bmatrix} \begin{bmatrix} y_t \\ x_t \end{bmatrix} = \begin{bmatrix} a_1 \\ a_2 \end{bmatrix} + \begin{bmatrix} u_{1t} \\ u_{2t} \end{bmatrix} , \tag{16}
$$

where a_1 and a_2 are constant terms. Granger proved that "x does not cause y" if and only if $c_{12}(L) = 0$ in equation (16).

Finally, Sims (1972) proved that y_t can be expressed as a one-sided distributed lag function of current and past x,

$$
y_t = a + \beta(L)x_t + \eta_t ,
$$

---

[15] There are many ways to parameterize a bivariate model such as equation (15). I have adopted Sims's (1972) specification that u_{1t} and u_{2t} are independent "white noise" series with unit variance for convenience. Pierce and Haugh (1977) discuss different parameterizations of this model in detail.

[16] Here I assume that processes have both MA and AR representations. See Box and Jenkins (1976) for a discussion of stationarity and invertibility in the context of univariate processes.

with a disturbance η_t which is uncorrelated with past or future x if and only if "y does not cause x." Note that the disturbance η_t can be serially correlated. All three of these representations of causality are equivalent to the definition that "x causes y" if the variance of y_t conditional on past y and past x is less than the variance of y_t conditional on past y alone:

$$\sigma^2 (y_t | y_{t-1}, \ldots, x_{t-1}, \ldots) < \sigma^2 (y_t | y_{t-1}, \ldots).$$

Thus, Granger causality exists if information about x provides more precise predictions about future movements of y than could be made by knowing just the past history of y.

Appendix B

Relationship Between Cross-Correlation Tests and Regression Tests

Suppose that two white noise series $\{a_{yt}\}$ and $\{a_{xt}\}$ are related through the one-sided distributed lag model,

$$a_{yt} = \sum_{i=0}^{M} v_i a_{xt-i} + \eta_t , \tag{17}$$

where M is a finite integer and η_t is an autoregressive-moving average disturbance.[17] Since $\{a_{xt}\}$ is serially uncorrelated, the least squares estimators of the regression coefficients, v_i, from the multiple regression (17) are identical to the estimators obtained from the sequence of simple regressions,

$$a_{yt} = v_i a_{xt-i} + \epsilon_{it} , \qquad i = 0,1,\ldots M. \tag{18}$$

The least squares estimator, $\hat{v}_i$, is proportional to the estimator of the cross-correlation coefficient between a_{yt} and a_{xt-i},

$$r_{a_y a_x}(i) = \hat{v}_i \, \frac{S(a_x)}{S(a_y)} , \tag{19}$$

where $S(a_x)/S(a_y)$ is the ratio of the sample standard deviations of a_x and a_y.

Box and Jenkins (1976, pp. 376-77) note that when a_y and a_x are uncorrelated at all lags,

$$\sqrt{T-i} \cdot r_{a_y a_x}(i) \overset{\sim}{} N(0,1) . \tag{20}$$

In other words, in large samples the cross-correlation coefficient estimator has a Normal distribution with mean of zero and a variance of $1/(T-i)$ when the

---

[17]The following analysis applies to the true innovations, but it also generally applies in large samples when residuals from ARIMA models (which are consistent estimators of the true innovations) are used instead.

two series are unrelated. This fact has led Haugh (1972, 1976) and Haugh and Box (1977) to suggest the statistic

$$S = T \cdot \sum_{i=0}^{M} [r_{a_y a_x}(i)]^2, \tag{21}$$

which has a chi-square distribution with $M+1$ degrees of freedom in large samples under the hypothesis that the series are uncorrelated at all lags.

Tests of Individual Coefficients

Note that (20) can be used to test whether any individual cross-correlation coefficient is different from zero by comparing the statistic $\sqrt{T-i}\, r_{a_y a_x}(i)$, with a standard Normal distribution. This is analogous to the t-ratio from the simple regression in (18), and these statistics are related in the following way. The estimator of the sampling variance of $\hat{v}_i$ from (18) is

$$S^2(\hat{v}_i) = \frac{S^2(\epsilon_i)}{(T-i)S^2(a_x)},$$

where $S^2(\epsilon_i)$ is the estimator of the variance of the disturbance in (18). Thus, the t-ratio from (18) is

$$t = \frac{\hat{v}_i}{S(\hat{v}_i)} = \frac{\sqrt{T-i}\, S(a_x)\hat{v}_i}{S(\epsilon_i)}. \tag{22}$$

Using the relationship in (19),

$$t = [\sqrt{T-i}\, r_{a_y a_x}(i)] \cdot \frac{S(a_y)}{S(\epsilon_i)},$$

where $S(a_y)/S(\epsilon_i)$ measures the degree of association between a_y and $a_{x\,t-i}$. For example, the coefficient of determination for (18) is defined as $R_i^2 = 1 - \dfrac{S^2(\epsilon_i)}{S^2(a_y)}$, so the t-ratio in (22) is equal to the cross-correlation test statistic divided by $\sqrt{1-R_i^2}$. In large samples, both the cross-correlation test statistic (20) and the regression test statistic (22) have standard Normal distributions under the null hypothesis that $v_i = 0$. However, whenever $\hat{v}_i$ is not exactly zero, and hence R_i^2 is positive, the regression test statistic will be larger than the cross-correlation test statistic. Therefore, the regression test will reject the null hypothesis more frequently at any level of significance. In other words, even though the cross-correlation test and the regression test have the same large sample distribution, in finite samples they must have different critical regions. The small sample properties of the tests are not well-known.

Note that if more than one of the distributed lag coefficients in (17) is nonzero, the t-ratios obtained from the multiple regression (17) will be larger than the t-ratios obtained from the sequence of simple regressions in (18). This occurs because the variance of the simple regression disturbance ϵ_{it} includes systematic variability due to other lagged values of a_x which are omitted from (18). In terms of the true parameters,

$$\sigma_{\epsilon_i}^2 = \sum_{\substack{j=0 \\ j \neq i}}^{M} v_j^2 \sigma_{a_x}^2 + \sigma_\eta^2 \, ,$$

so $\sigma_{\epsilon_i}^2$ is always larger than the variance of the disturbance from the multiple regression (17), σ_η^2, if more than one value of v_i is nonzero. Thus, tests of significance on individual lags are more powerful using the multiple regression model (17).

Tests of Sets of Coefficients

If one wants to test the joint hypothesis that a set of coefficients is equal to zero, there is relationship between cross-correlation and regression test statistics which is a direct extension of the previous case, where the tests involve only one coefficient. As mentioned above, the S-statistic defined in (21) has a χ_{M+1}^2 distribution in large samples under the hypothesis that $v_i = 0$ for all values of i. An alternative test is based on the F-statistic from the multiple regression (17)

$$F \equiv \frac{\hat{v}' X' X \hat{v}}{(M+1) S^2 (\eta)} \, ,$$

which has an F-distribution with $(M+1)$ and $(T\text{-}M\text{-}1)$ degrees of freedom. Note that $\underline{X}'\underline{X}$ is the cross-products matrix, which is just $T \cdot S^2(a_x) \cdot \underline{I}_{(M+1)}$, where $\underline{I}_{(M+1)}$ is an $M+1$ dimensional identity matrix, since $\{a_{x\,t}\}$ is serially uncorrelated with constant variance. Thus, it follows that

$$F = \frac{T \cdot S^2(a_x)}{(M+1)S^2(\eta)} \sum_{i=0}^{M} \hat{v}_i^2$$

$$= \frac{S^2(a_y)}{S^2(\eta)} \cdot \frac{1}{(M+1)} \cdot T \cdot \sum_{i=0}^{M} [r_{a_y a_x}(i)]^2$$

$$= \left(\frac{S^2(a_y)}{S^2(\eta)}\right) \cdot \left(\frac{1}{M+1}\right) \cdot S.$$

Therefore, the Haugh S-statistic in (21) is proportional to the multiple regression F-statistic:

$$S = \frac{S^2(\eta)}{S^2(a_y)} \cdot (M+1) \cdot F,$$

where the ratio $S^2(\eta)/S^2(a_y)$ is equal to one minus the coefficient of determination from (17), $(1\text{-}R^2)$. Because $(M+1) \cdot F$ has a $\chi^2{}_{M+1}$ distribution in large samples, both Haugh's S-statistic and the regression F-statistic have the same large sample distribution; however, the S-statistic is always smaller than the comparable F-statistic when R^2 is nonzero (Hsiao, 1977, p. 17, derives a similar result). Thus, the multiple regression F-test will reject the null hypothesis of no relationship more frequently than tests based on the S-statistic. This does not mean that the F-test is more powerful than Haugh's test; rather, it means that it is not really appropriate to use the same critical region for both tests. The small sample properties of these tests are as yet unknown.

Appendix C

Calculation of Implied Distributed Lag Coefficients

The distributed lag model for the original variables

$$y_t = a + \sum_{i=0}^{\infty} \beta_i x_{t-i} + \eta_t$$

$$= a + \beta(L)x_t + \eta_t \tag{23}$$

is related to the distributed lag model for the innovations of the original variables

$$a_{yt} = \sum_{i=0}^{\infty} v_i a_{xt-i} + N_t$$

$$= v(L)a_{xt} + N_t,$$

as seen in equations (1) and (3) in the text. Specifically, given the ARIMA models for y and x, represented by the autoregressive polynomials, $\phi_y(L)$ and $\phi_x(L)$, and the moving average polynomials, $\theta_y(L)$ and $\theta_x(L)$, the coefficients of $\beta(L)$ can be computed from the coefficients of $v(L)$, and vice versa, using the relationship

$$v(L) = \beta(L) \frac{\phi_y(L)}{\theta_y(L)} \frac{\theta_x(L)}{\phi_x(L)} .$$

For example, Table 3 contains estimates of v_i for $i = 0, 1, \ldots, 12$, based on the cross-correlations between the innovations of the inflation rate, a_y, and the innovations of the growth rate of the monetary base, a_x. The ARIMA models for these variables imply the following relationship between $\beta(L)$ and $v(L)$:

$$\beta(L) = v(L) \left\{ \frac{(1-0.88L)(1-0.94L^4)}{(1-L)(1-L^4)} \right\} \left\{ \frac{(1-L^{12})}{(1-0.89L^{12})} \right\}$$

$$= v(L) \left\{ \frac{1-0.88L-0.94L^4+0.83L^5-L^{12}+0.88L^{13}+0.94L^{16}-0.83L^{17}}{1-L-L^4+L^5-0.89L^{12}+0.89L^{13}+0.89L^{16}-0.89L^{17}} \right\}.$$

$$(24)$$

The coefficients of $\beta(L)$ can be obtained by calculating the coefficients of the right side of (24),

$$\beta_0 = v_0 ,$$

$$\beta_1 = \beta_0 + v_1 - 0.88v_0 ,$$

$$\beta_2 = \beta_1 + v_2 - 0.88v_1 ,$$

$$\beta_3 = \beta_2 + v_3 - 0.88v_2 ;$$

$$\beta_4 = \beta_3 + \beta_0 + v_4 - 0.88v_3 - 0.94v_0 ,$$

$$\beta_5 = \beta_4 + \beta_1 - \beta_0 + v_5 - 0.88v_4 - 0.94v_1 + 0.83v_0 ,$$

$$\beta_6 = \beta_5 + \beta_2 - \beta_1 + v_6 - 0.88v_5 - 0.94v_2 + 0.83v_1 ,$$

and so forth. Although this procedure is tedious when the ARIMA models for y and x are complicated, it is necessary to carry out this calculation in order to translate the cross-correlations of the innovations into the coefficients of the original model (23).

References

Basmann, R.L. (1965), "A Note on the Statistical Testability of Explicit Causal Chains against the Class of Interdependent Models," *Journal of the American Statistical Association*, **60**: 1080-93.

Box, G.E.P., and Jenkins, G.M. (1976). *Time Series Analysis*, revised ed. San Francisco: Holden-Day.

Box, G.E.P., and Pierce, D.A. (1970), "Distribution of Residual Autocorrelations in Autoregressive-Integrated-Moving Average Time Series Models," *Journal of the American Statistical Association*, **65**: 1509-26.

Fama, E.F. (1970), "Efficient Capital Markets: A Review of Theory and Empirical Work," *Journal of Finance*, **35**: 383-417.

_____(1975), "Short Term Interest Rates as Predictors of Inflation," *American Economic Review*, **65**: 269-82.

Feige, E.L., and Pearce, D.K. (1974), "The Causality Relationship between Money and Income: A Time Series Approach." Manuscript.

_____(1976), "Economically Rational Expectations: Are Innovations in the Rate of Inflation Independent of Innovations in Measures of Monetary and Fiscal Policy?" *Journal of Political Economy*, **84**: 499-522.

Fisher, I. (1930). *The Theory of Interest*. New York: Macmillan, reprinted A.M. Kelley, 1965.

Granger, C.W.J. (1969), "Investigating Causal Relations by Econometric Models and Cross Spectral Methods," *Econometrica*, **37**: 424-38.

Granger, C.W.J., and Newbold, P. (1974), "Spurious Regressions in Econometrics," *Journal of Econometrics*, **2**: 111-20.

Haugh, L.D. (1972), "The Identification of Time Series Interrelationships with Special Reference to Dynamic Regression." Ph.D. dissertation, Department of Statistics, University of Wisconsin.

Haugh, L.D. (1976), "Checking the Independence of Two Covariance-Stationary Time Series: A Univariate Residual Cross Correlation Approach," *Journal of the American Statistical Association,* **71**: 378-85.

Haugh, L.D., and Box, G.E.P. (1977), "Identification of Dynamic Regression (Distributed Lag) Models Connecting Two Time Series," *Journal of the American Statistical Association,* **72**: 121-30.

Hsiao, C. (1977), "Money and Income Causality Detection." Manuscript, Berkeley: University of California, Berkeley.

Muth, J. (1961), "Rational Expectations and the Theory of Price Movements," *Econometrica,* **29**: 315-35.

Nelson, C.R. (1973). *Applied Time Series Analysis.* San Francisco: Holden-Day.

_____(1975a), "Rational Expectations and the Predictive Efficiency of Economic Models," *Journal of Business,* **48**: 331-43.

_____(1978), "Granger Causality and the Natural Rate Hypothesis," *Journal of Political Economy,* **86**.

Nelson, C.R., and Schwert, G.W. (1977), "On Testing the Hypothesis that the Real Rate of Interest is Constant," *American Economic Review,* **67**: 478-86.

Pierce, D.A. (1975), "Forecasting in Dynamic Models with Stochastic Regressors," *Journal of Econometrics,* **3**: 349-74.

_____(1977a), "Relationships--and the Lack thereof--between Economic Series, with Special Reference to Money and Interest Rates," *Journal of the American Statistical Association,* **72**: 11-22.

_____(1977b), "Rejoinder," *Journal of the American Statistical Association,* **72**: 24-26.

Pierce, D.A., and Haugh, L.D. (1977), "Causality in Temporal Systems: Characterizations and a Survey," *Journal of Econometrics,* **5**: 265-93.

Plosser, C.I. (1976), "A Time Series Analysis of Seasonality in Econometric Models with an Application to a Monetary Model." Ph.D. dissertation, University of Chicago.

Plosser, C.I., and Schwert, G.W. (1977), "Estimation of a Noninvertible Moving Average Process: The Case of Overdifferencing," *Journal of Econometrics,* 6: 199-224.

_____(1978), "Money, Income, and Sunspots: Measuring Economic Relationships and the Effects of Differencing," *Journal of Monetary Economics,* **4**.

Rutner, J.L. (1975), "A Time Series Analysis of the Control of Money," *Federal Reserve Bank of Kansas City Monthly Review,* January: 3-9.

Sims, C.A. (1972), "Money, Income and Causality," *American Economic Review,* **62**: 540-52.

_____(1977b), "Comment," *Journal of the American Statistical Association,* **72**: 23-24.

Williams, D., Goodhart, C.A.E., and Gowland, D.H. (1976), "Money, Income, and Causality: The U.K. Experience," *American Economic Review,* **66**: 417-23.

Wold, H. (1954), "Causality and Econometrics," *Econometrica,* **22**: 162-77.

Yule, G.U. (1926), "Why Do We Sometimes Get Nonsense Correlations between Time Series? A Study in Sampling and the Nature of Time Series," *Journal of the Royal Statistical Society,* **89**: 1-69.

Zellner, A. (1977), "Comments on Time Series and Causal Concepts in Business Cycle Research," *New Methods in Business Cycle Research,* ed. C.A. Sims. Minneapolis: Federal Reserve Bank of Minneapolis.

_____(1979), "Causality and Econometrics," *Carnegie-Rochester Conference Series,* **10**, eds. K. Brunner and A.H. Meltzer. Amsterdam: North-Holland.

Further Reading

Additional material on aspects of time series analysis which are relevant to Granger causality, and some applications to a variety of economic time series are contained in the following references.

Auerbach, R.D. (1976), "Money and Stock Prices," *Federal Reserve Bank of Kansas City Monthly Review,* October: 3-11.

Bomhoff, E.J. (1977), "Money and the Economy: Causation or Reverse Causation?" Manuscript. Rotterdam: Erasmus University.

Box, G.E.P., and MacGregor, J.F. (1974), "The Analysis of Closed-Loop Dynamic-Stochastic Systems," *Technometrics,* 16: 391-98.

Caines, P.E., and Chan, C.W. (1975), "Feedback between Stationary Stochastic Processes," *IEEE Transactions on Automatic Control,* 20: 498-508.

Caves, D.W., and Feige, E.L. (1976), "Efficient Foreign Exchange Markets and the Monetary Approach to Exchange Rate Determination." Manuscript. University of Wisconsin.

_____(1977), "Efficient Markets, Stock Returns, the Money Supply, and the Economy: Which Tail Wags the Dog?" Manuscript. University of Wisconsin.

Cramer, R.H., and Miller, R.B. (1976), "Dynamic Modelling of Multivariate Time Series for Use in Bank Analysis," *Journal of Money, Credit and Banking,* 8: 85-96.

Durbin, J. (1970), "Testing for Serial Correlation in Least Squares Regression When Some of the Regressors are Lagged Dependent Variables," *Econometrica,* 38: 410-21.

Feige, E.L., and McGee, R. (1977), "Money Supply Control and Lagged Reserve Accounting," *Journal of Money, Credit and Banking,* 9: 536-51.

Frenkel, J. (1977), "The Forward Exchange Rate, Expectations, and the Demand for Money," *American Economic Review,* 67: 653-70.

Friedman, M. (1969). *The Optimum Quantity of Money and Other Essays.* Chicago: Aldine.

Geweke, J. (1977), "Testing the Exogeneity Specification in the Complete Dynamic Simultaneous Equation Model." Manuscript. University of Wisconsin.

Granger, C.W.J. (1977), "Comment," *Journal of the American Statistical Association,* 72: 22-23.

Granger, C.W.J., and Newbold, P. (1977), "Identification of Two-Way Causal Systems," *Frontiers of Quantitative Economics,* 3, ed. M.D. Intrilligator. Amsterdam: North-Holland.

Nelson, C.R. (1975b), "Rational Expectations and the Estimation of Econometric Models," *International Economic Review,* 16: 555-60.

_____(1977), "Recursive Structure in U.S. Income, Prices and Output." Manuscript. University of Washington.

Pierce, D.A. (1977c), "R^2 Measures for Time Series," Special Studies Paper No. 93, Washington, D.C.: Federal Reserve Board.

Rogalski, R.J., and Vinso, J.D. (1977), "Stock Returns, Money Supply and the Direction of Causality," *Journal of Finance,* 32: 1017-30.

Sargent, T.J. (1976a), "A Classical Econometric Model of the United States," *Journal of Political Economy,* 84: 207-37.

_____(1976b), "The Observational Equivalence of Natural and Unnatural Rate Theories of Macroeconomics," *Journal of Political Economy,* 84: 631-40.

Sargent, T.J., and Wallace, N. (1973), "Rational Expectations and the Dynamics of Hyperinflation," *International Economic Review,* 14: 328-50.

Sims, C.A. (1975), "Exogeneity Tests and Multivariate Time Series: Part I," Discussion Paper No. 75-54, Center for Economic Research, University of Minnesota.

_____(1977a), "Exogeneity and Causal Ordering in Macroeconomic Models," *New Methods in Business Cycle Research*, ed. C.A. Sims. Minneapolis: Federal Reserve Bank of Minneapolis.

DISCUSSION OF THE ZELLNER AND SCHWERT PAPERS

Charles R. NELSON*

University of Washington

Zellner reviews the causality concepts which have appeared in the econometric literature and compares them with definitions offered by philosophers of science. The Wiener-Granger notion of causality, which has led to a large number of empirical studies in recent years, receives particular attention. The philosophical definition of causality used by Zellner is drawn from H. Feigl, who defines causation as *predictability according to a law*. This concept is contrasted with the Wiener-Granger definition which says, briefly, that x is said to cause y if and only if *past x* helps to predict y in a predictive relation which includes past y. Zellner points out that Wiener-Granger causality implies temporal asymmetry, while the Feigl definition and others used in the econometric literature do not; instead, they allow the possibility of contemporaneous causal relations. Zellner also criticizes the Wiener-Granger concept for lack of reliance on economic laws. A *law* is generally defined as "a principle based on the predictable consequences of an act." To clarify the meaning of this, I think it is useful to supplement Feigl's definition of *causality* with an acceptable definition of *cause*.

A definition of cause which has its origin in the writings of Mill and Hume, and which is still regarded as the most satisfactory by modern philosophies of science (See Mackie, 1965) is simply that x is a cause of y if x is a necessary part of a condition which itself is sufficient though perhaps unnecessary for y. Thus, government acreage restrictions are said to cause a rise in the price of wheat, since the restrictions are *ceteris paribus* sufficient for a rise in price, though this is not the only possible circumstance in which the price of wheat will rise. This is clearly the concept of causation underlying the statement by George Stigler quoted by Zellner, namely that "unless one knows what 'causes' a particular phenomenon, one cannot effect or prevent its occurrence."

The obvious appeal of the Wiener-Granger definition is that it leads directly to empirical tests which can be applied to nonexperimental data. One need only examine the incremental predictive content of past x for y, given past y, to determine whether x "causes" y. The fact that x helps predict y, given past

*It is a pleasure to comment on these two very stimulating papers by Arnold Zellner and G. William Schwert which deal with the confusing and confused problem of causality in economics. Arnold Zellner was one of my teachers and without his strong influence on me as a student it is doubtful that I would have pursued a serious academic career. He is therefore a *cause* of my being a discussant of his paper. William Schwert was one of my students and I would like to believe that I in turn had some influence on his development.

y, is consistent with x causing y, but it is also consistent with y causing x, or with both being caused by other factors. Lack of Wiener-Granger predictability is consistent with contemporaneous causal relationships. Thus, wheat prices may rise contemporaneously with acreage restrictions, or even in advance of acreage restrictions (due to anticipations), though it is the restrictions which hl are the cause of the rise in price. To establish that x is sufficient, given certain conditions, for the occurrence of y is much more difficult and in general requires controlled experimentation.

Zellner justly criticizes econometrics texts for failing to discuss the concept of causation and the distinction between causation and correlation. These texts also fail to discuss the relation between *exogenous* variables and causation. *Exogenous* simply means *produced externally* (from the Greek equivalents), and exogenous variables are causes, or potential causes, in econometric models. A different definition of *exogenous* seems to have been adopted in much of the recent Wiener-Granger literature, starting with Sims (1972), where *exogenous* is used as shorthand for *not caused in the Wiener-Granger sense*. Thus, if x is not "caused" by y in the Wiener-Granger sense, then x is said to be exogenous in several recent papers. What this does mean, as Sims has shown, is that in a regression of y on all future, current, and past x, future x will not appear. This does not preclude the possibility of feedback from y to x, as Sims has indicated. Therefore, this use of *exogenous* is not equivalent to *generated outside*. The simplest version of this situation is one in which y and x are bivariate Normal and correlated, but serially random. Although it is well known that regressions of y on x and x on y will each produce residuals which are uncorrelated with the respective right-hand side variable, this, of course, tells us nothing about whether x or y, if either, is determined outside the relationship. If the truth were that $y = \beta x + u$, where x is exogenous, and u is independent of x, then deliberate manipulation of x would be associated with a (βx) change in y on average, while manipulation of y would produce no change in x. As Zellner points out, it may be possible in more complex systems to test for the exogeneity of a variable (without experimentation) provided there is enough information about the relevant structure and the identities of exogenous and predetermined variables to allow identification of particular parameters. Correlations per se, however, can tell us as little about exogeneity as they can about causation.

Zellner and Schwert both criticize the Wiener-Granger literature on the grounds that there has been little concern about the power of the statistical tests being used to determine the direction and presence of Wiener-Granger relationships. It is suggested that tests based on unconstrained regression or cross-correlations of "prewhitened data" lack parsimony and that low power resulting from lack of parsimony may account for the apparent difficulty in establishing the existence of *any* significant relationship in many contexts where theory would suggest that strong relationships are present. Schwert focuses on the "innovations" tests developed by Pierce and Haugh (1977), which utilize the fact that the direction of Wiener-Granger "causality" corresponds to the presence of leading or lagging cross-correlations between x and y after they have been prewhitened to remove serial correlation. By reference to several plausible examples, Schwert shows that relatively strong one-way causal relationships between an exogenous x and y can correspond to very weak relationships between innovations in the sense that correlation between innovations is weak at any individual lag and is spread out across many (possibly an infinite number of) lags. While the relationships between y and x could be estimated parsimoniously in terms of a few parameters in these examples, the cross-correlation tests ask the data to estimate a large number of parameters. Schwert's careful reexamination of evidence from studies by Feige and Pearce (1976) and by Pierce (1977) suggests that the small correlations which were found between innovations for inflation rates and money growth rates and for demand deposits and treasury bill rates are not inconsistent with strong relationships between the original variables. While Nelson and Schwert (1977) had found a significant predictive relation between interest rates and subsequent inflation rates based on a simple parametric model, Schwert shows that cross-correlations between the innovations of these series fail to detect that Wiener-Granger relation.

The lack of parsimony of cross-correlation and unconstrained regression tests can be seen in the following prototypical situation. Suppose that y_t and x_t are generated by a simultaneous system of the form

$$\Gamma \left({y \atop x} \right)_t = B \left({y \atop x} \right)_{t-1} + \left({u' \atop v'} \right)_t ,$$

(where u' and v' are independent random disturbances) with reduced form

$$\left({y \atop x} \right)_t = \left[{\phi_{11} \ \phi_{12} \atop \phi_{21} \ \phi_{22}} \right] \left({y \atop x} \right)_{t-1} + \left({u \atop v} \right)_t .$$

From the Wiener-Granger definition, it is clear that x does not "cause" y if and only if $\phi_{12} = 0$, y does not "cause" x if and only if $\phi_{21} = 0$, and that a complete lack of relationship between y and x corresponds to $\phi_{12} = \phi_{21} = \text{cov}(u, v) = 0$. The innovations for y and x are the disturbances, say a_t and b_t respectively, in their respective univariate representations which are given by

$$[(1-\phi_{11}L)(1-\phi_{22}L)-\phi_{12}\phi_{21}L^2]y_t = (1-\phi_{22}L)u_t + (\phi_{12}L)v_t = (1-G_yL)a_t$$

$$[(1-\phi_{11}L)(1-\phi_{22}L)-\phi_{12}\phi_{21}L^2]x_t = (1-\phi_{11}L)v_t + (\phi_{21}L)u_t = (1-G_xL)b_t,$$

where G_y and G_x are parameters implied by the sums of moving averages in u and v. Thus, the innovations a and b are related to the random disturbances u and v by the infinite lag relations

$$a_t = u_t + (G_y - \phi_{22}) \sum_{i=1}^{\infty} G_y^{i-1} u_{t-i}$$

$$+ \phi_{12} \sum_{i=1}^{\infty} G_y^{i-1} v_{t-i}$$

$$b_t = v_t + (G_x - \phi_{11}) \sum_{i=1}^{\infty} G_x^{i-1} v_{t-i}$$

$$+ \phi_{21} \sum_{i=1}^{\infty} G_x^{i-1} u_{t-i}.$$

Note that in general the cross-correlations between the innovations are infinitely two-sided even though the cross-correlations are only a function of a few underlying parameters. Thus, the Pierce-Haugh cross-correlation tests based on prewhitened data essentially substitute the estimation of an unlimited number of correlations in place of tests based on three parameters: ϕ_{12}, ϕ_{21} and $\text{cov}(u, v)$.

The unconstrained two-sided regressions of Sims (1972) are closely related to the above expressions for the innovations, since we can also write

$$a_t = \sum_{i=-\infty}^{\infty} \lambda_i \, b_{t-i} + \epsilon_t^a$$

$$b_t = \sum_{i=-\infty}^{\infty} \delta_i \, a_{t-i} + \epsilon_t^b \,,$$

in which the coefficients λ and δ are simply the cross-correlations between a and b scaled by their relative standard deviations. We now substitute y and x for a and b respectively using the univariate representations linking y to a and x to b. Because these are simply lag polynomials, the infinitely two-sided regressions relating a and b correspond to infinitely two-sided regressions relating y and x; thus we have

$$y_t = \sum_{i=-\infty}^{\infty} \lambda_i' \, x_{t-i} + \epsilon_t^y$$

$$x_t = \sum_{i=-\infty}^{\infty} \delta_i' \, y_{t-i} + \epsilon_t^x \,.$$

Hence, the Sims two-sided regression procedure also asks the data to estimate, in principle, an infinite number of parameters.

It is apparent that even for very simple systems neither the Pierce-Haugh procedure nor the Sims procedure will be parsimonious in the use of parameters. We would expect, therefore, that neither would be as powerful in detecting relationships as would tests based on the reduced form of the system. Further, the reduced form has the additional advantage of offering insight into the dynamic properties of the system, while the cross-correlations and two-sided regressions are much more difficult to interpret involving, as they do, rather complex mixtures of underlying parameters.

References

Feige, E.L., and Pearce, D.K. (1976), "Economically Rational Expectations: Are Innovations in the Rate of Inflation Independent of Innovations in Measures of Monetary and Fiscal Policy?" *Journal of Political Economy*, 84: 499-522.

Mackie, J.L. (1965), "Causes and Conditions," *American Philosophical Quarterly*, 2: 245-55, 261-64.

Nelson, C.R., and Schwert, G.W. (1977), "On Testing the Hypothesis that the Real Interest Rate is Constant," *American Economic Review*, 67: 478-86.

Pierce, D.A. (1977), "Relationships--and the Lack Thereof--Between Economic Time Series, with Special Reference to Money and Interest Rates," *Journal of the American Statistical Association*, 72: 11-22.

Pierce, D.A., and Haugh, L.D. (1977), "Causality in Temporal Systems: Characterizations and a Survey," *Journal of Econometrics*, 5: 265-93.

Schwert, G.W. (1979), "Tests of Causality: the Message in the Innovations," *Carnegie-Rochester Conference Series*, 10, eds. K. Brunner and A.H. Meltzer. Amsterdam: North-Holland.

Sims, C.A. (1972), "Money, Income, and Causality," *American Economic Review*, 62: 540-52.

Zellner, A. (1979), "Causality and Econometrics," *Carnegie-Rochester Conference Series*, 10, eds. K. Brunner and A.H. Meltzer. Amsterdam: North-Holland.

A COMMENT ON THE PAPERS BY ZELLNER AND SCHWERT

Christopher A. SIMS

University of Minnesota

The last paragraph of the paper by Schwert and the first part of the paper by Zellner have a common theme: Granger causality is not related to "*causality*" as the term is used, or ought to be used, by economists. Schwert suggests that the phrase "Granger causality" be replaced by the phrase "incremental predictive content." Schwert's proposed revisions in terminology amount, in my opinion, to suggesting that a spade be called a "short-handled digging implement."

While Granger's definition of causality does not cover every sense in which people use the notion of causality, and while tests for Granger causality have been misapplied and misinterpreted, Granger's definition does crystallize the central usage of the notion of causality as it has developed in scientific economics. Part of the confusion and uneasiness which the profession has evinced in dealing with the Granger definition arises from the fact that it forces us to deal explicitly with, and to subject to test, uses of the notion of causality which had previously been largely implicit. Economists ordinarily decide which variables to treat as exogenous in a model according to notions of which variables are causally prior in some sense. The statistical properties of an exogenous variable are exactly those of "Granger causal priority." It is true that there are some instances in which what we mean by "money is causally prior to income" is not the same as what we mean by "money is exogenous in the money demand equation," but this possibility was not given much analytical attention, until the advent of Granger's definition. By forcing us to consider explicitly the subtle but important distinctions among the ways we use the notion of causality, Granger's definition is having a healthy effect; if we try to pretend that Granger causality is "not causality," we obtain a spurious relief from an important challenge.

It may be helpful for me to explain why statistical exogeneity and hence Granger causal priority are such important notions in nearly all econometric work. Consider a standard simultaneous equation model

$$\Gamma y(t) = \beta Z(t) + u(t),$$

where the variables in the vector $Z(t)$ are the "predetermined" variables. In order to discuss the statistical properties of estimators Γ and β, we have to be able to characterize the likelihood function of the observed sample as a function of the unknown parameters and the data. This is ordinarily done in econometrics by dividing the elements of the Z vector into two categories–lagged endogenous variables and strictly exogenous variables. The latter are taken to have distributions independent of the disturbances $u(t)$, and the former are the same as elements of $y(t)$, but with different time arguments. These assumptions suffice to translate a hypothesis about the distribution of $u(t)$ for the values of t in the sample into a hypothesis about the conditional distribution of observed y's given the values of the exogenous variables. If there are variables which are not lagged endogenous, but not independent of the residuals u, we could not write down the likelihood for the y's without specifying the nature of the dependence between u's and these variables–i.e., without specifying additional equations in the model which convert these variables to endogenous or lagged endogenous. Thus, the notion of strict exogeneity is inescapable whenever we construct a model which does not "explain" every variable which appears in the model. As I showed in my *American Economic Review* paper (1972), if there is a model with a certain list of variables exogenous, then those variables are causally prior in Granger's sense; i.e., they cause the endogenous variables; they are not caused by the endogenous variables.

Schwert is therefore mistaken in suggesting that Granger's definition is of interest primarily to people engaged in forecasting. People engaged in policy analysis must use structural models. A critical array of identifying assumptions in most such models is embodied in the list of variables taken to be exogenous. Though these assumptions have seldom been tested, they are testable and are seldom so obviously true as to deserve the status of maintained hypotheses. The notion of Granger causality, because it points to a way of testing exogeneity assumptions, is of at least as much interest to policy analysts evaluating structural models as it is to forecasters.

This notion that tests for Granger orderings are useful and important tests of specification in structural modeling is not dealt with directly by either Schwert or Zellner. It is possible that neither would take issue with this notion, in which case my disagreement with either of them is in some sense narrow.

One can of course argue that exogeneity and causal ordering are really different things. There are two ways to argue this. First, one can argue that I am wrong to say that economists have usually decided which variables to take as exogenous using some notion of causal priority. This question concerns how economists usually think, and the reader will have to judge that for himself.

Alternatively, one can argue that Granger causality is discordant with uses of the notion of causality in philosophy, physics, and engineering. Zellner undertakes some discussion along these lines. Since discussion of these matters quickly grows complex, and I am not sure this kind of discussion is of much use to anyone, I will limit my comment to my main disagreements with Zellner. The logical support for my assertions is in an earlier paper of mine (1977), which the interested reader may want to consult.

Zellner holds up Feigl's definition of causality as a standard. Against this standard, he finds Simon's and Granger's definitions of causality wanting in serious respects. I have no objection to Feigl's definition, but only because, when properly interpreted, it is so general that it includes all of the other definitions Zellner discusses. Everything depends on what "predictability" and "law" mean, and these two terms are at least as ambiguous, in my view, as is "causality." In my paper on this subject (1977), I give an abstract set-theoretic definition of a causal relation which can quite naturally be paraphrased as "predictability according to a law." I then go on to explain how Granger and Wold-Simon causal orderings arise as special applications of this definition and how both relate to the notion of "structural identification" in econometrics and to notions of "causal operators" in physics and engineering. The interested reader should look at that paper to see why I do not believe that the Granger definition of causality is an unreasonable specialization of the general notion of causality.

Of course Granger's definition is a specialization, but so are any of the notions of causality which are actually applied in economics. Thus, for example, prices are in a legitimate sense causally prior in a system of demand equations: such equations are derived as descriptions of the behavior of individuals maximizing utility subject to given price vectors. In this sense, prices are "causally prior," and this fact even has implications for the way we should specify the equations to be estimated; e.g., we would not ordinarily write demand equations which have current prices as a function of lagged quantities. But, at least in the case of demand equations, economists are used to the idea that causal priority in this sense is not related to the choice of exogenous variables in a model of market demand. (Sometimes, however, it does seem that similar errors are made in other areas; e.g., equations with output on the left and inputs on the right are called production functions, and the same equations with inputs on the left are called input demand functions. The fact that policy variables are always in one sense causally prior to the other variables in a model is sometimes assumed to make it likely that they are Granger-prior, i.e., exogenous, in data used for estimation.)

Part of the purpose of my earlier paper is to display various ways in which the Granger definition of causality might turn out to be different from other specializations of the notion which arise in economics. I will not try to go through that discussion again here. The point is that, while there certainly is more than one notion of "causality" in economics, all are logically related, and it sometimes happens that they coincide. Economists have not been simply in error to think that economic reasoning about what is causally prior may be helpful in deciding which variables belong on the right-hand side of a regression. Granger's definition helps us understand what such reasoning involves and what its pitfalls may be.

Both Schwert and Zellner offer discussion of the methodology of testing for Granger orderings. This discussion can be considered apart from their views on whether "Granger causality" is "causality." Most of what Schwert says is sensible and worth reading. He is not harsh enough on the Pierce-Haugh methodology, however. Although he acknowledges that the methodology may be less powerful than others, his strongest objection to it is the one he puts in footnote 10: there is *no* statistical theory which would justify the tests used in the Pierce-Haugh methodology as a means to detecting causal orderings! The Pierce-Haugh methodology can only be justified as a means of detecting the existence of relations between series. If one is concerned that perhaps money supply and GNP are unrelated, the Pierce-Haugh methods are a way of testing that hypothesis. If one concludes that they are related, some other method must be found to test whether there is a causal ordering between the variables. Pierce has argued elsewhere (1977) that when relations between series are in fact weak, the Pierce-Haugh methods may not be badly misleading concerning causal orderings. This is true, but only in a trivial sense: when relations between series are weak, the Pierce-Haugh tests for causality will resemble correct tests in having low power. Pierce and Haugh's argument that methods other than theirs may be infected by a "spurious regression" problem is itself spurious. Any method which takes account of the possibility of general patterns of serial correlation avoids the spruious regression problem. Methods of testing based on direct estimation of vector ARMA models avoid the problem if they are used with proper caution to avoid excessively parsimonious parameterizations. Methods based on two-sided regression avoid it if they are used with proper caution to take account of serial correlation in residuals. Both methods are practical, being as easy or easier to implement than the Pierce-Haugh scheme, and both yield justifiable tests for causal ordering. For further discussion of these matters from a practical point of view, see John Geweke's recent paper (1977).

Zellner has many points to make about methodology. Most of them are general points about time series estimation, with application beyond the narrow field of causality testing. I will not try to argue each point on which I disagree with Zellner; my view is that the reader can best understand these matters by looking at some examples of applied work by Zellner and myself. This will do more to clarify our real differences on the issues of "parsimonious parameterization" and of the role of economic theory in the building of models than could reading an abstract debate on these issues.

I would, however, like to discuss one point which Zellner makes. He begins his discussion of empirical work by pointing to Haavelmo's classic paper and to the fact that, by embedding Haavelmo's first model in a more general model, a test of exogeneity is obtained. Not only is this observation correct, but it can be expanded to yield general methods for testing exogeneity in overidentified models. This insight has recently been pursued by Wu (1973) and Revankar (1978). As Zellner suggests, these tests are more powerful than methods which do not use overidentifying restrictions available from a priori theory. While this fact certainly gives these methods an important role, it is in some contexts also a defect. These methods cannot be employed unless the model is overidentified, and they must treat some of the identifying restrictions as maintained hypotheses, or rather, they can only test exogeneity jointly with some overidentifying restrictions. Thus, if we were to find in the example of the Haavelmo model that investment is not exogenous according to this test, we could either conclude that the Haavelmo model is correct and investment is not exogenous, or, if we thought exogenous investment likely, we might conclude that the test is actually rejecting the simple dynamic structure of the Haavelmo model. We would be as justified in concluding that we should stick with the first model, generalizing its lag structure, as in concluding that the second model which makes investment endogenous is correct. To resolve this dilemma, the tests based on the Granger definition are available. They exploit the fact that to test exogeneity, one needs no more identifying restrictions than that some lags of supposedly exogenous variables are known not to enter the reduced form. In particular, if the model relates current values of endogenous variables to current and past values of exogenous variables, tests based on the Granger definition are possible. In many applications overidentifying restrictions are so scarce or so dubious a priori that tests based on the Granger definition will be a welcome replacement for, or adjunct to, tests like those of Wu and Revankar.

References

Gewke, J. (1978), "Testing the Exogeneity Specification in the Complete Dynamic Simultaneous Equation," *Journal of Econometrics,* 7: 163-86.

Pierce, D.A. (1977), "Rejoinder," *Journal of the American Statistical Association,* 72: 24-26.

Revankar, N.S. (1978), "Asymptotic Relative Efficiency Analysis of Certain Tests of Independence in Structural Systems," *International Economic Review,* 19: 165-80.

Sims, C.A. (1972), "Money, Income and Causality," *American Economic Review,* 62: 540-52.

_____(1977), "Exogeneity and Causal Ordering in Macroeconomic Models," *New Methods in Business Cycle Research,* ed. C.A. Sims. Minneapolis: Federal Reserve Bank of Minneapolis.

Wu, De-Min (1973), "Alternative Tests of Independence Between Stochastic Regressors and Disturbances," *Econometrica,* 41: 733-50.

REJOINDER TO NELSON AND SIMS

Arnold ZELLNER
University of Chicago

I thank both Nelson and Sims for their thoughtful remarks on my paper. To make this exchange of views as fruitful as possible, I shall take this opportunity to respond to some of their comments.

First, both Nelson and Sims are concerned about the definition of a law; Sims, in addition, is concerned about the definition of predictability as related to confirmation of a law. Nelson writes, "A *law* is generally defined as 'a principle based on the predictable consequences of an act.'" This definition is close to that provided by Burks (1977) in his extensive discussion of the properties of laws of nature, namely, "A law of nature is a general principle, rule, or theory that describes many possible successions of complete states, holds for many possible boundary conditions, or covers many possible circumstances" (p. 426). Also Jeffreys (1967) states, "Hence a physical law is not an exact [deterministic] prediction, but a statement of the relative probabilities of variations of different amounts" (p. 13). While these definitions differ somewhat in their wording, their meanings are close enough to one another to constitute useful definitions for both physical and social scientific uses. As regards predictability and confirmation of a law, Burks (1977) writes, "To say that instance *I* confirms *L* [a law] is to say that the probability of *L* posterior to *I* exceeds the prior probability of *L*. . ." (p. 426), and "Instance-confirmation may be understood as an application of Bayes' Theorem" (p. 629). Burks and Jeffreys (1967, p. 43ff. and ch. V and VI) explain how observed facts and data, predicted by laws, alter the prior probabilities associated with them. These considerations do not lend support to Sims's assertion that there is ambiguity associated with the definitions of *laws* and *predictability*.

Second, Sims writes, "Part of the confusion and uneasiness which the profession has evinced in dealing with the Granger definition arises from the fact that it forces us to deal explicitly with, and to subject to test, uses of the notion of causality which had previously been largely implicit." This statement is just an *opinion* regarding the views of the profession. My own opinion is that the profession is uneasy with the Wiener-Granger definition because it does not mention the important role of economic theory and laws and gives the impression that causality can be established on purely statistical grounds. To appreciate this point, consider the application of the Wiener-Granger definition to just price and physical sales in a market without mentioning or taking account of the laws of supply and demand, income, other product prices, and cost and other factors affecting demand and supply. This example brings to the fore what I regard as the central problem of the Wiener-Granger definition. On the other hand, it is reassuring to learn from Sims's comment that his own "abstract set-theoretic definition of a causal relation. . .can quite naturally be paraphrased as 'predictability according to a law.'" This attests to the generality of Feigl's definition; however, Feigl's definition is not broad enough to include the Wiener-Granger and Simon definitions, as I pointed out in my paper.

This last statement should not be read as implying that appropriate modern time-series tests of hypotheses are not relevant or of interest in connection with the formulation of economic laws or models. The important consideration here, as emphasized at the end of my paper, is that appropriate modern time-series testing techniques be applied to carefully formulated hypotheses. The application of time-series testing techniques to a collection of time-series variables without explicit subject matter considerations is an exploratory data analytic exercise, as mentioned in my discussion of Pierce's work.

Third, Nelson's example of a bivariate normal distribution for x and y and its two associated regressions exhibits well the distinction between the Wiener-Granger concept of "exogenous" and the traditional concept, summarized by Nelson as "generated outside."

Fourth, in my paper I employed the Haavelmo example to illustrate how it is possible to test for exogeneity of a variable within the context of an economic model. Many more examples of this kind could have been provided that involve joint tests of hypotheses regarding the values of structural coefficients and disturbance covariances. Recent work by my student Reynolds (1977)[1] takes up some of the technical aspects of a subset of the problems in this area. The Haavelmo example was also put forward to indicate how economic considerations can be employed to construct meaningful tests of exogeneity that can be more powerful than others that have been employed to establish Wiener-Granger relationships. Indeed, in the last part of his comment, Nelson forcefully demonstrates the "lack of parsimony of cross-correlation and unconstrained regression tests" and the fact, mentioned in my paper, that these approaches involve introduction of a very large number of parameters. Thus, some reduction of the dimensionality of the parameter space is required to apply these approaches. It is my belief that introduction of well-thought-out economic restrictions on the parameter space that are compatible with serious subject matter considerations is much more satisfactory, statistically and economically, than the mechanical restrictions and other operations required

---

[1] Reynolds's paper has an important relationship to the work of Wu and Revankar.

to operationalize the cross-correlation and two-sided regression approaches. Last, as pointed out in Schwert's and my papers, the largely unexplored power characteristics of these latter testing procedures is a key issue.

References

Burks, A.W. (1977). *Chance, Cause, Reason: An Inquiry into the Nature of Scientific Evidence.* Chicago: University of Chicago Press.

Jeffreys, H. (1967). *Theory of Probability.* 3rd rev. ed. London: Oxford University Press.

Nelson, C.R. (1979), "A Comment on the Zellner and Schwert Papers," *Carnegie-Rochester Conference Series,* 10, eds. K. Brunner and A.H. Meltzer. Amsterdam: North-Holland.

Reynolds, R. (1977), "Posterior Odds for the Hypothesis of Independence between Stochastic Regressors and Disturbances," Manuscript. H.G.B. Alexander Research Foundation, Graduate School of Business, University of Chicago.

Sims, C.A. (1979), "A Comment on the Zellner and Schwert Papers," *Carnegie-Rochester Conference Series,* 10, eds. K. Brunner and A.H. Meltzer. Amsterdam: North-Holland.

Zellner, A. (1979), "Causality and Econometrics," *Carnegie-Rochester Conference Series,* 10, eds. K. Brunner and A.H. Meltzer. Amsterdam: North-Holland.

A PRODUCTION FUNCTION--NONACCELERATING INFLATION
APPROACH TO POTENTIAL OUTPUT
Is Measured Potential Output Too High?

Jeffrey M. PERLOFF

University of Pennsylvania

and

Michael L. WACHTER*

University of Pennsylvania

The size of the gap between potential and actual output and the associated slack in the labor market are two of the main targets of stabilization policy. Policymakers faced with forecasting unemployment and potential output immediately reach for Okun's law. Although we shall do the same, our primary concern is not to reestimate the traditional form of the equation, but to reconnect the potential output of Okun's law to a production function concept that is consistent with nonaccelerating inflation. Since our attempted amendments will take us somewhat far afield from policy questions, it is useful to provide our answers at the outset. We find that as of the fourth quarter of 1977 (1977:4) the GNP gap is approximately $22.2 billion. This gap is considerably below most other studies' calculations. This implies that as of 1977:4, the economy is close to an unemployment rate compatible with nonaccelerating inflation.

Our estimates of potential output are based on the following building blocks: a translog aggregate production function; three factor inputs--labor, capital, and energy; variable parameter elasticities that respond to market conditions; and an approximation to a nonaccelerating inflation rate of unemployment constructed by Wachter (1976). Our resulting potential output series differs from most prevailing estimates not only because it suggests that the economy has nearly completed its cyclical recovery as of 1977:4, but also because it traces out, in relation to GNP, a pattern of cyclical periods of excess demand as well as excess supply. Most prevailing estimates of potential output found in the literature largely pass through the peaks of business cycles. In this fashion they appear to provide an estimate of the production possibility supply[1] of the

*Funding was provided by the National Institutes of Child Health and Human Development and the General Electric Foundation. The authors wish to thank Ernst Berndt, Roberto Mariano, and the participants at the April, 1978 Carnegie-Rochester Conference for many helpful suggestions. Data were kindly supplied by Peter Clark, Paul Flaim, Robert Rasche, John Tatom, and Data Resources, Inc. Martin Asher, Choongsoo Kim, and Debbie Faigen provided exceptional research assistance.

[1] By the *production possibility supply*, we mean not the maximum supply that could be produced using inputs full time, but rather the supply which results from fixing hours of inputs at their noncyclical rates.

economy, rather than a potential output series which is historically consistent with stable prices.

The Council of Economic Advisers, in 1977, introduced a new potential series in which the 1977 GNP gap was virtually half of that implied by the historical series. We shall argue that even this gap may be too large and may need to be halved again.[2]

Although we estimate a specific level for the GNP gap, there are substantive and methodological problems in constructing a potential output series. The old CEA potential series was exogenous and grew along an exponential growth trend. Current definitions of potential, including our own, make that construct endogenous. Unfortunately, it is not possible to measure and/or to specify all the myriad factors that affect potential output. Most troublesome for policy purposes is that potential is a function of the policy variables themselves; that is, potential cannot be viewed as a target independent of the policy path chosen to achieve it.

I. Background

In the early 1960s, when activist stabilization policy was coming into vogue, a gap existed in the policy tool kit. While monetary and fiscal policies could be used to alter aggregate demand, the appropriate target for GNP was ill-defined. Arthur Okun's seminal work "Potential GNP: Its Measurement and Significance" (1962) was aimed at that problem. Okun derived the remarkably stable relationship which is now referred to as Okun's law:

$$QPOT = Q[1 + 0.032(U - U^*)] , \qquad (1)$$

where $QPOT$ is potential output or GNP, Q is actual GNP, U is measured unemployment, and U^* is the nonaccelerating inflation rate of unemployment-- assumed to be constant at 4 percent. Okun's law actually addressed two questions at once. First, and most important, it served as a method of calculating potential output, given GNP and unemployment. Second, and almost by accident, it developed into a method of predicting unemployment. Indeed, today, Okun's law is probably better known for this latter attribute.

---

[2]The new CEA series is discussed in the Annual Report of the Council of Economic Advisers, January, 1978, pp. 83-86. Their series, which is largely based on the work of Clark (1977), will hereafter be referred to as the Clark potential series. The historical potential output series was originally developed by the CEA during the 1960s. We hereafter refer to that series as the old CEA potential measure.

Since Okun's law (1) includes two unmeasured variables, $QPOT$ and U^*, one of the two variables must be supplied for the relationship to be used to predict the other. Thus, the use of Okun's law as a device for forecasting unemployment requires an estimate of potential output which is consistent with the hypothesized U^*. If we assume, for example, that U^* is still 4 percent, we should also assume that potential output is relatively large. If we assume that U^* has increased substantially above 4 percent, we should also expect a smaller potential output. As long as excess demand in the product and labor markets vary together, and the $(U^*, QPOT)$ pair are based on consistent assumptions, Okun's law will forecast unemployment accurately. The goodness of fit of the equation cannot be used to determine which of the many $(U^*, QPOT)$ pairs is the "correct" one.

This paper does not address the metamorphosis of Okun's law from a potential output equation conditional on unemployment to an unemployment equation conditional on potential output. Our major concern is with reconnecting Okun's law with a production function estimate of potential output based on an unemployment rate consistent with nonaccelerating inflation. We use the term *reconnecting*, because Okun, in his 1962 paper, clearly stated that potential output should be defined in terms of nonaccelerating inflation.[3]

The potential output measure, as an empirical construct, has undergone several transformations over the past 15 years. The prevailing view immediately after publication of Okun's article was that potential output could be empirically approximated by a fixed exponential trend. Since capital and labor inputs were subject to serious measurement errors, but appeared to grow at an unchanging rate, it seemed reasonable to forego estimating a production function and simply use the exponential trend to determine potential output. Furthermore, since the economy had a steady 1 percent inflation rate, it was possible to forego Okun's warning about the nonaccelerating condition.

More recently, as labor force growth has increased, and productivity growth has declined, the exponent of the potential output series has been adjusted several times to reflect these developments. The resulting series is an exponential trend with several distinct kinks. This series seems to have been unofficially used by the Council of Economic Advisers (CEA) during the 1960s and, until recently, was regularly published in *Business Conditions Digest* of the Department of Commerce.

---

[3]When Okun's paper was published, the notion of a nonaccelerating inflation rate of unemployment had not yet been developed in the literature. But Okun is clear that his gap concept should be constructed so as to be compatible with stable inflation rates.

In our approach, Okun's law disappears and is replaced by a production function,

$$Q = f(K, L, E) , \tag{2}$$

and a Phillips curve,

$$\dot{w} = g(U, \{\dot{w}_{t-i}\} , X) , \tag{3}$$

where Q is output, K is capital, L is labor, E is energy, $\dot{w}$ is the rate of wage inflation, $\{\dot{w}_{t-i}\}$ is a vector of lagged inflation rates which reflects an expectations formation process, or the inertia in labor markets as a result of long-term contracts, and X is a vector of other exogenous variables. Equation (3) may be solved for a U^* which is consistent with nonaccelerating inflation. The U^* so obtained may vary over time and, as is shown below, differs substantially from the constant 4 percent U^* of some earlier studies. Potential output is then obtained by inserting a potential labor series, L^*, which is consistent with U^*, into equation (2).[4]

A major result of our study is that our potential output series tends to be significantly below most previous measures of potential output. There are three major reasons for this difference.

First, many older studies assumed that U^* was constant at 4 percent over the postwar period. Okun's original estimates, the old CEA numbers, and Eckstein and Heien (1976), among others use the 4 percent figure.[5] Our estimated U^* increases substantially over the last quarter century. This increase leads to a lower potential output series.[6]

Second, many studies do not use an explicit production function, but rather, as discussed above, fit trend lines. Due to the nature of the technique,

---

[4]It would, in principle, be possible to adjust capital and energy in the same manner as labor. In practice, however, such adjustments are not feasible, since we lack reliable measures of capacity in general much less capacity measures which are consistent with nonaccelerating inflation. The issue of adjusting capital is discussed in more detail in Sections II and III.

[5]The assumption that U^* is approximately 4 percent from 1947 to 1960, the years used in Okun's study, is consistent with the U^* series which we use. See Section IV.

[6]Many recent studies, such as Perry (1977a, 1977b), Clark (1977), and Rasche and Tatom (1977a, 1977b), have used U^* series which trend upward over time. Because of the difficulty of estimating and inverting a Phillips curve, these studies have created proxies for a U^* series by controlling for demographic changes. This approach is discussed in greater detail in Section IV.

the fitted trend lines tend to hit only the peaks of the actual output series. As a result, the $QPOT$ numbers so obtained are almost always greater than or equal to the actual output, Q. In a production function approach, Q may be less than, equal to, or greater than $QPOT$. The $QPOT$ measure is not a ceiling.

Recently, Perry (1977a, 1977b) and Clark (1977) have developed techniques that lie somewhere between the mechanical trend fitting approach and the production function method. Both form an input index, which is then allowed to trend over time.[7]

Third, our production function uses a specification which is different from those used by other production function studies.[8] Our production function uses energy as well as labor and capital in a functional form which is less restrictive than that of the Cobb-Douglas function and is cyclically sensitive (i.e., the parameters may vary over the cycle).[9]

The remainder of this paper discusses the issues in detail and uses a production function and U^* estimates to construct potential output series. The production function estimation procedure is discussed in Section II. Section III presents our production function estimates. The construction of U^* is described in Section IV. The construction of our potential output series is discussed in Section V. In Section VI, our potential output series are compared with series calculated by other researchers. Section VII examines the labor market predictions obtained by using various potential output series in conjunction with Okun's law. Our conclusions are presented in Section VIII.

II. The Production Function

In order to calculate a potential output series, we estimated an aggregate capital, labor, and energy (KLE) production function, equation (2), for the private, nonagricultural sector of the United States. Unlike authors of earlier

---

[7]Perry uses only labor data, while Clark uses both labor and capital. Clark combines his labor and capital series into an input index by using a Cobb-Douglas production function with nonestimated parameters.

[8]Thurow and Taylor (1966), Eckstein and Heien (1976), and Rasche and Tatom (1977a, 1977b), have used a Cobb-Douglas or modified Cobb-Douglas production function methodology to estimate potential output. Thurow and Taylor do not use a concept of U^*; rather, they ask how output would change if labor and capital grew at different rates. By avoiding the use of U^*, they have implicitly built in a constant value for that term. Eckstein and Heien assume that U^* is 4 percent.

[9]Eckstein and Heien (1976) estimate a standard Cobb-Douglas production function with labor, capital, and raw materials (mostly energy), for the private, nonagricultural sector. Rasche and Tatom (1977a, 1977b) use a modified Cobb-Douglas production function for the private business sector. Labor and capital enter in the usual fashion as quantity measures. Rather than include the quantity of energy, they use the price of energy to the price of output of the private business sector as a proxy. Their use of prices instead of the quantity of energy has been criticized by de Leeuw (1977). Thurow and Taylor (1966) use a modified Cobb-Douglas production function for the private economy which allows for cyclical variations of a Hicks neutral nature. They use only labor and capital as inputs and substitute trend values of labor and capital for the actual numbers.

potential output studies, we have *not* imposed the arbitrary elasticity restrictions of the Cobb-Douglas or other similar function forms. Instead, we have used the translog production function, which is a second-order Taylor's series approximation in logarithms to an arbitrary production function:[10]

$$\ln Q = \beta_0 + \beta_1 t + \beta_2 t^2 + \beta_3 t^3 + \beta_4 I, \tag{4}$$

$$I = a_L \ln L + a_K \ln K + a_E \ln E + \frac{1}{2}\gamma_{LL}(\ln L)^2 + \gamma_{LK}\ln L \ln K +$$

$$\gamma_{LE}\ln L \ln E + \frac{1}{2}\gamma_{KK}(\ln K)^2 + \gamma_{KE}\ln K \ln E + \frac{1}{2}\gamma_{EE}(\ln E)^2, \tag{5}$$

where t represents a time trend (which is 0.25 in 1955:1 and grows by 0.25 each quarter), I is an index of inputs, and the Greek letters are technologically determined parameters (with symmetry conditions imposed: $\gamma_{ij} = \gamma_{ji}$, $i, j =$ K, L, E). The time trend terms (t, t^2, and t^3) were included in the production function to reflect Hicks neutral technological changes. The higher order terms (t^2 and t^3) allow for changes in the rate of technological progress during the estimation period.

Constant returns to scale were imposed on the production function by means of the following restrictions:[11]

$$a_L + a_K + a_E = 1,$$

$$\gamma_{LL} + \gamma_{LK} + \gamma_{LE} = 0,$$

$$\gamma_{LK} + \gamma_{KK} + \gamma_{KE} = 0,$$

$$\gamma_{LE} + \gamma_{KE} + \gamma_{EE} = 0.$$

---

[10] For a more thorough discussion of translog production functions see Christensen, Jorgenson, and Lau (1973), Berndt and Christensen (1973, 1974), Berndt and Wood (1975), and Humphrey and Moroney (1975). See Berndt and Khaled (1977) for a critical examination of the translog specification.

[11] See any of the references cited in footnote 10 for details. The β_4 term in equation (4) serves to scale measured Q so that it is consistent with the factor cost measure. Thus, the Q in equations (7) and (8) is the rescaled Q, and the constant returns to scale conditions hold.

If the log-quadratic terms are ignored (by setting $\gamma_{ij} = 0$, $i, j = K, L, E$), the translog is simply a three-input Cobb-Douglas function, where a_K, a_L, a_E are the output elasticities. If, however, any of the log-quadratic terms are nonzero, the translog differs from the Cobb-Douglas. Thus, the Cobb-Douglas restrictions are testable within the translog framework.

Assuming that input and product markets are competitive (or subject to constant markups), a necessary set of conditions for efficient production are the factor demand equations,

$$f_i = p_i, \qquad i = K, L, E, \tag{6}$$

where p_i is the factor price of the ith input relative to the price of output, and f_i is the marginal product with respect to the ith input. The marginal product of a translog production function is

$$f_i = \frac{Q}{i}(a_i + \sum_j \gamma_{ij} \ln j) > 0, \qquad i, j = K, L, E. \tag{7}$$

Substituting (7) into (6) and rearranging terms, we obtain the necessary conditions for economic efficiency in terms of distributive shares:

$$M_i = \frac{p_i i}{Q} = a_i + \sum_j \gamma_{ij} \ln j, \qquad i, j = K, L, E, \tag{8}$$

where M_i is the relative share of total cost for the ith input. Constant returns to scale and purely competitive markets assure that the sum of these shares exhausts total cost.

It is common practice in the translog literature to append to each of the equations in (8) an additive disturbance term which is said to represent random errors in cost-minimizing behavior. Aigner, Lovell, and Schmidt (1977), among others, have considered estimating stochastic frontier production function models by defining the disturbance term as the sum of symmetric normal and (negative) half-normal random variables. They estimate a value added per establishment production function of the Cobb-Douglas form and find that the one-sided component of the disturbance is relatively small.[12] While the implications of this literature for estimating a translog production function are not immediately obvious, we chose to follow the rest of the literature and assumed an additive error term at the end of each of the factor demand equations in (8). By estimating equations (8), rather than the production function directly (4), we are estimating a complete model of production, which includes the production possibility frontier and necessary conditions for producer equilibrium.

Since the cost shares of the three equations in (8) always sum to 1, the sum of the disturbances across the three equations is zero at each observation. Therefore, the disturbance covariance matrix is singular and nondiagonal. The linear homogeneity of the production function, together with the symmetry restrictions, guarantees that any two of the equations in (8) will exactly identify all the parameters of the production function. Thus, we drop one equation and one error term (arbitrarily, the energy equation). The disturbance column vector for the remaining error terms is specified to be independently and identically normally distributed with mean vector zero and nonsingular covariance matrix.

By stacking the remaining two equations (imposing symmetry conditions) and noting that their error terms are likely to be correlated (e.g., random deviations from profit maximization or cost minimization should affect both the markets for labor and capital), we can use Zellner's seemingly unrelated equation technique (ZEF) to obtain more efficient parameter estimates.[13]

The translog parameters are not independent of our choice of which two equations to estimate. It has been shown[14] that iterative Zellner's technique ($IZEF$) is computationally equivalent to maximum-likelihood. Thus, even though the ZEF parameter estimates depend on the omitted equation, the $IZEF$ estimates do not.

---

[12] See White (n.d.) for a discussion of the problems in estimating value added production functions. The approach used by Aigner, Lovell, and Schmidt ignores the efficiency conditions discussed above.

[13] Since there is no reason to believe that the input ratios are predetermined, an instrumental variables technique was tried on our preferred equation. The instruments used were the U.S. population 16 and older, government purchases of nondurables, government purchases of labor services, U.S. exports of goods and services, the capital stock lagged four quarters (Wharton Econometric Forecasting Associates, WEFA, data), the federal government's effective indirect business tax rate, state and local governments' effective indirect tax rate, an index of the rate of import duty, and the federal personal tax rate for bracket #3 (WEFA). These instruments are similar to the ones used by Berndt and Wood (1975). The results we obtained were virtually the same as those obtained with ordinary least squares (OLS) techniques. This result is not surprising since the $\bar{R}^2$ for the first stage for all variables was over 0.8 and for most was well over 0.9. For reasons of economy, we used the OLS approach rather than the more appropriate instrumental variables approach in the equations reported in Section III.

[14] See the Discussion in Berndt and Christensen (1973, pp. 88-89), which cites the work of Ruble and Kmenta and Gilbert.

Given our parameter estimates, it would be possible to estimate Allen partial elasticities of substitution between inputs i and j. The elasticities are calculated as[15]

$$\sigma_{ij} = \sum_k F_k k \, |\overline{F}_{ij}|/(ij \, |\overline{F}|) , \qquad i, j, k = K, L, E , \qquad (9)$$

where $|\overline{F}|$ is the determinant of the bordered Hessian $\overline{F}$,

$$|\overline{F}| = \begin{vmatrix} 0 & f_L & f_K & f_E \\ f_L & f_{LL} & f_{LK} & f_{LE} \\ f_K & f_{LK} & f_{KK} & f_{KE} \\ f_E & f_{LE} & f_{KE} & f_{EE} \end{vmatrix} , \qquad (10)$$

and $|\overline{F}_{ij}|$ is the cofactor of F_{ij} in $\overline{F}$.

So far, the procedure described for estimating a translog production function is quite standard. We now introduce a variation on the standard approach by allowing the elasticities of substitution between the various inputs to vary over the cycle. There are two major justifications for this approach. First, during various stages of the business cycle, labor-hoarding occurs in many markets. Second, the work of Nadiri and Rosen (1969) and others indicates that as the economy moves from one equilibrium to another, the rates of adjustment of labor and capital differ. If labor and capital were the only inputs in the production process, it would be possible to predict the effects of labor-hoarding and differential rates of adjustment on a theoretical basis. With three or more inputs, the effects cannot be unambiguously predicted.

In an attempt to capture the cyclical sensitivity of the production function, the parameters of the input function (5) are written as

$$a_i = a_i^0 + a_i^1 \, UGAP ,$$
$$\qquad\qquad i, j = K, L, E ,$$
$$\gamma_{ij} = \gamma_{ij}^0 + \gamma_{ij}^1 \, UGAP , \qquad (11)$$

[15] See Berndt and Christensen (1973, p. 97).

where $UGAP = 0.25$ x (U^*/U) is a measure of the cycle.[16] It would also be possible to view these parameters as functions of a capacity utilization index or other cyclical measures. We did not include the capacity utilization index, because there are theoretical problems with all current indexes and because most of the indexes are largely collinear with the $UGAP$ measure.

It should be noted that in deriving equations (8), we treated the input function's parameters as constants. If they are functions of $UGAP$, the parameters are functions of labor demand, since unemployment is a function of labor demand. We chose to treat the parameters as constants, however, since $UGAP$ is intended to be a proxy for cyclical fluctuations independent of a particular market.[17]

III. Empirical Results

We estimated our production function (4) in two steps. First, we estimated the factor share equations (8). Using these estimated parameters, we formed an input index (5) which was then used to estimate equation (4).

The data used in this study are discussed in the Appendix. Table 1 presents iterative Zellner ($IZEF$) estimates (which are computationally equivalent to maximum-likelihood estimates), with symmetry and constant returns to scale imposed.

Table 1 contains estimates of six types of production functions. The first is a translog production function with parameters which are a function of $UGAP_1$.[18] Henceforth, this will be referred to as the cyclically sensitive translog production function. The next two are standard production functions with our adjusted labor series (manhours measured in efficiency units) and the unadjusted labor series (official manhours). The fourth is a standard translog production function with what Berndt and Christensen (1973) call linear separability in energy imposed ($\gamma_{LE} = \gamma_{KE} = \gamma_{EE} = 0$). This restriction makes the production function Cobb-Douglas in energy and a composite input (K, L). If this restriction were true, it would be appropriate to estimate a subproduction function for K and L alone (as many past potential output studies have done).

---

[16] Since the Allen partial elasticities of substitution are nonlinear combinations of the parameters in (9), the linear specification of (9) leads to a nonlinear cyclical adjustment in the elasticities. If we were only interested in estimating these parameters, we would have employed a translog cost function instead, since the elasticities are linear functions of the parameters of the cost function. Preliminary experimentation indicates that more stable elasticity estimates may be obtained from cost functions.

[17] Of course, any given firm must treat the unemployment rate as a parameter of the system and not as a variable which it can control.

[18] $UGAP_1 = 0.25$ x (U_1^*/U), where U_1^* corrects for demographic changes in the composition of the labor force. See Section IV.

122

The fifth is a translog production function with Cobb-Douglas restrictions imposed ($\gamma_{ij} = 0$, $i, j = K, L, E$). The last is also a translog with Cobb-Douglas restrictions imposed. It differs from the preceding five production functions, since it uses an adjusted capital series (our capital stock series multiplied by the Federal Reserve Board's capacity utilization index). The cyclically sensitive translog production function was chosen for use in calculating potential output. The other production functions are provided so that our results can be compared more easily with those of the existing literature.

For the translog production function to make sense, the fitted cost shares should be positive and the production function convex at every data point. Convexity of the production function guarantees that the necessary conditions for profit maximization, (8), are also sufficient. The production function is convex if the bordered Hessian (10) is negative definite at every data point. Both the positivity and convexity conditions were met for all the estimated production functions reported in Table 1.[19] When capital was adjusted by the Federal Reserve Board's capacity utilization index, the resulting production functions failed the convexity criterion in many periods, which is one of the chief reasons we used unadjusted capital in our estimates.

To facilitate a comparison between the cyclically sensitive translog and the other production functions, the third column of Table 1 presents the intercept and slope coefficients for the cyclically sensitive translog evaluated at the nonaccelerating inflation rate of unemployment (i.e., $U = U_1^*$, $UGAP_1$ = 0.25).[20] It is immediately obvious that the various restrictions greatly affect the estimated parameters. The intercept or share coefficients (a_i) of the cyclically sensitive translog are different from those of the Cobb-Douglas production function. Labor's share is a little smaller and capital and energy's shares are larger than the Cobb-Douglas estimates imply. Further, the signs of the slope parameters of the cyclically sensitive production function's parameters are in some cases the opposite of those of the standard translog or the translog with linear separability of energy imposed.

To test whether the various restrictions are reasonable, we computed the relevant F-tests, as reported in Table 2. The Cobb-Douglas restrictions, which most of the potential output literature explicitly assumes, require that the production function be globally separable;[21] that is, all the Allen partial

---

[19] Convexity was tested in the cyclically sensitive production function case at both the actual $UGAP$ and at the nonaccelerating inflation level ($UGAP = 0.25$). The production function was found to be convex in both tests.

[20] That is, $a_i = a_i^0 + a_i^1 \times 0.25$, $\gamma_{ij} = \gamma_{ij}^0 + \gamma_{ij}^1 \times 0.25$, $i, j = K, L, E$.

[21] For a detailed description of the relevant tests, see Berndt and Christensen (1973). Denny and Fuss (1977) discuss hypothesis testing where the translog production function is considered an approximation to an arbitrary production function rather than an exact function as the Berndt and Christensen tests assume. The advantage of the Berndt and Christensen tests is that they are invariant to scaling.

TABLE 1

IZEF Estimates of KLE Translog Production Function
Parameters based on Equation (8)
U.S. Private, Nonagricultural Sector, 1955:1 - 1977:4
(Standard Errors in Parentheses)

| | Cyclically Sensitive Translog (U_1^*)† | | $U=U_1^*$ $UGAP_1=0.25$‖ | Standard Translog | Standard Translog# | Standard Translog with E Linearly Separable $f((L,K),E)$†† | Standard Translog with Cobb-Douglas Restrictions§§ | Standard Translog with Cobb-Douglas Restrictions§§,‖‖ |
	(1)‡	(2)§	(3)‖	(4)	(5)	(6)	(7)	(8)
α_L	0.7315 (0.06927)	-0.1049 (0.3293)	0.7053	0.7366 (0.01702)	0.7048 (0.02477)	0.6966 (0.009054)	0.7542 (0.002503)	0.7620 (0.001827)
α_K	0.4505 (1.1389)	-0.9259 (0.6121)	0.2190	0.2870 (0.03259)	0.2669 (0.02921)	0.2558 (0.008120)	0.1982 (0.001537)	0.1899 (0.001827)
α_E	-0.1820 (0.1786)	1.0308 (0.7993)	0.07570	-0.02365 (0.04625)	0.02829 (0.04887)	0.04760 (0.001953)	0.04757 (0.001117)	0.04812 (0.002583)
γ_{LL}	0.2756 (0.05440)	-1.1590 (0.2540)	-0.01415	0.015581 (0.01255)	0.03660 (0.01844)	-0.03126 (-0.004039)	0.0	0.0
γ_{LK}	-0.1453 (0.03863)	0.6617 (0.1802)	0.02013	-0.003365 (0.008189)	-0.00531 (0.01171)	0.03126 (0.004039)	0.0	0.0
γ_{LE}	-0.1303 (0.02550)	0.4973 (0.1214)	-0.005975	-0.01222 (0.007187)	-0.03107 (0.08559)	0.0	0.0	0.0
γ_{KK}	0.01224 (0.04054)	-0.1119 (0.1822)	-0.01574	-0.02169 (0.008503)	-0.01531 (0.008946)	-0.03126 (0.004039)	0.0	0.0
γ_{KE}	0.1331 (0.04191)	-0.5498 (0.1865)	-0.004350	0.02506 (0.01038)	0.02084 (0.01032)	0.0	0.0	0.0
γ_{EE}	-0.002760 (0.05436)	0.05250 (0.2469)	0.01589	-0.01284 (0.01458)	0.01023 (0.01373)	0.0	0.0	0.0
$\tilde{R}^2$##	0.6673			0.2550	0.2978	0.1226	---	---

124

TABLE 1 -- *Continued*

Note: The data used in these regressions are discussed in the Appendix. Except as indicated otherwise, all the regressions use adjusted labor. Manhours are adjusted for changes in the demographic composition of the labor force (i.e., manhours are measured in "efficiency" units). Also, except for the last regression, capital stock (based on DRI data) is used. Capital is *not* adjusted by a capacity utilization index unless otherwise noted.

†Here, the parameters vary with the cycle: $a_i = a_i^0 + a_i^1 UGAP_1$; $\gamma_{ij} = \gamma_{ij}^0 + \gamma_{ij}^1 UGAP_1$ (See equation 10). $UGAP_1 = 0.25 \times (U_1^*/U)$, where U_1^* is adjusted for demographic changes only (See Section IV).

‡Column 1 represents the a_i^0 and γ_{ij}^0 terms--that is, the part of the coefficients (a_i, γ_{ij}) which are constant (not varying with $UGAP_1$). See †.

§Column 2 represents the a_i^1 and γ_{ij}^1 terms--that is, the parts of the coefficients (a_i, γ_{ij}) which vary with $UGAP_1$. See †.

‖Column 3 evaluates the cyclically sensitive parameters ($a_i = a_i^0 + a_i^1 UGAP_1$; $\gamma_{ij} = \gamma_{ij}^0 + \gamma_{ij}^1 UGAP_1$) at the nonaccelerating inflation rate of unemployment: $U = U_1^*$.
When $U = U_1^*$, $UGAP_1 = 0.25$. Thus, $a_i = a_i^0 + 0.25 \times a_i^1$, $\gamma_{ij} = \gamma_{ij}^0 + 0.25 \times \gamma_{ij}^1$.

#Uses unadjusted labor (actual manhours data). See Appendix.

††The restriction that energy is linearly separable, $f((L,K),E)$, is imposed by setting $\gamma_{LE} = \gamma_{KE} = \gamma_{EE} = 0$.

§§The Cobb-Douglas restriction is imposed by setting $\gamma_{ij} = 0$, $i, j = K, L, E$.

‖‖The capital stock is adjusted by multiplying by the Federal Reserve Board's capacity utilization index (which is divided by 87.5--See Section V).

##Berndt's generalized R^2 measure: $\widetilde{R}^2 = 1 - \dfrac{|\hat{r}_1|}{|\hat{r}_0|}$, where $|\hat{r}_0|$ is the determinant of the residual covariance matrix when all "slope" coefficients are zero, and $|\hat{r}_1|$ is the determinant of the residual covariance matrix for the model being estimated. $\widetilde{R}^2 = R^2$ in only one equation is estimated. See Berndt and Wood (1977, p. 35).

elasticities of substitution between inputs (σ_{KL}, σ_{KE}, σ_{LE}) are equal to 1. Equivalently, the Cobb-Douglas hypothesis implies that $\gamma_{ij} = 0$, for all i, $j = K, L, E$.

The Cobb-Douglas restrictions were tested with respect to the standard translog and the cyclically sensitive translog. Test 1, in Table 2, shows that the Cobb-Douglas restrictions on the standard translog production function can be strongly rejected. The F-statistic is 14.49, while the critical value is 3.89. The Cobb-Douglas restrictions on the cyclically sensitive translog can be imposed in a weak and a strong form. Test 3 shows that the strong restriction that the production function be Cobb-Douglas with noncyclically sensitive parameters can be rejected. We can also reject the weaker hypothesis that the production function is Cobb-Douglas with cyclically sensitive parameters (Test 4).

Since the standard translog production function is nested within the cyclically sensitive production function, we can test the standard formulation by setting the coefficients $a_i^1 = \gamma_{ij}^1 = 0$, for all i, $j = K, L, E$, in the cyclically sensitive production function. As Test 5 shows, the standard translog hypothesis is rejected. The F-statistic is 23.14 while the critical value is 3.12.

Since much of the existing potential output literature leaves out energy, we have tested the condition that Berndt and Christensen have dubbed linear separability of energy: $Q = f((K,L), E)$; that is, $\gamma_{KE} = \gamma_{LE} = 0$ ($\sigma_{KE} = \sigma_{LE} = 1$). This restriction can also be rejected (Tests 2 and 6).[22]

We conclude from these tests that the cyclically sensitive translog production function is the proper choice for this study. We continue to present results from the other formulations for comparison purposes.

After estimating the factor share equations (8) and obtaining estimated parameters (see Table 1), we can now use the parameters to form an input index, I, (5). Given the input index, I, we can estimate the production function (4).[23] Table 3 presents estimates from the second stage of the estimating procedure. Because we assume that the error term, if any, associated with equation (4) is independent of the errors associated with equations (8), our estimates of (4) are consistent.[24] To allow for Hicks neutral technological progress, we have included a time trend term (t) in equation (4). To allow for varying rates of technological growth, we have also included time squared (t^2) and time cubed (t^3) terms. The coefficients on the time squared and time cubed terms tend to

---

[22] Berndt and Christensen (1973) have noted that energy may be separable if a nonlinear condition holds. This condition requires that $\sigma_{KE} = \sigma_{LE} \neq 1$. Since the existing literature generally assumes a Cobb-Douglas formulation, this restriction does not seem to be a particularly relevant one to test here (though it, too, is rejected by the data).

[23] The coefficient on the input index is not equal to 1 because of the arbitrary scaling of output.

[24] See also footnote 27.

TABLE 2

Significance Tests for *KLE* Translog Production Functions
(with and without cyclically sensitive parameters)

Test	Restrictions	Degrees of Freedom	Critical Value	Test Statistics
Standard Translog				
(1) Cobb-Douglas	3	179	3.89	14.49
(2) Linear separability $f((L,K),E)$	2	179	4.73	9.56
Cyclically Sensitive Translog				
(3) Cobb-Douglas (cyclically sensitive share parameters)	6	174	2.91	19.90
(4) Cobb-Douglas (share parameters not cyclically sensitive)	8	174	2.61	22.78
(5) Parameters are not cyclically sensitive, i.e., standard translog	5	174	3.12	23.14
(6) Linear Separability $f((L,K),E)$, (parameters not cyclically sensitive)	7	174	2.75	21.31

Note: Significance level = 0.01 for all tests. $F(m, n - k)$, m = number of restrictions, $n - k$ = degrees of freedom in the unrestricted case.

TABLE 3

KLE Translog Production Functions, Equation (4)
(Standard Errors in Parentheses)

	Cyclically Sensitive Translog *,†,§	Standard Translog †,§	Standard Translog †,§	Standard Translog with E Linearly Separable $f((L,K),E)$†,§,‖	Standard Translog with Cobb-Douglas Restrictions †,‡,#	Standard Translog with Cobb-Douglas Restrictions †,#,**	Cyclically Sensitive Translog *,†,§,††	Cyclically Sensitive Translog *,†,§,‡‡
Constant	4.9391 (0.09501)	-2.5588 (0.6878)	0.2882 (0.5515)	-0.5271 (0.5515)	-1.9522 (0.6366)	0.5967 (0.2536)	4.8403 (0.1178)	4.8670 (0.1296)
t (time)	0.02862 (0.002701)	0.02057 (0.002664)	0.02433 (0.002596)	0.02070 (0.002740)	0.02074 (0.002656)	0.02264 (0.001760)	0.2731 (0.005924)	0.02836 (0.005702)
t^2	0.3582×10^{-3} (0.3142×10^{-3})	-0.9649×10^{-5} (0.3460×10^{-3})	0.1164×10^{-2} (0.3858×10^{-3})	-0.1647×10^{-3} (0.3657×10^{-3})	-0.8228×10^{-4} (0.3480×10^{-3})	0.3698×10^{-3} (0.2748×10^{-3})	0.3390×10^{-3} (0.6290×10^{-3})	0.2889×10^{-3} (0.6069×10^{-3})
t^3	-0.1112×10^{-4} (0.9479×10^{-5})	-0.2189×10^{-4} (0.9435×10^{-5})	0.2089×10^{-4} (0.1099×10^{-4})	-0.1461×10^{-4} (0.1009×10^{-4})	-0.1932×10^{-4} (0.9504×10^{-5})	-0.2652×10^{-4} (0.5863×10^{-5})	-0.8409×10^{-5} (0.1818×10^{-4})	-0.7896×10^{-5} (0.1774×10^{-4})
I (Input Index)	0.2568 (0.01896)	1.7807 (0.01395)	1.2192 (0.08930)	1.3481 (0.1101)	1.6987 (0.1323)	1.1741 (0.05290)	0.2780 (0.02370)	0.2719 (0.02607)
$\bar{R}^2$	0.996	0.995	0.996	0.995	0.996	0.998	0.999	0.999
SEE	0.01658	0.01724	0.01649	0.01771	0.01718	0.01132	0.007740	0.007482
DW	0.231	0.293	0.213	0.293	0.276	0.392	1.540	2.105

128

TABLE 3 -- *Continued*

* Parameters vary with $UGAP_1$.

† Uses adjusted labor (manhours measured in efficiency units): manhours are adjusted for changes in the demographic composition of the labor force. See Appendix.

‡ Uses unadjusted labor (actual manhours). See Appendix.

§ Uses a capital stock index based on DRI data (See Appendix). Capital is *not* adjusted by a capacity utilization index.

‖ The restrictions that energy is linearly separable, $f((L,K),E)$, is imposed by setting $\gamma_{LE} = \gamma_{KE} = \gamma_{EE} = 0$.

The Cobb-Douglas restriction is imposed by setting $\gamma_{ij} = 0$, $i, j = K, L, E$.

** The capital stock is adjusted by multiplying by the Federal Reserve Board's capacity utilization index (divided by 87.5--See Section V).

†† First-order Cochrane-Orcutt autocorrelation, $\rho = 0.881$.

‡‡ Second-order Cochrane-Orcutt autocorrelation, $\rho_1 = 1.101$, $\rho_2 = -0.249$.

129

be small and statistically insignificant at the 0.05 level.[25] The coefficients on the time trends in the cyclically sensitive translog production function indicate a rate of Hicks neutral technological progress which is slightly under 3 percent.

The $\bar{R}^2$ of each of the production functions is essentially equal to 1. An examination of the plots of estimated output against actual output indicates that the cyclically sensitive translog production function is by far the best for picking the turning points.

The regressions presented in the first six columns of Table 3 suffer from autocorrelation. Although the coefficient estimates are consistent, the standard errors are biased. More efficient estimates could be obtained by using a generalized least squares approach (which was not taken, because it is computationally impractical). Columns 7 and 8 of Table 3 present cyclically sensitive translog estimates with first- and second-order Cochrane-Orcutt autocorrelation adjustments. The coefficient estimates do not vary greatly between the unadjusted (column 1) and adjusted (columns 7 and 8) estimates.[26] We have not used the adjusted estimates because the errors do not follow a simple first- or

---

[25] In some of the specifications, the coefficient on time cubed was statistically significant. Because of the nonlinear time trend, some of the intercept terms are negative. If only a single time trend term is included, all the intercept terms would be positive. Because of autocorrelation, these statistical tests should be viewed with caution.

[26] The resulting potential output series (which are calculated in the manner explained in the following section) are quite similar. The potential output series based on the unadjusted estimates has a correlation coefficient of 0.99854 with the potential output series based on a first-order correction and a correlation coefficient of 0.99857 with the potential output series based on a second-order correction. The auto-correlation adjustment has the effect of smoothing the cyclical fluctuations, and the small difference between the resulting adjusted and unadjusted potential series are highly correlated with cyclical variables; that is, the Cochrane-Orcutt corrections generally slightly reduce the GNP gap series.

second-order process.[27] Nonetheless, if we had used the estimates from columns 7 or 8, the qualitative conclusions of the paper would not have been altered, since the series are virtually identical.

IV. Nonaccelerating Inflation Rate of Unemployment

Potential output is that output which society could produce with the labor supply which is consistent with nonaccelerating rates of inflation. Thus, to provide estimates of potential output, we need, besides the aggregate production function, an equation which determines the natural rate U^*.

Three approaches have been adopted in the literature for dealing with the problem of estimating U^*. The first is to adjust the unemployment rate for demographic changes in the population and for changes in relative unemployment among the various age-sex groups. This approach is described in Wachter (1976) and was used to produce the series used in the previous section as parameters of the factor elasticities. This demographic normalization of the

---

[27]We can rewrite (4) as

$$\ln Q = \beta_0 + \beta_1 t + \beta_2 t^2 + \beta_3 t^3 + \beta_4 \hat{I} + \beta_4 \epsilon_t, \tag{12}$$

where

$$\epsilon_t = I \cdot \hat{I},$$

and $\hat{I}$ is the estimated input index.
Let

$$z_t = \begin{pmatrix} \ln L \\ \ln K \\ \ln E \\ 1/2 \ln L^2 \\ \ln L \ \ln K \\ \ln L \ \ln E \\ 1/2 \ln K^2 \\ \ln K \ \ln E \\ 1/2 \ln E^2 \end{pmatrix} \qquad \delta = \begin{pmatrix} a_L \\ a_K \\ a_E \\ \gamma_{LL} \\ \gamma_{LK} \\ \gamma_{LE} \\ \gamma_{KK} \\ \gamma_{KE} \\ \gamma_{EE} \end{pmatrix},$$

then,

$$\operatorname{var} \epsilon_t = E \epsilon_t^2 = z_t' V_{\hat{\delta}} z_t, \tag{13}$$

and

$$\operatorname{cov}(\epsilon_t, \epsilon_s) = z_t' V_{\hat{\delta}} z_s, \tag{14}$$

where $V_{\hat{\delta}}$ is $\hat{\delta}$'s variance-covariance matrix.
As equation (14) shows, there is autocorrelation. From equation (13) we know that there is also heteroscedasticity. A simple OLS estimate of (12) will lead to consistent estimates of the coefficients. To obtain efficiency, a generalized least squares approach should be used (which is beyond our computer capabilities at this time). A simple first- or second-order Cochrane-Orcutt adjustment will, therefore, not be appropriate. We wish to thank Roberto Mariano for making this point.

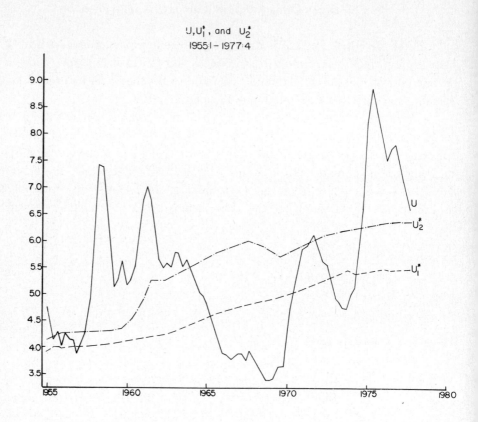

Figure 1

unemployment rate, denoted U_1^* and plotted in Figure 1, is developed outside of any wage or price equation and is thus only an indirect approximation to the U^* concept.[28]

The technique of using a demographic adjustment to the unemployment rate in constructing potential output series is followed by Clark (1977), Rasche and Tatom (1977a, 1977b),[29] and Perry (1977a, 1977b). The Clark and Rasche-Tatom series are similar in methodology to the Wachter (1976) series. The Perry construct, based on his 1970 work, differs theoretically in that it is based on a fixed weighting scheme using relative wage rates among demographic groups. Our series is based on a variable weighting scheme using relative unemployment rates among demographic groups. Empirically, the approaches differ from each other. The important distinction, for our purposes, is that in our series, U^* increases 1.5 percentage points between 1955 and 1977, while in the other series, U^* increases by only 1.1 percentage points.[30]

The second approach to U^* is to confront the nonaccelerating inflation constraint directly; that is, a wage or price equation is estimated directly, with nonaccelerating inflation imposed in the form $\dot{w}_t = \dot{w}_{t-1} = \ldots = \dot{w}_{t-n}$ or $\dot{p}_t = \dot{p}_{t-1} = \ldots = \dot{p}_{t-n}$. The equation can then be inverted to solve for the equilibrium U^*. Numerous problems with this approach account for its lack of popularity. The primary disagreements center on how to specify the inflation equations, in terms of both functional form and explanatory variables.

For our purposes, it was better to experiment with a wage rather than a price equation. Price inflation is more susceptible to exogenous shocks, which are very difficult to quantify. Wage inflation is less sensitive to weather, international trade, and oil price increases. A series of short-run shocks may be averaged out over the relatively long-term contracts which are important in the labor market. The result is that the wage series will vary more with longer-run influences, and the underlying U^* will be more stable and less subject to the vagaries of variables, which are difficult to quantify.

---

[28] Wachter (1976) specifically refers to this construct as a normalized unemployment rate to distinguish it from a nonaccelerating inflation rate of unemployment. For a review of the demographic adjustments of the unemployment rate series, see Flaim (1977). For a general discussion of the U^* debate, see Gordon (1976).

[29] Rasche and Tatom use Clark's series.

[30] One reason for the difference between our series and Clark's series is that he adjusts his unemployment rates for the change in the labor force and unemployment definitions that occurred in 1967. We did not make any adjustment because it is unclear what type of adjustment should be made. Overlapping data are available for only one year, and the Bureau of Labor Statistics determined that the differences were not significant enough to enable them to revise their earlier numbers. A standard correction in the literature is the use of the ratio of the old and new unemployment series to alter the pre-1967 numbers. For a variety of reasons which go beyond the scope of this paper, we believe that the change in the definition would not translate into a constant ratio revision of the pre-1967 data. Making this adjustment would tend to understate the change in relative unemployment rates. On the other hand, it is possible that making no revisions somewhat overstates these changes.

To illustrate this method, we estimate a series of relatively simple Phillips curves of the general form[31]

$$\dot{w}_t = a_0(\tau) + a_1(\tau) \, UGAP + \Sigma \, \beta_i \dot{w}_{t-i} \, , \tag{15}$$

where U_1^* is the normalized unemployment rate series discussed above, and the τ's indicate that the coefficients on the constant and the unemployment term may vary over time. We allowed for several different schemes for the varying parameters and also introduced a variable to capture the Phase I through IV controls period.[32] We imposed the assumption of nonaccelerating inflation by subtracting the lagged dependent variables(s) and their coefficients from both sides so that the resulting dependent variable is in the form $\dot{w}_t - \Sigma \, \beta_i \dot{w}_{t-1}$. The nonaccelerating inflation rate is imposed with reference not to the previous quarter, but to a weighted average of previous inflation rates. Allowing parameters to vary with time and imposing $\Sigma \, \beta_i = 1$, we obtain the non-accelerating inflation rate of unemployment

$$U^* = \frac{-a_1(\tau) \, U_1^*}{a_0(\tau)} \, .$$

In virtually all of these equations, the resulting U^* series is above the demographic adjustment U_1^* series. This result is anticipated by Wachter (1976), who finds that the nonaccelerating inflation rate of unemployment for 1975 is 6.04 (for a long-run productivity growth rate of 2.5 percent), compared to a U_1^* of approximately 5.5 percent. As long as the coefficients in the wage equation are allowed to vary over time, the demographic U_1^* series will, in general, not equal the U^* which solves the equation. The average U^* calculated across alternative parameter schemes tends to be approximately 6.25 in 1977 and about 0.5 to 1.0 percent higher than the U_1^* series.

---

[31] The wage equation can be specified in many different ways. See, for example, the articles contained in Brunner and Meltzer (1976a, 1976b). Most Phillips curves contain one or more measures of unemployment and either lagged wages or prices. There is a tradeoff, however, between adding extra independent variables to proxy unemployment and lagged effects and adding time varying parameters. If one believes that the U^* series changes over time, but that it is difficult to quantify the underlying causal mechanism, equation (15) has appeal.

[32] The variable, which is the same as that used in Wachter (1976), is designated NIXCON.

It is useful to illustrate the types of results that emerge from this approach, for both U^* and potential output. The underlying wage equation is a particularly simple one:

$$\dot{w} - \sum_{i=1}^{12} \beta_i \dot{w}_{t-i} = \underset{(0.4813)}{1.848} \; UGAP - \underset{(0.1080)}{0.4361} \; DUM1 - \underset{(0.1273)}{0.3716} \; DUM2$$

$$- \underset{(0.1212)}{0.4000} \; DUM3 - \underset{(0.2182)}{0.7898} \; NIXCON \qquad\qquad (16)$$

$$\bar{R}^2 = 0.223 \qquad D.W. = 2.37 \; ,$$

where

$$DUM1 = \begin{cases} 1 & 1955{:}1 - 1960{:}4 \\ 0 & 1961{:}1 - 1977{:}4 \end{cases}, \; DUM2 = \begin{cases} 1 & 1961{:}1 - 1968{:}4 \\ 0 & \begin{cases} 1955{:}1 - 1960{:}4 \\ 1969{:}1 - 1977{:}4 \end{cases} \end{cases}$$

$$DUM3 = \begin{array}{ll} 1 & 1969{:}1 - 1977{:}4 \\ 0 & 1955{:}1 - 1960{:}4 \end{array} \; ,$$

and the β_i follow a harmonic series and sum to unity. The equation is thus a kind of second difference, where the lagged $\dot{w}_{t-i}$ term reflects the formation of expectations and/or inertia in the labor market resulting from long-term contracts. The dummy variables were chosen to conform to election years when the presidency changed between Democratic and Republican administrations. The exception is 1977, which is included in the prior dummy variable because of the shortness of the time period. Solving the wage equation for U, assuming $\dot{w} - \sum_{i=1}^{12} \beta_i \dot{w}_{t-i} = 0$ and $NIXCON = 0$, results in a U^* series. Since the dummy variables create arbitrary discontinuities in the U^*, we smoothed the jumps using a five-quarter centered moving average.[33] The resulting construct, denoted U_2^*, is plotted in Figure 1 along with U_1^* and the measured unemployment rate. It has a value of 4.17 percent in 1955:1, goes above 5 percent in 1961:2,

---

[33]We tend to believe that the underlying U^* is subject to important short-run discontinuities. We are not optimistic, however, about our ability to represent those spikes with exogenous variables or to determine exactly when they occur. An alternative approach to the problem of connecting labor or product market gaps with inflation is presented in Meltzer (1977).

reaches 6.05 percent in 1971:4, and settles at 6.35 percent in 1977:4. Figure 1 shows that U_2^* is always above U_1^*, and the difference is greatest in the middle of the period, reflecting the low absolute value of the coefficient on $DUM2$. Since the absolute value of the $DUM3$ coefficient is greater than that of the $DUM2$ coefficient, the U_2^* series grows more slowly than U_1^* after 1969:1.

The third approach to calculating a U^* series is to estimate an unemployment equation and attempt to isolate the disequilibrium component of unemployment from the equilibrium component (U^*). One way to accomplish this would be to invert the Phillips curve and reestimate using unemployment as the independent variable:

$$U = f(U_1^*, \dot{w}_t, \Sigma \, \beta_i \dot{w}_{t-i}) \, . \tag{17}$$

As with the Phillips curve, other variables such as minimum wages (Gramlich, 1976) and "surprises" in the money supply (Barro, 1977) could be added to this equation.

The error structures of (15) and (17) are different, with the latter exhibiting severe autocorrelation when estimated in quarterly form. When equations of the form (17) are estimated, there is an unsettled question as to whether the lagged dependent variables, which are used to absorb the autocorrelation, should be viewed as part of the equilibrium U^* component.[34] If the lagged dependent variables are interpreted as reflecting equilibrium changes, the resulting U^* trails after U, thus exhibiting considerable cyclical sensitivity. This U^* series is very different from the U_1^* derived from the demographic adjustment or the U_2^* derived from the wage equation (16). In the equations of form (17) that we estimated, the resulting U^* was again, if averaged over the cycle, above the U_1^* demographic series. Since we are unsure how to divide the autoregressive component, we have omitted any U^* series constructed by the direct estimation of an unemployment equation.

V. Constructing Potential Output Series

In the approach that we have adopted here, the major ingredient in developing a potential output series from an estimated production function relationship is a potential labor series. Our favored series combines U_1^* as a measure of U^* and the translog production estimates based on cyclically

---

[34] This is the technique adopted by Sargent (1973).

sensitive parameters. To derive potential labor, we first regressed manhours in the private, nonagricultural economy, adjusted for demographic shifts (denoted L) on a constant, $UGAP_1$ (=0.25 x U_1^*/U) and time trends.

$$L = -40.72 + 36.90\, UGAP_1 + 266.77t - 180.36t^2 + 41.56t^3,\,^{35}$$
$$(41.83)\quad(2.42)\qquad\qquad(74.19)\quad(43.60)\quad(8.43)$$

(18)

$$\bar{R}^2 = 0.980, \qquad SEE = 0.9517, \qquad D.W. = 0.536.$$

The potential L_1^* results are obtained by setting $UGAP_1 = 0.25$, which is equivalent, due to the scaling of $UGAP$, to setting $U = U_1^*$ for every quarter.[36] The method for constructing the adjusted L series is described in the Appendix.

As a substitute for equation (18), we estimated separate equations for hours and employment. Since this does not significantly alter the resulting potential labor series, we used equation (18) to create L_1^*.

A similar regression was used to obtain potential manhours using an unadjusted labor series. The adjusted and unadjusted potential L series resulted in similar measures of potential. Since we believe that the labor series should be adjusted for changes in the demographic characteristics of the labor force, we report the results from that series.

The potential output series is obtained by replacing actual manhours (L) with the potential manhours (L^*) derived from (18) and by setting the cyclically sensitive coefficients of the translog (11) equal to their equilibrium values where $U = U_1^*$ or $UGAP = 0.25$. That is;

$$a_i = a_i^0 + 0.25\, a_i^1 ,$$

$$i, j = K, L, E .$$

$$\gamma_{ij} = \gamma_{ij}^0 + 0.25\, \gamma_{ij}^1,$$

In addition to using a potential manhours series, we also experimented with a potential capital series. We assumed that the measured capital series

---

[35] Here the time trend started at 1.00 and grew by 0.01.

[36] A similar method has been used in many studies. See, for example, Rasche and Tatom (1977a, 1977b).

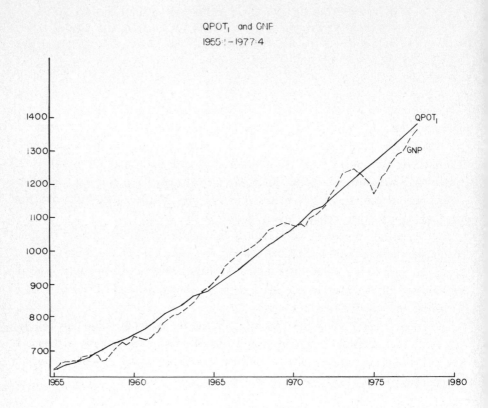

QPOT$_1$ and GNP
1955:1 – 1977:4

Figure 2

138

is the potential, and we used adjusted capital to estimate production functions, where

$$\text{adjusted capital} = \text{measured (or potential) capital} \times \frac{\text{capacity utilization}}{87.5},$$

where 87.5 was assumed to be the *nonaccelerating inflation rate of capacity utilization* over the sample period. The use of adjusted capital in the production function estimation in place of observed capital yielded unsatisfactory parameter estimates in many cases.[37] Consequently, our preferred potential output series does not distinguish between potential and adjusted capital.[38]

As discussed above, the calculations are performed for the private, nonagricultural economy. Following the literature, we assume that actual output in both agricultural and governmental sectors equaled potential output in those sectors. The potential output series for the overall economy is obtained by adding the actual output of those two sectors to the potential output of the private, nonagricultural economy. The series based on the cyclically sensitive translog is denoted $QPOT_1$.

VI. Alternative Measures of Potential Output

In this section, we compare our various potential output series with those found in the literature. First, we examine the relationship between $QPOT_1$[39] and GNP. Second, we compare $QPOT_1$ with other potential series in the literature; namely, those created by the old CEA, Clark, Perry, and Rasche and Tatom. Third, we present an alternative potential series based on a standard translog production function and $QPOT_2$.[40] These series are compared with $QPOT_1$.

A. $QPOT_1$

Our preferred potential output series, $QPOT_1$, is plotted in Figure 2 against GNP. While traditional potential output series imply that the economy

---

[37] Translog production functions estimated using adjusted capital failed to exhibit convexity at every data point.

[38] This adjustment was used in only one of the Cobb-Douglas estimates to provide a comparison with the technique used in Clark (1977) and Rasche and Tatom (1977a, 1977b).

[39] $QPOT_1$ is derived from a translog production function with parameters that vary cyclically with U_1^*/U.

[40] $QPOT_2$ is derived from a translog production function with parameters that vary cyclically with U_2^*/U.

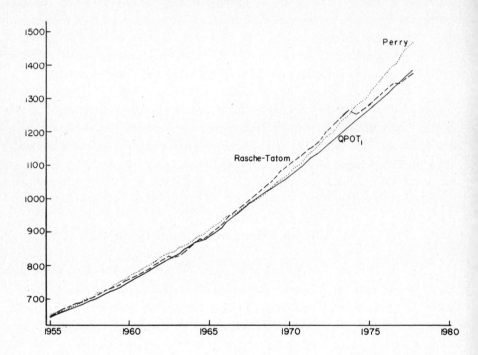

QPOT$_1$, Rasche-Tatom, and Perry Potential Output Series
1955:1 – 1977:4

Figure 3

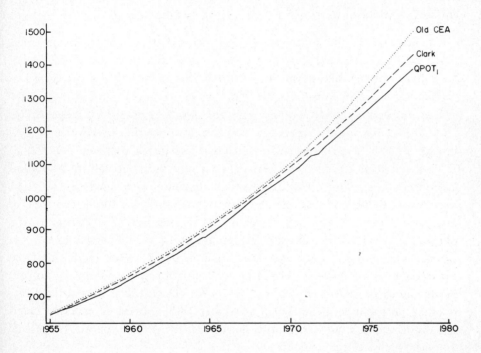

QPOT$_i$, Clark and Old CEA Potential Output Series
1955:1 – 1977:4

Figure 4

141

is almost always below potential, $QPOT_1$ allows for expansions and recessions. As indicated in Figure 2, GNP fluctuates around $QPOT_1$, exhibiting significant periods of excess demand ($Q > QPOT_1$) as well as excess supply ($Q < QPOT_1$). Although it is not clear from the graph, the early period, 1955:2 through 1956:2 is a period of excess demand or $Q > QPOT_1$. Between 1956:3 and 1957:1, the economy is in approximate equilibrium in the sense that $Q \sim QPOT_1$. A long and deep period of excess supply begins in 1957:2 and lasts until 1964:2. The depth of this downturn is reached in 1961:1, when the percentage gap $\dfrac{QPOT_1 - Q}{Q}$, is 5.37 percent, and the dollar gap, $QPOT_1 - Q$, is \$39.56 billion. An extended period of excess demand begins in 1964:3 and lasts through 1970:1. As a consequence of the mini-slowdown of 1967, this expansion has two peaks in the gap series, 1966:1 and 1968:3. The percentage gaps are -4.39 and -4.04 percent, respectively, and the dollar gaps are -\$40.77 and -\$41.20, respectively.

The economy experienced a very shallow downturn between 1970:2 through 1972:1, a relatively steep but short expansion between 1972:2 and 1974:1, and then a very deep, but still relatively short, downturn. The mini-downturn of the early 1970s registered a maximum percentage gap of 2.56 percent in 1970:4, but that was the only quarter in which the percentage gap was above 2 percent. The dollar gap in that quarter was \$27.4 billion. In the following expansion, the maximum percentage gap was -3.49 percent in 1973:1, and the associated dollar gap was -\$41.5 billion. $QPOT_1$ series implies that the expansion of 1972-1974 marked a greater deviation from potential than did the downturn of 1970-1971. As will be shown below, this is in sharp contrast to other potential series in which the early 1970s period of excess demand virtually disappears, and the entire decade of the 1970s appears to be one prolonged period of economic slack.

The $QPOT_1$ series does track a very deep recession beginning in 1974. At the depth of the downturn, 1975:1, the gap is \$92.3 billion, or 7.89 percent. This percentage gap is the largest positive or negative gap in the post-1955 period. By 1977:4, however, most of the gap has been closed, so that $QPOT_1 - Q$ is only equal to \$22.2 billion.

B. *Other Potential Series: Old CEA, Clark, Perry, and Rasche-Tatom*

As shown in Figures 3 and 4, with a few minor exceptions, $QPOT_1$ lies below the old CEA, Clark, Perry,[41] and Rasche-Tatom potential series. The old CEA, Clark, and Perry measures are almost always higher than actual output.

---

[41] In order to compare $QPOT_1$ to Perry's series, we interpolated his annual potential series to obtain quarterly data.

Recessions, measured in terms of their GNP gap series, are always long and deep, whereas expansions are brief and shallow. To illustrate this, the lowest of the three, the Clark potential series, is plotted in Figure 5 against GNP. With the exception of the late 1960s there are no significant periods in which GNP is greater than Clark's measure of potential. What holds for the Clark potential series holds a fortiori for the Perry and old CEA series (See Figure 6). If $QPOT$ is defined as the level of output at which the inflation is constant, how do these series explain the rise in the inflation rate over the past decade?

An inspection of the Clark quarterly and Perry annual data confirms the lack of periods when $Q > QPOT$. Clark's "minimum estimate" potential series is slightly below Perry's figures. Clark calculates that $Q > QPOT$ in 1955, 1965-69, 1972, and 1973 (See Figure 5). When his "maximum estimate" is used, 1955, 1972, and 1973 disappear as years of excess demand. In either case, the size of the positive GNP gaps, in the few years in which they are positive, are always swamped by the adjacent years in which they are negative.

Perry's potential is only below GNP during the period 1965 through 1969 and in 1973. But in 1973, the dollar difference, $QPOT(\text{Perry}) - Q$, is only equal to -$3.7 billion. In 1972, on the other hand, the dollar gap is $14.0 billion, and in 1975 it is $136.7 billion. The 1973 expansion, therefore, is indeed a very mild period of excess demand. To illustrate the difference between Perry's potential and $QPOT_1$, our largest percentage gap during the 1972-73 expansion is larger than Perry's largest percentage gap during the 1965-69 years of excess demand.

The Rasche-Tatom potential series is, on average, above the Clark estimates until the 1973 oil price jump. It is only since 1973 that the "pessimistic" Rasche-Tatom series generates relatively low estimates of potential output. Their GNP gap prior to 1973 indicates considerable slack.

The Rasche-Tatom series is of special interest for two reasons. First, their current estimates of potential output are the closest to $QPOT_1$. Second, they estimate a production function, which includes an energy proxy, as a basis for their potential series. They use relative price of energy in their production function with the quantities of labor and capital. Since the price of energy moves sharply upward beginning in late 1973, their potential series is adjusted sharply downward. Given the least squares fit of the production function, the downward tilt of their fitted series after 1973 results in an upward tilt prior to 1973. This helps explain, in part, why their pre-1973 potential series tends to be above Clark's estimates.

We use the quantity of energy, rather than its relative price, with the quantities of labor and capital. The quantity of energy, as distinct from its

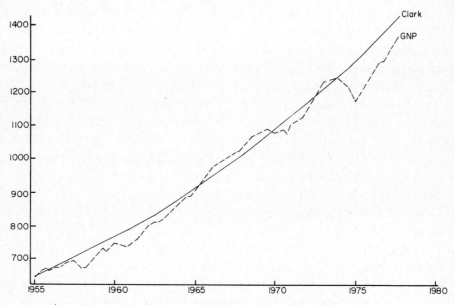

Clark's Potential Output and GNP[1]
1955:1–1977:4

[1]This series lies between his minimum and maximum series and is the one
used in the 1977 CEA report.

Figure 5

144

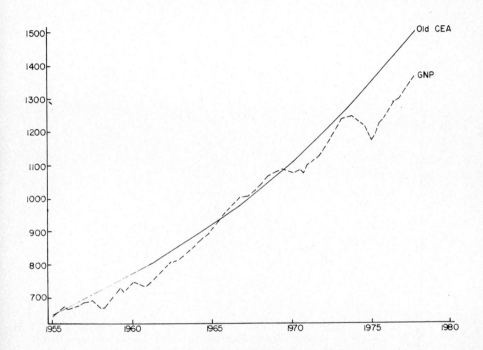

Old CEA Potential Output and GNP
1955·1-1977·4

Figure 6

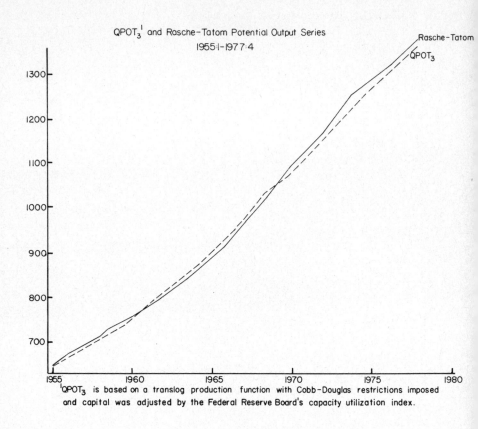

QPOT$_3^1$ and Rasche-Tatom Potential Output Series
1955:1-1977:4

^{1}QPOT$_3$ is based on a translog production function with Cobb-Douglas restrictions imposed and capital was adjusted by the Federal Reserve Board's capacity utilization index.

Figure 7

146

relative price, did not deviate greatly from its trend value in 1973; hence, unlike Rasche and Tatom, we do not get a large jump in 1973-1974.[42]

To further compare our work with that of Rasche and Tatom, we placed Cobb-Douglas restrictions on the parameters of the translog and multiplied capital by the Federal Reserve Board's capacity utilization index.[43] We retain U_1^* as the measure for U^*. As might be expected, the resulting series, denoted $QPOT_3$, falls somewhere between the Rasche-Tatom and $QPOT_1$ potential series. The $QPOT_3$ series is plotted against the Rasche-Tatom potential in Figure 7. The cyclical pattern of $QPOT_3$ is similar to that of $QPOT_1$; for example, it retains a noticeable period of $Q > QPOT$ in 1972-1973. The Rasche-Tatom potential series has only one period (1965-1969) of shallow excess demand $(Q > QPOT)$. The $QPOT_3$ series is uniformly below Rasche-Tatom's series beginning in the late 1960s. They are, however, approximately equal immediately before the oil price increase, and again in 1977:4.

To summarize, the prevailing measures of potential output (the old CEA, Clark, Perry, and Rasche-Tatom measures) indicate only one expansionary period during the last 20 years. Even during the period 1965 through 1969, the size of the gap is small relative to the excess supply gap immediately prior to 1964 and after 1969. These four potential output series appear to bound GNP from above. Indeed, most recent studies have used special dummy variables for 1974 to keep their output from becoming "too large." In general, these series are almost certainly higher than a nonaccelerating inflation rate of potential output. It is difficult to reconcile accelerating inflation between 1965 and 1977 with an estimated potential which shows deep and long periods of excess supply and shallow and brief periods of excess demand.

As a result, it appears that the prevailing measures of potential output are rooted more in a physical capability than on a nonaccelerating inflation basis. Only $QPOT_1$, relative to GNP, generates the kind of alternating excess demand and supply gaps that could be consistent with periods of rising and falling inflation.

A summary comparison of the compound annual growth rates of the various potential output series is shown in Table 4. Although there are only small differences in the rates of growth across series, these small differences translate into large changes in the potential output levels.

---

[42]See de Leeuw (1977) and Perry (1977b) for objections to the Rasche-Tatom technique of using the relative price of energy.

[43]Thus, we have estimated a Cobb-Douglas production function in labor, adjusted capital, and energy. Our estimate differs from that of Rasche and Tatom in that energy enters as a quantity and the production function was estimated in the translog framework rather than directly.

TABLE 4

Compound Annual Growth Rates of Various
Potential Output Series

Potential Series	1956:1 - 1977:4	1956:1 - 1960:4	1961:1 - 1964:4	1965:1 - 1969:4	1970:1 - 1973:2	1973:3 - 1977:4
GNP (actual)	3.48	1.87	4.83	4.04	3.88	2.25
Rasche-Tatom	3.33	2.95	3.24	4.43	3.76	2.26
$QPOT_1$	3.42	3.05	3.46	3.79	3.57	3.28
Clark	3.58	3.45	3.67	3.69	3.55	3.55
Perry	3.69	3.46	3.39	3.48	4.24	4.02
Old CEA	3.79	3.59	3.64	3.82	4.02	4.02

Note: Compound annual growth rate = $\left(\left(\dfrac{QPOT}{QPOT(-N)}\right)^{4/N} - 1\right) \times 100$, where N is the number of quarters of growth.

Over the full period, the Rasche-Tatom potential series grows the slowest, with our $QPOT_1$ a close second (See the second and third rows of Table 4). The old CEA, Perry, and Clark potential series grow faster than actual GNP. It is clear (See, for example, Figures 5 and 6) that this tendency for their potential series to grow faster than actual GNP washes out most of the cycles.

Analysis of growth rates during subperiods reveals important differences among the series. For example, the old CEA measures grow faster than most other potential measures in every subperiod. The Perry measure, which largely reflects labor force growth, grows relatively slowly from 1956 through 1964, and rapidly thereafter. The Clark potential, on the other hand, tends to grow at approximately the same rate over the entire period. The Rasche-Tatom potential, on the other extreme, grows rapidly, relative to the other potential series, between 1965-1973 and then very slowly thereafter. The largest difference among the series occurs in the post-1973 period and reflects the varying treatment of the productivity slowdown in 1974. The old CEA and Perry series ignore this productivity slowdown entirely, which explains their 4 percent plus growth rates of the past few years. Rasche and Tatom capture the productivity slowdown with their relative price term. Since energy prices in the U.S. are likely to rise due to deregulation or government taxes, even if world prices fall, Rasche and Tatom's relative price term implies a permanent drop in potential. Our $QPOT_1$ series does not give any special treatment to 1974. The slowdown in capital growth and productivity is thus captured in the coefficients of the production function.[44] As a result, our growth rate for the most recent period is above that of Rasche and Tatom, but below those of the old CEA and Perry.

---

[44]The cyclically sensitive translog shows less of a slowdown than does the standard translog (See Section C).

C. *Other Measures of Potential Using the Translog Production Function*

In this section we introduce two alternative potential output series. In the first, we omit the cyclically sensitive parameters and use a standard translog. In the second, we use the cyclically sensitive translog, but replace U_1^* with the U_2^* series, which is discussed in Section IV.

The potential series which results from using the standard translog with U_1^* is denoted $QPOT_4$ and is plotted together with GNP in Figure 8. Both $QPOT_1$ and $QPOT_4$ show a similar cyclical pattern and differ from the previous estimates, shown in Figures 3 and 4, by allowing for both recession and expansions. $QPOT_4$ and $QPOT_1$, which are virtually identical in the early period, diverge slightly in the 1970s, with $QPOT_1$ going slightly above $QPOT_4$. The result is that the 1974-1977 period of excess supply ends for $QPOT_4$ in early 1977. Our preferred series, $QPOT_1$, still indicates excess supply in 1977:4. Thus, the introduction of cyclically sensitive parameters into the translog yields a more moderate slowdown in potential output growth over the past decade.

The change from U_1^* to U_2^* as the underlying level of the nonaccelerating inflation rate of unemployment has a dramatic effect on the resulting new potential series, $QPOT_2$. While most of the potential output series found in the literature tend to bound GNP from above, $QPOT_2$ does the same from below.[45] Since, by construction, U_2^* is calculated so that $\dot{w} = \sum_{i=1}^{12} \beta_i w_{t-i}$, with $\Sigma \beta_i = 1$, it increases rapidly over the estimation period in tandem with the growing inflation rate. With $QPOT_2$, the 1965-1970 expansion now looms large compared to the small recessions in the 1950s and even the 1974-1977 downturn. Indeed, $QPOT_2/Q$ indicates nearly as large a percentage gap, in absolute value, for the 1972-1973 expansion as it does for the 1974-1977 recession.

If potential output is defined, following Okun (1962), as requiring a nonaccelerating inflation constraint, rather than a physical capacity constraint, then $QPOT_2$ has appeal relative to some of the existing potential series. Since the ongoing inflation rate is considerably higher today than it was in the mid-1950s, the economy's actual output is likely to have been, on average, above potential output, where the latter term is defined as the nonaccelerating inflation ceiling for GNP.

Needless to say, other specifications of the wage equation (15) could result in measures of potential closer to $QPOT_1$. Much more research is required on measuring U^* and in quantifying the variables that may underlie the shifting Phillips curve coefficients. Given the sensitivity of U_2^* to the particular specification of the wage equation and the greater acceptance of U_1^*-type corrections in the literature, we chose $QPOT_1$ as our preferred series.

---

[45] See Figure 9.

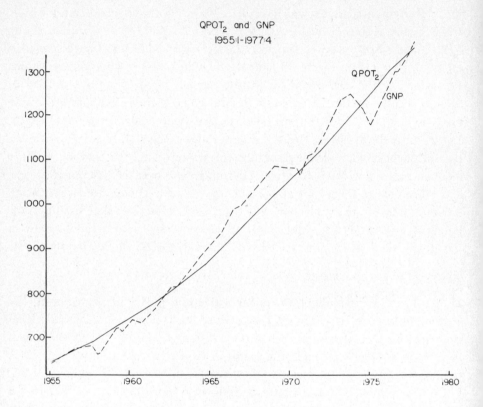

Figure 8

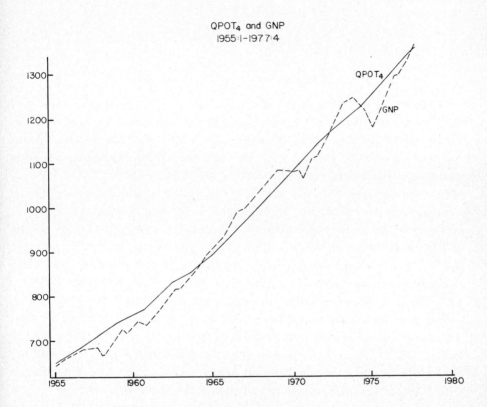

Figure 9

VII. The Okun Equation and Forecasts of the Current Unemployment Rate

In this section, we calculate a series of Okun's law equations over the various unemployment rates and potential output series. The general equation is of the form

$$U - U^* = a + \beta \; \frac{QPOT}{Q}^{.46}. \tag{19}$$

From our derivation of $QPOT$ and our production function explanation of Q, it is clear that we do not agree with the specification of (19). In addition, as shown elsewhere, even when using an Okun's law approach as a shorthand approach to predicting unemployment, we would include additional variables and make adjustments for lagged effects and autocorrelation.[47] Our interest in (19) is based largely on the fact that this specific form is still widely used as a forecasting device. For our purposes, three interesting questions can be asked of this equation. They are related to the consistency between any given pair of U^* and $QPOT$ series, the prediction of the current state of the labor market (that is, the forecast of U given U^* and $QPOT/Q$), and the stability of the β coefficient over time and across equations.

First, as discussed above, the Okun equation by mapping the product market gap into a labor market gap provides a rough consistency check between a GNP and an unemployment forecast or between an estimate of potential output and U^*. To illustrate these points, we shall compare our series with the old CEA estimate of potential output, which was used by Okun in his studies and is still perhaps the most widely used measure of potential output.

The first two rows of Table 5 indicate the results obtained by assuming that U^* is constant at 4 percent over the 1954-1977 period. The dependent variable in (i) and (ii) is U rather than U - 4. Rows 3-4 and 6-8 use the U_1^* variable with different measures of potential output. Row 5 uses the U_2^* series which was constructed from the inverted Phillips curve of Section IV. The traditional Okun's law equation (i) is fitted using the old CEA exponentially growing time trend (with a few shifts in its exponential rate of growth).[48] Equation (i) remains relatively close to the original Okun fit obtained 15 years

---

[46] See Summers (1968) on the implications of estimating Okun's law in the form of (19) instead of estimating it with $QPOT/Q$ on the lefthand side.

[47] See Friedman and Wachter (1974).

[48] The old CEA series is updated beyond 1973 by continuing the 4 percent exponential growth rate.

TABLE 5

Alternative Okun's Law Equations (19): 1955:1 - 1977:4

Equation	Dependent Variable	Measure of Potential	Constant (a)	β	$\bar{R}^2$	Predicted Unemployment Rate 1977:4 †
i	U	old CEA	-26.1902	30.3055	0.882	7.24
ii	U	$QPOT_1$	-35.5430	40.6331	0.777	5.75
iii	$U - U^*_1$	$QPOT_1$	-40.6179	41.0013	0.872	6.55
iv	$U - U^*_1$	old CEA	-25.1306	24.7670	0.645	7.69
v	$U - U^*_2$	$QPOT_2$	-43.9741	44.2582	0.900	6.49
vi	$U - U^*_1$	Clark	-36.5230	36.2408	0.813	7.07
vii	$U - U^*_1$	Rasche-Tatom	-36.9181	36.8537	0.664	5.80
viii	$U - U^*_1$	Perry	-28.8134	28.7187	0.807	7.63

†Actual unemployment rate in 1977:4 was 6.63 percent.

153

ago. The coefficients, $\beta + a$, sum to 4.12, which is the implicit and constant measure of U^*. The fit of the equation is quite good; in fact, it is the second best of the eight equations shown in this table. This is the "consistency check" discussed in Section I. The old CEA potential series is "consistent" with a constant U^* equal to 4 percent.

An almost identical $\bar{R}^2$ can be obtained from a very different Okun's law equation, one which uses the (demographic adjusted) U_1^* and $QPOT_1$ series, (iii). While U_1^* and $QPOT_1$ are very different from U and the old CEA potential, both pairs are internally consistent. If you believe that U^* has been constant at 4 percent since 1955, you might also believe the old CEA potential series. If you believe that U^* has increased gradually from about 4 percent to 5.5 percent between 1955 and 1977, you might choose $QPOT_1$ as your potential series.

The highest $\bar{R}^2$ is obtained from equation (v), which combined U_2^* and $QPOT_2$. The U_2^* variable, which is based on an inverted Phillips curve, has a value of 6.35 percent in 1977:4. As a result, this series suggests that the economy has now returned to the nonaccelerating inflation level of economic activity. According to both $QPOT_2$ and U_2^*, the 1974-1977 recession is over. The consistency check of Okun's law confirms this fact; Q and U are approximately equal to $QPOT_2$ and U_2^*, respectively. The fact that (v) has the highest $\bar{R}^2$ of the eight equations and that (i), with the old CEA potential and $U^* = 4$, has the second highest shows that the Okun equation cannot distinguish among very different $(U^*, QPOT)$ pairs.

The problems encountered by mixing U^* and potential series are shown in equations (ii) and (iv). In equation (ii), where U is regressed on $QPOT_1/Q$, the implicit U^* is forced to be a constant. The decline in $\bar{R}^2$ suggests that $QPOT_1$ is not consistent with a constant U^*. On the other hand, (iv) combines U_1^* with the old CEA potential. The drop in $\bar{R}^2$ illustrates the fact that the old CEA estimate works better in Okun's equation with a constant U^* than with U_1^*.

The second issue involves the implications of these Okun's law equations for the state of the labor market in the most recent period. The $QPOT_1$ series results in a positive output gap of \$22.2 billion in 1977:4. This is considerably below the old CEA gap of \$136.1 billion. The last column of Table 5 indicates the translations of these GNP gap figures into unemployment prediction for 1977:4. Our U_1^* and $QPOT_1$ series, used together (iii), have a predicted value for unemployment in 1977:4 of 6.55 percent. Since the actual value was 6.63 percent for that quarter, the last quarter's residual is small. The old CEA potential regressed on unemployment alone, equation (i), yields a predicted unemployment rate of 7.24 percent. This is an unusually large residual for the equation, especially in the midpoint of a recovery. Forecasters who still use the old CEA potential series made 1977 unemployment rate predictions which were systematically above the published unemployment rate of the Bureau of Labor Statistics.

The projections of unemployment in 1977:4 for equations (vi) through (viii), using $U - U_1^*$ as the dependent variable,[49] shows the relationships between the Clark, Rasche-Tatom, and Perry potential series and U_1^*. As would be expected, the ordinal ranking of these unemployment predictions is directly related to the size of their potential. The forecasted unemployment rates are 7.63 percent for Perry's potential,[50] 7.08 percent for Clark's potential, and 5.80 percent for Rasche-Tatom's potential.

Perhaps the only surprise is the Rasche-Tatom equations. The low $\bar{R}^2$ reflects a significant discrepancy between movements in labor and product market tightness. The Rasche-Tatom series uses Clark's U^* series, which reflects only demographic factors. The Rasche-Tatom potential series, however, has a sharp break attributed to the change in the price of oil in 1973. If the product and labor market gaps are to maintain their pre-1973 functional form, the kink in Rasche-Tatom's potential series should eventually be mirrored in an increase in U^* above the demographic adjustment.

The third issue of interest is the coefficient, β, on the gap term. The Okun relationship can be rewritten in the form

$$QPOT = Q[\ \frac{a}{\beta} + \frac{1}{\beta}\ (U - U^*)]\ . \tag{20}$$

In his original article, Okun estimated a coefficient of 0.032 for $1/\beta$, giving rise to the famous 3 to 1 relationship between output and unemployment. Extending the data period through 1977:4 does not change the result. In equation (i), the basic Okun form, $1/\beta$ is 0.033, remarkably close to the original 0.032. In our basic equation, (iii), the $1/\beta$ equals 0.024. In this case, a 1 percent increase in U increases the output gap by 2.4 instead of 3.3 percent. To restate the result in a more optimistic fashion, the lowering of unemployment by

---

[49] Note that we are using U_1^* rather than the U^* which the Clark, Perry, and Rasche-Tatom series actually use.

[50] This number is based on a quarterly interpolation of Perry's series, as noted above.

1 percent requires that output growth exceed potential growth by only 2.4 percent, instead of 3 percent.[51]

VIII. Conclusion

Our paper presents a new potential output series that is an approximation to the maximum output consistent with nonaccelerating inflation. It is developed from a translog production function with estimated parameters that vary over the cycle and a measure of the nonaccelerating inflation rate of unemployment. Our series lies below other potential measures found in the literature. We argue that these latter series should probably be viewed as output levels consistent with physical capacity constraints.

Most of the older potential output series were constructed by fitting trend lines through cyclical peaks in actual output. As a result, these series indicate that actual output was consistently below potential, except for the years 1965 through 1969. In addition, most series indicate a relatively small negative GNP gap, $QPOT < Q$, between these years. A GNP gap that is almost always positive, $QPOT > Q$, is not consistent with the increase in the inflation rate experienced by the U.S. economy over the past twenty years.

Our $QPOT_1$ series allows for sizeable expansions as well as recessions. It indicates that $QPOT \leq Q$ between 1955:2 - 1957:1 and between 1972:2 - 1974:1 as well as between 1964:3 - 1970:1. In addition, the periods of excess demand have relatively large GNP gaps in absolute size. Our $QPOT_1$ series confirms that the 1974-1977 downturn was the largest absolute deviation from potential output over the postwar period. Our estimate of the gap during

---

[51] Since U is 1.05 above U_1^* in 1977:4, and $1/\beta$ equals 0.024, the GNP gap should be approximately 2.4 percent. In fact, the gap $[(QPOT_1 - Q)/Q]$ in 1977:4 is equal to 1.67 percent. Part of this difference is due to the fact that α and β are not constrained to be equal, as they are in Okun (1962). Consequently, α/β serves the role of a scaling factor. For example, when the labor market is in equilibrium, in the sense that $U = U_1^*$, (20) implies that

$$Q \times \frac{\alpha}{\beta} = QPOT.$$

According to (iv) of Table 5, the $QPOT_1$ which is consistent with $U_1^* = U = 5.5$ percent in 1977:4 is $1395.8 billion. The difference between this adjusted $QPOT_1$ and Q thus implies a gap of $35.6 billion rather than $22.7 billion in 1977:4.

Alternatively, if $Q = QPOT$, then

$$\beta - \alpha + U^* = U$$

so that U^* is 5.88 percent in 1977:4 rather than 5.5 percent.

156

1977:4, however, is approximately $22.2 billion, well below that obtained from most other estimates of potential. This small gap indicates that the economy is close to the level of economic activity which is compatible with nonaccelerating inflation.

Although we estimate a specific level for the GNP gap, we suggest a degree of caution in using our potential series or any potential series as a guide to policy. In order to calculate a potential output series, one must estimate a nonaccelerating inflation rate of unemployment. This rate, U^*, is in part determined by government policies such as the variance of the money supply, minimum wage levels and coverage, the size of the armed forces, the allocation of Labor Department funds between manpower training programs and direct job creation, and so forth.

In addition, U^* may be a function of the rate of inflation or the expected rate of inflation. In his Nobel Prize speech, Milton Friedman (1977) argued that the long-run Phillips curve may be upward sloping due to the manner in which governments respond to inflation. At least implicit in the work of Okun (1975) and Wachter and Williamson (1978) is the notion that inflation interacting with induced changes in institutional methods of labor and product market contracting may also cause an upward sloping Phillips curve.

As a result, U^* and potential output in any given period will depend upon private market and governmental responses to inflation and to the government policy mix in general. Any potential output series is thus conditional on existing institutional rules and government policies. Projections of this series are, therefore, a useful target for stabilization policy only if these rules and policies are not substantially altered from those existing during the estimation period.

Appendix
The Data

All the data used in this study pertain to the U.S. private, nonagricultural sector, unless otherwise noted. The basic factor inputs are divisia indexes.

Berndt (1976) argued convincingly that production function coefficients may be very sensitive to the capital series used. A good capital series uses the real rate of return and effective tax rates. The best series available to us were obtained from Data Resources, Inc. (DRI). The DRI data included a net stock and rental price series for producers' durable equipment and nonresidential structures. The capital stock data are end-of-quarter and are depreciated by the usual perpetual inventory method. Rental prices are Jorgensonian in nature (though altered somewhat). These series were combined to form a divisia index.

We used two different labor series (called labor and adjusted labor). The labor series is the basic manhours series for the private, nonagricultural sector. This series is based on government data, but transformed by Wharton Econometric Forecasting Associates (WEFA). The adjusted labor series was constructed to control for demographic shifts in the labor force.

We first calculated an employment index (E):

$$E = \sum_i w_i(E_i - E_i^{gov}),$$

where E_i is the total nonagricultural employment of demographic group i,[52] E_i^{gov} is the ith demographic group's government employment, and w_i are weights formed by taking the ratio of full-time, year-round, total money income of the ith demographic group to the money income of males 25-64. This index is intended to represent efficiency units of employment in terms of prime-age males.

The employment series was multiplied by the average hours worked by prime-age males[53] to form an adjusted labor series.

The energy divisia index was formed by combining data on various types of energy. The data series used were[54] millions of short tons of bituminous coal

---

[52]Males 16-19, males 20-24, males 25-64, males 65+, females 16-19, females 20-24, females 25-64, and females 65+.

[53]The hours data, which are unpublished, were obtained from the Labor Department. The data represented average hours in May. These data were interpolated into a quarterly series by using the average hours worked in the manufacturing sector series.

[54]Most of the data were obtained from the *Commodity Yearbook*, but the ultimate source is indicated in parenthesis after the data set.

(Bureau of Mines), the average wholesale price of bituminous coal (Bureau of Labor Statistics), millions of barrels (42 gallons) of domestic production of crude oil (BOM), the average price of crude petroleum at wellhead, Oklahoma-Kansas wells (BLS), millions of barrels of imported crude petroleum (from three different Bureau of the Census publications), revenues from imported crude petroleum (from three different Bureau of the Census publications), trillions of BTUs of natural and "manufactured and mixed gas" used commercially and by industry (American Gas Association), revenues from total utility gas for commercial and industrial uses (AGA), millions of kilowatt hours of electricity used by commercial and industrial establishments (hydro as prime mover) (BLS),[55] and the average price of all sources of electric power (BLS).

It should be noted that our energy index does not include most electrical power. We had hoped to include all electricity which was not produced using our other energy measures. Since we could not obtain measures of nuclear produced electricity (which is presumably a small part of the total), we only included hydro electricity. Thus, our measure of the energy share is much smaller than that used by others.[56] Yet, to include the other sources of electricity seems to be a form of double counting.

Our output series is real GNP originating in the domestic, business, nonfarm sector, where an implicit price deflator was used. The unemployment rate comes from *Employment and Earnings*. All data were seasonally adjusted.

---

[55] This figure was calculated by multiplying total hydro electricity by 65 percent, which is the relatively constant ratio of commercial and industrial total electrical usage.

[56] Our energy share would almost double if all electricty were included. See Hudson and Jorgenson (1974) for a detailed discussion of energy issues and comparison figures. See Berndt and Wood (1975, 1977) for a discussion of the problems associated with including energy in a production function.

References

Aigner, D., Lovell, C.A., and Schmidt, P. (1977), "Formulation and Estimation of Stochastic Frontier Production Function Models," *Journal of Econometrics,* **6**: 21-37.

Annual Report of the Council of Economic Advisers (1978). Washington, D.C.: U.S. Government Printing Office, January, 1978.

Barro, R.J. (1977), "Unanticipated Money Growth and Unemployment in the United States," *American Economic Review,* **67**: 101-15.

Berndt, E.R. (1976), "Reconciling Alternative Estimates of the Elasticity of Substitution," *Review of Economics and Statistics,* **58**: 59-68.

Berndt, E.R., and Christensen, L.R. (1973), "The Translog Function and the Substitution of Equipment, Structures, and Labor in U.S. Manufacturing, 1929-1968," *Journal of Econometrics,* **1**: 81-114.

_____(1974), "Testing for the Existence of a Consistent Aggregate Index of Labor Inputs," *American Economic Review,* **64**: 391-404.

Berndt, E.R., and Kahled, M.S. (1977), "Energy Prices, Economies of Scale and Biased Productivity Gains in U.S. Manufacturing, 1947-71," University of British Columbia, Department of Economics Discussion Paper No. 77-23. Vancouver: University of British Columbia.

Berndt, E.R., and Wood, D.O. (1975), "Technology, Prices, and the Derived Demand for Energy," *Review of Economics and Statistics,* **57**: 259-68.

_____(1977), "Engineering and Econometric Approaches to Industrial Energy Conservation and Capital Formation: A Reconciliation," Massachusetts Institute of Technology, Energy Laboratory Working Paper No. MIT-EL 77-040WP. Cambridge, Mass.: Massachusetts Institute of Technology.

Brinner, R. (1978). *Technology, Labor, and Economic Potential,* Data Resources Study, **29**. Lexington, Mass.: Data Resources, Inc.

Brunner, K., and Meltzer, A.H., eds. (1976a). *The Phillips Curve and Labor Markets,* Carnegie-Rochester Conference Series on Public Policy, vol. 1. Amsterdam: North-Holland.

_____ (1976b). *The Economics of Price and Wage Controls,* Carnegie-Rochester Conference Series on Public Policy, vol. 2. Amsterdam: North-Holland.

Christensen, L.R., Jorgenson, D.W., and Lau, L.J. (1973), "Transcendental Logarithmic Production Frontiers," *Review of Economics and Statistics,* **55**: 28-45.

Clark, P.K. (1977), "Potential Gap in the United States, 1948-1980," in *U.S. Productive Capacity: Estimating the Utilization Gap,* Center for the Study of American Business, Washington University Working Paper 23, December 1977, 21-66. St. Louis: Washington University.

Commodity Year Book. New York: Commodity Research Bureau, Inc., various years.

de Leeuw, F. (1977), "Comments on Rasche and Tatom," *U.S. Productive Capacity: Estimating the Utilization Gap,* Center for the Study of American Business, Washington University Working Paper 23, December 1977, 137-45. St. Louis: Washington University.

Denny, M., and Fuss, M. (1977), "The Use of Approximation Analysis to Test for Separability and the Existence of Consistent Aggregates," *American Economic Review,* **67**: 404-18.

Eckstein, A.J., and Heien, D.M. (1976), "Estimating Potential Output for the U.S. Economy in a Model Framework," *Achieving the Goals of the Employment Act of 1946--Thirtieth Anniversary Review,* U.S. Congress, Joint Economic Committee, 94th Congress, 2nd Session, December 3, 1976, 1-25.

Flaim, P.O. (1977), "Impact of Demographic and Other Noncyclical Factors on the Unemployment Rate." Prepared for the Office of the Assistant Secretary of Labor for Policy Evaluation and Research. Mimeographed.

Friedman, B., and Wachter, M.L. (1974), "Unemployment: Okun's Law, Labor Force, and Productivity," *Review of Economics and Statistics,* **56**: 167-76.

Friedman, M. (1977), "Nobel Lecture: Inflation and Unemployment," *Journal of Political Economy* **85**: 451-72.

Gordon, R.J. (1976), "Recent Developments in the Theory of Inflation and Unemployment," *Journal of Monetary Economics,* **2**: 185-219.

Gramlich, E.M. (1976), "Impact of Minimum Wages on Other Wages, Employment, and Family Incomes," *Brookings Papers on Economic Activity,* **2**. Washington, D.C.: The Brookings Institution.

Hudson, E.A., and Jorgenson, D.W. (1974), "U.S. Energy Policy and Economic Growth, 1975-2000," *Bell Journal of Economics and Management Science,* **5**: 461-514.

Humphrey, D.B., and Moroney, J.R. (1975), "Substitution Among Capital, Labor, and Natural Resource Products in American Manufacturing," *Journal of Political Economy,* **83**: 57-82.

Meltzer, A.H., (1977), "Anticipated Inflation and Unanticipated Price Change," *Journal of Money, Credit and Banking,* **9**: *182-205.*

Nadiri, M.I., and Rosen, S. (1969), "Interrelated Factor Demand Functions," *American Economic Review,* **59**: 457-71.

Okun, A.M. (1962), "Potential GNP: Its Measurement and Significance," *Proceedings of the Business and Economics Section,* 98-104, Washington, D.C.: American Statistical Association.

_____(1975), "Inflation, Its Mechanics and Welfare Costs," *Brookings Papers on Economic Activity,* 2. Washington, D.C.: The Brookings Institution.

Perry, G.L. (1977a), "Potential Output and Productivity," *Brookings Papers on Economic Activity,* 1. Washington, D.C.: The Brookings Institution.

Perry, G.L. (1977b), "Potential Output: Recent Issues and Present Trends," *U.S. Productive Capacity: Estimating the Utilization Gap,* Center for the Study of American Business, Washington University Working Paper 23, December, 1977, 1-20. St. Louis: Washington University.

Rasche, R.H., and Tatom, J.A. (1977a), "Energy Resources and Potential GNP," *Federal Reserve Bank of St. Louis Review,* **59**: 10-23.

_____ (1977b), "Potential Output and Its Growth Rate--The Dominance of Higher Energy Costs in the 1970s," *U.S. Productive Capacity: Estimating the Utilization Gap,* Center for the Study of American Business, Washington University Working Paper, 23, December, 1977, 67-106. St. Louis: Washington University.

Sargent, T.J. (1973), "Rational Expectations, the Real Rate of Interest, and the Natural Rate of Unemployment," *Brookings Papers on Economic Activity,* 2. Washington, D.C.: The Brookings Institution.

Summers, R. (1968), "Further Results in the Measurement of Capacity Utilization," *Business and Economic Statistics Section Proceedings,* 25-34, Washington, D.C.: American Statistical Association.

Thurow, L.C., and Taylor, L.D. (1966), "The Interaction Between the Actual and the Potential Rates of Growth," *Review of Economics and Statistics,* 48: 351-60.

Wachter, M.L. (1976), "The Changing Cyclical Responsiveness of Wage Inflation over the Postwar Period," *Brookings Papers on Economic Activity,* **1**. Washington, D.C.: The Brookings Institution.

Wachter, M.L., and Williamson, O.E. (1978), "Obligational Markets and the Mechanics of Inflation," *Bell Journal of Economics and Management Science,* 8: 549-71.

White, Lawrence J. (undated), "Value Added Production Functions: How Good are Least Square Estimates of Scale Economies and Technological Change?" Mimeographed. Princeton, N.J.: Princeton University.

THE MEANING AND MEASUREMENT OF POTENTIAL OUTPUT
A Comment on the Perloff and Wachter Results

John A. TATOM*

Federal Reserve Bank of St. Louis

Perloff and Wachter have produced an interesting and thought provoking study of the nation's production frontier. The study is a contribution to the literature both in terms of its conclusions and its technical analysis. The most relevant conclusion is the 1977:4 GNP gap of about \$22 billion, which is far below the gap estimated by several other studies. Since recent estimates using a modified version of the methods explained by Rasche and Tatom (1977b, 1977c) indicate a similar gap, I will not question this basic conclusion. Instead, I would like to focus upon the assumptions, data, and technical analysis used in the study to arrive at this conclusion.

The major contributions of the Perloff and Wachter study are (*a*) the suggested shift in emphasis from a high-employment measure of potential output to a nonaccelerating inflation rate (NIR) measure; (*b*) the relatively successful use of a production function approach to such measures; (*c*) the use of the translog specification of the function as well as the inclusion of cyclically sensitive production function parameters; and (*d*) the evidence provided in support of recent "low" estimates of potential output as opposed to "high" estimates offered in other studies. The first contribution is the most novel aspect of the paper and deserves comment before the more technical aspects are taken up.

1. Potential Output Measures: NIR vs. High-Employment Benchmarks

The notion that measures of potential output are most useful when constructed using the relatively more sustainable criterion of nonaccelerating inflation is a novel departure from the existing literature. The concept of potential output as developed and measured by Okun (1962), and later by others, is based upon a high-employment benchmark. The appeal of Okun's 4 percent unemployment rate benchmark was that it was "a reasonable target under existing labor market conditions" (Okun, 1962, p. 98), and that any other unemployment rate benchmark could be used without affecting the method of measuring potential output. As Perloff and Wachter indicate, the benchmark has been adjusted in recent years by various researchers, but in each case the

---

*The author wishes to thank Allan H. Meltzer, Robert H. Rasche, Jeffrey M. Perloff, and Michael L. Wachter for comments on an earlier draft, and Marcus Courtney for research assistance.

effort was based upon measuring an unemployment rate which held "labor market tightness" the same as in 1955, i.e., equivalent to Okun's benchmark.

The recent efforts of some researchers to utilize a production function to measure potential output have required the assumption of a high-employment capital utilization benchmark. For example, the capacity utilization rate benchmark employed in some of the Perloff and Wachter experiments of 87.5 percent, as measured by the Federal Reserve Board Index, has been used by Rasche and Tatom (1977b, 1977c) on the grounds that it is about the rate observed at peacetime peaks and is the rate which prevailed in mid-1955.

Perloff and Wachter develop two alternative unemployment rate benchmark series. The first one, U_1^*, only accounts for demographic changes in order to remain comparable to a 4 percent rate in 1955. A second series, U_2^*, is based upon a nonaccelerating inflation rate criterion. The first series is similar to the high-employment unemployment rate benchmark series developed by others. Perloff and Wachter's choice of U_1^* as the appropriate benchmark for measuring labor employment at potential output appears to be inconsistent with their claim of measuring NIR potential output.

Because Perloff and Wachter do not employ a capital utilization rate adjustment in their preferred production function, they do not require an NIR benchmark for utilization. Where they do experiment with such an adjustment, the utilization benchmark used, a high-employment measure, is too high to be regarded as an NIR criterion. A simple monetary explanation of capacity utilization suggests the appropriate NIR benchmark is much lower than 87.5 percent. Suppose that departures from the natural capacity utilization rate, C_n, are only secured by monetary surprises, but capacity utilization, C, only adjusts to its equilibrium level with a lag. Let the anticipated rate of monetary (M1) growth equal its trend rate of growth in the recent past (5 years), $\bar{\dot{M}}_{t-1}$. Such a model can be written as

$$\hat{C} = C_n + \beta_o (\dot{M}_t - \bar{\dot{M}}_{t-1}) \qquad \text{and}$$

$$\Delta C_t = \lambda(\hat{C}_t - C_{t-1}) \qquad \text{or}$$

$$\Delta C_t = \lambda C_n + \lambda\beta_o (\dot{M}_t - \bar{\dot{M}}_{t-1}) - \lambda C_{t-1}.$$

An estimate of such an equation using annual data for the period 1954-77 yields

$$\Delta C_t = 45.30 + 1.48 \, (\dot{M}_t - \dot{M}_{t-1}) - 0.55 \, C_{t-1}$$
$$(3.27) \; (2.93) \qquad\qquad (-3.33)$$
$$\overline{R}^2 = .53 \qquad d = 2.00 \qquad S.E. = 3.64 \, ,$$

where t-statistics are indicated in parentheses. The natural capacity utilization rate which would prevail in the steady state with a constant anticipated rate of money growth and inflation is 81.9 percent ($S.E.$ = 1.13 percent). Thus, a t-test of the hypothesis that the NIR capacity utilization is 87.5 percent indicates that it can be rejected.[1]

Such an explanation is also important to an understanding of the meaning of NIR output and unemployment. The Perloff and Wachter view appears to be that when NIR measures are exceeded, the relatively low levels of slack in the economy cause accelerating inflation. The alternative view, suggested in the simple model above, is that an unanticipated acceleration in money growth will temporarily lead to a capacity utilization rate, and other real activity measures, in excess of the natural rate, until such monetary growth comes to be anticipated. The difference depends on how NIR measures are considered. Are they permanent measures, attainable and sustainable in the absence of additional inflation rate "surprises," or they are intended simply to provide a necessary benchmark for assessing the prospects for the inflation rate? Do differences in actual and NIR output explain the outlook for the inflation rate, as Perloff and Wachter appear to indicate, or do such differences indicate an unsustainable response to past policy induced changes in the inflation rate? Until the direction of causation is clear, the relevance of NIR measures for policy target discussions will be ambiguous.

On the NIR criterion, the Perloff and Wachter unemployment benchmark ($U_2^* = 6.35$) and natural capacity utilization rate above of 82 percent were virtually achieved in the fourth quarter of 1977 ($U = 6.6$, $C = 83$ percent).

---

[1] This model is a simplification of Barro's (1977) unemployment rate model. The major simplification is that anticipated money growth is hypothesized to equal the recent trend growth rate of the money stock, M1. A similar result is obtained if anticipated money growth and inflation are assumed to be the existing rate of inflation. The selection of the five-year trend is not completely arbitrary. Unemployment in the Barro model ultimately depends on a weighted sum of the current and past four year rates of growth of the money stock. A test of whether the natural rate is systematically different in the latter half of the sample period is rejected using a dummy variable. The natural capacity utilization rate appears to be quite stable.

Their measure of the gap of $22 billion at the time--based upon an unemployment benchmark of 5.5 percent--appears to be the usual high-employment type of estimate, not the NIR measure which they claim it to be. If the NIR gap is zero or negative, the meaning and significance of an NIR measure, as opposed to a high-employment measure, becomes more critical for policymakers.

2. Technical Aspects of the Perloff and Wachter Estimates

The translog production function for the nonagricultural business sector which Perloff and Wachter use includes a time (t) trend which is related, for no apparent a priori reason, to t, t^2, and t^3 terms. The function is estimated indirectly by estimating the input parameters from the first-order conditions for profit-maximization. The inputs included in the study are capital, labor, and energy.

Such a method raises serious conceptual problems. The use of the first-order conditions for the only three inputs in the model appears to involve two questionable assumptions: (a) The firms involved are always in long-run equilibrium in all factor markets, and (b) the nonagricultural business sector is essentially a price-taker in all three resource markets. This appears to be the case since the first-order conditions take relative factor prices as given and allow the optimal choice of each of the three inputs. Such an approach is not typical since potential output is usually viewed as a short-run concept.[2]

Such a criticism has been made of other production function studies. Perloff and Wachter, for example, note that Perry (1977b) and de Leeuw (1977) criticized the imposition of a first-order condition only for energy demand as a constraint in the estimation of a production function by Rasche and Tatom (1977b, 1977c). The alternative, that factor use adjusts to the profit maximizing rate only with a considerable lag, appears more likely to be the case for labor inputs and especially capital inputs than for energy.[3] The estimation of translog production function parameters using such factor share equations and time series data has also been questioned by Griffin and Gregory (1976), who develop the contradictory conclusions which may result from such a method.

The more serious limitation of the approach is its reliance upon factor share data and resource input data which had to be constructed, in particular

---

[2]The introduction of cyclically sensitive shares in the estimation of the share equations, however, can be viewed as a method of relaxing the long-run equilibrium condition, although it lacks theoretical justification.

[3]Experiments with lagged adjustment of output to energy price changes in the Rasche-Tatom production function failed to indicate that the imposition of the short-run first-order condition was inappropriate, although essentially the same results are obtained with the use of a one-quarter lag of energy price in the energy demand formulation as with the current quarter price of energy. Similar tests of a lagged response of private sector output to utilized capital indicate such a response also can be rejected. The production function parameters were estimated from the production function estimation itself in the Rasche-Tatom studies, so the absence of bias due to omitting lagged effects on output may not carry over when the parameters are estimated from factor share equations which assume long-run equilibrium.

the energy input and its factor share.[4] Perloff and Wachter note some of the limitations of the energy divisia index which they use as well as one of the many arbitrary assumptions used to allocate energy to productive uses (versus household consumption) by various organizations which maintain energy data. Moreover, data limitations do not allow them to remove primary coal and petroleum energy used for the production of household energy (for example, electricity and gasoline) from their energy quantity series. To the extent that household demands for energy are more price inelastic and/or to the extent that regulations retarded the advance of household energy prices relative to business use, their energy quantity index would not be capable of measuring the size of the reduction of energy use in the nonagricultural business sector since 1973.

The difficulties of obtaining a measure of energy use compatible with existing series on output and capital and labor inputs can be avoided by the use of the first-order condition for energy when a Cobb-Douglas function is used. This lack of appropriate energy data was the primary motivation for the use of the first-order condition in the Rasche and Tatom studies (1977b, 1977c). As noted in these studies, such an approach does not introduce detectable biases in the parameter estimates for which independent evidence is available. Nonetheless, the use of a Cobb-Douglas production function reinforces the criticism of Perry (1977b) and de Leeuw (1977), since it implies larger reductions in energy use (since 1973) than the critics and Perloff and Wachter believe have been observed. Such criticisms miss the point, however, since all that is essential is that the use of the Cobb-Douglas approximation provides an unbiased measure of the effect of a rise in energy prices on output, and no evidence has been presented which conflicts with the effect or its size as hypothesized by Rasche and Tatom (1977a, 1977b, 1977c).[5]

A look at the production function estimates in Table 3 of Perloff and Wachter's paper reveals considerable support for the Rasche-Tatom estimates. Of the first six production function estimates, the best fit is obtained by using the standard translog with Cobb-Douglas restrictions and the adjustment used

---

[4] Perloff and Wachter's concern for double counting in measuring energy appears to be unwarranted. First, they do not explain the role of the energy inputs they omit in the construction of the price deflator and output measures upon which they rely. Second, even if double counting were a problem, the same considerations affect the energy inputs they do include, as well as the capital input measure.

[5] Indeed, de Leeuw presents three implications of our work which have been supported: a reduction in labor productivity, which he accepts and which Rasche and Tatom demonstrated (1977a); a reduction in output per unit of utilized capital, which was observed and explained in Rasche and Tatom (1977b and 1977c); and a rise in output per unit of energy, which de Leeuw (1977) indicates occurred, although to a considerably smaller extent than a strict interpretation of the Cobb-Douglas assumption would imply.

by Rasche and Tatom (1977b, 1977c) to measure utilized capital.[6] Moreover, the relevant energy coefficient, the output elasticity of energy, is supportive of that obtained by Rasche and Tatom. The a_E estimate in the last column of Perloff and Wachter's Table 1 is significant and equals 0.048. Adjusting for the input coefficient β_4 of 1.17 in Table 3 and for Perloff and Wachter's comment in their Appendix that the gross share of energy in factor cost is twice as large as their a_E estimate, the relevant output elasticity in the Cobb-Douglas form $(\beta_4 \cdot a_E)$ is 11.3 percent. This estimate is very close to the 10.4 percent estimate, using quarterly data, or the 12 percent estimate, using annual data, found by Rasche and Tatom (1977b).[7]

Since Perloff and Wachter prefer the cyclically adjusted translog function, some comments on it are warranted. After estimating the parameters given in their Table 1, several hypotheses of their model could have been tested and rejected. The share equations could have then been reestimated to include only the statistically significant parameters. Of the nine production function parameters presented in the first two columns of their Table 1, four (a_K, a_E, γ_{KK}, γ_{EE}) have neither significant cyclical nor significant permanent components. Additional statistical investigation might reveal whether some or all of these four parameters should be omitted from the production function.[8] In addition, because a_L is apparently not cyclically sensitive, its cyclical component could be set equal to zero in the reestimation of the share equations.

Finally, a major concern in recent studies of productivity and potential output has been the explanation of productivity developments in recent years (See Clark, 1977a, 1977b and Rasche and Tatom, 1977a, 1977b, 1977c). Because of the evidence pointing to a drop in labor and capital productivity, it is unfortunate that Perloff and Wachter do not test their share and preferred production

---

[6]The F-tests which Perloff and Wachter show in Table 2 are derived from, and apply to, the estimated share equations which are not presented. If such estimates exhibit the same degree of autoregression as the production function estimates, the tests are biased.

[7]It should be noted that the output variables are different in the two studies, since Perloff and Wachter exclude agricultural output, treating it as fixed and independent of resource usage in the short-run. Also, the Perloff-Wachter production function uses an adjusted labor series, but they note that such an adjustment makes little difference in the potential output estimates.

[8]The standard errors of the estimates of the production function parameters measured at high employment are not indicated in their Table 1. A test of whether all the γ coefficients are zero at high employment would provide important information on whether the Cobb-Douglas form is appropriate for estimating potential output.

function estimates for structural changes or note the presence or absence of unusual productivity or factor share errors in recent years.[9]

3. The Quantitative Significance of the Perloff and Wachter Innovations for Another Approach to Measuring Potential Output

The Rasche-Tatom production function specification can be derived from that used by Perloff and Wachter under some assumptions supported by their work. Moreover, such a derivation provides a test of the usefulness and impact of their innovations on the study of an alternative and broader measure of real output, that of the private business sector. To derive the Rasche-Tatom specification, only the first-order condition for energy is imposed and γ_{EE} is assumed to be zero.[10] Using Perloff and Wachter's constraints and letting β_4 in (4) equal unity, the Perloff and Wachter production function (4 - 5) may be rewritten as

$$(\ln Q - \ln K) = \beta_0 + \beta_1 t + \beta_2 t^2 + \beta_3 t^3 + \frac{a_L}{1-x}(\ln L - \ln K)$$

$$-\frac{(\gamma_{KL} + \frac{\gamma_{KK}}{2})}{1 - x}(\ln L - \ln K)^2 - \frac{x}{1-x}\ln P_e + \frac{x}{1-x}\ln x ,$$

$$(1)$$

where

$$x = [a_E - \gamma_{KE}(\ln L - \ln K)] \qquad (2)$$

---

[9] Section VII on the unemployment rate and Okun's law equations using various measures of potential output cannot be discussed in detail here. It should be noted, however, that each of the equations presented in Table 5 is probably misspecified by omitting a significant lagged measure of the GNP gap. This result is indicated in Tatom (1978) for at least two of the equations examined there as well as for the equation Okun originally used to estimate the responsiveness of unemployment to growth. While Perloff and Wachter indicate that such misspecification exists, they do not point out that it means that the discussion of the unemployment rate equation is not helpful in providing support for one or another potential output measure.

[10] The motivation of this assumption, other than simplicity, is that γ_{EE} is not significantly different from zero in any of the estimates in Table 1. The significance of γ_{EE} is a critical issue for the related matter of how large a reduction in energy use is associated with a given reduction in potential output due to a rise in the relative price of energy resources. Observations that output per unit of energy has not risen proportionately with the rise in the relative price of energy require (for the first-order condition to hold), given the rate of usage of labor and capital at potential output, that γ_{EE} be significantly negative and larger in size the smaller is the reduction in energy usage. Of course, if the capital stock declined when the energy price rose, then $\gamma_{KE} < 0$ (which Perloff and Wachter find to be the case) may be sufficient to reconcile this discrepancy. Obviously, further investigation of the translog specification could shed more light on the nature of the response to a higher energy price as well as the mechanism by which this change is translated into a decline in productivity of existing labor and capital.

is the share of energy in factor cost, and P_e is the relative price of energy.[11] Since the share of energy is a fraction, the last term in equation (1) may be written as the series $(-x + 1/2 \, x \, (x-1) - 1/3 \, x \, (x-1)^2 + 1/4 \, x \, (x-1)^3 - 1/5 \, x \, (x-1)^4 + \ldots)$.[12] Substituting (2) into this series indicates that the last term is a constant plus a series of terms in powers of $(\ln L - \ln K)$. Thus, equation (1) may be estimated as

$$(\ln Q - \ln K) = \beta_0 + \beta_1 \, t + \beta_2 \, t^2 + \beta_3 \, t^3 + \beta_4 \, (\ln L - \ln K)$$

$$+ \beta_5 \, (\ln L - \ln K)^2 + \ldots + \beta_{n+3} \, (\ln L - \ln K)^n$$

$$+ \beta_{n+4} \, \ln P_e . \tag{3}$$

To determine whether the use of the translog specification adds significantly to the explanation of the broader output measure, private business sector output, this equation was estimated over the sample period 1955:1-1977:4. None of the coefficients $(\beta_5 \ldots \beta_{n+3})$ are significant for values of n up to and including 5.[13] Thus, the appropriate structure of (1) for the private business sector appears to be

$$(\ln Q - \ln K) = \beta_0 + \beta_1 \, t + \beta_2 \, t^2 + \beta_3 \, t^3 + \beta_4 \, (\ln L - \ln K) + \beta_5 \, \ln P_e ,$$

$$\tag{3}$$

---

[11] The energy input is eliminated by the use of the first-order condition, rewirtten as $\ln E = \ln Q - \ln P_e + \ln x$, where x is the share of energy. The input function (Perloff and Wachter's equation 5) may be written as $(I = a_L \ln L + a_K \ln K + 1/2 \, \gamma_{LL} \, (\ln L)^2 + 1/2 \, \gamma_{KK} \, (\ln K)^2 + \gamma_{LK} \ln L \ln K + x \ln Q - x \ln P_e + x \ln x)$. The remaining substitutions necessary for (1) are $[(a_K + a_L) = 1 - a_E = 1 - x + \gamma_{LE} \ln L + \gamma_{KE} \ln K]$ or since $\gamma_{KE} = -\gamma_{LE}$, $[a_K + a_L = 1 - x - \gamma_{KE} (\ln L - \ln K)]$, $\gamma_{LL} = -2 \gamma_{KL}$, and $\gamma_{KL} = -\gamma_{KE} = \gamma_{LE}$.

[12] This result follows from the approximation which holds for $2 > x > 0$: $\ln x = (x - 1) - 1/2 \, (x - 1)^2 + 1/3 \, (x - 1)^3 \cdot \ldots$.

[13] This conclusion holds for adding the indicated variables to the three production function estimates shown in Table 1. The criterion used to reach this conclusion is an F-test of the significance of the addition of the variables to equations shown. In every case, the hypothesis that the coefficients on the additional variables are zero is not rejected at the 95 percent confidence level.

which is the equation used by Rasche and Tatom (1977b, 1977c), except for the squared and cubed time terms. One method of obtaining (3) as the appropriate specification of the production function is to invoke a Cobb-Douglas specification; another is simply to assume γ_{KE} in equation (1) equals zero.[14] Then the coefficient on the relative price of energy may be used to find the share of energy, and a_L may be found from β_4 and β_5. The evidence in Rasche and Tatom (1977b, 1977c) indicates that the hypothesis, a_L is labor's share in factor cost, cannot be rejected, as is required by the Cobb-Douglas specification. It cannot be overemphasized, however, that the use of equation (3) does not rule out the presence of a more sophisticated technology, such as the translog specification indicates; instead, the test supports the quantitative unimportance of the specification, and this conclusion may only apply to the production of the broader output aggregate used here and not to the output studied by Perloff and Wachter.

To assess the importance of the introduction of the additional time variables and cyclically sensitive factor shares, equation (3) was estimated with and without each feature. The production function estimates are given in Table 1. Cyclically sensitive labor and capital shares and the time coefficients are statistically significant. When the excess unemployment variable ($UN = U - U_F$, where U_F is a demographically adjusted benchmark roughly equal to U_1^*) is added to equation (A), it is insignificant, indicating the absence of additional cyclical sensitivity of output per unit of capital. How important are these adjustments to measures of potential output?

To provide information on this question, three measures of potential output are constructed using each production function in Table 1. The method follows Rasche and Tatom (1977c) with one exception. Since no aggregate evidence could be found relating the civilian labor force to the excess unemployment rate, UN, the distinction between the potential and actual labor force seems unnecessary and is not used. The high-employment benchmarks are those supplied by Clark (1977b) for labor and an 87.5 percent capacity utilization rate for capital.

Estimates of potential output for the first quarter in several years are given in Table 2. When each measure is compared with the latest Rasche-Tatom estimates for the longer period beginning in 1948, none of the estimates are as much as 1 percent different in any quarter since 1958. The notable discrepancy, indicated only in the first row of Table 2, is in the period 1955:1-1958:2 when the

---

[14] If γ_{KE} is assumed to be zero, the absence of a significant coefficient on the squared logarithm of the labor-capital term implies that γ_{KK}, γ_{KL}, γ_{LL} may not be zero in the translog form. Even if γ_{KE} is non-zero, the assumption that x is a constant may be sufficiently close to reality that equation (3) cannot be rejected.

TABLE 1

Alternative Production Function Estimates
for the Private Business Sector
(1955:1-1977:4)

(A) $\ln Q = 1.4962 + 0.0102\,t - 0.0001\,t^2 + 0.79 \times 10^{-6}\,t^3 + 0.6475 \ln L$
  $(11.5283)\quad(5.1746)\quad(-3.0540)\quad(2.8103)\quad\quad(14.6586)$

  $+ 0.3525 \ln K - 0.1035 \ln P_e - 0.0033\,UN \ln L + 0.0033\,UN \ln K$
  $(7.9789)\quad(-4.2132)\quad(-2.4133)\quad\quad(2.4133)$

  $\bar{R}^2 = 0.98 \qquad d = 2.10 \qquad S.E. = 0.0060 \qquad \hat{p} = 0.84$

(B) $\ln Q = 1.5430 + 0.6531 \ln L + 0.3469 \ln K - 0.0964 \ln P_e + 0.0041\,t$
  $(13.5929)\quad(14.7130)\quad(7.8147)\quad(-4.5175)\quad\quad(9.2798)$

  $- 0.0037\,UN \ln L + 0.0037\,UN \ln K$
  $(-2.5979)\quad\quad(+2.5979)$

  $\bar{R}^2 = 0.98 \qquad d = 2.05 \qquad S.E. = 0.0062 \qquad \hat{p} = 0.90$

(C) $\ln Q = 1.6080 + 0.7264 \ln L + 0.2736 \ln K - 0.0913 \ln P_e + 0.0047\,t$
  $(14.3138)\quad(20.8002)\quad(7.8332)\quad(-4.3070)\quad\quad(12.5312)$

  $\bar{R}^2 = 0.98 \qquad d = 1.90 \qquad S.E. = 0.0064 \qquad \hat{p} = 0.89$

Note: t - statistics are given in parentheses.

TABLE 2

Alternative Measures of Potential Output
in First Quarters of Selected Years

	Using RT Method (Table 1, Equation C)	With Cyclically Sensitive Shares (Table 1, Equation B)	With Cubic Time Trend (Table 1, Equation A)	Most Recent RT Estimates (from period 1948 to present)
1955	645.2	643.8	610.2	645.3
1960	755.5	754.4	757.0	755.7
1965	889.4	887.7	897.0	889.4
1970	1101.2	1103.4	1100.7	1101.7
1973	1230.9	1230.1	1219.3	1229.4
1974	1263.9	1260.6	1247.6	1258.0
1975	1285.4	1281.5	1268.8	1276.8
1976	1319.2	1313.3	1303.6	1309.3
1977	1357.1	1348.3	1343.8	1345.3
(1977:4)	1386.8	1376.1	1377.8	1373.4

measures obtained from Equation (A) are markedly below other measures. The difference between the series which includes the cubic time trend and the Rasche-Tatom measures diminishes from about 5.5 percent early in 1955 to 1 percent in 1958:2. The annual average for 1955, when the cubic time trend is included, is $624.5 billion, which is far below actual GNP in 1955 or the measures of potential constructed by Perry (1977a), Rasche and Tatom (1977b, 1977c), Clark (1977a, 1977b) or the old CEA series. The latter measures range from about $651-$658 billion. While the cubic time trend is statistically significant, its usefulness appears limited since it yields such dubious results early in the sample period and there is no a priori motivation for its inclusion.[15] Beyond 1958, neither adjustment (time trend or cyclically sensitive shares) appears to have an appreciable effect on potential output measures.

4. Summary

Perloff and Wachter's study of U.S. potential output raises important theoretical and empirical issues and comes to the conclusion that there is considerably less slack in the economy (1977:4) than many observers and policymakers believe. The major theoretical issue raised concerns the meaning and significance of NIR measures of potential output. Unfortunately, the benchmark assumption used for constructing potential output is essentially a high-employment benchmark assumption comparable to that used by others. Regardless of the significance of NIR output, such measures would apparently be considerably smaller and the NIR gap would currently be closed.

The Perloff and Wachter production function analysis suggests the use of a more sophisticated technology than has previously been used in potential output studies. In addition, they argue for the consideration of cyclically sensitive factor shares and a more complicated time trend for technological progress. All three features have been examined here for the same period, but using data for the private business sector and a less restrictive approach to the estimation of the production function parameters. Although the latter two features appear to be significant in a statistical sense, they do not appear to have much effect on potential output measures for recent years. The use of their time trend specification is suspect in this instance, however, because it leads to unusual measures in the early years of the series and because it lacks underlying theoretical support.

The consideration of a translog technology is an important issue which has not been fully resolved. Their evidence as well as that presented here

---

[15]The annual rate of technological change, according to Perloff-Wachter's Table 3, column 1, has other dubious characteristics. The rate begins at 2.9 percent per year in 1955:1, rises to a peak of 3.2 in late 1963, and then falls, reaching 2.8 percent at the end of 1977. The rate of technological change in equation (A) actually shows a reverse pattern, falling until 1963 and then rising ad infinitum.

supports the use of Cobb-Douglas restrictions. It is shown above that a specification of the production function which is consistent with Cobb-Douglas assumptions is supported by private business sector data, but that this specification can be regarded as an approximation of a translog production function as well. The statistical evidence presented does not discriminate between the two technological hypotheses, although the Cobb-Douglas restrictions cannot be rejected.

A final issue which is not resolved by the Perloff and Wachter study concerns the loss in potential output in 1974 due to the large increase in the relative price of energy. Their $QPOT_1$ series does not indicate such a loss. The statistical problems indicated above for their share and production function estimates, as well as the data limitations cited, leave open the possibility that their approach may eventually provide evidence on this issue.

References

Barro, R.J. (1977), "Unanticipated Money Growth and Unemployment in the United States," *American Economic Review,* **67**: 101-15.

Clark, P.K. (1977a), "A New Estimate of Potential GNP." Unpublished Memorandum, Council of Economic Advisers, January 27, 1977.

_____(1977b), "Potential GNP in the United States, 1948-1980," *U.S. Productive Capacity: Estimating the Utilization Gap.* Center for the Study of American Business, Washington University Working Paper 23. St. Louis: Washington University.

de Leeuw, F. (1977), "Comments on Rasche and Tatom," *U.S. Productive Capacity: Estimating the Utilization Gap.* Center for the Study of American Business, Washington University Working Paper 23. St. Louis: Washington University.

Griffin, J.M., and Gregory, P.R. (1976), "An Intercountry Translog Model of Energy Substitution Response," *American Economic Review,* **66**: 845-57.

Okun, A.M. (1962), "Potential GNP: Its Measurement and Significance," *Proceedings of the Business and Economics Section,* 98-104. Washington, D.C.: American Statistical Association.

Perloff, J.M., and Wachter, M.L. (1979), "A Production Function-Nonaccelerating Inflation Approach to Potential Output: Is Measured Potential Output Too High?" *Carnegie-Rochester Conference Series,* **10**, eds. K. Brunner and A.H. Meltzer. Amsterdam: North-Holland.

Perry, G.L. (1977a), "Potential Output and Productivity," *Brookings Papers on Economic Activity,* **1**. Washington, D.C.: The Brookings Institution.

_____(1977b), "Potential Output: Recent Issues and Present Trends," *U.S. Production Capacity: Estimating the Utilization Gap.* Center for the Study of American Business, Washington University Working Paper 23. St. Louis: Washington University.

Rasche, R.H., and Tatom, J.A. (1977a), "The Effects of the New Energy Regime on Economic Capacity, Production, and Prices," Federal Reserve Bank of St. Louis *Review*, May, **59**: 2-12.

_____(1977b), "Energy Resources and Potential GNP," Federal Reserve Bank of St. Louis *Review,* June, **59**: 10-23.

_____(1977c), "Potential Output and Its Growth Rate--The Dominance of Higher Energy Costs in the 1970s," *U.S. Productive Capacity: Estimating the Utilization Gap.* Center for the Study of American Business, Washington University Working Paper 23. St. Louis: Washington University.

Tatom, J.A. (1978), "Economic Growth and Unemployment: A Reappraisal of the Conventional View," Federal Reserve Bank of St. Louis *Review,* October, **60**: 16-22.

POTENTIAL GNP: ITS MEASUREMENT AND SIGNIFICANCE
A Dissenting Opinion

Charles I. PLOSSER and G. William SCHWERT*

University of Rochester

The concept of potential output has played a central role in discussions and the implementation of economic policy for at least fifteen years. The paper by Perloff and Wachter (1979) is the most recent in a series of efforts to bring improved economic theory and statistical methods to bear on the measurement of potential output. Before we discuss some of the specific issues raised by Perloff and Wachter, we would like to address a recurring problem that has plagued the interpretation of econometric results found in the literature on potential output since the work of Okun (1962).

1. Inverting Regressions

Many of the recent attempts to estimate potential output, including Clark (1977) and Perry (1977), follow the procedure outlined by Okun (1962) of using estimated regressions of unemployment on output to "solve out" for "potential output" as a function of actual output and a measure of the deviations of the unemployment rate from some "full-employment" rate or "natural rate" of unemployment.[1] Unfortunately, what appears to be a rather simple algebraic manipulation of the relationship between unemployment and output represents poor econometrics in practice, and can have important implications for the interpretation of subsequent results.

What Okun and others wish to do is to take a deterministic function relating two variables, Y and X,

$$Y = \beta X,$$

and invert it to get the relationship between X and Y,

$$X = \frac{1}{\beta} Y.$$

*The National Science Foundation provided support for this research. Comments from Karl Brunner, Ronald Hansen and Clifford Smith are gratefully acknowledged.

[1] Perloff and Wachter use a similar procedure in equation (15) and the equation following (15) to estimate a "nonaccelerating-inflation rate of unemployment."

Unfortunately, regression relationships cannot be manipulated this way. The linear regression of Y on X (where we assume both Y and X have means of zero for convenience),

$$Y = \beta X + \epsilon,$$

has a slope coefficient $\beta = \rho(Y,X) \cdot \sigma(Y)/\sigma(X)$, where $\rho(Y,X)$ is the correlation coefficient between Y and X, and $\sigma(Y)$ and $\sigma(X)$ are the standard deviations of Y and X, respectively. Hence, the expected value of Y given X is βX. On the other hand, the regression of X on Y,

$$X = \gamma Y + \eta,$$

has a slope coefficient $\gamma = \rho(Y,X) \cdot \sigma(X)/\sigma(Y)$, and the expected value of X given Y is γY. It would be incorrect to use $\dfrac{1}{\beta} Y$ as a measure of the expected value of X given Y. It is easy to see that

$$\gamma = \frac{1}{\beta} \cdot \rho^2(Y,X).$$

Consequently, only in the case where $\rho(Y,X) = \pm 1$ will the regression of X on Y have a slope coefficient equal to the reciprocal of the slope coefficient in the regression of Y on X. In other words, only if Y and X are perfectly correlated (so both regressions are, in fact, deterministic) will such a procedure be valid.

In order to see the importance of this point, consider the simple Okun procedure for estimating potential output. Okun regresses quarterly changes in the unemployment rate (ΔU) on quarterly percentage changes in real GNP, $[\dfrac{\Delta Y}{Y}]$. We have estimated this equation using data from the first quarter of 1953 through the last quarter of 1970,

$$\Delta U = 0.261 - 0.301 \, [\frac{\Delta Y}{Y}], \tag{1}$$
$$(0.050) \ \ (0.039)$$

$$\bar{R}^2 = 0.469, \quad \hat{\sigma} = 0.309, \quad D\text{-}W = 2.25,$$

180

where standard errors are in parentheses, $\bar{R}^2$ is adjusted for degrees of freedom, $\hat{\sigma}$ is the standard deviation of the residuals, and $D\text{-}W$ is the Durbin-Watson statistic. Equation (1) implies that given a 1.0 percent increase in real GNP, the unemployment rate can be expected to fall by 0.3 percent. It is not correct to infer that given a 1.0 percent increase in the unemployment rate, real GNP can be expected to fall by 3.3 percent, which is the famous (infamous) 3 to 1 relationship between output and the unemployment rate called Okun's law.

If one is interested in the expected value of $\dfrac{\Delta Y}{Y}$, given ΔU, that is, the expected movement in real GNP conditional on some observed movement in the unemployment rate, it is appropriate to estimate the regression of the percentage change in real output on the change in the unemployment rate,

$$[\frac{\Delta Y}{Y}] = 0.857 \quad - \quad 1.58 \ \Delta U, \tag{2}$$
$$\phantom{[\frac{\Delta Y}{Y}] = } (0.087) \qquad (0.206)$$

$$\bar{R}^2 = 0.469, \quad \hat{\sigma} = 0.708, \ D\text{-}W = 2.25 \ .$$

Hence, given a 1.0 percent increase in the unemployment rate, real GNP is expected to fall by 1.6 percent, *not* 3.3 percent!

Using Okun's assumption that a 4.0 percent unemployment rate is the "desired" or "full-employment" rate, Okun's estimate of the gap, G, between "potential output," P, and actual output, Y, is calculated from

$$P - Y = \quad G = 0.033 \ (U - 4) \cdot Y \ .$$

If the unemployment rate is 1.0 percent above the 4.0 percent "full-employment" rate, the "gap" is 3.3 percent of actual GNP. However, using the correct estimate of the effect of unemployment on output from equation (2), the "gap" is calculated from

$$G = 0.016 \ (U - 4) \cdot Y \ .$$

That is, the output gap is cut approximately in half.[2] Thus, the lax econometric procedures followed by Okun and others can have substantial implications for policy.

The above discussion is not meant to suggest that we believe that obtaining correct estimates of potential output is simply a matter of turning around a regression equation. To the contrary, we feel there are many important conceptual and statistical problems that must be overcome before a meaningful interpretation can be given to estimates of inherently unobservable measures like potential output.

2. Econometric Problems in the Perloff and Wachter Paper

The Perloff and Wachter approach to calculating potential output involves the estimation of a translog production function for the economy, equations (4) and (8), and a wage equation (16) from which they construct their "nonaccelerating-inflation rate of unemployment." Potential output is obtained by substituting the potential labor force obtained from a labor (supply or demand?) equation (18) into the aggregate production function (4).

Unfortunately, we feel that there are important statistical problems with the empirical analysis conducted by Perloff and Wachter. For example, it is not clear that the "cyclically-sensitive translog production function" provides a better description of the time series behavior of aggregate output than simpler models. Comparison of the first six columns of Table 3 reveals that the estimated production function with the smallest residual variance is the Cobb-Douglas model in column (6). In fact, it has a residual variance at least 30 percent less than any of the other specifications. It is unfortunate that Perloff and Wachter do not estimate this Cobb-Douglas model, correcting for autocorrelation, so it can be compared to the corrected, cyclically-sensitive translog models that are presented in the last two columns of Table 3.

Another disturbing aspect of the results in Table 3 is that the cyclically-sensitive production functions typically place more weight on the time trend terms (particularly the linear term, t) than on the term representing the factor inputs. Moreover, the estimated cyclically-sensitive models imply severe diminishing returns to scale. That is, the coefficient of the index of factor inputs is substantially below 1.0 (the value which seems to be implied by the production function model). This suggests that the estimates of the cyclically-sensitive model are not consistent with the theory.

There is an additional point regarding Perloff and Wachter's empirical analysis which we feel is of interest. To obtain a potential output series, a

---

[2] Of course, if the "full-employment" rate of unemployment is larger than 4.0 percent, the "gap" will be reduced, whether the estimates from equation (1) or (2) are used.

potential labor series, L^*, is constructed using (18) and setting $UGAP_1 = 0.25$. Aside from the severe autocorrelation problems present in the estimated model (as evidenced by a very low Durbin-Watson statistic), it should be noted that substituting $UGAP_1 = 0.25$ into (18) implies that the potential labor series simply follows a deterministic cubic time trend. Given that potential labor is a time trend, that labor makes the largest contribution to the index of inputs (See Table 1), and that output itself is further influenced by time trends (See Table 3), our interpretation is that Perloff and Wachter have obtained a measure of potential output which is dominated by a deterministic time trend. We doubt that Perloff and Wachter believe that these polynomials in time represent true models of economic activity, because they imply an explosive and *deterministic* growth path for the economy (Cowden, 1963, describes the perils of using regressions which are polynomial functions of time). An alternative view might be to consider actual output being associated with a particular growth *rate,* but not a deterministic growth *path* to which output tends to return. Such an alternative view would lead to models of output that appear to be more nearly like random walks with drift (where the drift is the expected growth rate), rather than deterministic time trends.

Despite the use of the time trends to represent the nonstationary behavior of output over time, the Durbin-Watson statistics for the first six columns in Table 3, which estimate the production function (4), are between 0.2 and 0.4, implying first-order serial correlation in the residuals of about 0.9 or 0.8. As a result of discussion which occurred at the Carnegie-Rochester Conference, Perloff and Wachter also estimate the cyclically-sensitive production function using first- and second-order Cochrane-Orcutt models for the regression residuals in the last two columns of Table 3. In these models, the quadratic and cubic time trend coefficients are insignificant and the autoregressive coefficients for the residuals are close to unity, implying close to nonstationary behavior. Perloff and Wachter argue that their regression estimates are consistent, even though they are not efficient. We believe, however, that the severe residual autocorrelation exhibited in the Perloff and Wachter regressions should not be dismissed so lightly. As we have argued in detail elsewhere (Plosser and Schwert, 1978), the costs of ignoring highly autocorrelated residuals can be very large in terms of statistical inference. If the residuals from the regressions in Table 1 are as highly autocorrelated as those in Table 3 (as we suspect), all of the statistical tests reported by Perloff and Wachter, in particular, the F-tests which compare various production function specifications in Table 2, grossly overstate the level of significance of their results.

One positive suggestion, which would provide a crude test of the specification of these models, is to estimate all of the models in terms of the first differences of the data. This would probably yield valid statistical tests (because the residuals would probably not be highly autocorrelated), and the comparison of the levels regressions with the differences regressions may indicate other possible specification errors. For example, if output follows a random walk with drift, the residuals from the differences model would be serially uncorrelated.

3. Conceptual Problems with Defining Potential Output

Even if all of these estimation problems can be overcome, there are serious problems with the meaning and usefulness of a concept like "potential output." We believe that a supply-oriented concept such as "potential output" has little operational significance. It is not an equilibrium concept, since there is no relationship with aggregate demand. Consequently, "potential output" cannot be viewed as representing the level of output which would prevail in the absence of any unexpected random shocks to aggregate supply or demand.

While the Perloff and Wachter measure of potential output seems to behave like "normal output" (for example, the level of output that would prevail if there were no unexpected monetary or fiscal shocks), because it allows for both positive and negative "gaps," the similarity is only superficial. For example, given that there is no aggregate demand in their model, all deviations of actual output from potential output implicitly arise from aggregate demand fluctuations. Therefore, demand management stabilization policies are the logically consistent way to control economic fluctuations and restore the economy to its "equilibrium" growth path. In fact, this would be true of any measure of so-called "potential output." However, aggregate demand policies are not necessarily appropriate in a world where actual output is viewed as the outcome of the interaction between supply and demand in both factor and product markets.[3] In such an equilibrium model "potential output" ceases to have any significance, and even measures of "normal output" are difficult to operationalize because they require comparing the relative merits of various equilibria.

Suppose one could model "potential output" as Perloff and Wachter are attempting to do. Lucas (1976) has argued that traditional econometric models cannot be used to design control policies because rational economic agents will react to the change in control regimes, thus changing the parameters of the econometric model. Perloff and Wachter recognize this problem in the last sentence of the paper: "Projections of this series are, therefore, a useful

---

[3]In a recent paper, Lucas (1978) has expressed similar doubts about the operational definition of full-employment and its usefulness as a theoretical construct or policy guide. For example, one possible definition of "potential output" is the level of gross national product which would result if all persons over 16 years old worked 24 hours a day, every day of the year. This extreme definition illustrates the futility of defining potential output without reference to utility maximizing behavior.

target for stabilization policy only if these rules and policies are not substantially altered from those existing during the estimation period." If Lucas's argument about econometric policy evaluation is correct, then policy-oriented uses of "potential output" are not only futile, they can be seriously misleading.

Perhaps attempts to estimate "potential output" should best be viewed as exercises in economic history, describing what existed under past policy regimes. Perloff and Wachter explicitly recognize the possibility that different regimes of government policy can influence their econometric models.[4] Nevertheless, most analysts, including Perloff and Wachter, would like to use estimates of potential output to guide future policy decisions. Unfortunately, even if the dummy variables and the cyclically-sensitive parameters capture the effects of past policies on the models' estimates, these models cannot be used to predict the future path of output under different policy regimes.[5] It would seem, therefore, that modeling "potential output" is an exercise with little merit, serving only to perpetuate the idea that its use as a policy guide can be justified through economic theory.

4. Conclusions

In this paper we have tried to point out some of the econometric and conceptual difficulties with defining and measuring potential output. In brief, most efforts to estimate potential output, including the paper by Perloff and Wachter, are essentially equivalent to trend extrapolation of output. The details of different approaches really amount to questions about whether the trend line should pass through the peaks of past output (as Okun's approach implies when the "full-employment" unemployment rate is set equal to a low 4.0 percent) or through the middle of past output (as Perloff and Wachter's approach implies). The former approach produces an "output gap" which is always positive, implying a continual need for stimulative government policies, while the latter approach implies that the "output gap" can be both positive and negative.

In general, the Perloff and Wachter estimates of potential output are well below the estimates produced by the Council of Economic Advisers (CEA). For example, Perloff and Wachter estimate a "gap" between potential and actual

---

[4] For example, the translog production function (4) has coefficients which are allowed to vary linearly with the "unemployment gap," which they rationalize through a "labor hoarding" argument. The wage equation (16) has dummy variables to represent different average changes in growth rates of wages during different presidential administrations and a dummy variable representing Phase I to Phase IV of price controls.

[5] For example, suppose that instead of wage and price controls, the economy is subjected to TIP (Tax-Based Income Policies). One could not use the Perloff and Wachter results to obtain measures of the future path of actual or potential output because TIP would affect the "full-employment" rate of unemployment.

output of $22.6 billion as of the fourth quarter of 1977, which is substantially below the CEA estimate of $136.1 billion. While we concur that the economy is probably not in need of the kind of fiscal or monetary stimulus implied by the huge CEA estimate of the output gap, we feel that the Perloff and Wachter study is deficient in its empirical analysis and leaves a number of important conceptual questions unanswered.

References

Clark, P.K. (1977), "Potential Gap in the United States, 1948-1980," in *U.S. Productive Capacity: Estimating the Utilization Gap*, Center for the Study of American Business, Washington University Working Paper 23: December 1977, St. Louis: Washington University.

Cowden, D.J. (1963), "The Perils of Polynomials," *Management Science*, **9**: 546-50.

Lucas, R.E. (1976), "Econometric Policy Evaluation: A Critique," *The Phillips Curve and Labor Markets,* Carnegie-Rochester Conference on Public Policy, vol. 1, eds. K. Brunner and A.H. Meltzer. Amsterdam: North-Holland.

_____(1978), "Unemployment Policy," *American Economic Review,* **68**: 353-57.

Okun, A.M. (1962), "Potential GNP: Its Measurement and Significance," *Proceedings of the Business and Economics Statistics Section of the American Statistical Association*: 98-104.

Perloff, J.M., and Wachter, M.L. (1979), "A Production Function-Nonaccelerating Inflation Approach to Potential Output: Is Measured Potential Output Too High?" *Carnegie-Rochester Conference Series,* **10**, eds. K. Brunner and A.H. Meltzer. Amsterdam: North-Holland.

Perry, G.L. (1977), "Potential Output and Productivity," *Brookings Papers on Economic Activity*, **2**. Washington, D.C.: The Brookings Institution.

Plosser, C.I., and Schwert, G.W. (1978), "Money, Income, and Sunspots: Measuring Economic Relationships and the Effects of Differencing," *Journal of Monetary Economics,* **5**: 637-60.

A COMMENT ON THE PERLOFF AND WACHTER PAPER

Robert J. GORDON

Northwestern University and *the National Bureau of Economic Research*

The paper by Perloff and Wachter is interesting, sophisticated, and basically correct in its policy implications. It presents a full agenda of issues for both the policy-oriented and the technically-oriented discussant. In the limited time available for preparation of this comment, I can touch only on some of the more important of these issues.

1. Semantics

Originally in the early 1960s, there was no natural rate hypothesis of unemployment. The idea that inflation would continually accelerate below some unemployment rate had not yet made its appearance, and the stable Phillips tradeoff curve reigned supreme. Since the tradeoff curve provided a menu of possible choices for policymakers, the selection of a single point on the curve depended only on the tastes of society and/or its policymakers, and not on any dividing line between points of acceleration or deceleration of inflation. The selection in the early 1960s of a 4.0 percent unemployment rate as a definition of "full employment," and the accompanying output as society's "potential," was entirely arbitrary. No production function or wage equation estimates led to the choice. In fact the label "potential" was a misnomer, with its connotation of capacity limitations, and the original Okun-Heller concept should have been called not "potential output," but "arbitrarily-defined full-employment output."

The macroeconomic revolution associated with the natural rate hypothesis rendered obsolete the arbitrary 4.0 percent full employment unemployment target, as well as the associated measure of potential output. It was widely recognized by the early 1970s that the dividing line between accelerating and decelerating inflation rates was considerably higher than 4.0 percent; as early as 1971, equations constrained to be consistent with the natural rate hypothesis yielded a natural unemployment rate estimate of 5.5 percent.[1] Thus the earlier potential output concept no longer represented the economy's true potential in any meaningful sense, because an attempt to maintain actual output permanently equal to potential would cause a continuous acceleration of inflation.

---

[1] Gordon (1971, p. 139, n. 41).

A major surprise was the failure of the Republican economic policy-making establishment of 1968-76 to abandon the obsolete potential output concept, since official adoption of a new, less ambitious target variable would have added support to its own policies of economic restraint in 1970 and 1974. A shift to a consistent Federal budget measure would have helped to gain support for its policies of expenditure restraint. Ironically, the Republican regime issued a new, less ambitious set of output and budget numbers as its dying gasp in January, 1977, but it continued to use the misleading nomenclature "potential output," and its methodology did not tie the new measure to the behavior of wages and prices.[2]

Thus, my first quarrel with the paper by Perloff and Wachter is its adherence to the discredited and obsolete word "potential" as the output concept to be made consistent with the natural rate of unemployment. It is by now well understood that the word "natural" means equilibrium, in the sense of the absence of pressure for an acceleration or deceleration of inflation. It does not mean "optimal" or "immutable." Thus, I will apply the short and simple phrase "natural output" to the real GNP series derived by the procedures Perloff and Wachter adopt, and the phrase "natural employment surplus" to the Federal budget concept consistent with natural output.

2. How Much Methodology is Really Necessary?

The policy implications of a new and less ambitious natural output series are obvious and important. The GNP gap which once seemed gigantic now looks tiny, while the previously modest full employment deficit is replaced by a gigantic natural employment deficit. Ironically, though, nothing in Perloff and Wachter's paper makes a crucial contribution to the new chosen series $QPOT_1$. The war is over before the fighting commences, through the authors' choice of a particular natural unemployment (U^*) series developed in a previous paper by Wachter (1976). Taking this set of data on U^*, one can compute an acceptable and consistent natural output series without any use of production functions at all. First, one can establish benchmarks in quarters in which actual unemployment equals U^*, and then run a trend between the value of actual real GNP achieved in those quarters. Extra information is needed only to extrapolate the series in the most recent period since the last benchmark quarter.

How does this "simpleminded natural output series" (Q^*) compare to the $QPOT_1$ series which emerges from Perloff and Wachter's paper? I have just published such a quarterly Q^* variable for 1947-77 based on a U^* variable

---

[2] The 1977 potential output variant is that labelled "Clark" in Perloff and Wachter (1979).

similar (but not identical) to that of Perloff and Wachter. Table 1 shows the percentage differences between the two series for selected quarters:[3]

TABLE 1

Percentage Differences between Gordon and Perloff-Wachter Series for Selected Quarters

	Gordon Q^* Gap	Perloff-Wachter $QPOT_1$ Gap	Gordon Minus Perloff-Wachter
1956:3-1957:1	- 0.16	~0	~0
1961:1	6.00	5.37	0.63
1966:1	- 4.20	- 4.39	0.19
1968:3	- 4.35	- 4.04	- 0.31
1970:4	3.04	2.56	0.48
1973:1	- 2.45	- 3.49	1.04
1975:1	9.80	7.89	1.91
1977:4	3.42	1.63	1.79

Since the underlying natural unemployment series (U^*) used to create Q^* and $QPOT_1$ are so similar, and since the differences between the two resulting natural output variables are so minor before 1973, we can conclude that the validity and credibility of the Perloff and Wachter policy conclusions depend much more heavily on their techniques for estimating U^* than on their production function approach for translating U^* into $QPOT_1$. The main contribution of the production function appears to be a rather pessimistic estimate of the growth rate of $QPOT_1$ in the period since 1973.

3. Robustness of Estimates of the Natural Unemployment Rate

One peculiar feature of Perloff and Wachter's presentation is that considerable effort is devoted to the estimation of a natural unemployment series U_2^*, based on econometric wage equations, but the favored natural output series is based not on U_2^*, but on a U_1^* measure which is not explained; it simply appears like a *deus ex machina* from one of Wachter's earlier papers. This suggests three questions: How trustworthy is U_1^*, given its crucial contribution to the overall conclusion of the paper? How reliable is U_2^*? Which of the two natural unemployment series is to be preferred?

The computation of U_1^* begins from the premise that the unemployment rate of some demographic subgroup of the labor force bears a more stable

---

[3] The Q^* series for 1947:1 through 1977:4 appears in Gordon (1978, Table B-2, pp. xviii-xxi). Since I did not have Perloff and Wachter's $QPOT_1$ series when preparing this comment, comparisons are made only for those quarters for which explicit figures on the percentage gap are given in their paper. The percentage gap concept defined by Perloff and Wachter is $(Q^*-Q)/Q$, instead of the more conventional $(Q^*-Q)/Q^*$. It appears that before 1973 the differences between the Q^* and $QPOT_1$ series are extremely minor, well below 1 percent, while in the 1975-77 interval, the difference has grown to about 2 percent.

statistical relationship to accelerations and decelerations of inflation than the aggregate unemployment rate. Wachter (1976), for instance, uses a wage equation to estimate a natural unemployment rate for the prime-aged male subgroup. He then converts this into an aggregate natural rate concept (U_1^*) by estimating auxiliary equations which explain movements in the unemployment rates of the other subgroups as a function of the demographic variables and the unemployment rate of the chosen subgroup.

The problem with this technique is that its resulting aggregate U^* estimate appears to be very sensitive to the choice of the particular labor market control subgroup. I showed (1977) that, without making any statistically significant difference in a wage equation, one could come up with an estimated increase in U^* between 1956 and 1974 ranging anywhere from 0.58 to 1.61 percentage points, with the smallest increase occuring for all employees aged over 20 as the subgroup, and the largest increase for males aged 25 and over. Furthermore, unpublished tests indicate that there is additional sensitivity of the results, depending on the form of the basic wage equation, and on whether wages or prices are chosen as the dependent variable. One interesting feature of alternative estimates is that they appear to raise the estimated U^* in the mid-1950s almost as much as they lower it in the 1970s. These alternative estimates make sense, mainly because actual unemployment never falls below Wachter's U_1^* series in the mid-1950s, thus leaving unanswered the question as to why inflation accelerated as it did in 1955 and 1956. An alternative U^* concept based on one of the other subgroups would yield an associated natural output series which is lower in the 1950s and higher in the 1970s, and which would thus exhibit a faster trend rate of growth than $QPOT_1$.

When the U_1^* variable is used by Perloff and Wachter to explain wage acceleration directly, it appears that a set of dummy variables is necessary to correct a downward bias in U_1^*. Put another way, the U_1^* concept created to divide the regions of accelerating and decelerating inflation consistently underestimates wage acceleration, and the explanation of wage behavior is improved when U_1^* is replaced by the U_2^* variable which incorporates the dummy variables. A prime mystery of the Perloff-Wachter presentation is why the natural output series $(QPOT_1)$ associated with U_1^* is "favored" by the authors over the alternative $QPOT_2$, since their own results appear to show that wages tend to accelerate when the economy is operating at U_1^*. Either Perloff and Wachter should come up with a wage or price equation which shows that U_1^* is consistent with nonaccelerating inflation, or they should drop both U_1^* and $QPOT_1$.

My suspicion is that U_1^* is closer to the "truth" than U_2^*, but for reasons which are not evident in the Perloff-Wachter paper. I would guess that the dummy variables in the Perloff-Wachter equation (16) biased upward the resulting U_2^* estimate, because variables are omitted which contribute to wage acceleration. Among these are the rates of change of the effective social security payroll tax, the effective minimum wage, and prices relative to wages, and the change in the U^*/U ratio. If, for instance, the massive increase in the effective minimum wage in 1956:1 or the increase in aggregate prices relative to wages in 1973-74 really explain part of the acceleration of wages in those periods, then the omission of these variables by Perloff and Wachter requires that wage behavior be explained by an increase in the contribution of the dummy variables. In my own experimentation with equations similar to (16), I have found that it is possible to obtain a U_2^* series *below* U_1^*, depending on the exact specification used.

4. The Translation from U^* to $QPOT$

The above comparison of Q^* and $QPOT_1$ indicates that the production function approach of Perloff and Wachter does not make much practical difference for policy, compared to the simpler trend-through-benchmarks method; nevertheless, the use of a production function and data on nonlabor inputs is superior in principle and may be of practical importance for forecasting in the future. Here I applaud most of the choices made in the Perloff-Wachter paper.

Labor input is estimated from a regression of hours on the unemployment gap and several time trends, with "natural" hours then calculated by solving the estimated equation for a zero gap. The role and significance of the estimated time trends is unclear. No standard errors are given for the quadratic terms, which pick up changes in the trend growth of the labor force participation rate and hours per employee. Future forecasts of natural labor input based on this equation will tend to extrapolate the recent rapid growth in the secondary labor force participation rate, in contrast to the alternative hypothesis proposed by Wachter himself (1977) that the growth in the labor force will slow down in the 1980s, partly because of the improved relative wages of secondary workers. This contributes one reason to expect that the relatively slow recent growth of $QPOT_1$ will decelerate even further in the future.

The capital input series was obtained from DRI, and the main question which can be raised is whether government-mandated investment expenditures for environmental, health, or safety purposes are included in the capital stock. Since these forms of capital do not contribute to real output as presently measured, any capital stock measure which includes them will tend to overstate the growth rate of natural output in the 1970s relative to earlier periods. This is another source of possible upward bias in the recent growth rates of $QPOT_1$.

191

The authors are correct to include in capital input the entire capital stock rather than only the capital stock which is utilized. Today's natural output level depends on the amount of the capital input which is available today at the "natural capacity utilization rate," not at today's lower capacity utilization rate. Nevertheless, because the size of the capital stock is endogenous and responds to the output and unemployment gaps, the growth in capital input achieved during a slack period like 1975-77 understates the growth in capital input and natural output which would occur if the economy were operating continuously at a zero gap. For this reason, the Perloff-Wachter $QPOT_1$ series understates the true underlying natural rate of output growth.

The authors deserve praise for realizing that to include all forms of primary energy as well as electricity would involve counting twice the true contribution of energy to output growth. Perhaps more important, they have rightly entered the quantity of energy directly into the production function, thus allowing the data to determine how long it takes for the increased relative price of energy to reduce energy consumption per unit of output. This is far superior to the Rasche-Tatom procedure which assumes that the impact of a relative price increase on energy consumption is instantaneous, and that the elasticity of substitution between energy and other inputs is unity.

5. The Cyclically Sensitive Translog

A major innovation in the Perloff-Wachter procedure is the estimation of cyclically sensitive production function coefficients. The F-tests of Table 2 provide convincing evidence that the production function parameters do vary cyclically, which should be old news to Walter Oi (1962) and his followers who have emphasized the role of labor hoarding as a source of cyclical fluctuations in productivity, profits, and labor's share. It is no surprise that equations which attempt to explain labor's share as a function of a constant and the slowly changing capital and energy variables yield a significant coefficient on the cyclical variable.

There are several possible interpretations of this, however. The authors appear to regard competitive factor pricing as holding continuously, while the underlying technological parameters undergo cyclical shifts. An alternative interpretation, consistent with the disequilibrium approach to macroeconomics associated with the work of Barro and Grossman (1976), is that a cyclical decline in sales combined with wage and price inflexibility introduces a sales constraint which forces firms off their notional labor demand curves. Workers are no longer hired up to the point where their marginal product equals the real wage. Along the "effective" (constrained) labor demand curve, the marginal product of an additional worker is zero. Although the choice between these two interpretations is important for microeconomic production theory, it has no bearing on the overall conclusions of the present paper. The allowance for cyclical sensitivity in factor shares improves the estimates of the constant zero-gap translog parameters, which in turn are used to weight together the separate estimates of labor, capital, and energy input.

It is ironic that, despite the superiority of the cyclically-sensitive explanation of income shares, the resulting input series yields an explanation of output in Table 3 which is plagued by serial correlation, and which appears to fit substantially less well than the standard translog with Cobb-Douglas restrictions. The Perloff-Wachter paper can be faulted for its failure to reestimate these equations with corrections for serial correlation, and to exhibit the *QPOT* series corresponding to the better-fitting Cobb-Douglas variant.

6. Conclusion

Overall, the authors have presented an innovative paper. Nevertheless, there are a number of areas where the data cannot distinguish between alternative estimates of the level of growth rate of natural output. At present, it is not possible to pin down the natural unemployment rate to a single point; the wage and price data appear consistent with a range of possibilities from 5 to 6 percent. Similarly, the evidence in Table 3 suggests that a number of possible weighting schemes are capable of explaining the relation of output to input with approximately the same goodness of fit. The paper would be improved if the authors could provide a matrix of possibilities for different combinations of the natural unemployment concept and production function variants, in order to help policymakers assess the width of the band spanning reasonable estimates of natural output and its rate of growth. Significance tests for each element in the matrix could be developed by using the associated output gap measure directly in wage or price equations.

References

Barro, R.J., and Grossman, H.I. (1976). *Money, Employment, and Inflation.* Cambridge: Cambridge University Press.

Gordon, R.J. (1971), "Inflation in Recession and Recovery," *Brookings Papers on Economic Activity,* 2. Washington, D.C.: The Brookings Institution.

_____(1977), "Structural Unemployment and the Productivity of Women," *Optimal Policies, Control Theory and Technology Exports,* Carnegie-Rochester Conference Series, vol. 7, eds. K. Brunner and A.H. Meltzer. Amsterdam : North-Holland.

_____(1978). *Macroeconomics.* Boston: Little, Brown and Company.

Oi, W. (1962), "Labor as a Quasi-Fixed Factor," *Journal of Political Economy,* 70: 538-55.

Perloff, J., and Wachter, M. (1979), "A Production Function--Nonaccelerating Inflation Approach to Potential Output: Is Measured Potential Output Too High?" *Carnegie-Rochester Conference Series,* 10, eds. K. Brunner and A.H. Meltzer. Amsterdam: North-Holland.

Wachter, M.L. (1976), "The Changing Cyclical Responsiveness of Wage Inflation Over the Postwar Period," *Brookings Papers on Economic Activity,* 7. Washington, D.C.: The Brookings Institution.

_____(1977), "Intermediate Swings in Labor-Force Participation," *Brookings Papers on Economic Activity,* 8. Washington, D.C.: The Brookings Institution.

REPLY

Jeffrey M. PERLOFF
University of Pennsylvania

and

Michael L. WACHTER
University of Pennsylvania

The comments by Gordon, Tatom, and Plosser and Schwert raise many issues. The three comments run almost as long as our original paper and, in many cases, oppose each other. Therefore, we will not try to deal with every point. The various issues can be grouped into two large categories: conceptual questions and econometric issues. The conceptual issues which were raised are relevant and deal largely with the validity of the potential output construct. The econometric considerations have mostly been dealt with in our original paper. None have empirical significance for our measure of potential output.

1. Conceptual Questions

We defined potential output ($QPOT$) as that output which is consistent with the nonaccelerating inflation rate of unemployment (U^*). From the manner in which we define U^*, it should be obvious that we are not implying that a large GNP gap will "cause" further inflation.

In our paper, we calculated various potential output series under alternative assumptions to demonstrate the sensitivity of our potential output series to these assumptions. Two measures of U^* were used: U_1^*, which corrects for demographic variations over time, and U_2^*, which was based on an estimated Phillips curve.

As Figure 1 in our paper shows, the two series differ substantially. The existing Phillips curve studies, with which we are familiar, produce estimates somewhere within the range between U^*_1 and U^*_2; thus, we felt that these two series effectively bound the relevant range. While the differences between $QPOT_1$ and $QPOT_2$ (based on U^*_1 and U^*_2 respectively) are not as great, they are still substantial from a policy perspective. Both Gordon and Tatom question our choice of the $QPOT_1$ series as our preferred series. Our choice was partially based on U^*_2's sensitivity to the specification of the Phillips curve and our priors that U^*_1 is closer to U^* than is U^*_2.

Gordon agrees with us on the sensitivity of U^*_2 and notes that U^*_1 is closer to U^* by his priors as well. His claim that he can find a specification of the Phillips curve which yields a U^* as low as U^*_1 is not too surprising. We were not able to accomplish this feat, but, then, we did not try every possibility. Indeed, across all our specifications the average U^*_2 was above 6.3, and we assume that Gordon's estimate was his lowest rather than his average point estimate across specifications.

Gordon also debates our demographic correction to form U^*_1, by indicating that the choice of a benchmark group (we used males 25 to 54) influences U^*_1. We agree that U^* is somewhat sensitive to the choice of the benchmark. Our argument, advanced in Wachter (1974) is that the prime-age male group, which is the demographic age group least likely to be influenced by government labor market social legislation, is the best group to serve the role of a fixed benchmark. Our method is not an optimal solution to measuring U^*; much could be learned from further work on the responsiveness of prime-age male labor force and unemployment to different government programs.[1]

Gordon notes that the important factor in our new, lower potential output series is a higher U^* series than that used by Perry, Clark, and others. While he grants that in theory and practice the use of production function is a superior means of moving from a U^* estimate to $QPOT$, he suggests that relatively crude techniques might work almost as well within the historical period. The basic problem with that approach, as he indicates in his textbook (1978), is that in order to produce "reasonable" numbers, one must change the slope of the trend line over time. There is no problem with this method in producing ex post $QPOT$ figures, but it will be of little value to policymakers who are interested in the current level of the GNP gap. In any case, one thrust of our work was to indicate that potential output does respond to the business cycle and to other economic variables.

Both Gordon and Tatom raise questions about the use of capital in our methodology. Gordon suggests that there may be a feedback through capital which we have ignored. We agree with him that such feedback may have long-run significance and that more work should be done in estimating capital investment equations (such as those of Jorgenson, 1971) simultaneously with the other equations we estimated.

Tatom estimates how an existing capacity utilization measure varies with surprises in the money supply. As our methodology does not use capacity utilization, his comments are relevant to the Rasche-Tatom technique rather than our own. We ignored capacity utilization numbers since there are both

---

[1] See Perloff and Wachter (1979c).

conceptual and practical problems with using existing series (as explained by Gordon in his comment and by us in our paper).

The major conceptual issue, however, is whether a potential output series construct is useful given the ability of the government to affect the economy. Simply put, the value of a potential output series depends on the stability of underlying structural relationships. If these relationships are not invariant to policy changes, potential output may not be uniquely defined. Plosser and Schwert, in opposition to Gordon and Tatom, have questioned the usefulness of a potential output series. There are two basic responses to the points which they raise: one theoretical and the other empirical.

First, we examined potential output over the historical period. Thus, government policy was predetermined. Most of the objections Plosser and Schwert raise seem better directed at projections of potential output into the future. As we have argued elsewhere (Perloff and Wachter, 1979b), if the government reacts to a potential output target projected into the future, the target itself may change (i.e., potential output may not be uniquely defined). It is not possible, however, for 1955 policy to respond to out output series, so this objection is largely irrelevant for our historical estimates. To the extent that government policy rules changed over the estimation period and affected structural relationships, we would have obtained more precise estimates by allowing for more of these changes than we did. Our limited attempts at subdividing the period did not indicate sufficient parameter instability to cause significant changes in the underlying potential series.

Second, the contention which Plosser and Schwert make is on relatively weak empirical grounds. Even granting their theoretical point--the endogeneity of U^* and potential output to government policies--any simultaneity biases may be relatively minor in practice. Many economists, such as B. Friedman, have argued that economic actors adjust slowly as they attempt to decipher the myriad statements that are made by administrators, Congressmen, the Federal Reserve, OPEC, and other policy-setting individuals or groups.

If expectations adjust slowly, in a fashion not captured by our equations, then our potential output will drift from its "true" value. There is no reason to presume that the drift will be in sudden or very rapid spurts. As a remedy, we suggest that parameter estimates need to be continually updated as new data become available. Presumably, if large, discontinuous policy actions are not only announced (a frequent occurrence), but also put into effect (a rare occurrence), one should be wary of future projections (though not necessarily historical analyses). We attempted to take account of these factors by introducing policy variables into our Phillips curve and cyclical variables into our production function.

Given these adjustments, it would be useful if Plosser and Schwert could indicate the empirical importance of their argument. Essentially, we believe that all that they have argued is that our adjustments *might* be inappropriate.

Indeed, Plosser and Schwert are of two minds on this issue. First, they argue that there are conceptual problems in defining a construct called potential output. Then, after essentially stating that there is no such animal as potential output, they suggest that, due to econometric mistakes, we do not measure it properly. Finally, they concede that even though we have mismeasured a non-existent creature, our conclusions are correct: ". . .[W]e concur that the economy is probably not in need of the kind of fiscal and monetary stimulus implied by the huge CEA estimate of the output gap. . . ."

2. Econometric Issues

A large number of technical points were raised in the comments. For the most part, these points strike us as being of secondary importance, except for the issue of the price versus the quantity of energy which Tatom raises. Since all of these technical issues were dealt with in the original paper, we will only briefly discuss them here.

All the commentators raised the question of the seriousness of autocorrelation problems in our estimates. In the final version of our paper, we dealt with this question in some detail. There are three points that need to be made: First, as noted by Plosser and Schwert, our estimation techniques are consistent, even if there are autocorrelation problems. Second, if we make a first- or second-order autocorrelation adjustment, we obtain very similar potential output series: the correlation coefficients between the first- or second-order autocorrelation adjusted potential output series and $QPOT_1$ is 0.999. Thus, this theoretical point has very limited empirical significance. Third, as we show in footnote 27, a first-order autocorrelation adjustment may even be inappropriate since the error term is also heteroscedastic. It therefore does *not* follow that the first-order autocorrelation adjustment will necessarily be superior to the unadjusted estimate.

The suggestion of Plosser and Schwert that we use a first-difference estimation technique seems ill-advised, since that approach assumes a first-order autocorrelation adjustment coefficient of negative one which will (except on a set of measure zero) always be wrong. Further, this adjustment is not appropriate due to the heteroscedasticity problem. Tatom suggests that because of autocorrelation, the various test statistics may overstate our case. Although his theoretical point is correct, it should be noted that, for example, in Table 2, the test statistics are gigantic--even a significant bias in the standard errors is not likely to change the results.[2]

All three comments contend that the Cobb-Douglas has the best "fit" in Table 3. It does not follow from such an observation, however, that the Cobb-Douglas is the appropriate form to use. All the regressions reported in Table 3 have $\bar{R}^2$ s in excess of 0.955, and, hence, "explain" virtually all of the variance. Further, the comparisons of $\bar{R}^2$ s as a means of specification choice is unjustified on statistical grounds since, in most cases, the equations are not of the nested hypothesis form. Indeed, different input series are used in the various regressions as explained in the table. Finally, an $\bar{R}^2$-test does not measure the success with which a series picks up turning points. As we noted in our paper, the cyclically sensitive translog is the most successful in this regard.

Since we used a two-step production function estimation technique in which the second step was identical in all cases and only the first steps differed, it is appropriate to test for specification in the first step. The proper *nested* hypothesis test of the Cobb-Douglas versus the translog or cyclically sensitive translog, as Gordon points out, is presented in Table 2. The *F*-test on the Cobb-Douglas restrictions (within the translog formulation) is almost 3-3/4 times as great as the critical value. The comparable test of the Cobb-Douglas restrictions against the cyclically sensitive translog produces a test statistic almost 7 times as great as the critical value. Even given some serial correlation, the Cobb-Douglas restrictions must be rejected.

Tatom and Plosser and Schwert also question our use of cubic time trend terms in our second step. Plosser and Schwert point out that such time trends, if projected far enough into the future, imply an explosive growth path. Of course we agree with that point, however, it does not follow that such approximations are unreasonable *within* the sample period. Furthermore, as we show in Perloff and Wachter (1979b), if a single time trend term is used instead of the cubic, our potential output series is not significantly altered.[3]

Both Tatom and Plosser and Schwert have misinterpreted the Okun's law section of our paper. They argue that Okun's law is misspecified. Of course, Okun's law is misspecified: Okun noted this point in his original article in 1962. The question he raised was whether his simple equation could explain unemployment changes as well as more complicated schemes. Others, including Friedman

---

[2]See Berndt and Christensen (1974, p. 399) who make this argument as well.

[3]If both a single time trend and an autocorrelation adjustment are used, the resulting potential output series has a correlation coefficient of over 0.99 with $QPOT_1$. Thus, these issues are not of great importance.

and Wachter (1974) and Tatom (1978) have attempted to improve on Okun's law as a method of explaining unemployment. The point that we raised in Section III had nothing to do with the specification arguments raised by Tatom and Plosser and Schwert. Our point was that Okun's law, could not be used to test the reliability of the old CEA potential output series or indeed any other potential series. Specifically, any pair of U^* and $QPOT$, which are constructed from similar assumptions, produce a high $\bar{R}^2$ in the Okun's law type equation.

Plosser and Schwert, however, go further and suggest that many authors such as Clark, Perry, and Okun have been careless in deciding which side of the Okun's law relation the additive error term should be placed on and that we similarly make this "error." We believe that the first section of the Plosser and Schwert comment in which they discuss this point is largely irrelevant to our paper, since we do not specifically use the Okun's law relationship. Further, we raised exactly the same point in our paper. We cited an article by Robert Summers (1968), in which he examined the implications of placing the error term on the "other" side of Okun's law relationship ten years before Plosser and Schwert rediscovered this issue.

In his comment, Tatom compares the Rasche and Tatom approach to calculating potential output to ours. Rasche and Tatom essentially estimated a hybrid production-cost function using quantity measures of labor and capital (adjusted by a capacity utilization measure)[4] and the price of energy in a Cobb-Douglas framework. As we have already argued, the translog formulation is econometrically superior to the Cobb-Douglas (which is, after all, a special case of the translog).

A more fundamental difference concerns our use of the quantity of energy rather than its price. Like Gordon, we prefer our constructed energy measure to the price-proxy approach of Rasche-Tatom. For example, that specification implies instantaneous responses to price changes. Much of Tatom's comment is a useful defense of their technique.[5] Obviously, neither side had managed to convince the other.[6]

As we pointed out in our original paper, the Rasche and Tatom potential output series is the closest to ours of any existing series. Except for the late

---

[4]Tatom appears to argue in his comment that such an adjustment is wrong.

[5]In Section II of his comment where he purports to show that the relevant output elasticity in the Cobb-Douglas form is 11.3 percent, Tatom's reasoning is incorrect. As we explain in our paper, we use a more restrictive definition of energy than Rasche and Tatom. Tatom mistakenly concludes from our Appendix that the gross share of energy in factor cost is twice as large as our factor share estimate. To the contrary, we claim our study does not *double count* the quantity of energy. In many studies of energy, the quantity measures essentially count the coal or gas which is used to produce electricity twice. We do not do that. Thus, it is incorrect for Tatom to double our output elasticity as he does.

[6]Perhaps the most careful work on the energy and GNP issue has been done by Hudson and Jorgenson. See, for example, Hudson and Jorgenson (1978).

1960s and early 1970s (where their use of the price of energy causes a sudden jump in their potential output measure), the two series are very close (see Figure 3). Thus, effectively, it makes little differences which of our two approaches is followed except in explaining the impact of OPEC on potential output.

We do have some serious objections to the way Tatom uses our equations. He examines the significance of the cyclically sensitive parameters and cubic time trends in a version of our equations. His modifications, however, result in a misspecification of our approach; hence, his comparisons are misleading. For example, he argues that the cubic time trends produce "too low" numbers for 1955 (see his Table 2): 610.2 versus 645.2 using the Rasche-Tatom methodology. Using our equations, both the cubic time trend and the single time trend specifications produce numbers within 1 percent of the Rasche-Tatom number for that year. Thus, his results are due to the misspecification he introduces rather than to our methodology.

References

Berndt, E.R., and Christensen, L.R. (1974), "Testing for the Existence of a Consistent Aggregate Index of Labor Inputs," *American Economic Review,* 64: 391-404.

Friedman, B., "Optimal Expectations and the Extreme Information Assumptions of 'Rational Expectations' Macromodels," *Journal of Monetary Economics,* forthcoming.

Friedman, B., and Wachter, M.L. (1970), "Unemployment: Okun's Law, Labor Force, and Productivity," *Review of Economics and Statistics,* 56: 167-76.

Gordon, R.J. (1978). *Macroeconomics.* Boston: Little-Brown.

_____(1979), "A Comment on the Perloff and Wachter Paper," *Carnegie-Rochester Conference Series,* 10, eds. K. Brunner and A.H. Meltzer. Amsterdam: North-Holland.

Hudson, E.A., and Jorgenson, D.W. (1978), "Energy Prices and the U.S. Economy, 1972-1976," Harvard Institute of Economic Research Discussion Paper, No. 637, July, 1978. Cambridge: Harvard University.

Jorgenson, D.W. (1971), "Econometric Studies of Investment Behavior: A Survey," *Journal of Economic Literature,* 9: 1111-47.

Okun, A.M. (1962), "Potential GNP: Its Measurement and Significance," *Proceedings of the Business and Economics Section,* 98-104. Washington, D.C.: American Statistical Association.

Perloff, J.M., and Wachter, M.L. (1979a), "A Production Function-Nonaccelerating Inflation Approach to Potential Output: Is Measured Potential Output Too High?" *Carnegie-Rochester Conference Series,* 10, eds. K. Brunner and A.H. Meltzer. Amsterdam: North-Holland.

_____(1979b), "Alternative Approaches to Forecasting Potential Output, 1978-1980," forthcoming in *American Statistical Association Proceedings.*

Perloff, J.M., and Wachter, M.L. (1979c), "An Evaluation of Unemployment Data Needs in Macro Models," forthcoming in the National Commission on Employment and Unemployment Statistics volume.

Plosser, C.I., and Schwert, G.W. (1979), "Potential GNP: Its Measurement and Significance: A Dissenting Opinion," *Carnegie-Rochester Conference Series,* **10**, eds. K. Brunner and A.H. Meltzer. Amsterdam: North-Holland.

Summers, R. (1968), "Further Results in the Measurement of Capacity Utilization," *Business and Economic Statistics Section Proceedings,* 25-34. Washington, D.C.: American Statistical Association.

Tatom, J.A. (1978), "Economic Growth and Unemployment: An Assessment of "Okun's Law." April 11, 1978. Manuscript.

_____(1979), "The Meaning and Measurement of Potential Output: A Comment on the Perloff and Wachter Results," *Carnegie-Rochester Conference Series,* **10**, eds. K. Brunner and A.H. Meltzer. Amsterdam: North-Holland.

Wachter, M.L. (1974), "Primary and Secondary Labor Markets: A Critique of the Dual Approach," *Brookings Papers on Economic Activity.* Washington, D.C.: The Brookings Institution.

INSTITUTIONAL CHANGES, REPORTED UNEMPLOYMENT, AND INDUCED INSTITUTIONAL CHANGES

Kenneth W. CLARKSON
University of Miami

and

Roger E. MEINERS*
Texas A&M University

Prompted by an increasing number of criticisms of official government unemployment statistics, Congress, in 1976, established a National Commission on Employment and Unemployment Statistics (NCEUS) to "identify the needs of the Nation for labor force statistics and assess the extent to which current procedures, concepts, and methodology in the collection, analysis, and preservation of such statistics constitute a comprehensive, reliable, timely and consistent system of measuring employment and unemployment and indicating trends therein" (Public Law No. 94-444 § 13(c) (1)).

Some of the criticisms have been summarized by the chief of the Division of Employment and Unemployment Analysis of the Bureau of Labor Statistics (BLS). He reports a number of challenges to the usefulness of the current unemployment figures. For example, there have been many arguments in favor of broadening the concept of unemployment to capture some measure of hardship or inadequacy in labor supply. This might be accomplished by measures combining employment and earning status, including "discouraged" workers or involuntary part-time workers, or other measures reflecting certain labor supply concepts (Bregger, 1977, p. 16).

Missing from both the congressional mandate creating NCEUS and the debate on the validity and accuracy of unemployment statistics, are questions relating to the impacts of certain government actions on the unemployment rate. These actions include: (*a*) manpower training and public service employment programs; (*b*) changes in the minimum wage law; (*c*) changes in unemployment compensation; (*d*) changes in duration of unemployment payments; and (*e*) various work registration measures that accompany federal programs.

This paper focuses on the effects of institutional factors that cause changes in the measurement of the reported official employment labor force

---
*Special thanks are due Walter Oi and William Poole for their valuable suggestions.

statistics. Particular emphasis will be given to work registration requirements that accompany various federal welfare programs. It is our hypothesis that the measured high rate of unemployment, especially in recent years, can be explained in large part by a number of federal programs that directly and indirectly cause recipients to report themselves as unemployed when they are not seeking work, or to engage in activities prolonging the period of unemployment (Clarkson and Meiners, 1977a, 1977b). These individuals, who were previously not included in the labor force, now are counted in the official unemployment statistics.

After presenting some empirical estimates of the magnitude of measurement error attributable to the work registration requirements, we investigate the relationship between reported unemployment figures and new institutional programs designed to reduce unemployment.

I. Why Is Unemployment So High?

In the twenty-five years before 1972, official unemployment averaged 4.7 percent. In the five years after 1972, unemployment averaged over 6.7 percent, an increase of over 40 percent in measured unemployment.[1] Much unemployment is, of course, due to natural market activity: people are fired or laid-off temporarily; some leave jobs voluntarily to search for new employment; there are new entrants in the labor market who are still searching for their first job; and there are those who, after leaving the job market at some time, have decided to return and are searching for jobs.[2] Change in the composition of the labor force is another natural phenomenon which causes measured unemployment to vary. From 1957 to 1977 the female portion of the labor force increased from 31 percent to 40 percent. During the same period the portion of the labor force composed of individuals aged 16 to 24, who, like females, tend to enter and leave the job market more frequently than adult males, increased from 17 percent to 24 percent. Although the impact of this change on measured unemployment is uncertain, Phillip Cagan (1977, p. 38) estimated that the change in the composition of the labor force from 1956 to 1973 caused measured unemployment to be 0.46 percentage points higher in the latter year. A Bureau of Labor Statistics economist estimates the impact to be an even greater increase of 0.75 percentage points from 1957 to 1973, and 1.04 percentage points from 1957 to 1976 (Flaim, 1977, Table 1).

---

[1] All unemployment figures are from U.S. Department of Labor, Bureau of Labor Statistics, *Employment and Earnings*, various issues, unless otherwise stated.

[2] These are the traditional categories or reasons for unemployment used by the Bureau of Labor Statistics. For further discussion of the economic sense of voluntary unemployment, see Alchian (1970), and Lippman and McCall (1976).

These factors, however, only partially account for the change in reported unemployment since 1972. A primary source of the increase in reported unemployment is higher unemployment compensation benefits (Feldstein, 1973, 1974, 1976). Unemployment insurance also subsidizes job search. Workers can afford to remain unemployed longer while searching for a better job.[3] Equally important, individuals who are not really in the labor force, especially students and seasonal workers, can collect unemployment insurance as long as they claim they are looking for work, hence, they are counted as unemployed. Feldstein (1976, p. 33) estimates that in 1971, unemployment insurance accounted for half of temporary unemployment. His study suggests that since temporary layoff unemployment was about 1.6 percent, 0.8 percentage points of measured unemployment were attributable to this aspect of unemployment compensation.

The impact of increases in unemployment compensation benefits since 1972 is difficult to assess. Cagan (1977, pp. 32-33) estimates that from 1957 to 1973 the gradual expansion of unemployment insurance increased measured unemployment by 0.08 percentage points. He also estimates that the 1974 and 1976 federal legislation expanding the number of workers covered by unemployment compensation added 0.06 percentage points to measured unemployment. In 1974 and 1975, federal legislation temporarily extended unemployment compensation benefits from 26 to 65 weeks. Another study (O'Neill et al., 1974) estimates that a 13-week increase in unemployment benefits would increase measured unemployment by 0.4 percentage points. Finally, Alfred Tella (1976, editorial page) has estimated that the impact of the 1975 change in unemployment benefits increased reported unemployment by 0.2 percent.

Economic theory also leads one to the conclusion that minimum wages will increase unemployment. The total effect of minimum wages on measured unemployment is unclear, since the law forces some individuals who would be working out of the labor force entirely. Jacob Mincer's study (1976) of minimum wage legislation from 1954 to 1969 demonstrates that the largest impacts of the wage floor are on nonwhite teenagers, white teenagers, and young men and women. Using Mincer's estimates, Cagan (1977, p. 35-36) computes an increase in all measured unemployment of between 0.30 and 0.43 percentage points from 1956 to 1973 and between 0.45 and 0.63 percentage points from 1956 to 1974, due to the effect of the minimum wage on the younger age groups alone.

Walter Williams (1977) attributes the twenty-five year decline in labor force participation by black youths and the large increase in black youth

---

[3]Ehrenberg and Oaxaca (1976) found that unemployment insurance increases the expected duration of unemployment.

unemployment, in both absolute and relative terms when compared to white youth, to the federal minimum wage. Williams's study is supported by another recent empirical study of the impact of minimum wage laws, which estimates that "the youth unemployment rate [would have been] 3.8 percentage points lower," were it not for the 1966 amendments to the wage legislation (Ragan, 1977, p. 136).[4]

In Cagan's review (1977, esp. pp. 38-39) of the sources of change in the measured rate of unemployment, he concludes that from 1956 to 1977 the "full-employment" unemployment rate may have increased from 1.23 to 1.60 percentage points.[5] Hence, if 4.7 percent unemployment was noninflationary or frictional in 1956, the rate of unemployment in 1977 would have been around 5.9 or 6.3 percent. Besides the impact of a change in the composition of the labor force and of changes in the minimum wage and unemployment insurance since 1956, Cagan also notes that welfare work registration requirements have increased measured unemployment. He cites the 1976 *Annual Report of the Council of Economic Advisers,* which noted the 1972 welfare work registration requirement for Aid to Families with Dependent Children (AFDC) recipients, and estimated that the requirements increased measured unemployment by 0.2 percentage points.[6] While we recognize the importance of the institutional factors identified by Cagan, we believe that the effects of the work registration requirements are substantially greater than 0.2 percentage points, as claimed in the Council of Economic Advisers' report.

II. Work Registration Requirements

Since July 1, 1972, work registration requirements have been in effect for the two largest federal income transfer programs, food stamps and AFDC.[7] By the terms of 1971 amendments to both programs, certain beneficiaries of the programs must register with the employment service for work (Public Law No. 91-671 for food stamps; Public Law No. 92-223 for AFDC). The intent of both

---

[4] Like Mincer, Ragan concludes, "Minimum wage legislation reduces youth employment; males, especially non-white males, are the hardest hit." (1977, p. 135). See also Welch (1974).

[5] For alternative estimates of the total impact of many of the variables on unemployment, see Perloff and Wachter (1979).

[6] Cagan also cites Tella's estimate that enrollment in federal manpower programs may reduce unemployment, perhaps by 0.3 percentage points in 1976.

[7] Work registration is required for several other federal welfare programs, such as railroad unemployment insurance, trade readjustment assistance, and some Indian programs. These programs are not included here because they were instituted at different points in time and are trivial in magnitude compared to AFDC and food stamps.

program requirements was clear to the sponsor of the legislation, Senator Talmadge (D-Ga.). In hearings before the registration requirements became effective (July 1, 1972), the Senator said, "When we enacted this provision, we contemplated a registration procedure similar to the way persons register for unemployment compensation, namely, the individual would provide information on his or her work experience, and, if ready to be placed in employment immediately, an attempt would be made to place the individual in a job" (U.S. Congress, Senate Finance Committee, 1972, p. 15). It was estimated at that time that 1.5 million of the 12.6 million AFDC recipients would register for work through the Work Incentive Program (WIN).[8]

The work registration requirements have not changed significantly since their introduction. The major provisions for food stamp program registration are:

Refusal to register for or accept employment....

(1) Unless otherwise exempted by the provisions of paragraph (2), no household shall be eligible for assistance if it includes a physically and mentally fit person between the ages of eighteen and sixty who (i) refuses at the time of application and once every six months thereafter to register for employment in a manner determined by the Secretary; (ii) refuses to fulfill whatever reasonable reporting and inquiry about employment requirements as are prescribed by the Secretary; (iii) is head of the household and voluntarily quits any job without good cause, unless the household was certified for benefits under this chapter immediately prior to such unemployment: *Provided*, That the period of ineligibility shall be sixty days from the time of the voluntary quit; or (iv) refuses without good cause to accept an offer of employment at a wage not less than the higher of either the applicable State or Federal minimum wage, or 80 per centum of the wage that would have governed had the minimum hourly rate under the Fair Labor Standards Act of 1938, as amended, been applicable to the offer of employment, and at a site or plant not then subject to a strike or lockout.[9]

---

[8] The WIN program was established in 1968 for AFDC recipients. It provided job training for about 100,000 AFDC recipients up to the time of the 1972 work registration requirement (U.S. Congress, Senate Finance Committee, 1972, p. 51). Since 1972 the WIN program has focused on work registration and short-term training for jobs. The food stamp program had no prior work registration or employment programs.

[9] The term *strike* does not include a strike which has been determined to be unlawful by court decision.

(2) A person who otherwise would be required to comply with the requirements of paragraph (1) of this subsection shall be exempt from such requirements if he or she is (A) currently subject to and complying with a work registration requirement under Title IV of the Social Security Act, as amended, or the Federal-State unemployment compensation system; (B) a parent or other member of a household with responsibility for the care of a dependent child under age twelve or of an incapacitated person; (C) a parent or other caretaker of a child in a household where there is another able-bodied parent who is subject to the requirements of this subsection; (D) a bona fide student enrolled at least half-time in any recognized school, training program, or institution of higher education; (E) a regular participant in a drug addiction or alcoholic treatment and rehabilitation program; or (F) employed a minimum of thirty hours per week or receiving weekly earnings which equal the minimum hourly rate under the Fair Labor Standards Act of 1938, as amended, multiplied by thirty hours. (7 U.S.C.A. § 20.5(d), 1978)

Similarly, AFDC applicants and registrants must register for manpower services, training, and employment as a condition of eligibility for AFDC unless they are

1) under age 16;
2) regularly attending school and age 16 but not yet 21 years;
3) ill (medical evidence required);
4) incapacitated (medical evidence required);
5) 65 years or older;
6) too remote from a WIN office;
7) a caretaker in the home of another household member who requires such care (medical evidence required); or
8) a mother or other female caretaker of a child, when the nonexempt father or other nonexempt adult male relative in the home is registered and has not refused to participate in the program or to accept employment without good cause. (29 C.F.R. § 56.20(b), 1976)

A better understanding of how the registration procedure works in practice can be gained by reading the various manuals issued to government workers who are responsible for implementing the law.[10] Both the Department of Labor's *WIN Handbook* and the U.S. Department of Agriculture's *Food Stamp Certification Handbook* cite the legislation establishing work registration and make clear its purpose. For instance, "the Food Stamp Act requires that all able-bodied adults who are members of eligible households, with few exceptions, register for work and accept suitable employment. . . .It prevents participation by those persons who would refuse to pursue gainful employment in order to obtain program benefits. . . ."(U.S. Department of Agriculture, 1975, p. 40).[11]

The food stamp handbook notes that the work registration requirement is prerequisite to certification for food stamp eligibility. It is a requirement which cannot be waived. With the exception of the large majority of food stamp recipients who are exempt from the registration requirements, recipients must complete a work registration form (FNS-284 or an equivalent). A copy of the form is sent to the Employment Service (ES). Applicants must register at least every six months. Some states require reregistration more often. An applicant who is already registered for work because of participation in the WIN program is not required to register for food stamps, hence, double counting of registrants is eliminated. Each person required to register for work is also required to:

(1) Report for an interview to the Federal or State ES office where he is registered upon reasonable request.
(2) Respond to a request from the Federal or State ES office requiring supplemental information regarding employment status or availability for work.
(3) Report to an employer to whom he has been referred by such office.
(4) Accept a bona fide offer of suitable employment to which he is referred by such office.
(5) Continue suitable employment to which he was referred by such office. (U.S. Department of Agriculture, 1975, pp. 46-47)

---

[10]Several critics of our earlier works suggested that in practice the work registration procedure for welfare recipients may be less formal than that for unemployed individuals who voluntarily register with the employment service. This section demonstrates that the procedures are identical.

[11]See also U.S. Department of Labor, *The WIN Handbook* (1977b, ch. I).

Employment is not suitable if the wages are too low (e.g., below the minimum wage), if there is a strike at the place of employment, if union membership is required or is not allowed, if the job is too dangerous, if the person is not physically or mentally fit for the job, or if the location is too far from the person's home. Persons who fail to comply with any of the provisions outlined in *The Food Stamp Certification Handbook* will be suspended from participation in the food stamp program until they comply or for one year, whichever is earlier.

Applicants and recipients of AFDC go through a similar work registration procedure for the WIN program. Like food stamp recipients, only a small portion of AFDC beneficiaries are required to register for work. In addition, approximately 20 percent of the 2.1 million registrants in fiscal 1976 were voluntary registrants, that is, AFDC recipients who were legally exempt but registered for the WIN program anyway (U.S. Department of Labor, *WIN in 76, The Work Incentive Program*, 1976, p. 6). Voluntary registrants need not comply with the work requirements to retain AFDC benefits. The remaining 80 percent represent mandatory registrants in 1976.

AFDC applicants complete work registration the same day they register for AFDC benefits. At registration the MA5-95 or equivalent registration form is completed. Except for some personal information, the essence of the form is as follows:

> THE WORK INCENTIVE PROGRAM (WIN) IS DE-
> SIGNED TO HELP PEOPLE RECEIVING ASSISTANCE TO
> BECOME EITHER PARTIALLY OR COMPLETELY SELF
> SUPPORTING THROUGH EMPLOYMENT.
> IF IT IS DETERMINED THAT YOU ARE A
> *MANDATORY* WIN REGISTRANT, YOUR APPLICATION
> FOR AID MAY BE AFFECTED UNLESS YOU ARE
> REGISTERED IN THE WIN PROGRAM. 'FAILURE TO
> COOPERATE WITH WIN CAN AFFECT THE AMOUNT OF
> YOUR GRANT. (U.S. Department of Labor and Department
> of Health, Education and Welfare, 1977, p. 3-52)

The registrant then checks a box acknowledging mandatory registration and participation, or he or she may volunteer to register despite exemption. Like food stamp recipients, AFDC recipients are registered with the Employment Service. WIN registrants complete form ES-511, "the basic record of all individuals served by the ES, and is completed on all individuals who contact a local office seeking assistance in finding employment or seeking employability development" (U.S. Department of Labor and Department of Health, Education and Welfare, 1977, p. 3-72). On this form the registrant notes whether or not he or she is a mandatory WIN registrant or a food stamp work registrant. The form is the basis of the record kept by state employment agencies of the applicant's employment and training history and the services provided to him or her.

At the time of WIN registration, the person is told about the program, what it does, and what he or she must do. The registrant is provided job market information and referral services when appropriate. The job services provided by WIN sponsors

will consist of, but are not limited to:

(1) Information on jobs available through listings with the WIN sponsor, and an explanation of how to use the Job Bank system, if one is available, to obtain job information;

(2) Screening of the individual's work application against current job orders by WIN staff and referral to employers as appropriate;

(3) Individual job development efforts if indicated by the individual's work experience and current labor demands;

(4) Providing leads to job opportunities not listed with the WIN sponsor, and methods of seeking out such job opportunities;

(5) Career guidance information and other job-related information such as announcements of Civil Service examinations; and

(6) Placing the individual's work application in WIN sponsor files to permit further exposure to job openings from file search activities. (U.S. Department of Labor, 1977b, pp. iv, 7-8)

Failure to comply with WIN program procedures will lead to denial of AFDC benefits after a field investigation and hearing procedure.

III. Measuring Unemployment

Each month the Bureau of Labor Statistics analyzes and publishes information on population, labor force, and unemployment. The information is collected according to a variety of social, demographic, and economic characteristics. The statistics that concern us here, however, are derived from the Current Population Survey that is conducted by the Bureau of the Census for the Bureau of Labor Statistics. In this survey, unemployment is defined by the BLS as follows:

> *Unemployment*: Unemployed persons include those who did not work at all during the survey week, were looking for work, and were available for work during the reference period except for temporary illness. Those who had made specific efforts to find work within the preceding 4-week period--such as by registering at a public or private employment agency, writing letters of application, canvassing for work, etc., are considered to be looking for work. (U.S. Department of Labor, Bureau of Labor Statistics, 1976, p. 5)

Three key elements determine whether an individual surveyed by the Bureau of the Census is counted as unemployed: not working, available for work, and looking for work. Since the first two requirements are satisfied by registering for work as part of the eligibility for the particular public program, we will concentrate on what constitutes "looking for work." Some hint is given in the Bureau of Labor Statistics, *BLS Handbook of Methods*, particularly the definition cited above. More importantly, the *Current Population Survey: Interviewer's Reference Manual* (U.S. Department of Commerce, Bureau of the Census, 1976, p. D6-9) explicitly states that "registration in a public or private employment office" constitutes looking for work. With respect to the AFDC and the WIN programs, unemployment includes situations in which the individual is receiving either institutional training or working on special work projects. In particular, the *Interviewer's Reference Manual* specifies that persons in the WIN program should be treated as follows:

> Classify persons receiving public assistance or welfare who are referred and placed in an on-the-job or skill training program as *employed* if receiving on-the-job training or *unemployed*

if receiving institutional training only. Consider persons receiving public assistance or welfare who are placed on special work projects which involve no pay other than welfare itself as unemployed. (p. D6-15)

An important issue is raised here; i.e., whether these regulations cause individuals who must register at the Employment Service to respond that they are looking for work when canvassed by the Bureau of the Census. Some individuals who registered for work because of food stamps or AFDC may not report themselves to be unemployed when the canvasser from the Bureau of the Census asks them if they are unemployed. The incentives and pressures, however, are against such behavior. They have been told by one government official that they must be actively seeking work or they will lose their benefits. They have signed forms acknowledging the work requirement and its relation to the receipt of benefits. They have registered with the Employment Service, and they have been given various job-seeking advice and assistance. When another government worker comes to the door and asks them if they are actively seeking employment, they would minimize their risk, at no cost, by answering in the affirmative.

A Available evidence supports the proposition that work registration imposes considerable pressure on individuals to find jobs. In fact, from the beginning of the food stamp work registration requirements through March, 1976, more households failed to comply with the requirements (and had their benefits terminated) than obtained jobs (U.S. Congress, House, Food Stamp Act of 1976, p. 38).

A study prepared for the Department of Labor provides some insights into the precise activities of welfare recipients subject to the work registration requirements (Evans, et al., 1976). The study was designed to consider the merits of alternative methods of increasing the pressure on work registrants to search the labor market more diligently and to accept more jobs. In examining this problem, the authors sought to determine "whether existing work tests affected the timing and quality of jobs found after a period during which a person received welfare benefits and had to register with the Employment Service (ES) in connection with their receipt" (Evans, et al., 1976, pp. 1-2).

The study was conducted by analyzing three cities which had different forms of enforcement of the food stamp work registration program and two cities which had different AFDC work test implementation procedures. For example, one city with AFDC work registration required registrants to appear at the Employment Service to review job listings while picking up their welfare

215

checks. The other city required registrants to search for job openings and report to the employment service for a review of such search efforts. In each of the five cities, the authors identified six measurable aspects of the work tests that could be applied to an individual. These included the following: *a*) called-in to the Employment Service office; *b*) called-in frequently; *c*) questioned about job search activities; *d*) asked for proof of job search activities; *e*) referred to a job; and *f*) pressured to accept a job (Evans, et al., 1976, p. 3).

The study's analysis of these factors showed that there were substantially different levels of enforcement among the three cities which had food stamp work tests. The study also revealed evidence of pressure on registrants who remained unemployed, but that the success of these efforts was very slight. In most cases, the tendency of such pressure to increase the probability of returning to work was not statistically significant (Evans, et al., p. 5).

Large numbers of individuals must register for work and, as a result, be counted in the official unemployment statistics. If these individuals generally prefer not to work at existing wage rates and welfare benefits, or are largely unemployable, the work registration requirements will permanently increase the natural rate of unemployment. This means that the unemployment data collected since the implementation of the work registration programs are not comparable to the data collected before that time. More importantly, the data collected are invalid for public policy purposes, since they are now based on incorrect notions of what the unemployment figures represent. On this basis alone, it can be argued that individuals registered as unemployed under work registration requirements should be reported separately.

The effectiveness of the various work registration programs in inducing recipients to become employed is an important question. The available evidence reveals that the existing registration program has not had a high rate of success. One researcher concluded that "[o]nly about 10 percent of adult recipients are regarded as ready to participate in WIN. That is, 328,000 welfare recipients were certified as entering WIN in fiscal 1975, while there continued to be over 3 million heads of households receiving AFDC. . . .the figures. . .indicate that about three-quarters of AFDC adults. . .were regarded as unsuited for employment. . . ."(U.S. Department of Labor, 1977c, pp. 5-6). Further, "women who went through WIN and did not get work at the end had become markedly more dependent on welfare than they were when they started" (p. 21). One study of WIN "graduates" who became employed showed considerable turnover. "Four months after job entry, more than half of them had left. Of those who left, half had quit, almost one-third had been laid off, and the others had been fired" (p. 23).

In addition, a U.S. Department of Labor working paper (1975, pp. 22-23) provides further evidence that work registrants are generally not available for jobs:

> The net result. . .is that an undetermined percentage--perhaps the majority–of the food stamp work registrant population are individuals who are not really available for work or acceptable to employers. Yet the processing of registrations goes on and the volume of registrants on file continues to swell.

IV. Empirical Estimation of the Effects of Work Registration Requirements

Since the effects of minimum wages and unemployment compensation on the unemployment rate are discussed above, this section will estimate the effects attributable to work registration requirements. Following this estimation, we turn our attention to the joint determination of various institutional and noninstitutional factors and their relative impacts on the reported unemployment rate.

A preliminary estimate of the impact of the work registration requirements on the measured unemployment is straightforward. Using data available from the Department of Labor and official Bureau of Labor Statistics publications,[12] corrected rates of unemployment for the years 1972 through 1977 were determined. Table 1 gives these estimates as well as the official measured unemployment. Corrected rates for years prior to 1972 were not calculated because the work registration requirements were not in force. In each case the corrected number of unemployed persons was determined by subtracting the average total active food stamp and AFDC work registrants from the average official number of unemployed persons. The number of work registrants is estimated by using the active file for those on the food stamp program and the mandatory file for those receiving AFDC benefits. Both of these files represent less than the total number of welfare recipients who must register for work prior to receiving benefits. In September, 1976, for example, there were 3.7 million initial food stamp registrants, but only 1.2 million active food stamp work registrants (Clarkson and Meiners, 1977a, pp. 15, 17). The average number of food stamp and AFDC registrants was subtracted from the average

---

[12] Data on work registrants are available from Employment Series Automated Reporting Systems (ESARS) Tables compiled by the Department of Labor. Employment and labor force data are available from various issues of *Employment and Earnings*.

TABLE 1

Employment and Unemployment: A Comparison

Year	Civilian Employment as a Percentage of Total Non-Institutional Population Age 16 and Over	Measured Unemployment as a Percentage of Civilian Labor Force	Corrected Unemployment as a Percentage of Civilian Labor Force
Low Employment Periods			
1950	55.25%	5.3%	n.a.*
1955	55.15	4.4	n.a.
1966	55.57	3.8	n.a.
1971	55.49	5.9	n.a.
Average	55.37	4.9	n.a.
1975	55.25	8.5	6.6%
Medium Employment Periods			
1956	56.06	4.1	n.a.
1968	56.00	3.6	n.a.
1972	56.05	5.6	5.1†
Average	56.04	4.4	n.a.
1976	56.06	7.7	5.7
High Employment Periods			
1969	56.52	3.5	n.a.
1974	56.98	5.6	4.2
1977	57.11	7.0	5.2‡

Source: Calculated from *Economic Report of the President, 1978*, p. 288; National Center for Social Statistics, *The Work Incentive Program*, Report E-5; and Employment Series Automated Reporting Systems, Department of Labor (unpublished statistics).

* n.a.: Not applicable.

† Based on data from July-December 1972.

‡ Based on data from January-July 1977.

civilian labor force to determine the corrected average civilian labor force.[13] The ratio of the corrected average number of unemployed persons to the corrected average civilian force yielded the corrected unemployment rate. For example, in 1976 the average number of work registrants was 2,025,000. Subtracting this figure from the average official unemployment of 7,288,000 yields the corrected unemployment of 5,263,000. The corrected average civilian labor force is determined by subtracting the average number of work registrants from the official average civilian labor force of 94,773,000 which yields a corrected average civilian labor force of 92,748,000. Thus the corrected rate of unemployment is 5.7 percent (5,263,000 ÷ 92,748,000 = 0.0567).

Table 1 also shows civilian employment as a percentage of total noninstitutional population ages 16 and over. The corrected unemployment rates are more consistent with the relationship between the ratio of civilian employment to the noninstitutional population and measured unemployment to the civilian labor force, which had been quite stable since World War II until the last few years. Thus during periods of low employment (55.15 to 55.57 percent), measured unemployment averaged 4.9 percent of the civilian labor force. Yet in 1975 a similar rate of employment (55.25 percent) was associated with measured unemployment rate of 8.5 percent. Our corrected 6.6 percent rate of unemployment is more consistent with previous relationships between employment and unemployment. Similar results hold for periods of medium and high employment.

Additional evidence confirms the hypothesis that the work registration requirements cause welfare recipients to report more unemployment than individuals who are not on welfare but are in similar situations. For example, Table 2 shows the results of a study of various characteristics of individuals participating in the food stamp and food distribution programs during November, 1973. Since food stamp recipients are subject to work registration requirements, and food distribution recipients are not, our theory implies that unemployment would be higher among the former than among the latter. That implication is confirmed by the figures in Table 2. Approximately 30.2 percent of food stamp recipients were unemployed, compared to 24.5 percent of the individuals in the food distribution program.[14] Since monthly incomes, employment status,

---

[13]Individuals subject to the work registration requirements of both the food stamp and AFDC programs were counted only once.

[14]Calculated from data in U.S. Congress, Joint Economic Committee, *Studies in Public Welfare* (1974, pp. 42.45).

219

and demographic characteristics were similar for these groups, this difference is important confirming evidence.[15]

TABLE 2

Monthly Income and Employment Status,
November 1973

Category	Food Stamp Recipients	Food Distribution Recipients
Total Monthly Income	$364	$373
Unemployment Rate	30.2%	24.5%
Labor Force Participation		
Persons Employed		
Full Time	11.4%	11.6%
Part Time	9.7%	9.6%

Source: Calculated from data in U.S. Congress, Joint Economic Committee, *Studies in Public Welfare*, Paper No. 17, December, 1974.

Additional evidence is provided by the special August, 1975 Current Population Survey that contains information on participation in the food stamp and AFDC programs. An examination of the data taken from that survey[16] reveals that in all income classes, the unemployment rate for those individuals on welfare programs with work registration requirements was significantly higher than the rate for those individuals in the same income class who did not participate in welfare programs with work registration requirements. For instance, Table 3 shows that those individuals who reported monthly incomes of between $100 and $199 had unemployment rates of 11.5 percent, while those in the same income class who were not participating in welfare programs averaged 5.5 percent unemployment. Overall unemployment based on this sample was 11.7 percent for individuals who participated in one or more welfare programs with work registration requirements. This can be compared with an unemployment rate of 4.1 percent for individuals who are not in welfare programs with work registration requirements.

---

[15] It is interesting to note that the Department of Agriculture used an incorrect definition of employment in this publication. Table 8 of their published document reports that the "unemployment" rate of those seeking work among recipients of the food stamp program was 9 percent, and among participants in the food distribution program it was 7 percent. The definition of the unemployment implicitly used by the Department of Agriculture in this report, however, is the ratio of those unemployed to the total population (not the labor force) of recipients of the individual welfare programs (U.S. Congress, Joint Economic Committee, 1974, Table 8).

[16] Data were taken from those households that provided complete information on income; participation or nonparticipation in food stamp, AFDC, or general assistance welfare programs; and employment status. If information from any one of these categories was missing, the household was omitted from the sample. The analysis of these data is not complete, since the tapes sent from the Department of Labor did not contain an end of file marker and we have been able to analyze only the first 17,428 observations.

TABLE 3

Unemployment and Welfare Status, August 1975

Monthly Income	Individuals on Welfare Programs with Work Registration Requirements			Individuals Not on Welfare Programs		
	Labor Force	Number Unemployed	Percentage	Labor Force	Number Unemployed	Percentage
Less than $100	63	9	14.29%	207	17	8.21%
100 - 199	270	31	11.48	384	21	5.47
200 - 299	335	36	10.75	702	40	5.70
300 - 399	270	33	12.22	851	64	7.52
400 - 499	209	23	11.00	1,064	86	8.08
500 - 599	150	20	13.33	1,190	71	5.97
600 - 749	107	17	15.89	1,493	75	5.02
750 - 999	106	11	10.38	2,330	114	4.89
1,000 - 1,249	54	3	5.56	2,109	67	3.18
1,250 - 1,499	25	2	8.00	2,100	69	3.29
1,500 and more	24	3	12.50	3,249	98	3.02
Income Not Reported	16	2	12.50	120	10	8.33
TOTAL	1,629	190	11.66	15,799	732	4.13

Source: Computed from August, 1975 Current Population Survey data tapes.

Calculations taken from the August, 1976 Current Population Survey reveal similar results. Overall unemployment among individuals who are participating in welfare programs with work registration requirements was 11.5 percent, as shown in Table 4. Unemployment among individuals who did not participate in welfare programs with work registration requirements was 4.2 percent.[17] With the exception of one income class, those who earn between $600 and $749 a month, the rate of unemployment was greater for individuals who participated in welfare programs with work registration requirements than for individuals not on welfare.

Finally, an examination of the impact of work registration requirements for AFDC mothers provides additional support for the hypothesis that the work registration requirements will increase the number of individuals who indicate they are "looking for work" and consequently are reported as unemployed. In 1971, one year prior to the institution of work requirements for AFDC recipients, unemployment among mothers in the AFDC program who were living at home was 5.7 percent (Council of Economic Advisers, 1974, p. 172), 1.2 percentage points below the average female unemployment of 6.9 percent for that year (U.S. Department of Labor, Bureau of Labor Statistics, *Employment and Earnings*, 1972, Table A-33). In 1973, the first full year after the institution of work registration requirements for AFDC mothers, unemployment among this group was 11.5 percent (Council of Economic Advisers, 1974, p. 172) and 5.5 percentage points above the unemployment rate for females in general, 6.0 percent (*Employment and Earnings*, 1974, Table A-33). This change provides more evidence that the primary impact of the work registration requirement on AFDC mothers was to encourage more of them to claim that they were actively seeking work, whether or not they were actually doing so.

We now turn our attention to the simultaneous estimation of the relative effects of various insitutional and noninstitutional factors on monthly changes in the overall labor force participation rate. Factors, which in the aggregate are likely to have, or have been hypothesized to have, impacts on changes in the level of labor force participation have been included in our determination.

---

[17] For August, 1976 only the first 21,437 cases were analyzed, since these types were also missing an end of file marker.

TABLE 4

Unemployment and Welfare Status, August 1976

Monthly Income	Individuals on Welfare Programs With Work Registration Requirements			Individuals Not on Welfare Programs		
	Labor Force	Number Unemployed	Percentage	Labor Force	Number Unemployed	Percentage
Less than $100	61	10	16.39%	218	25	11.47%
100 - 199	245	36	14.69	463	18	3.89
200 - 299	315	43	13.65	793	44	5.55
300 - 399	352	54	15.34	1,030	73	7.09
400 - 499	294	24	8.16	1,271	65	5.11
500 - 599	158	14	8.86	1,367	68	4.97
600 - 749	136	8	5.88	1,897	117	6.17
750 - 999	134	10	7.46	2,678	118	4.41
1,000 - 1,249	80	4	5.00	2,540	86	3.39
1,250 - 1,499	35	7	20.00	2,797	87	3.11
1,500 and more	36	1	2.78	4,383	102	2.33
Income Not Reported	17	4	23.53	137	17	12.41
TOTAL	1,863	215	11.54	19,574	820	4.19

Source: Computed from August, 1976 Current Population Survey data tapes.

The variables that we have examined are specified in Table 5, and their relationship to changes in participation rate is given in equation (1):[18]

$$X_1 = \gamma_1 + \gamma_2 X_2 + \gamma_3 X_3 + \gamma_4 X_4 + \gamma_5 X_5 + \gamma_6 X_6 + \gamma_7 X_7 + \gamma_8 X_8$$

$$+ \gamma_9 X_9 + \gamma_{10} X_{10} + \underset{\sim}{e}, \tag{1}$$

where the expected signs are $\gamma_1 > 0$, $\gamma_2 > 0$, $\gamma_3 \geqslant 0$, $\gamma_4 > 0$, $\gamma_5 < 0$, $\gamma_6 < 0$, $\gamma_7 ? 0$, $\gamma_8 < 0$, $\gamma_9 < 0$, and $\gamma_{10} > 0$.

Changes in industrial production are included to reflect differences in real aggregate output, and we postulate the standard positive relationship between it and changes in labor force participation. Similarly, we have included changes in the wholesale price level. The ratio of women to men in the labor force was included to reflect both overall increased participation as well as potential substitutability of female for male workers. That ratio is expected to be positive. A negative relationship is postulated for the effect of changes in the number of members of the armed forces. For the official rate of unemployment, which reflects the probability of receiving a job, we postulate the sign to be negative. The expected sign for changes in the real level of the minimum wage is ambiguous, since higher minimum wages, which provide increased incentives to enter the labor force, simultaneously decrease those incentives as unemployment increases. Changes in both the number of Old Age and Survivors Insurance (OASI) recipients and Disability Insurance (DI) recipients are included, and the expected signs are negative in each case. Finally, the relative number of welfare registrants is included, and the postulated coefficient for this institutional variable is positive.

---

[18] In our original specification we estimated $U = \gamma_0 + \gamma_1 F + \gamma_2 I + \gamma_3 P + \gamma_4 M + \gamma_5 B + \gamma_6 D + \gamma_7 W + \underset{\sim}{e}$,
where U is the official rate of unemployment, F is the percentage of females in civilian labor force ages 20 and over, I is the monthly change in industrial production (1967 = 100), P is the monthly change in wholesale price index (1967 = 100), M is the minimum wage in constant dollars (1967 = 100), B is the unemployment benefits as a percent of average weekly wage, D is the average duration of unemployment compensation, and W is the percentage of welfare work registrants in civilian labor force and the expected signs are $\gamma_1 \geqslant 0$, $\gamma_2 \leqslant 0$, $\gamma_3 \leqslant 0$, $\gamma_4 \geqslant 0$, $\gamma_5 > 0$, $\gamma_6 > 0$, $\gamma_7 > 0$. The estimated coefficients with their associated t values in parentheses using data from January, 1967 to July, 1977 are:

$$U = 0.0074 - 0.2068F - 0.0010I - 0.0008P + 0.0283M + 0.1388B + 0.0013D$$
$$ (0.51) (0.85) (0.83) (1.34) (1.29) (2.52)$$

$$+ 1.4531W; \qquad R^2 = 0.51, \text{ and } D.W. = 1.43.$$
$$(2.77)$$

TABLE 5

Definition of Variables
(All First Differences)

Variable Name	Definition (and Source)*	Mean	Standard Deviation
X_1	Labor Force Participation Rate	0.0003	0.0019
X_2	Industrial Production (1967 = 100) (*Economic Report of the President*)	0.3984	1.2493
X_3	Wholesale Price Index (1967 = 100) (*Economic Report of the President*)	1.2459	1.7503
X_4	Women/Civilian Labor Force	0.0004	0.0012
X_5	Armed Forces/Civilian Labor Force	-0.0000†	0.0007
X_6	Official Unemployment Rate	0.0002	0.0197
X_7	Minimum Wage in Constant Dollars (1967 = 100) (*Statistical Abstract and Economic Report of the President*)	-0.0027	0.0388
X_8	OASI Recipients/Civilian Labor Force (*Social Security Bulletin*)	0.0001	0.0012
X_9	DI Recipients/Civilian Labor Force (*Social Security Bulletin*)	0.0002	0.0002
X_{10}	Welfare Work Registrants/Civilian Labor Force (ESARS and *Employment and Earnings*)	0.0003	0.0009

*Monthly first differences $(X_t^i - X_t^{i-1})$ are computed from June, 1972 through July, 1977. All data are calculated from *Employment and Earnings* unless otherwise stated.

†Less than - 0.00005.

The estimated coefficients with their associated t values (using data from June, 1972 to July, 1977) are given in equation (2):[19]

$$X_1 = 0.00023 + 0.00009X_2 + 0.00004X_3 - 0.01846X_4$$
$$(0.75) \qquad (0.44) \qquad (0.16)$$

$$+ 0.13836X_5 + 0.00297X_6 - 0.00438X_7$$
$$(0.59) \qquad (0.40) \qquad (1.10)$$

$$- 1.48125X_8 + 0.49381X_9 + 0.26626X_{10} \qquad\qquad (2)$$
$$(8.89) \qquad (0.63) \qquad (1.61)$$

$$R^2 = 0.72 \qquad D.W. = 2.25$$

An inspection of equation (2) reveals that only the ratio of OASI recipients to the civilian labor force (X_8) and the work registration (X_{10}) variables are significant at the 10-percent level. Overall, this regression provides additional confirming evidence that the work registration requirement increases the official rate of unemployment, since overall participation should not be altered if the work registration requirements merely resulted in the unemployed seeking food stamp or AFDC benefits.

V. Measured Unemployment and Public Policy

The use and misuse of unemployment statistics by politicians is well established common practice. Recently, however, legislators have been explicitly tying federal spending to measured unemployment. As noted by the Commissioner of the Bureau of Labor Statistics, "In recent years, another use of statistical indicators has emerged: large sums of money are being transferred among different groups of Americans on the basis of movements of these statistics. Thus in 1977 alone, over $16 billion has been allocated to States and communities on the basis of unemployment statistics" (Shiskin, 1977, p. 4).

This expenditure may also represent a lower bound on the total spending of the federal government in an attempt to lower measured unemployment to

---

[19] We would prefer to calculate equations using data for different age and sex groups, as work registrants are not normally distributed among the various age and sex groups represented in the work force. Unfortunately, data in the required form are not available, so disaggregated estimation is not possible at this time.

"traditional" levels. For instance, in 1975 unemployment was reported as 8.5 percent, the highest since the depression.[20] This figure spurred arguments for new federal programs to combat unemployment and for a general increase in federal spending to stimulate economic activity. The billions of dollars spent by the federal government because of the unusually high measured unemployment figures during this period are impossible to estimate. It is clear that higher levels of unemployment have given added strength to the call for passage of the Humphrey-Hawkins Full Employment and Balanced Growth Act to guarantee jobs for all.

Several federal programs specifically provide for the allocation of funds to states and local areas based on official unemployment statistics.[21] The first federal legislation which specified funding according to the level of unemployment reported by the Bureau of Labor Statistics was Title IV of the Public Works and Economic Development Act of 1965 (Public Law No. 89-136).[22] Designed to "enhance the domestic prosperity," this legislation allocated about $0.5 billion in fiscal 1966 to provide federal financial assistance to areas "suffering substantial and persistent unemployment and underemployment" (Public Law No. 89-136 § 2).[23] Administered by the Economic Development Agency in the Department of Commerce, the program provides funds to qualified state and local governments to help in the construction of public works projects. To qualify for federal funds as a "redevelopment area," the geographical area covered must have averaged 6 percent unemployment for the past year and have had an annual average rate of unemployment at least 50 percent above the national average for three of the past four years, 75 percent above the national average for two of the past three years, or 100 percent above the national average for one of the past two years. A 1976 amendment to this legislation provides extra federal grants for areas with a rate of unemployment of at least 7 percent during the most recent quarter (Public Law No. 94-487 § 122). Funding is terminated when the national unemployment rate drops below 7 percent for one quarter.

[20]Although generally ignored, it should be remembered that the official unemployment statistics of the depression have been attacked as inaccurate. See Michael R. Darby (1976).

[21]It is not the purpose of this paper to criticize any of the programs discussed here. Besides these programs, there is pending legislation to further expand the role of the federal government in reducing unemployment. See D.I. Meiselman (1978).

[22]Other federal programs at various times may have tied federal spending to reported unemployment. The programs discussed here are those reported by the Deputy Commissioner for Data Analysis, Bureau of Labor Statistics, as having legislative requirements for local area unemployment data. See J.L. Norwood (1977, p. 9).

[23]An "underemployed person" means "(1) A person who is working part-time but has been seeking full-time work, and who is a member of a family whose total annual income during the 12 months prior to application. . .does not exceed the poverty level determined. . .by OMB. (2) A person who is working full-time and who is a member of a family whose total annual income during the 12 months prior to application. . .does not exceed the poverty level determined. . .by OMB." (29 C.F.R. § 94.4 (fff) 1977).

The Comprehensive Employment and Training Act (CETA) of 1973, designed to provide job training and employment opportunities for economically disadvantaged unemployed and underemployed persons, is the largest federal program to rely on unemployment statistics as a fund dispersal qualification (Public Law No. 93-203). Title I of CETA, Comprehensive Manpower Services, provides funding for state and local programs which train and retrain people, help them find jobs, and promote job creation and development. Some of the funding for this part of CETA is allocated on the basis of the relative number of unemployed persons living in the governmental area compared to the number in all other areas.

Title II of CETA, Public Employment Programs, is administered, as are all other sections of the legislation, by the Employment and Training Administration of the Department of Labor. This program provides unemployed and underemployed persons with transitional employment in public services in areas of substantial unemployment. Almost all of the funding for this program is based on reported unemployment. An area of "substantial unemployment" is "any area of sufficient size and scope to sustain a public service employment program and which has a rate of unemployment equal to or in excess of 6.5 per centum for three consecutive months. . . ." (Public Law No. 93-203 § 204(c), 1973. The area, which may contain multiple governmental units, must have a population of at least 50,000 in order to qualify for funding.

Title VI of CETA was added by the Title I of the Emergency Jobs and Unemployment Assistance Act of 1974 (Public Law 93-567). With authorization of $2.5 billion for fiscal 1975, the Emergency Jobs Programs Act provides transitional public service employment for unemployed and underemployed persons and funding for manpower services to help people qualify for nonpublic service employment. Funding for the local public service jobs programs is also based on a formula. Fifty percent of the funds are allocated on the basis of unemployment in the area, relative to unemployment in all other areas. Twenty-five percent of the funds are allocated to areas with "substantial unemployment," which is 6.5 percent or more. The other twenty-five percent of the funds are allocated "on the basis of the relative excess number of unemployed persons" in the area. "Excess number" means "unemployed persons in excess of 4.5 per centum of the labor force" in the area (Public Law No. 93-567 § 603(2)(C), 1974). At the time this legislation was extended by the Emergency Jobs Programs Extension Act of 1976, it was financing $2.2 billion of the $2.6 billion spent by the federal government on public service jobs, the other $400 million being financed by Title II of CETA (*Legislative History*, Public Law No. 94-444, 1976). In fiscal 1977, $3.5 billion was budgeted for continuing Title VI.

Title II of the Emergency Jobs and Unemployment Assistance Act of 1974 provides temporary federal funding of state unemployment compensation programs for individuals who have exhausted their benefits. The funds are provided when, for the past three months, the national unemployment rate averaged 6 percent or more, or the unemployment rate in the area in question averaged 6.5 percent or more. These benefits extended state compensation payments by 26 weeks.

The Public Works Employment Act of 1976 (Public Law No. 94-369) has two main provisions, both of which allocate funds based on reported unemployment. Title I, Local Public Works, allocated $2 billion for the fiscal year ending September 30, 1977. The federal government paid 100 percent of the cost of public works projects qualifying for funding. Seventy percent of the funds were allocated to state and local governments on the basis of priority according to the level of unemployment. Top priority was given to areas in which unemployment was both over 6.5 percent and above the national average. Second priority was given to areas with unemployment over 6.5 percent, but less than the national average. The remaining funds were to be dispersed on the basis of other criteria. The Public Works Employment Act of 1977 (Public Law No. 95-28), an amendment to the 1976 Act, provided an additional $6 billion for the period ending December 31, 1978. The allocation of the funds was changed so that 65 percent of the funds would be paid according to the relative level of unemployment in each area when compared to the national average. The other 35 percent of the funds are for areas with an unemployment rate above 6.5 percent for the last year.[24]

Title II, Anti-Recession Provisions, of the Public Works Employment Act of 1976 provided an additional $1.25 billion for state and local governments during the five quarters beginning July 1, 1976 in an attempt to stimulate the economy. A base of $125 million was provided in each quarter plus an additional $62.5 million for every one-half percentage point that the national unemployment rate was above 6 percent during the last quarter. The shares for state and local areas are equal to the "excess unemployment percentage" multiplied by their revenue sharing base.[25] This program was amended by the Intergovernmental Anti-Recession Assistance Act of 1977, which is Title VI of the Tax Reduction and Simplification Act of 1977 (Public Law No. 95-30).

---

[24]This change in the allocation formula may have represented a recognition by Congress that measured unemployment was on the decline, which would have eliminated many areas from funding under the 6.5 percent minimum guideline.

[25]"Excess unemployment percentage" is equal to the difference resulting from the subtraction of 4.5 percentage points from the unemployment rate for the governmental unit, but not less than zero. A government would get no funds if its unemployment rate fell below 4.5 percent. Local government will receive two-thirds of the total funds.

An additional $2.25 billion was authorized to be spent in the five quarters beginning July 1, 1977. The amended program provided the same base of $125 million per quarter, plus an additional amount equal to $30 million multiplied by the number of one-tenth percentage points the national unemployment rate was above 6 percent during the previous quarter.[26]

These programs reveal the importance of the reported levels of unemployment to various government officials. Could the direct link between official unemployment levels and certain payments to states explain the nearly complete dismissal of the work registration unemployment hypothesis by politicians and government officials?

Our initial evidence indicates that states have come to recognize the importance of these statistics to their fiscal status. Due to a change in the statistical technique used in the calculation of the unemployment rate in New Jersey, that state lost $20 to $25 million in CETA funds. New Jersey unsuccessfully sued the Department of Labor in *Hoffman* v. *Dunlop* (U.S. Department of Labor, 1977a, p. 72). This case serves to illustrate the financial and political importance of unemployment statistics. When money is allocated on the basis of official unemployment rates, more attention will be paid to their collection and estimation. Because there is a direct budget payoff, state and local officials have an incentive to see that welfare work registration yields more "unemployed" individuals.

Perhaps we should worry about the incentives to suppress actions that would lower the official rate of unemployment. Certain changes in the rules for distributing funds to states would weaken the resistance to corrections in the unemployment rate that lower the overall level. Although some of the programs tied to the unemployment rate were designed to terminate once the national level of unemployment dropped below 6 or 6.5 percent, the tendency has been to lower the numerical criteria for funding as the rate of unemployment declines. Some programs, despite their "temporary" nature, appear to have become permanent. For example, the Temporary Employment Assistance program had an outlay of $2,340 million in fiscal 1977. The estimated outlay for fiscal 1978 is $4,765 million; for fiscal 1979 it is $5,956 million (Office of Management and Budget, 1978, pp. 617-18). Expected expenditures on training, employment, and labor services also continue to rise. The actual outlays in fiscal 1977 were $7,251 million. Estimated future outlays are: $11,370

---

[26] This amendment foresaw the problem of inaccurate local unemployment rates. In Section 602(d) it provides that the Secretary of Labor may reject the official unemployment rate for a governmental unit and assign it the number he thinks is more accurate. For example, the New York regional office of the Bureau of Labor Statistics recently decided to stop publishing its monthly unemployment estimate for New York City because the estimate was not considered sufficiently accurate for researchers (*New York Times*, September 7, 1977).

million, fiscal 1978; $13,264 million, fiscal 1979; $14,738 million, fiscal 1980 (Office of Management and Budget, 1978, p. 165).

VI. Conclusion

Future research on unemployment will surely yield more accurate estimates of the magnitudes of error attributable to work registration requirements and other federally instituted programs. However, it seems unlikely that our general conclusions will be altered. There has been a permanent increase in the number of individuals included in the unemployment statistics. The increase represents individuals excluded from the labor force (the minimum wage law), individuals who find work less attractive (the magnitude and duration of unemployment benefits), and individuals who are not seeking work, but must register for work as a condition for receiving welfare benefits (the work registration requirement). Thus, we find the circle is complete: changes in our institutions (the work registration requirements) have permanently altered official unemployment statistics (a permanent higher reported level), which in turn can be linked to new changes in institutions (public programs to reduce unemployment).

References

Alchian, A.A. (1970), "Information Costs, Pricing, and Resource Unemployment," *Microeconomic Foundations of Employment and Inflation Theory,* ed. E.S. Phelps. New York: W.W. Norton and Company.

Bregger, J.E. (1977), "Establishment of a New Employment Statistics Review Commission," *Monthly Labor Review,* **100**: 14-20.

Cagan, P. (1977), "The Reduction of Inflation and the Magnitude of Unemployment," *Contemporary Economic Problems,* ed. W. Fellner. Washington, D.C.: American Enterprise Institute.

Clarkson, K.W., and Meiners, R.E. (1977a). *Inflated Unemployment Statistics: The Effects of Welfare Work Registration Requirements.* Coral Gables, Florida: Law and Economics Center.

_____(1977b), "The Spurious Increase in the Unemployment Rates," *Policy Review,* **1**: 27-51.

Code of Federal Regulations (1978). Washington, D.C.: U.S. Government Printing Office.

Council of Economic Advisers (1974). *Economic Report of the President, 1974.* Washington, D.C.: U.S. Government Printing Office.

Darby, M.R. (1976), "Three-and-a-Half Million U.S. Employees Have Been Mislaid: Or, An Explanation of Unemployment, 1934-1941," *Journal of Political Economy,* **84**: 1-16.

Ehrenberg, R.G., and Oaxaca, R.L. (1976), "Unemployment Insurance, Duration of Unemployment, and Subsequent Wage Gain," *American Economic Review,* **66**: 754-66.

Evans, R., Jr., et al. (1976), "The Impact of Work Tests on the Employment Behavior of Welfare Recipients." Study prepared for the U.S. Department of Labor, Manpower Administration, Washington, D.C. Mimeographed.

Feldstein, M. (1973), "The Economics of the New Unemployment," *Public Interest,* **33** : 3-42.

_____(1974), "Unemployment Compensation: Adverse Incentives and Distributional Anomalies," *National Tax Journal,* **27**: 231-44.

_____(1976), "The Effect of Unemployment Insurance on Temporary Layoff Unemployment." Discussion Paper No. 520. Cambridge: Harvard Institute of Economic Research.

Flaim, P. (1977), "The Impact of Demographic Changes on the Unemployment Rate." Mimeographed.

Lippman, S.A., and McCall, J.J. (1976), "The Economics of Job Search: A Survey," *Economic Inquiry,* **14**: 347-68.

Meiselman, D.I. (1978). *Welfare Reform and the Carter Public Service Employment Program: A Critique.* Coral Gables, Florida: Law and Economics Center.

Mincer, J. (1976), "Unemployment Effects of Minimum Wages," *Journal of Political Economy,* **84**: 87-104.

Norwood, J.L. (1977), "Reshaping a Statistical Program to Meet Legislative Priorities," *Monthly Labor Review,* **100**: 9.

Office of Management and Budget (1978). *The Budget of the United States Government, FY 1979.* Washington, D.C.: U.S. Government Printing Office.

_____(1978). *The Budget of the United States Government, FY 1979,* Appendix. Washington, D.C.: U.S. Government Printing Office.

O'Neill, D., Classen, K., and Holen, A. (1974), "Effects of the 1974 UI Extensions on Unemployment." Washington, D.C.: Public Research Institute of the Center for Naval Analyses.

Perloff, J.M., and Wachter, M.L. (1979), "A Production Function-Nonaccelerating Inflation Approach to Potential Output: Is Measured Potential Output Too High?" *Carnegie-Rochester Conference Series,* 10, eds. K. Brunner and A.H. Meltzer. Amsterdam: North-Holland.

Ragan, J.F., Jr. (1977), "Minimum Wages and the Youth Labor Market," *Review of Economics and Statistics,* 59: 136.

Shiskin, J. (1977), "A New Role for Economic Indicators," *Monthly Labor Review,* 100: 4.

Tella, A. (1976), "Analyzing Joblessness," *New York Times,* October 27, 1976, editorial page.

U.S. Code Annotated (1978). St. Paul, Minn.: West Publishing Company.

U.S. Congress, House (1976). *Food Stamp Act of 1976.* 94th Congress, 2d Session, H.R. 94-1460, September 1, 1976.

U.S. Congress, Joint Economic Committee (1974). *Studies in Public Welfare.* Calculated from data in U.S. Congress, Paper No. 17, December, 1974.

U.S. Congress, Senate Finance Committee (1972). *Work Incentive Program: Hearing Before the Committee on Finance.* Washington, D.C.: U.S. Government Printing Office.

U.S. Department of Agriculture (1975). *The Food Stamp Certification Handbook.* Food and Nutrition Service, No. 732-1. Washington, D.C.: U.S. Government Printing Office.

U.S. Department of Commerce, Bureau of the Census (1976). *Current Population Survey: Interviewer's Reference Manual.* CPS-250, rev. August, 1976. Washington, D.C.: U.S. Government Printing Office.

U.S. Department of Labor (1975). *The Food Stamp Work Requirements in Perspective.* Unpublished working paper, Manpower Administration, May, 1975.

U.S. Department of Labor (1976). *WIN in 76, The Work Incentive Program,* Seventh Annual Report to the Congress. Washington, D.C.: U.S. Government Printing Office.

_____(1977a), "Significant Decisions in Labor Cases," *Monthly Labor Review,* **100**: 72.

_____(1977b). *The WIN Handbook,* No. 318, Chapter I. Washington, D.C.: U.S. Government Printing Office.

_____(1977c). *The Work Incentive (WIN) Program and Related Experiences.* R&D Monograph 49, Employment and Training Administration. Washington, D.C.: U.S. Government Printing Office.

U.S. Department of Labor, Bureau of Labor Statistics. *Employment and Earnings,* various issues. Washington, D.C.: U.S. Government Printing Office.

_____(1976). *BLS Handbook of Methods.* Washington, D.C.: U.S. Government Printing Office.

U.S. Department of Labor and Department of Health, Education and Welfare (1977). *WIN Technical Assistance Guide, Volume I.* Washington, D.C.: U.S. Government Printing Office.

Welch, F. (1974), "Minimum Wage Legislation in the United States," *Economic Inquiry,* **12**: 285-318.

Williams, W.E. (1977), "Government Sanctioned Restraints That Reduce Economic Opportunities for Minorities," *Policy Review,* **2**: 7-30.

GOVERNMENT LABOR POLICIES AND
EQUILIBRIUM UNEMPLOYMENT RATES
A Comment on Clarkson and Meiners

Walter Y. OI

University of Rochester

In their paper, "Institutional Changes, Employment Statistics, and Induced Institutional Changes," Kenneth Clarkson and Roger Meiners try to persuade us that (*a*) the work registration requirements embedded in the Federal Food Stamps and AFDC welfare programs have increased the official unemployment rate, (*b*) the impact of these two programs is considerably greater than the 0.2 percentage point increment estimated by P. Cagan, and (*c*) the resulting higher equilibrium unemployment rates have induced further Federal programs to bring down unemployment rates. In their language,

> It is our hypothesis that the measured high rate of
> unemployment, especially in recent years, can be explained
> in large part by a number of federal programs that directly
> and indirectly cause recipients to report themselves as
> unemployed when they are not seeking work, or to engage
> in activities prolonging the period of unemployment.

At the outset, let me review the paper which can be divided into its four major sections as follows:

A. *Why is Unemployment so High?* In this section, the authors review several studies which have estimated the quantitative impact of several conventional variables affecting the aggregate unemployment rate. The kinds of variables examined include (*a*) the demographic composition of the labor force, (*b*) unemployment insurance, and (*c*) minimum wage rates. Reference is made to the study by Phillip Cagan (1977) who concluded that these three factors accounted for a rise of 1.23 to 1.60 percentage points in the equilibriun unemployment rate at full employment. The authors disagree with Cagan's estimate that work registration programs are responsible for only a 0.2 percentage point rise in the unemployment rate.

B. *Work Registration Requirements.* In this section, the authors describe the compliance requirements which were imposed on Food Stamps and AFDC recipients on July 1, 1972. They discuss the ways in which mandatory work registration requirements can be expected to expand the nominal number of unemployed persons.

C. *Empirical Estimation of the Effects of Work Registration Requirements.* Two procedures which I shall call (*a*) the assignment method, and (*b*) the regression method are developed to quantify the extent to which work registration requirements have inflated official unemployment rates. Three other bodies of data, (*a*) Food Stamps vs. food distribution recipients, (*b*) welfare recipients with and without work registration requirements, and (*c*) AFDC mothers, before and after the requirements, are examined to infer the direction of change in measured unemployment.

D. *Measured Unemployment and Public Policy.* In the final section, the authors turn to the induced institutional changes; CETA and various public works and public service employment programs are described with emphasis placed on the criteria for allocating Federal monies to local governmental units. The authors imply that these "new programs" of the mid-1970s were the results of the inflated unemployment rates which were generated by the earlier vintage of Federal programs.

The AFDC and Food Stamps programs examined in this paper were primarily designed to redistribute income. The particular ways in which the programs were implemented resulted in the possibly regrettable outcome of higher *measured* unemployment rates. In my comments on the paper, I first review the concept of an equilibrium unemployment rate. In Parts 2 and 3, I criticize the two empirical procedures used to estimate the *partial* effects of these two programs on measured unemployment rates. The two concluding parts deal with the authors' views on the impact of these programs on subsequent government labor policies.

1. Determinants of Equilibrium Unemployment Rates

In *University Economics*, Alchian and Allen (1967) tell us that all of the churches are empty almost all of the time. The family car sits in splendid idleness 95 percent of the time. Firemen polish their equipment and play volleyball. Neoclassical economic theory has always embraced the principle that apparent idleness or unemployment does not *imply* inefficiency. Inventories of goods and football players on the bench serve the useful productive function of "availability." Soldiers on garrison duty may seem to be unemployed but they provide a deterrent service.

In the last two decades, economists have reembraced the concept of *frictional unemployment*--the principle that unemployment can be voluntary and productive. Transfers to different jobs, migration to different labor markets, movements between home production and labor market production, can often be most "economically" accomplished by spreading out the adjustments over time. The time that is allocated to make these transitions to different jobs, labor markets, or activities can be called *search*. In a world characterized by uncertain changes in tastes and technologies, human and nonhuman resources may appear to be unemployed while they are involved in optimal transitional adjustments to different employments.

The concept of frictional unemployment can be found in the writings of Adam Smith, Nassau Senior, Alfred Marshall, and others. An excellent analysis of the principle of productive idleness is provided by W.H. Hutt (1977).[1] The unemployed worker in a state of pseudo-idleness can properly be said to be "productive" when he is *prospecting* for a job.[2] Thus, in a dynamic world, it will be socially optimal to have some workers who are productively unemployed while they prospect for preferred jobs with higher expected returns.

The concept of an equilibrium unemployment rate U^* at "full employment" (whatever that might mean) appears to have been generally accepted by the economics profession. In the context of the so-called Phillips curve, U^* may be called the *natural* rate of unemployment or the noninflationary unemployment rate. But there are some unresolved issues. When taste changes lead to shifts in product demands, or technological advances shift supply prices, labor and nonhuman resources must be transferred to preferred employments. Certain groups of workers--the young and those with less permanent (casual) ties to the labor market--have historically borne the brunt of these adjustments to changing demand/supply conditions. Some conjectural hypotheses can be advanced to explain why the equilibrium, full employment unemployment rates, U_j^*, ought to be higher for these particular demographic groups. For expository purposes, let the j-th group refer to teenaged males, 16-19 years of age. Individuals in this group have little specific human capital in their existing jobs if they hold them. Their wages are low so that the opportunity costs of prospecting are small. These two facts imply that teenaged males have more to gain from job shifts and should thus devote more time to prospecting. In addition, if there are some exogenous risks of unpredictable demand/supply

---

[1]*The Theory of Idle Resources* was first published in 1939. An expanded edition with appendix notes has been recently issued by the Liberty Press (1977).

[2]In my opinion, the term *prospecting*, which was used by Mr. Hutt, is preferable to the term *search* as a description of states of productive unemployment. I search for the manuscript which I mislaid and the child who has wandered away from the picnic grounds. But when I go prospecting, there is no hint of an earlier mistake.

shifts calling for job switching, socially optimal allocation schemes would assign these risks to individuals with the *least* risk aversion. There is abundant evidence indicating that the attitudes toward risk-bearing systematically vary over the life cycle. Young aggressive males generally prefer risks; they are, after all, the ones who engage in crime,[3] volunteer for our Armed Forces, and have the highest accident rates. The implicit employment practices which seem to characterize the larger firms seem to assign the risks of involuntary job losses to young males and casual workers with only loose ties to the labor market. Such practices are surely optimal from the viewpoint of minimizing the psychic costs of risk-bearing.

Conceptually, one could develop several definitions for the equilibrium unemployment rate at "full employment"; some examples might include (1) U_0 = the socially optimal rate which maximizes the expected present value of total product given the uncertainties in the world, (2) U_c^* = the competitive equilibrium rate that would have been generated by competitive market forces in the *absence* of government intervention and monopolistic influences, or (3) U_a^* = the actual market equilibrium rate that results from market forces which incorporate the monopolistic influences of large corporations and unions as well as the constraints imposed by various government labor policies. The discussion in the preceding paragraph of this comment implied that the socially optimal unemployment rate, U_0^*, would vary across individuals, being higher for those persons who incur low adjustment costs to job changes or who prefer risk-bearing. If the aggregate competitive market equilibrium rate, U_c^*, reflects the behavior of fully informed economic agents, variations in the characteristics of the work force will also lead to changes in the equilibrium rate, U_c^*. To the extent that younger males and women returning to the labor force have more to gain from prospecting for preferred jobs, larger fractions of them in the labor force ought to be accompanied by higher equilibrium unemployment rates, both from a socially optimal viewpoint, U_0^*, as well as for the hypothetical competitive equilibrium viewpoint, U_c^*.

It has been argued that an unbridled competitive equilibrium rate U_c^* might fall below a socially optimal rate U_0^* because some unemployed workers will be forced to accept nonoptimal job offers when they lack the funds to sustain further prospecting. In this event, some program of unemployment insurance and compensation to unemployed persons could lead to a higher expected total product. However, benefit levels that are set "too high" could induce inordinately long periods of unemployment so that the actual market

---

[3]G.S. Becker (1968) has shown that if the supply response of criminal offenses is more elastic with respect to the probability of arrest vs. the fine if arrested, then the criminal's utility function of wealth must involve an increasing marginal utility of wealth; i.e., criminals must prefer risks. The empirical evidence evidently corroborates this relationship.

equilibrium unemployment rate U_a^* could exceed a socially optimal rate U_0^*. A slightly different argument applies to the way in which minimum wage rates affect U_a^*. Even in a two-sector model, Mincer (1976) argues that a rise in the minimum wage rate could generate more unemployment as potential workers enter longer queues for the higher paying jobs.[4] A binding minimum wage can thus be expected to raise U_a^* above both the socially optimal U_0^* and unbridled competitive U_c^* equilibrium unemployment rates.

Clarkson and Meiners correctly argue that the provisions of various government programs can affect the actual equilibrium unemployment rates U_a^*. The Work Registration Requirements in the Food Stamps and AFDC programs tend to expand the number of persons who report themselves as "unemployed." But other Federal programs, notably Social Security retirement and disability programs, operate in an opposing direction tending to lower actual unemployment rates.[5] In trying to decide if the gap between measured unemployment rates U (which presumably approximate U_a^* at "full employment") and some other benchmark like a socially optimal rate U_0^*, has widened or narrowed as a result of government policies, we should acknowledge the effects from the totality of all Federal and State government policies. Let me turn now to some specific comments on the paper.

2. Assignment of Work Registrants to Unemployment

The first procedure for estimating the effects of work registration requirements invokes a strong assumption. Specifically, the authors assume that all of the R_t work registrants represent *net increments* to the numbers of persons in both the labor force L_t and the pool of unemployed persons X_t. According to their first procedure, the *actual* equilibrium rate U^* that would have prevailed in the absence of work registration requirements can be calculated by subtracting the number of work registrants R_t from both the numerator and denominator of the official unemployment rate U_t.

---

[4]The reasoning behind the Mincer model appeared earlier in the rent-seeking society of Krueger (1974). Krueger's model implies that if unionism or other noncompetitive factors result in wages that contain substantial amounts of economic rents, individuals will join queues to compete for those jobs. In equilibrium, the "expected" returns will be equalized in jobs with and without economic rents. However, unemployment will be generated by those individuals who join the queues to get jobs with economic rents. Thus, it is just not the minimum wage rate, but the entire structure of market wage rates which affect the actual market equilibrium rate U_a^*.

[5]In order to qualify for benefits under either early retirement or disability insurance, the recipient must comply with an earnings test requirement. The recipient's benefits will be taxed if his wage earnings exceed $3,000 per year. (The allowable earnings limit in 1950 was only $600.) Confer *Social Security Bulletin*, *Annual Statistical Supplement*, 1975, p. 29).

TABLE 1

Work Registrants and Employment Statistics for Selected Years

		1967	1970	1973	1974	1975	1976
Population and Employment (000)							
(1)	Civilian Adult Population P	133,319	140,182	148,263	150,827	153,449	156,048
(2)	Labor Force L	77,347	82,715	88,714	91,011	92,613	94,773
(3)	Employed Persons E	74,732	78,627	84,409	85,935	84,783	87,485
(4)	Unemployed Persons X	2,975	4,088	4,304	5,076	7,830	7,288
(5)	Work Registrants R*	n.a.	n.a.	1,235.0†	1,308.5	1,838.9	2,025.0
Measured Rates (percent)							
(6)	Unemployment rate $U = (X/L)$	3.85	4.94	4.85	5.58	8.45	7.69
(7)	LFPR, $\theta = L/P$	58.02	59.00	59.84	60.34	60.35	60.73
(8)	Employment rate, $\epsilon = E/P$	55.78	56.09	56.93	56.98	55.25	56.06
(9)	Work Reg. Rate, $W_1 = R/P$	n.a.	n.a.	0.83	0.87	1.20	1.30
(10)	Work Reg. Rate, $r = R/L$	n.a.	n.a.	1.39	1.44	1.98	2.14
(11)	Corrected Unemployment rate $U* = (X-R)/(L-R)$	3.85	4.94	3.51	4.20	6.60	5.67

*Data estimated from figures reported in Table 1 of Clarkson and Meiners (1979).

†Obtained from *Manpower Report of the President*, 1974.

242

$$U_t^* = \frac{X_t - R_t}{L_t - R_t} = \frac{U_t - r_t}{1 - r_t}, \tag{1}$$

where $U_t = (X_t/L_t)$ is the official unemployment rate, and $r_t = (R_t/L_t)$ is the ratio of mandatory work registrants to the labor force.[6] In Table 1, I show the two measures of the unemployment rates on lines (6) and (11), where I infer the figures for R_t from Table 1 of Clarkson and Meiners (1979).

According to this assignment method, 27.8 percent of this 7.3 million unemployed persons in 1976 would *not* have been counted as unemployed if there had been no work registration requirements for the Federal AFDC and Food Stamps programs. The assignment method thus yields a "corrected" unemployment rate of $U^* = 5.67$ percent vs. the official unemployment rate of $U = 7.69$ percent. This first procedure would evidently blame the work registration requirements for a 2.0 percentage points increment to the measured, official unemployment rate in 1976.[7]

An implication of the assignment method is that the work registrants resulting from the compliance requirements of AFDC and Food Stamps should have increased *both* the official unemployment rate, $U = (X/L)$, *and* the labor force participation rate, $\theta = (L/P)$. Moreover, those subgroups which contain larger fractions of work registrants ought to exhibit proportionally larger increases in both U and θ. Based on an admittedly casual examination of the data, I get the impression that the cyclical behavior of unemployment rates has not substantially changed since the cycles of the mid-1950s. The one notable exception is in the unemployment rate of married males with spouse present. This group has historically exhibited the smallest fluctuations in unemployment rates--they are even more stable than the prime age males who are used as the base for the Perloff-Wachter (1979) and Perry (1977) weighted unemployment rates. The unemployment rate of married males with spouse present climbed from 2.3 percent in 1973 to 5.1 percent in 1975; this group probably had the smallest proportion of work registrants.[8]

---

[6] The adult population can be divided into three mutually exclusive groups: X = unemployed persons, E = employed persons, and N = *not* in the labor force. The labor force is simply, $L = X + E$. In their later regression model, Clarkson and Meiners do not measure the importance of work registrants by $r = (R/L)$, but rather by $W = (R/P)$. The two measures are related by

$$r = W/\theta$$

where $\theta = (L/P)$ is the labor force participation rate.

[7] In the Cagan study cited earlier in their paper, work registration requirements were responsible for only a 0.2 percentage point rise in U. Clarkson and Meiners do not tell us whether the "corrected" rates shown in Table 1 have to be adjusted further for the changing demographic mix of the labor force or for changes in unemployment insurance benefits and coverage.

[8] *Economic Report of the President 1976*, Table B-24, p. 199.

Reference to Table 1 reveals that the labor force participation rate θ (See line 7) rose in the period following the work registration requirements, July 1, 1972. This squares with the Clarkson-Meiners assignment method, but it fails to examine the time path for subgroups. Participation rates of adult males over 20 years of age and of older women 45 and over have declined since 1960. Further, the participation rates of teenaged males and of women under 45 have been rising for two or more decades. In the absence of data on the ratio of work registrants to population, (R/P) for subgroups, one cannot test the validity of the maintained assumption in the assignment method--namely do registrants represent net increments to both X and L? I would like to see this test performed.

Finally, the authors seem to be assuming that the number of work registrants in each period, R_t, is exogenously determined by budget authorizations or other features of the two Federal programs. If R_t is positively correlated with the unemployment rate U_t, this correlation should be netted out in making the adjustments to estimate "corrected" unemployment rates U^*.

3. A Monthly Regression Model

The second procedure for estimating the effects of work registration requirements on unemployment statistics was based on a single equation regression model. In the original Conference paper, the authors developed a model in which the official unemployment rate U_t was regressed on seven explanatory variables: (1) F = the percentage of females in the civilian labor force; (2) I = the *change* in the monthly index of industrial production; (3) P = the *change* in the wholesale price index; (4) M = the minimum hourly wage rate in constant dollars; (5) B = the ratio of weekly unemployment benefit payments to the weekly wage; (6) D = the duration of unemployment of insured workers; and (7) $W = R/P$ = the ratio of work registrants to the population over 20 years of age. This estimated regression which now appears in footnote 18 of the revised manuscript is reproduced below.[9]

$$U_t = 0.0074 - 0.2068F_t - 0.0010I_t - 0.0008P_t + 0.0283M_t + 0.1388B_t$$
$$(0.51) \quad\quad (0.85) \quad\quad (0.83) \quad\quad (1.34) \quad\quad (1.29)$$
$$+ 0.0013D_t + 1.4531W_t \cdot [R^2 = 0.51, D\text{-}W = 1.43, \text{monthly data,}$$
$$(7.52) \quad\quad (2.77) \quad\quad\quad\quad\quad \text{Jan. 1967-June 1977]}$$
$$(2)$$

---

[9] The authors have apparently rejected the monthly unemployment rate model and have replaced it with a model which presumably "explains" the first-differences in labor force participation rates. I have revised my remarks about the unemployment rate model of footnote 18 in the text of Part 3. My comments on the revised first-difference model appear in the postscript to these comments. Since my remarks in Part 4 of my comments were based on the original conference paper, I felt that this procedure would be acceptable.

Several critical remarks can be made about the specification of this unemployment equation. The use of only contemporaneous measures of aggregate demand I_t and inflation P_t differs from other models. Only the female component in the demographic composition of the labor force is explicitly acknowledged. No attempt is made to adjust for teenaged labor force participation or for employment in the Armed Forces. Finally, the inclusion of the duration of unemployment on the right side is likely to induce a simultaneous equations bias.

The authors follow a familiar pattern in specifying single equation regression models, namely, they include "relevant" explanatory variables in a *linear* model without examining what the theory implies about functional forms. In their first assignment method, the authors identify two measures of unemployment rates--an offical rate U_t and a corrected rate U_t^* which are related via the identity

$$U_t = (1\text{-}r_t)U_t^* + r_t \, , \tag{3}$$

where $r_t = R_t/L_t = W_t/\theta_t$ is the ratio of work registrants to the civilian labor force. The corrected rate U_t^* presumably measures the unemployment rate that would have prevailed in the absence of a work registration requirement. Consequently, U_t^* ought to be related to some vector of explanatory variables X_t whose elements incorporate the influences of changes in aggregate demand, anticipated inflation, returns from unemployment insurance programs, etc. Thus, the theory implies some structural equation of the form

$$U_t^* = X_t\beta + u_t \, . \tag{4}$$

If some behavioral equation like this is substituted into equation (3), one can obtain a reduced equation in which the official and observable monthly unemployment rate U_t could be related to observable variables, X_t, and the ratio of work registrants to the civilian labor force, r_t

$$U_t = (1\text{-}r_t)(X_t\beta + u_t) + r_t = r_t + X_t\beta - r_t X_t\beta + (1\text{-}r_t)u_t \, . \tag{5}$$

Notice that in this model, r_t enters first with a prior coefficient of unity and later in interaction with X_t. I do *not* recommend that this suggestion be followed. Over the eleven years covered by the data, we have experienced many changes in government policies as well as in the composition of the U.S. adult population. I doubt that *one* structural equation could accurately track the path of the official unemployment rate.[10]

4. Impact of Government Programs on Unemployment

Government policies dealing with employment and income maintenance are intended to affect the equilibrium unemployment rate. But unemployed persons are not all alike, and only some are "involuntarily" unemployed. According to Clarkson and Meiners, Food Stamps and AFDC program participants who register at U.S. Employment Services in order to comply with program requirements, represent *net additions* to the measured number of unemployed persons; they can thus be viewed as increments to voluntary unemployment. I agree with the authors that the registration requirements will inflate measured unemployment, but I do not believe the magnitude of the estimated effects.

If we are interested in estimating the *partial effects* of particular government programs on the equilibrium unemployment rate, we should begin with a behavioral model. Given prices, wage rates, tastes and expectations, individuals will presumably distribute themselves across three mutually exclusive states (X, E, N) where X = unemployed, E = employed, and N = *not* in the labor force. Income maintenance and government employment/training programs surely affect the benefits and costs of locating in each of these three states. Expansions in unemployment insurance benefits and coverage reduce the opportunity costs of prospecting thereby tending to lengthen the duration of unemployment spells. When Social Security raised the benefit levels for disability and early retirement, it increased the gains of withdrawing from the labor force and entering the N state.[11] The effects of wage rate changes (including but not limited to the minimum wage rate), educational and training opportunities,

---

[10]Given the flaws in the model's specification, one cannot take the parameter estimates seriously. The coefficient of + 1.4531 for W_t does, however, come close to the first assignment method's result. If W_t = 1.30 for 1976 is substituted into their equation (2), it means that an elimination of the work registration requirements would lower U_t by 1.89 percentage points. I still believe that this is too large an imputation to give to the work registration requirements, but in fairness, the closeness of the two approaches is surprising.

[11]Social Security beneficiaries under early retirement and disability insurance must comply with a severe earnings test; i.e., if their wage earnings exceed a rather modest limit, they are taxed at rates of 50 percent and higher. Thus, entry into these programs means virtual withdrawal from the labor force. The data suggest that in response to higher benefit levels, there has been a sharp increase in the numbers in both Social Security programs.

employment in the Armed Services, etc. should also be incorporated into the analytical model. I would have liked to have seen the authors embed their estimation methods into a model wherein individuals optimally choose to register and possibly be counted as unemployed. This was simply not done in their paper. Their estimates that work registration requirements added 1.9 to 2.0 percentage points to the measured unemployment rate in 1976 appear to be implausibly high. In addition to the work registration requirements, factors such as (a) the changing demographic mix of the labor force which now has more individuals with higher labor turnover rates, (b) larger unemployment insurance benefit levels, and (c) higher minimum wage rates are believed to be responsible for increments of 1.23 to 1.60 percentage points in the equilibrium unemployment rate U_a^* at full employment.[12] When these adjustments are added to the Clarkson-Meiners correction, the equilibrium unemployment rate in 1976 should have been in the interval of 4.1 to 4.5 percent; i.e., if we had the labor force composition, unemployment insurance benefits, and minimum wages that prevailed in 1960, and if we had had *no* work registration requirements (but we still had Food Stamps and AFDC) the market forces would have produced an unemployment rate around 4.3 percent. It is simply *not* a credible estimate for the impact of these programs, at least in terms of my subjective estimates.

5. The Data and the Dollars--Program Evaluation

In their concluding section, Clarkson and Meiners write, "Recently, however, legislators have been explicitly tying Federal spending to measured unemployment." Formulas which relate government spending to measurable variables have historically been created and used to legitimize various allocative schemes. The State of New York pays each private university a bounty of Y_1 dollars for each baccalaureate, Y_2 for each masters, and Y_3 for each doctorate awarded during the year with $Y_1 < Y_2 < Y_3$. The variables which determine the amounts paid under the formula can and often are manipulated. Every good dean knows that publication lists will become longer and are more likely to be partly fabricated when merit pay increases are linked to the number of publications.

The allocative schemes which tie Federal spending to measured unemployment rates can be of two types: (a) to determine the *size* of the income maintenance/employment program in question in relation to other programs

---

[12]Clarkson and Meiners cite Cagan (1977) as the source for this range of 1.23 to 1.60 percentage points. In their paper for this conference, Perloff and Wachter estimate that the changing demographic mix, unemployment insurance, and minimum wages are responsible for a rise of 1.0 to 1.5 percentage points in U^*, the full employment or noninflationary unemployment rate.

such as housing subsidies, defense, ports and harbors, etc., or (*b*) to distribute the fixed budget for a program of a given size across competing governmental units. If the formula is mainly intended to allocate monies across competing jurisdictional units, the policymaker should only be concerned about "relative biases." Thus, when all jurisdictions fudge their unemployment statistics in roughly the same direction and magnitude, the *ex post* allocation may end up being the same as that which would have prevailed with honest, unbiased data.

Even when the data forming the bases for the allocative formulas are used to fix program size, Congress and the President must still work within the confines of a loosely defined budget constraint. If program budgets grow because of inflated, fabricated statistics, subsequent budget authorizations may contain provisions which incorporate the anticipated funding of the data. Indeed, the language in some legislation often puts eligibility in *relative* terms, i.e., ". . .have an average unemployment rate at least 50 percent above the national average. . . ," etc. When corrective language like this fails to achieve the intended allocative schemes, the government can take at least two kinds of alternative actions. First, the government can change the formula linking monies to other, hopefully more predictable, variables. In fact, Clarkson and Meiners point out that ". . .the Secretary of Labor may reject the official unemployment rate for a governmental unit and assign the number he thinks is more accurate." This provision can assure that the formula will achieve the desired allocations, at least from the Secretary's viewpoint.[13] A second option available to the policymaker is to leave the formula unchanged, but to use other programs to offset the misallocations resulting from an ill-conceived formula and program. Local government units can be equated to the "rotten kids" in G.S. Becker's "Theory of Social Interactions" (1974). The Federal government can be put in the role of a Super Mom who constructs an intricate system of incentives and penalties which are designed to maximize some master global objective function.[14] Thus, if Oblong receives inordinately large sums for public service employment because of its high measured unemployment rate, a central planner could rig the mass transit subsidies so that Oblong receives very little from this latter program.

On the basis of my review of the Clarkson-Meiners paper, the central theme is that the "costs" of the work registration requirements, which were

---

[13]Discretionary actions of this type (substituting a personal estimate of the New York City unemployment rate for the B.L.S. estimate) can probably be done only once or twice. The legitimacy of the resulting allocations would be questioned and ultimately rejected.

[14]The empirical verification of the theory of demand or cost curves depends on the stability of certain key behavioral equations and objective functions. I would conjecture that the meager progress which economists have made in explaining government policies is partly due to the instability of government objective functions.

tied to the Food Stamps and AFDC programs as of July 1, 1972, exceeded any possible "benefits." The authors pointed out that very few of the program participants ever got jobs and became gainfully employed. Presumably, through compliance with the work registration requirement as a condition for program participation, the recipients would gain job information. On the other side of the ledger, the "costs" of work registration ought to include at least (a) the adminstrative costs incurred by the bureaucracy, (b) the money and implicit time costs of recipients who were coerced into registering, and (c) the indirect costs of the so-called "induced institutional changes." In the concluding part of the paper, the authors claim that the high measured unemployment rates in 1975 and 1976 were *mainly* due to the work registration requirements. Moreover, these high rates *caused* the proposal and passage of several pieces of legislation that were intended to reduce the unemployment rate. In the authors' view, CETA, public service employment, person-power training programs, etc. were evidently unnecessary and would *not* have been funded by Congress *if* (and it is a very big IF) Congress and the President's economic advisers had been supplied with "accurate" unemployment data. The authors have not tried to estimate the indirect costs of these "induced institutional changes," nor have they convinced this reader that these "induced institutional changes" were *caused* by the work registration requirements.

Seemingly innocent provisions in hastily conceived legislation may lead to some unpredictable and undesirable by-products. Clarkson and Meiners are to be applauded for the care with which they have examined the provisions in the enabling legislation requiring work registration by AFDC and Food Stamps recipients. The evidence assembled in Tables 2, 3, and 4 (and the discussion accompanying these tables) supports the thesis that the requirement has inflated the measured unemployment rate. The empirical estimation of the aggregate effects of work registration requirements on measured unemployment is less satisfactory. If an analytic model of program participation had been developed, we could have examined the characteristics of the kinds of persons who would choose to register. An estimation method that is embedded in such a model is likely to provide more plausible estimates of the program's impact on measured unemployment. Finally, it is regrettable that the authors did not extend the analysis to provide an overall, systematic assessment of the benefits and costs of the work registration requirements in these two income maintenance programs.

6. Postscript

In revising their paper, the authors have radically altered the monthly regression model discussed in Part 3 above. The model no longer tries to explain the time path of the official unemployment rate U_t. The dependent variable is now defined as the first difference in monthly estimates for the labor force participation rate, $X_{1t} = \theta_t - \theta_{t-1}$, where $\theta = (L/\pi)$ is the proportion of the population base π that is *in* the labor force of employed E and unemployed X persons, $L = X + E$. Given this switch in the dependent variable, it is not surprising to find that the explanatory variables are also different. The ratio of U.I. benefits to weekly wages B and the duration of unemployment D have been dropped, although a plausible theory could be constructed in which at least B would be positively related to θ. In their revised labor force participation rate (LFPR) model, the authors treat the official unemployment rate U as an exogenous explanatory variable. Three additional variables which were mentioned in Part 4 above [X_5 = (armed forces/labor force), X_8 = (OASI recipients/labor force), and X_9 = (DI recipients/labor force)] were added to an ad hoc single equation model.

The econometric specification of the LFPR model differs from that for the original unemployment rate model of footnote 18 in two respects. First, *all* of the variables in the LFPR model are defined in terms of first differences of monthly observations. Second, the authors have dropped all of the data from 1967-71. The first change could possibly be justified if the model in original level values exhibited truly serious positive serial correlation. The second change (omitting some of the sample data) might be justified on the grounds that there was no work registration requirement before 1972. The authors do not explain their reasons for their choice of this particular econometric specification. Judged by the Durbin-Watson statistics, the serial correlation coefficients for the unemployment rate and LFPR models are roughly of the same absolute size.

Two of the explanatory variables [X_8 = (OASI/labor force) and X_{10} = (work registrants/population)] were found to have significant effects on the monthly changes in the labor force participation rate. This finding prompted the authors to conclude,

> Overall, this regression provides additional confirming evidence that the work registration requirement increases the official rate of unemployment since overall participation should not be altered if the work registration requirements merely resulted in the unemployed seeking food stamps or AFDC benefits.

The authors do not remark on the size of the regression coefficients, $\gamma_8 = -1.48$ and $\gamma_{10} = 0.27$. The former implies that each additional OASI recipient reduces the labor force by 1.48 persons, while each added work registrant contributes only 0.27 persons to the labor force. The latter is very different from the assumed one-to-one increment in the assignment method. The official unemployment rate appears in this LFPR model as a separate explanatory variable so that the model cannot give us implications about how X_{10} affects X_6. In all respects, I am of the opinion that this revised LFPR model is even less informative than the unemployment rate model of footnote 18. My remarks in Part 4 above still apply; namely, we need a behavioral model of expected utility maximization to evaluate the partial effect of the work registration requirement on unemployment statistics.

References

Alchian, A.A., and Allen, W.R. (1967). *University Economics,* Belmont, Calif.: Wadsworth Publishing Co.

Becker, G.S. (1974), "A Theory of Social Interactions," *Journal of Political Economy,* **82**: 1063-93.

_____(1968), "Crime and Punishment: An Economic Approach," *Journal of Political Economy,* **76**: 169-217.

Cagan, P. (1977), "The Reduction of Inflation and the Magnitude of Unemployment," *Contemporary Economic Problems 1977,* ed. W. Fellner. Washington, D.C.: American Enterprise Institute.

Clarkson, K.W., and Meiners, R.E. (1979), "Institutional Changes, Reported Unemployment and Induced Institutional Changes," *Carnegie-Rochester Conference Series,* **10**, eds. K. Brunner and A.H. Meltzer. Amsterdam: North-Holland.

Hutt, W.H. (1977). *The Theory of Idle Resources.* Indianapolis: Liberty Press.

Krueger, A.O. (1974), "The Political Economy of the Rent-Seeking Society," *American Economic Review,* **64**: 291-303.

Mincer, J. (1976), "Unemployment Effects of Minimum Wages," *Journal of Political Economy,* **84**: S87-S104.

Perloff, J.M., and Wachter, M.L. (1979), "A Production Function Non-Accelerating Inflation Approach to Potential Output: Is Measured Potential Output Too High?" *Carnegie-Rochester Conference Series,* **10**, eds. K. Brunner and A.H. Meltzer. Amsterdam: North-Holland.

Perry, G.L. (1977), "Potential Output and Productivity," *Brookings Papers on Economic Activity,* **2**. Washington, D.C.: The Brookings Institution.

NORTH-SOUTH ECONOMIC AND POLITICAL RELATIONS
How Much Change?

Rachel M^cCULLOCH*
Harvard University

I. Introduction

"North-South economic relations. . .have come to the forefront of inter-national economics and politics," observed Jagdish Bhagwati in his introduction to a recent conference volume on the New International Economic Order proposals.[1] By 1978, however, it is more accurate to add "and have again receded into relative obscurity." The New International Economic Order is no longer new, if indeed it ever was, and its ubiquitous acronymic designation has become yet another tidbit in the alphabet soup of world politics. We still hear from time to time about progress or the lack of it in the "ongoing North-South dialogue," but whatever the negotiators have to say to one another at this stage, it no longer rates headlines. Despite dire threats a few years back of many new OPECs and of the imminent exhaustion of world resources, prices of most primary commodities have fallen well below the historic peaks reached during 1972-74. Even the price of oil has fallen in real terms, and the issue of indexation of commodity export prices has dropped from view.

Of the specific proposals associated with demands for the establishment of a new order more consistent with the economic and political requirements of the less-developed countries (LDCs), most have been relegated to the limbo of international task forces, working groups, and consultations. Only in the area of commodity exports and LDC debt does there appear to be any intention on the part of the industrialized nations to accede to LDC demands, and even in these areas, the concessions offered fall far short of the goals set by the developing nations. The slow recovery of the industrialized nations from the recession of the mid-1970s has resulted in the indefinite tabling of proposals to facilitate the expansion of LDC manufactured exports. Instead, the LDCs are now struggling to retain market positions already achieved, in the face of threatened new protectionist moves by Northern nations. The industrialized world appears unwilling or unable to cope with the internal economic and political consequences of increased imports.

---

*This is a revised version of the paper presented at the Conference. In recent usage, "North" designates collectively the industrialized economies, located mainly in the Northern hemisphere; "South" denotes the less-developed countries, located mainly in the Southern hemisphere. Comments of the Conference partici-pants are gratefully acknowledged. I am also indebted to Jorge Dominguez and Albert Hirschman for their comments on the earlier version, and to Jagdish Bhagwati and Robert Repetto for helpful conversations.

[1] Bhagwati (1977, p. 1).

However, despite the very modest record achieved thus far by the South in advancing the specific programs of the NIEO, it would be erroneous to conclude that nothing "new" has come onto the international scene. In fact, there are three important developments which have come about or at least been pressed forward as a result of the protracted NIEO negotiations. These concern the perceived requirements for LDC economic progress and even the appropriate ways in which this progress should be gauged, the actual and potential importance of the LDCs as a force in the international economy, and the political role of the LDCs in the major international organizations.

This paper analyzes the underlying forces which promoted the dramatic confrontations of 1973-75 and assesses the consequences of these and subsequent developments for North-South political and economic relations. The discussion focuses upon three aspects of the drive for a NIEO:

Political evolution. The initial demands of the South upon the North, as well as the initial response from the North, reflected the nexus of two key developments. The emergence of an effective economic and political coalition of LDCs allowed these nations to address the North with a single voice; conditions in world commodity markets gave Northern policymakers an unprecedented interest in listening closely to that voice. However, just as altered perceptions on the parts of both South and North led to the sudden emergence of the NIEO as a world issue, subsequent modifications of those perceptions have caused its relegation to a lower position on the international agenda. Furthermore, not only the perceived distribution of economic and political power has changed, but also the focus of the debate itself. Many NIEO sympathizers in the North, convinced of the failure of traditional growth-oriented development strategies to aid the world's poorest inhabitants, began by taking the rhetoric of the North-South debate at face value. But neither the specific proposals nor the general thrust of the NIEO drive could long support the illusion that real progress for that billion or so living in conditions of absolute poverty was either a primary motivation or a likely outcome of the NIEO. Many Northern supporters of traditional development ends have thus withdrawn their approval from the NIEO proposals and have pressed instead for a different kind of initiative.

Economic issues. The most conspicuous aspect of the ongoing NIEO drive has been the somewhat lengthy list of specific economic proposals covering trade, aid, investment, and technology transfer. That list has gradually evolved, with some proposals coming into sharp focus and others fading into the background, as a result of changing economic conditions and perceived bargaining strength. It now appears that representatives of North and South have agreed, at least tacitly, to turn the New International Economic Order into a rescue operation for the old political order. Fundamental changes crucial to long-run economic prospects for growth--in particular, reduction of barriers to trade--as well as fundamental changes crucial to elimination of absolute poverty--structural reforms *within* developing countries--have been pushed aside in favor of proposals less potentially disruptive to the current distribution of wealth and power, in both North and South. The focus of negotiations has been wealth transfers rather than wealth creation, redistribution rather than development.

Contradictions and conflicts. While North-South negotiations have focused primarily upon specific proposals for changes in international economic and political relations, some basic conflicts and contradictions on broader questions have emerged in the process. These conflicts and contradictions are as likely to divide North from North as North from South. Central issues raised concern the appropriate role of market forces in determining incomes of individuals and of nations, the relationship between market allocation of scarce resources and the theoretical benefits of perfect competition, the implications of the Southern quest for national sovereignty, and the distinction between inequality and inequity.

II. Political Evolution

The ability of the developing nations to bring their drive for establishment of a new order to the forefront of world politics--if only for a limited time--reflected two quite separate developments, one largely political, the other economic. The first was the gradual emergence, beginning in the 1960s, of an effective coalition of LDCs capable of maintaining a unified position in negotiations with the industralized nations. This development has been called the rise of LDC "trade unionism."[2] Second, the stage was set for the LDC "strike" by the commodity boom of 1972-74, fueled by rapidly increasing growth in the industrialized nations, the Arab oil boycott of 1973, and the subsequent OPEC success in achieving unilaterally a massive increase in the price of oil.

The emergence of an effective bloc enabled the LDCs to speak with a single voice, while events in world markets for primary commodities gave the industrialized nations new reason to listen. Following the oil crisis of 1973, control over primary commodities came to be seen as a major source of power. Dependence upon imported raw materials was thus viewed as entailing important constraints upon political or economic actions which might antagonize the

---

[2]Ibid.

suppliers of these imports.[3] However, a subsequent reevaluation of the nature of "commodity power" has led to major shifts in the positions of both Northern and Southern negotiators.

A. Emergence of a Unified "South"

The formation of an LDC political-economic bloc goes back at least as far as the 1950s, when the United States and the U.S.S.R. vied for allies among the newly independent nations.[4] The Bandung Conference in 1955, attended by representatives of 29 African and Asian developing nations, may have been the first formal exploration of the potential gains from such cooperation. Toward the end of the 1950s, national leaders including Nasser, Nehru, Nkrumah, Sukarno, and Tito gained prominence in their roles within the non-aligned group. Four "summit conferences" of the nonaligned nations were held between 1961 and 1973, with the number of nations represented increasing over that period from 25 to 75. The initial philosophy of the nonaligned movement was political rather than economic, centering upon decolonization and independence on one hand and on neutrality in the East-West rivalry on the other. However, nearly three-fourths of the developing nations had become members of the nonaligned group by 1973.

The shift within the nonaligned bloc from a largely political orientation to one stressing economic issues came with the 1970 Lusaka summit meeting, attended by representatives of 53 nations. The emphasis at this meeting was upon individual and collective self-reliance, after the Chinese example. Disappointed with the meager results from bilateral aid programs and efforts through the United Nations Conference on Trade and Development (UNCTAD) during the 1960s, the members now sought to take development "into their own hands"[5] through various forms of increased cooperation among developing nations. With the receding of East-West tensions, the political objectives of the nonaligned movement were less pressing, and it had become increasingly obvious that "sovereignty, to be meaningful, requires economic decolonization and a developed economy."[6] An economic declaration adopted at the Lusaka summit gave special attention to the issue of natural resources.

The specifically economic objectives of the developing nations have been expressed in the international community through the Group of 77. This bloc

---

[3]Nye (1976, p. 133).

[4]On the political evolution of the nonaligned bloc, see Jankowitsch and Sauvant (1976).

[5]Ibid., p. 19.

[6]Ibid.

first coalesced at the 1963 UN General Assembly session with a membership of 75, and grew to 77 by the time of the first UN Conference on Trade and Development (UNCTAD I) in 1964.[7] The group continued to add members as more nations achieved independence, so that the 77 were in fact more than 100 by the early 1970s.

By the time of the Algiers summit conference of nonaligned nations in September, 1973, many of the economic goals of the Group of 77 had become an integral part of the non-aligned position. While the Lusaka statement on economic issues had stressed collective self-reliance, the central theme of the Algiers declaration was gains to the developing nations from solidarity in confrontations with the industrialized nations. The document emphasized improved terms of trade for commodity exporters, a central concern of the Group of 77 since UNCTAD I.

With the Algiers summit, the originally political nonaligned bloc and the economically-oriented Group of 77 effectively joined forces in what became a highly conspicuous political *and* economic pressure group within and outside the UN. That the coalition had political as well as economic objectives has tended to be overlooked by both supporters and critics of the NIEO drive. While most of the specific proposals put forth have concerned global economic arrangements and the LDC demand for a larger share of world wealth, a collateral goal has been the achievement of full political status within the community of nations. Thus, full participation in the decision-making process has been sought "not merely to ensure that the developing countries' interests are safeguarded but equally as an assertion of their rights as members of an international community."[8]

If the emergence of a unified South, ready to seize upon a uniquely propitious moment in world events, puzzled some Northern observers, all the more puzzling has been continued Southern solidarity in the face of obvious sources of internal strain. Given a group of more than 100 nations including the oil-rich, the "middle-income" nations with other important primary exports or considerable industrial capacity, and the 40 or so poorest nations with GNP per capita less than $200, important divergences of interest are inevitable. Yet despite some internal disagreements over such issues as generalized debt relief and seabed mineral exploitation, the bloc has found more reason to agree than to disagree. As one writer sums up, "What do Iran, Peru, Zambia, and Sri Lanka have in common? Perhaps only a shared sense of relative deprivation vis-à-vis

---

[7]Nye (1974).

[8]Bhagwati (1977, p. 1).

257

the OECD countries." In fact, however, Southern tacticians have succeeded to some extent in tailoring bloc strategy to the needs of the diverse subgroups. Differential treatment of the poorest nations has been consistently sought, and OPEC has linked oil price negotiations with Northern consuming nations to the full range of NIEO demands.[9]

B. Commodities and OPEC

Developing nations' exports of primary commodities have been a leading issue in negotiations with the industrialized nations for many years, predating even the founding of the UN. It is, therefore, natural that the events which brought the LDCs' demands into the headlines centered upon commodity markets. The Arab oil embargo and OPEC price hike were not the first but perhaps the most dramatic of the events which made many policymakers in the industrialized nations believe that market relationships had undergone a permanent fundamental change. The prices of many primary commodities had risen rapidly in the 1972-73 period, most reaching their 1972-75 peaks before the oil boycott. The publication of *The Limits to Growth*[10] in 1972 was accompanied by widespread fears that rapid economic growth in the industrialized nations would imminently deplete world supplies of many exhaustible primary commodities and outstrip the growth of world food production, leaving much of the world to suffer progressive starvation. Whatever the scientific shortcomings of the analysis, rising prices for virtually every primary commodity seemed to arrest at least temporarily the effectiveness of rational counterarguments.

The oil boycott and subsequent quadrupling of the price of oil took the consuming nations by surprise, although in retrospect there was ample prior warning of OPEC's intent and considerable evidence of its increasing collective power.[11] The immediate effects of the oil crisis were mixed. While talk of "commodity power" and "many new OPECs" motivated some in the industrialized nations to pay greater attention to the demands of the LDCs, others, firm believers in the strength of market forces, remained confident that OPEC's disintegration would not be long in coming and even proposed a variety of strategies intended to hasten that end.[12]

---

[9] Hansen (1977, p. 9). On Southern solidarity, also see Branislav and Ruggie (1976).

[10] Meadows et al. (1972).

[11] See Vernon (1976, esp. pts. 1 and 2).

[12] One strategy proposal still in vogue is the use of sealed bids to encourage "cheating" by members of the cartel.

With the passage of time, both positions have been modified. Despite attempts by the producers of other primary commodities to emulate OPEC, prices of most primary commodities fell dramatically as the industrialized nations' demand dropped, in part reflecting substitution and conservation, but mainly as a result of the worldwide recession. But OPEC was able to maintain and even raise the price of oil in the face of declining world consumption. Most observers have concluded that oil is indeed a special case and that OPEC's success depends critically upon specific supply and demand conditions not common to other commodities. But while the ability of other commodity producers to sustain large unilateral price increases is no longer perceived as a significant threat, their power to inflict costly short-term supply interruptions may be considerable. Thus, there is continuing interest, although at a somewhat lower level than in previous years, in reaching some compromise in negotiations with the developing nations.

C. Response of the Industrialized Nations

The Algiers conference marked the beginning of a two-year period of escalating confrontation, mainly rhetorical in nature, between the LDCs and the industrialized nations. The UN General Assembly somewhat hastily arranged a Sixth Special Session devoted to raw materials and development for April, 1974, although a special session on development had already been planned for 1975. It was at the Sixth Special Session that the General Assembly adopted a "Declaration on the Establishment of a New International Economic Order," thus officially christening the LDCs' drive for a fundamental restructuring of the international system.[13] A few months later, the General Assembly passed a second resolution, a "Charter of Economic Rights and Duties of States," in which the LDCs sought to establish the "right" of commodity producers to band together to achieve more favorable terms, as well as the "duty" of the consuming nations to refrain from retaliatory actions. From several other LDC-dominated conferences similar principles and programs emanated, along with rhetorical calls for Third World unity. But the cycle of confrontation and escalation came to an abrupt end with the Seventh Special Session of the UN General Assembly in September, 1975.[14]

The NIEO was put forward on the heels of an unprecedented increase in the world price of oil and at a time when the prices of many other primary

---

[13] The phrase had, however, already appeared in documents of the Algiers conference.

[14] On the events leading up to the Seventh Special Session, see McCulloch (1977) and references cited there.

commodities were near historic peaks. Furthermore, the NIEO proposals were accompanied by a quite open threat of the further exercise of commodity power by the LDCs in the event of noncooperation on the part of the industrialized nations. Thus, the responses from the developed nations reflected at least in part the degree of their dependence upon primary commodity imports. When the UN General Assembly adopted the Charter of Economic Rights and Duties of States by a roll-call vote, there were 120 votes in favor, 10 abstentions, and 6 against. These 6 were Belgium, Denmark, Federal Republic of Germany, Luxembourg, the United Kingdom, and the U.S. (The earlier Declaration on the Establishment of a New International Economic Order had been adopted without a vote over the objections of a number of industrialized nations.)

The official position initially adopted by the U.S. was uncompromisingly negative.[15] Not only the specific proposals of the NIEO were rejected, but also the underlying assumption that major structural modifications of the international system were required to eliminate biases against the economic interests of the poorer nations. At least rhetorically, the U.S. became the champion of free markets. Many in the government and outside firmly believed that OPEC would soon crumble as a consequence of internal conflicts. Furthermore, among the major developed nations, the U.S. relied to a relatively small degree on imported raw materials other than oil. An early 1975 U.S. government task force report set U.S. dependence on imports at 15 percent of total requirements of key raw materials, while the corresponding figures for Western Europe and Japan were 75 and 90 percent.[16] Thus, U.S. policymakers were better able to risk the political and economic consequences of alienating the developing nations.

Within the U.S. government, the Treasury supported a free market approach, particularly in primary commodity trade, while the State Department favored a more flexible negotiating stance. In May, 1975, Secretary of State Kissinger made the first official step toward accommodation of LDC goals by announcing that the U.S. was ready to discuss commodity arrangements on a case-by-case basis, although Treasury officials remained adamant in their opposition. Secretary Kissinger's speech for the UN Seventh Special Session in September, 1975 gave an even clearer indication of a major shift in U.S. policy. Written in a positive and even conciliatory tone, the speech contained numerous specific proposals, endorsed by both State and Treasury department officials, aimed principally at increasing financial resource flows to the developing

---

[15] A detailed account of U.S. policy formation in response to Southern demands is given in Cohen (1977, ch. 6).

[16] Cited in Council Report No. 16, United States-Japan Trade Council, March 12, 1975.

nations. But with regard to commodity agreements, Treasury officials continued to insist on free markets. As late as January, 1976, Assistant Treasury Secretary Gerald Parsky reiterated Treasury's refusal to go along with LDC demands for a system of commodity agreements.[17]

The official U.S. position on commodities had moved slightly, but significantly, by the time of UNCTAD IV in May, 1976. Although the agenda of the month-long meeting included many other issues, particularly those relating to debt moratorium and transfer of technology, commodities again were the central focus. The U.S., along with West Germany, Japan, and the U.K., agreed to participate in further meetings to discuss the establishment of a "common fund" to support world commodity prices through buffer stock arrangements. However, one U.S. delegate emphasized at the close of the session that the U.S. had agreed only to "consultations prior to a decision whether to enter into negotiations" on a common fund.[18] Secretary of State Kissinger's speech to UNCTAD IV had also proposed the establishment of an International Resources Bank to promote resource development in LDCs, but the conference failed to endorse even a resolution to examine the Kissinger proposal. Opponents believed that the bank proposal was intended to undermine LDC efforts to establish a common fund.

Although the nations of the European Community (EC) supported the U.S. in rejecting many of the NIEO proposals, the EC nations were more attuned in attitude and practice to socialist planning concepts and hence less alarmed than the U.S. by the frankly interventionist tone of the NIEO program. While American policymakers were still expressing unqualified opposition to almost any sort of international commodity agreement, the nine EC nations were negotiating the terms of a major trade and aid agreement with 46 African, Caribbean, and Pacific (ACP) developing countries, including former colonies and Commonwealth states. Under the Lomé Convention, signed on February 28, 1975, the EC extended to these 46 LDCs (and another 6 added later) some of the same benefits sought on a global basis by the Group of 77. Perhaps most important, the agreement provided the ACP countries with completely free and unlimited access to the enlarged EC market for all exports except some agricultural products covered by the EC's Common Agricultural Policy (CAP). In contrast to earlier EC agreements with some of the same countries, no reverse preferences were required of the ACP countries. For beef, sugar, rum, and bananas, special supply-purchase agreements were concluded. The Lomé Convention also established an export earnings stabilization facility (Stabex)

---

[17]Cohen (1977, pp. 83-85).

[18]*Wall Street Journal*, June 1, 1976.

covering 14 primary commodities. Under Stabex, export earnings from sales to the EC are stabilized on a commodity-by-commodity basis; members become eligible for loans or grants when earnings fall short of their average over the four preceding years. Finally, the Lomé Convention included a number of provisions intended to facilitate industrialization through financial and technical assistance.[19]

D. North-South Dialogue Outside the United Nations

After the initial confusion that followed the Arab oil embargo and OPEC price increases, the major consuming nations sought ways to protect themselves against future supply interruptions and to negotiate a lowering of oil prices. In November, 1974, the International Energy Agency (IEA) was formed under U.S. leadership. The 16 member nations included all the major oil consumers except France, together accounting for about 80 percent of world oil imports.[20] The IEA was in part an attempt to create a "counter cartel" to negotiate more effectively with OPEC,[21] but its major focus was cooperative action in the face of any future embargo. Target stocks and reserve capacity sufficient for 60 days consumption were designated, along with guidelines for reduction of demand and allocation of supplies in the event of a reduction in import supplies.[22]

U.S. efforts to initiate bilateral negotiations with OPEC on the oil price issue alone did not succeed. As it became clear to American and European policymakers that the collapse of OPEC was not imminent, the IEA members acceded to OPEC insistence on linking progress on oil to other agenda items of the NIEO. The new forum was to include not only energy producers and consumers, but also representatives of the non-OPEC developing nations. The Paris-based Conference on International Economic Cooperation (CIEC), which came to be known as the North-South Dialogue, was formally initiated in December, 1975. CIEC was made up of 8 representatives of the North, including the U.S., 7 OPEC delegates, and 12 representatives of the non-OPEC developing nations. Although CIEC was not part of the UN machinery, observers from various UN agencies were invited. At the initial meeting, four commissions--on energy, raw materials, development, and finance--were established.

---

[19] For details of the Lomé Convention, see Bywater (1975) and *IMF Survey*, July 4, 1977, p. 210.

[20] Vernon (1976, p. 212).

[21] Ibid.

[22] Ibid., p. 262.

The final session of CIEC was postponed until the end of May, 1977 to allow the new Carter administration time to formulate its position on North-South issues. Nevertheless, there was little to show for 18 months of negotiations. By mid-1977 it had become clear that international negotiations would have little effect on oil prices; at the same time, the consuming nations found themselves living "permanently" with high-priced oil with less disastrous political and economic consequences than initially envisioned. The non-OPEC developing countries came away with two minor concessions from the North. First, an additional $1 billion in emergency aid for the poorest nations had been pledged. The industrialized nations also gave ground, at least in principle, on the common fund issue by agreeing that such a fund should be a "key instrument" in achieving LDC goals of stable prices and higher earnings from commodity exports.[23] If the concrete accomplishments of CIEC were at best minor--a *Japan Times* editorial[24] described the final results as "a productive deadlock"--the conciliatory tone of the proceedings provided a significant contrast to the rhetorical skirmishes characteristic of UN forums, even in the relatively calm post-Seventh Special Session period.

Yet another "North-South dialogue," this time free not only of official ties to the UN but also to individual nations, was instituted in December, 1977. The independent Commission on International Development Issues, promoted and financed by the World Bank, is a "blue-ribbon" group headed by former West German Chancellor Willy Brandt and including no less than three other former prime ministers among its seventeen members.[25]

Perhaps significantly, on December 19, 1977, the UN General Assembly passed a resolution affirming that "all negotiations of a global nature on establishment of the new international economic order should take place within the framework of the UN system."[26] UNCTAD V has been scheduled for May, 1979, and a special session of the General Assembly to assess progress toward establishment of the NIEO has been set for 1980.

E. Redistribution for Whom?

An early response by Northern critics to the NIEO centered upon its actual redistributive consequences once the broad categories of North and South were appropriately broken down into groups of countries with differing

---

[23] *Wall Street Journal*, June 2, 1977.

[24] Quoted in Council Report No. 31, United States-Japan Trade Council, June 24, 1977.

[25] *Newsweek*, December 12, 1977, p. 70.

[26] *UN Chronicle*, January, 1978, p. 56.

economic and social conditions. For example, it was widely appreciated that generally higher prices for primary commodities would hurt the very poorest developing nations, many of which are dependent upon imports of food and fuel. The Kissinger strategy for splitting the Southern bloc rested upon the design of North-South redistributive programs with specific appeal to different national groupings within the unified South. However, this approach proved unsuccessful, presumably because Southern nations saw greater potential gains from maintaining bloc solidarity than through notoriously fickle Northern generosity.

A different distributional issue led some dedicated Northern supporters of international redistribution to oppose the NIEO. The NIEO rhetoric relies upon the ethical appeal of redistribution from rich to poor, that is, from rich to poor people, the rectification of supposed inequities resulting from inequality of opportunity (as distinct from inequality of ability or effort). But the actual proposals put forward by the South focus entirely upon international redistribution, and, as Peter Kenen has noted, "governments that have done little indeed to rectify internal inequality are not embarrassed to demand an international rectification."[27] In fact, international resource transfers might in some cases even be used to shore up the position of entrenched Southern elite groups.

A growing number of those Northerners who advocate special or preferential policies to promote development goals--as opposed to a completely laissez-faire approach--have adopted a new outlook which has become known as a "basic human needs" (BHN) orientation. Rather than relying upon overall growth to yield "trickle-down" benefits, the BHN strategy seeks direct means to improve the circumstances of those one billion or so now living in "absolute poverty." In contrast to the recent LDC emphasis upon increased unconditional North-South resource transfers, BHN would make such transfers conditional upon implementation of programs to improve nutrition, sanitation, health care, and basic education for the poorest of the poor. Apart from questions of feasibility and effectiveness, BHN presents obvious conflicts with the Southern goal of increased national sovereignty, as well as with the usual economic analysis of redistributive transfers. These issues are addressed in a later section.

III. Specific Proposals

By the time of UNCTAD IV in May, 1976, most of the vaguely worded demands contained in the "Programme of Action on the Establishment of a New International Economic Order" adopted at the Sixth Special Session two

---

[27] Kenen (1977, p. 53).

years earlier had become concrete proposals. The integrated program for commodities was viewed by most as the central issue at UNCTAD IV and remained a top agenda item in North-South negotiations subsequently. The two other key topics at UNCTAD IV were generalized debt relief and transfer of technology. In these three areas, varying degrees of compromise were achieved. The industrialized nations conceded to LDC demands to the extent of agreeing on steps "towards the negotiation of a common fund" for financing of buffer stocks, thus moving a small but significant distance toward eventual implementation of the integrated program. No accord was reached on the subject of debt relief, with the creditor countries declining the overall approach favored by the LDCs and maintaining their position that action should be taken as required on a case-by-case basis, rather than through such general measures as a special debt conference.[28] With respect to technology transfer, the private ownership of most Northern scientific and technical knowledge of interest to LDCs precluded any major accomplishments, but a compromise program to facilitate LDC development and adaptation of "appropriate" technology with Northern support and assistance was adopted.[29]

UNCTAD IV reaffirmed the perennial LDC goal of expanding industrial exports to the developed countries with resolutions on preferential access, internal adjustment by developed countries to permit "redeployment" of less internationally competitive industries to LDCs, and special and preferential treatment of LDCs within the General Agreement on Tariffs and Trade (GATT) multilateral trade negotiations.[30] Secretary of State Kissinger also gave token attention to the trade issue with a number of specific proposals to improve LDC access to the markets of the industrialized nations. But both at UNCTAD IV and thereafter, the issue of trade in manufactured goods has been relegated to a position on the North-South agenda clearly below that of the common fund for generalized debt relief.

In light of the potential importance of expanded LDC industrial exports in achieving development goals, the low priority currently accorded the trade issue deserves comment. Stabilization of commodity prices and generalized debt relief are measures which minimize disruptions of present LDC internal economic arrangements. In contrast, gains through expansion of industrial output in the LDCs require significant internal transformations of those economies, and thus may carry with them potent threats to current regimes.

---

[28]Council Report No. 38, United States-Japan Trade Council, July 2, 1976.

[29]*UN Chronicle*, June, 1976, p. 43.

[30]Ibid., p. 37.

From the Northern perspective, commodity agreements could bring short-term relief from troublesome price fluctuations, while the cost of these efforts is at least partially hidden from consumers and taxpayers. In contrast, the gains from freer trade in processed primary commodities and manufactured goods may appear slight in comparison with the immediate economic and political costs of internal adjustment.

A. *Primary Commodities and the Common Fund*

The "Programme of Action" adopted at the Sixth Special Session was organized under ten headings. "Fundamental problems of raw materials and primary commodities as related to trade and development" was the first of these ten. Included among the proposed measures in this section was the "preparation of an over-all integrated program. . .for a comprehensive range of commodities of export interest to developing countries." The UNCTAD secretariat subsequently produced the "Integrated Programme for Commodities,"[31] which was to become a central issue in North-South negotiations for several years.

While proposals to achieve development aims through commodity agreements are hardly new, having been debated at great length since UNCTAD I in 1964 and even earlier, the approach of linking together a large group of commodities to be covered by a common set of arrangements is a significant departure from past efforts. The program, initially envisioned as covering a list of 18 products (bananas, bauxite, cocoa, coffee, copper, cotton, hard fibers, iron ore, jute, manganese, meat, phosphates, rubber, sugar, tea, tropical timber, tin, and vegetable oils), is intended to raise and stabilize export earnings of LDC producers and to increase the degree of processing in the producing countries. As originally set forth, the program consisted of five elements: creation of buffer stocks for 10 storable commodities, financing of the buffer stock operation through a "common fund" to which both producers and consumers would contribute, improved and expanded export earnings stabilization, long-term supply and purchase agreements, and expansion of processing in LDC producing nations.

Negotiations concerning the integrated program have centered primarily upon the proposed establishment of the common fund. LDC negotiators see the fund as critical to the success of the buffer stock operations, since past buffering attempts have failed primarily as a result of inadequate resources.[32] Also, supporters say, a common fund available to stabilize each of the 10 commodities

---

[31] UNCTAD (1975).

[32] *IMF Survey*, July 4, 1977, p. 221.

would not have to be as large as the sum of adequate separate funds for each individually and would be more credit-worthy than individual funds because of diversification. The actual amount required for the fund was calculated by UNCTAD at $6 billion, $3 billion to be provided initially and another $3 billion "on call."[33]

Initial Southern emphasis upon a "just and equitable relationship" between the prices of commodity exports and those of food and manufactured goods imported by the LDCs created some confusion as to whether buffer stock floor and ceiling prices would be designated through indexation. Later documents have clarified that restrictions on exports and production would be employed in conjunction with buffering if participants in a given agreement should establish a target price higher than the long-run market equilibrium price "in order to protect the purchasing power of the commodity."[34]

By the end of 1977, opposition in principle to the common fund proposal on the part of the U.S. and the European Community had given way to protracted but inconclusive negotiations on the specifics of the financing and use of the fund. The LDCs sought direct contributions from consuming countries, while the industrialized nations offered only to pool the resources of existing commodity arrangements, along with those of any established in the future.[35] Disagreement over the uses for which the fund would be available has centered on the "second window" proposal. Originally the fund was viewed as a common source from which individual buffer stocks could obtain necessary financing. However, the Group of 77 subsequently sought to earmark part of the fund for other uses, including research and development, marketing arrangements, and commodity diversification.[36]

Extensive buffer stock operations are the central feature of the proposed integrated program. The shortcomings of commodity buffer stock arrangements as a means of achieving greater price stability are by now familiar.[37] First, designating appropriate floor and ceiling prices around the long-term equilibrium price requires operators to distinguish successfully between short-run price fluctuations and changes in fundamental market relationships, a task which is unlikely to be performed with much success. Second, to the extent that a buffer facility actually increases total stocks held worldwide, a real resource cost is

---

[33]Ibid.

[34]Ibid.

[35]*Wall Street Journal*, December 2, 1977.

[36]*Economist*, March 25, 1978, pp. 91-92.

[37]See, for example, Johnson (1977).

entailed. However, the establishment of official buffer stocks may depress private holding of inventories. This would reduce the social resource cost of a buffer of a given size, but also reduce its effects on price stability. Third, even if floor and ceiling prices are appropriately designated, an open-ended source of financing and stored commodities is required to ensure success. In the absence of these, speculative pressures will undermine the operation whenever either constraint is approached. Finally, suppression of underlying instability eliminates any market premium for risk-bearing. Thus, a successful buffer may depress the long-term price trend of a particular commodity by in effect providing a subsidy to a risky undertaking.

With respect to the proposed single common fund, several further problems arise. First, because much of the movement of primary commodity prices is tied to the world business cycle, the advantages from pooling and diversification would probably be minor. Second, if, as in all past buffering arrangements, total resources prove inadequate, rules for allocating the available funds across the various individual buffers will be a perennial source of conflict. Third, there appears to be no particular reason why financing for auxiliary commodity-related activities ought to be tied to the buffer stock finance. Finally, while the avowed purpose of the buffer stock arrangements is price stabilization, a $6 billion fund could be managed in such a way as to produce quite sizable price movements--up or down--in any one commodity.

All this takes as given the objective of reducing commodity export price fluctuations, yet there is little evidence that export price instability is, in itself, an obstacle to economic development.[38] Instability of export earnings may be a problem for undiversified LDC economies with limited access to private capital markets. However, direct control over price movements is not required to provide export earnings stabilization, as this can be done through contingent loans based upon export earnings shortfalls below trend.

Two earnings stabilization arrangements are already in existence. Under the Stabex system established by the Lomé Convention, 52 developing nations are eligible for loans or grants to make up for earnings shortfalls on a commodity-by-commodity basis, relative to exports to the EC during the four previous years.[39] The export earnings stabilization facility of the International Monetary Fund (IMF) recently liberalized and expanded, allows commodity producers to smooth overall earnings shortfalls reflected in balance of payments deficits. The shortfalls are measured relative to a five-year average centered in

---

[38] See Kreinin and Finger (1976) and sources cited there.

[39] Bywater (1975).

the current year.[40] UNCTAD's integrated program includes several proposals for further liberalization of access to the IMF facility. One proposed revision would take account of changes in the import purchasing power of a country's exports, thus providing stabilization of real rather than nominal earnings.

B. Trade in Manufactures

Traditional theories of development have emphasized the expansion of industrial output, either through import substitution or, more recently, through export promotion. For several decades, the LDCs have sought preferential access for their manufactured exports to the protected markets of the industrialized nations. This was the basic objective of the Generalized System of Preferences (GSP), promoted within UNCTAD by the Group of 77. Under the GSP, LDC exports would enter industrialized markets duty-free or at reduced tariff rates.[41] After more than a decade of opposition in principle, particularly on the part of the U.S., followed by protracted negotiations over specifics, all the major industrialized nations have now implemented some type of GSP arrangement.[42] On January 1, 1976, the U.S. became the last nation to offer this special treatment.

GSP systems have two quite different effects on "beneficiary" nations. For any given level of LDC exports, they raise the net revenue accruing to the exporter by the amount of the tariff reduction. Furthermore, the system tends to increase eligible exports in the same way as an export subsidy. But whatever the theoretical merits of the GSP, actual gains have been rather meager, thanks to the many restrictions imposed upon eligibility of countries and of particular exports. Especially important is the exclusion from eligibility of a number of import-sensitive items which have caused severe internal adjustment problems for the industrialized nations in recent years. In effect, precisely those labor-intensive manufactures in which the LDCs have already achieved considerable market penetration in the absence of special treatment--i.e., those in which they have the greatest demonstrated comparative advantage--are explicitly omitted from preferential treatment. Of these, by far the most important is textiles, where even the present high level of imports by industrialized nations, limited by both high tariffs and pervasive quantitative

---

[40]On the IMF facility and the effect of the December, 1975 liberalization on subsequent operations, see *IMF Survey*, March 7, 1977, pp. 65-69.

[41]On development of the preference issue, see Wall (1971).

[42]For details of the various national schemes, see *IMF Survey*, June 23, 1975, pp. 188-89, and July 4, 1977, p. 214.

restrictions, greatly understates the already established export potential of the LDCs in this area.

The GSP depends for its effect on preferential treatment of LDC exports. A second type of approach with potential benefits to LDCs is multilateral most-favored-nation (MFN), i.e., nondiscriminatory, tariff reductions on products of greatest interest to present and potential LDC suppliers.[43] However, the emphasis placed by the LDCs upon preferential and nonreciprocal treatment left them at the sidelines in the Tokyo Round negotiations. These talks, while having the expansion of trade with LDCs as one stated goal, nonetheless focused primarily upon those products of greatest interest to the industrialized nations. One critique of the NIEO proposals[44] suggests that the LDCs may have done themselves considerable damage by insisting upon their right to maintain their own high tariff walls. Not only has this deprived them of a potentially useful bargaining tool within the GATT framework, but it has also slowed the growth of intra-LDC trade.

The "Lima Declaration," adopted by the Second General Conference of the UN Industrial Development Organization (UNIDO) in 1975, noted that developing nations constitute 60 percent of the world's population but account for only 7 percent of total world industrial output. The declaration proposed an increase in LDC industrial output to bring that share to 25 percent by the year 2000. Coming at a time when policymakers in most industrialized countries were already confronting unmanageable internal adjustment problems in import-competing industries, this new "threat" from the LDCs received widespread attention.

The issue raised by the Lima Declaration is central not only to development prospects but to the continued growth and prosperity of the industrialized nations themselves. Despite the implementation of "trade adjustment assistance" in the U.S. and similar policies in other industrial nations, the developed world has failed to solve the key problem of making smooth and politically acceptable changes in the internal allocation of resources in response to shifts in international comparative advantage. Instead, pressure for new trade barriers in the U.S. and Europe has slowed, and threatens even to reverse, the gradual movement toward freer trade of the post-World War II period. The increasing resort to elaborate nontariff arrangements to limit competition from abroad has had three important effects. First, prospects for expanded industrial exports by the LDCs, even without preferential treatment, are diminished. Second, a political

---

[43] For a comparison of LDC benefits from GSP and nondiscriminatory trade liberalization, see Baldwin and Murray (1977).

[44] Kreinin and Finger (1976).

atmosphere conducive to pleas for special protection diverts entrepreneurial attention from productivity improvements to lobbying efforts. Finally, by restricting the ability of other nations to sell their exports, each country forgoes possible opportunities for expansion of its own export sector. Thus, true long-run adjustment, in which resources are drawn from declining industries into more productive uses, is aborted.

The argument is sometimes made that expanding the market for LDC manufactured exports in the industrialized nations results in gains to those who are already most prosperous in the LDCs, while the cost is borne primarily by the least affluent workers in the industrialized nations. A large fraction of LDC exports to the developed nations come from that handful of nations which have already made substantial progress in industrialization, mainly but not exclusively "middle income" developing nations. Furthermore, in almost every developing nation, urban industrial workers have incomes far above those earned by workers in rural areas. It is also true that workers displaced from the labor-intensive import-competing industries in the industrialized nations are typically older and less well educated than the average worker in manufacturing as a whole; a disproportionate number are female or members of minority groups. Thus, these workers already earn wages which are low by national standards.

However, these facts do not constitute a case for increased protectionism on the part of the industrialized nations. Empirical evidence has accumulated to support the thesis that export promotion is an effective growth strategy.[45] Thus, while relatively few LDCs have succeeded in following this route in the past, there is an important argument for keeping it open for other nations. Second, while the typical displaced worker has labor market characteristics commanding a relatively low wage, workers with the same characteristics do earn higher incomes in expanding industries. Hence, while there is surely an argument, politically as well as in terms of national equity, for measures to ensure some sharing of the adjustment burden, workers may be harmed rather than helped in the longer run by policies which perpetuate their employment in declining industries. Furthermore, the higher real cost of many goods which results from protection is reflected in lower real earnings for all workers. This hidden cost may constitute a large loss for the poorest residents of the industrialized nations.

C. LDC Debt

Although the sharply increased oil price produced a surge of borrowing by developing nations in the mid-1970s, rapid growth of LDC debt had already

---

[45] Bhagwati and Srinivasan (1977).

begun during the 1960s. Total LDC indebtedness grew from approximately $40 billion in 1967 to nearly $100 billion by 1973. Private lenders played an important role in promoting this growth of debt, much of which reflected accelerating development in the middle-income LDCs.[46] By the end of 1977, total debt of non-OPEC LDCs had climbed to nearly $250 billion, according to one source,[47] as LDC oil importers borrowed to maintain their growth rates and to postpone adjustment to reduced real incomes. Huge current account deficits in the period after the oil price increase raised increasing doubts about the LDCs' ability to repay these loans. Throughout 1977, newspaper accounts forecast massive LDC defaults in the absence of drastic new measures to alleviate the debt overhang. Then, almost as quickly as it had come into the public eye, the debt issue seemed to vanish. LDCs succeeded far more rapidly than expected in reducing their current account deficits; some loan terms were renegotiated to ease the immediate burden. By early 1978, bankers were reported to be "wincing" as LDCs prepaid their high interest balance of payments loans.[48]

Renegotiation of debt terms on a case-by-case basis has been an established practice in both official and private lending to LDCs. What is new in recent years is the Southern proposal to grant generalized debt relief for all LDCs or at least for broad groups, rather than on the basis of individual circumstances, and without the imposition of new requirements by the lender upon the borrower. While the "Programme of Action" called only for "debt renegotiation on a case-by-case basis with a view to concluding agreements on debt cancellation, moratorium, rescheduling, or interest subsidization," at UNCTAD IV a number of general debt relief measures were proposed by the Group of 77. These included waiver of interest payments until 1980 for bilateral loans, cancellation of the debts of the poorest LDCs, and establishment of a new international fund to refinance private credits over longer periods.[49] These proposals were rejected by the industrialized nations; opposition appeared even from some developing nations worried about their own future access to private capital markets in the event that general debt relief was granted. All that emerged from UNCTAD IV was an agreement to continue negotiations on appropriate guidelines for considering debt problems on a country-by-country basis. But little progress was made thereafter. When the final session of CIEC

---

[46] Fishlow (1978b, p. 135).

[47] UNCTAD estimate, as reported in *Wall Street Journal*, March 13, 1978. This figure includes short-term trade credits.

[48] *Business Week*, February 27, 1978, p. 86.

[49] Council Report No. 38, United States-Japan Trade Council, July 2, 1976.

came to a close, careful wording papered over many remaining North-South differences, but "there wasn't any language that could be found to cover up industrial lands' absolute refusal to forgive debts generally." Only case-by-case consideration was offered, although the industrial nations did pledge a new $1 billion aid package for the poorest nations, enough to cover debt repayment obligations for one year.[50]

In subsequent months, several nations moved unilaterally to provide generalized relief on their own government loans to LDCs. By March, 1978, Sweden, Canada, the Netherlands, and Switzerland had converted to grants all past loans to the poorest LDCs. The relief thus granted was relatively small in total magnitude--the largest debts are those of the middle-income LDCs--but the move was a positive response to the Southern call for an across-the-board approach. At an UNCTAD ministerial meeting on debt in March, the U.S. relaxed its previously stated opposition to relief other than on a case-by-case basis and agreed to seek congressional authorization for a moratorium on outstanding official debt of LDCs with per capita incomes of less than $280 per year. However, U.S. cancellations would still be made on an individual basis, with "cancellation contingent upon agreement on the worthiness of projects getting the money."[51]

As the events of recent years suggest, the debt problem has two quite distinct aspects. The crisis problem of countries like Zaire and Peru is that of meeting immediate commitments on scheduled payments of interest or principal to creditors. Where long-term prospects for economic growth are favorable, as in the case of countries with undeveloped mineral wealth, adjustment of terms is sufficient to eliminate the problem. The second problem, that of the poorer oil-importing LDCs, is one of reduced real income. Debt repayments must be accommodated through increased exports or decreased imports during future periods, even though borrowing to finance oil deficits has created no new sources of wealth. This situation need not produce financial crisis, but a reduced living standard in an already poor nation may create a political crisis.

Debt relief constitutes a resource transfer based upon loans outstanding from official or commercial sources. This would appear to be an unpromising criterion for the allocation of current official development assistance, yet there are strong political reasons for choosing this allocational rule. For Northern creditors, debt relief on past official loans eases the problems of LDC debtors in meeting the terms of outstanding commercial loans. Thus, ominous threats to the stability of the international financial system are lessened, even if terms

---

[50]*Wall Street Journal*, June 2, 1977.

[51]*New York Times*, March 6, 1978.

on commercial borrowings are unchanged. For the Southern nations, debt relief obviates some of the need for belt-tightening policies to achieve balance of payments adjustment through trade alone. In terms of political stability, an option which does not require reduced living standards is highly desirable. Obviously, the appeal of this argument is less for those nations who now enjoy ready access to commercial capital markets. The one-time transfer of resources implied by a debt moratorium might well be overshadowed by losses from reduced future availability of commercial financing.

Those who emphasize the harm done to the economic prospects of oil-importing LDCs by the OPEC price hike should note that generalized relief on resulting debt transfers part of that burden to the industrialized nations. (Of course, there still remains a permanent reduction in real income of LDC oil importers as a consequence of the higher price.) Thus, the debt relief proposal may play a role in cementing Southern solidarity, and it is perhaps not surprising that the debt issue played such a prominent role in the CIEC negotiations. A similar interpretation could also be placed upon the Witteveen facility of the IMF, a recently created $10 billion fund, financed equally by OPEC and OECD nations, the purpose of which is to provide medium-term debt relief for oil-importing nations.[52]

IV. Contradictions and Conflicts

The lengthy negotiations on specific NIEO proposals have brought to light conflicting beliefs of the participants on basic economic and political questions. By their very nature, such conflicts are more difficult to resolve or even to identify than differences on the narrower technical issues. Nevertheless, an appreciation of these underlying sources of conflict may illuminate the positions maintained by the negotiators and facilitate evaluation of the NIEO proposals.

Goals of the NIEO. Despite the outpouring of speeches and documents on the NIEO, there is still little agreement as to its basic objectives. This failure to clearly identify goals necessarily complicates the problem of evaluating alternative measures. Sympathetic Northerners tend to view NIEO in terms of its ultimate effects on the interpersonal distribution of income and particularly upon the living standard of the poorest inhabitants of the South. But for Southern policymakers, national sovereignty and international redistribution appear to be the major goals.[53] While some Southern nations also seek actively

---

[52]Some OPEC nations have also become major sources of official development assistance, particularly but not exclusively for Muslin LDCs.

[53]Krasner (1977).

to promote interpersonal redistribution, for others it is seen as a threat to current economic and political relationships rather than as a desired outcome.

Markets and perfect competition. Much of the opposition to the NIEO proposals rests upon the assumed superiority of markets to political institutions as alternative means of allocating scarce resources. Economic theory has established that perfectly competitive markets have certain desirable efficiency properties. However, reliance upon the market does not ensure conditions approximating perfect competition. In many cases, the absence of political institutions governing resource use simply clears the way for oligopolistic market structures, the efficiency properties of which are less well understood. The case for reliance upon markets cannot rest primarily upon the beneficial consequences of perfect competition. The relevant comparison is between the performance of actual markets and actual political institutions.

With respect to the distribution of benefits, a key issue in the North-South debate, market outcomes have no particular relationship to perceived "neediness" of transactors. Rather, the distributive impact, both within and between nations, will depend primarily upon the distribution of property rights. However, two arguments can be made for market institutions in terms of their distributive consequences. To the extent that overall efficiency is in fact promoted, total world wealth is increased, yielding benefits through the familiar but somewhat discredited "trickle-down" channel. More important, the absence of centralized economic power in the form of political institutions controlling resource use reduces the ability of already rich and powerful elite groups to further improve their lot through nonmarket wealth allocations.[54]

Equity and equality. In the North-South debate, these terms are often used interchangeably. It may be more useful to distinguish equality of opportunity and equality of outcome. Unequal outcomes play a key role in the efficient functioning of any economic system, while unequal opportunities do not. Progress toward distributive goals might thus be most appropriately measured in terms of potential economic mobility rather than actual earnings. Advocates of the basic human needs approach have stressed that, to be meaningful, equality of opportunity probably requires some minimum level of nutrition, health, and basic education. Less often stressed are the preconditions of civil and economic liberties. It should be noted that barriers to free international migration constitute the single most important current source of inequality of opportunity.

National sovereignty and income distribution. As part of the NIEO stress upon national sovereignty, Southern nations have asserted their desire

---

[54] On the economic and political benefits of market institutions, see Brunner (1976).

for expanded multilateral and unconditional resource flows. At first glance this proposal appeals to economic theory along the lines of the negative income tax analysis: if transfers are to be made, they should be made in such a way as to maximize their utility to the recipient. However, this overlooks the role and nature of interdependent utility functions. Northern taxpayers are unlikely to be indifferent about the way in which funds are used. Defense expenditures which raise collective utility for an LDC or its ruling elite may rank lower than improvements in nutrition, sanitation, or literacy. Thus, the tying of aid flows to achievement of specific objectives may be appropriate. However, the problems of enforcing aid ties are likely to be formidable. In particular, merely associating loans or grants with specific projects would not be sufficient to ensure that funds allocated result in greater accomplishment in target areas.[55] And, as has already been emphasized, transfers between rich and poor *nations* do not in themselves ensure or even necessarily promote redistribution between rich and poor *people* if powerful elites control the allocation of resources.

How much change? Those who support the NIEO as well as those who resist its establishment seem to have taken at face value, or nearly so, much of the rhetorical debate of recent years. Yet a truly radical break with the past is not on the agenda of the South.[56] As has been frequently pointed out, the specific NIEO proposals contain little that is fresh. Perhaps more to the point, most of the proposals remain well within the framework of current international relationships.[57] The South is not looking for a new order, but, rather, jockeying for a better position in the old one. Similarly, while the most vehement Northern critics of the NIEO invoke the imminent demise of the capitalist system, most of the NIEO proposals would simply apply, in an international setting, interventionist policies which the "market" economies have already endured for many years. This is not to defend the wisdom of these policies, but merely to indicate that under all the verbal fireworks, North and South are not so very far apart.

---

[55]On the conflict between national sovereignty and achievement of specific basic human needs objectives, see Hansen (1977).

[56]Fishlow (1978a, p. 18).

[57]An alternative and more radical Southern approach is discussed by Diaz-Alejandro (1978).

A Chronology of North-South Relations

1961	Sept. 1-6 Belgrade	First summit conference of nonaligned countries
	Dec. 19	General Assembly designates UN Development Decade
1964	Mar. 23-June 16 Geneva	First UN Conference on Trade and Development (UNCTAD 1); 77 developing nations issue joint declaration proclaiming "a new era in the evolution of international co-operation in the field of trade and development"
	December	UNCTAD institutionalized as UN organ
1967	Oct. 10-25	Group of 77 ministerial meeting in preparation for UNCTAD II
1968	Feb. 1-Mar. 29 New Delhi	UNCTAD II
1970	Sept. 8-10 Lusaka	Third summit conference of nonaligned countries adopts "Declaration on Non-Alignment and Economic Progress"
	October 24	General Assembly proclaims Second UN Development Decade
1972	Apr. 13-May 21 Santiago	UNCTAD III
1973	Sept. 5-9 Algiers	Fourth summit conference of nonaligned countries reaffirms national sovereignty over natural resources, recommends establishment of "a new international economic order" to achieve their objectives

1973	Sept. 12-14 Tokyo	Formal opening of Tokyo Round of multilateral trade negotiations under GATT, with emphasis on securing additional benefits for developing countries
	October 27	Arab petroleum exporting countries impose output and destination restrictions
	Dec. 22-23 Teheran	OPEC ministers set new posted prices to become effective January 1, 1974
1974	Apr. 9-May 2	UN General Assembly Sixth Special Session on raw materials and development adopts "Declaration on the Establishment of a New International Economic Order" and "Programme of Action"
	December 12	General Assembly adopts "Charter of Economic Rights and Duties of States"
1975	Jan. 15-16	International Monetary Fund raises quotas of major oil producers
	Feb. 4-8 Dakar	Conference of Developing Countries on Raw Materials calls for linking of energy negotiations to other North-South issues
	February 28 Lomé, Togo	EC and 46 African, Caribbean, and Pacific (ACP) nations sign Lomé Convention, major trade and aid package including commodity export earnings stabilization and free access to EC market for ACP exporters
	March 4-6 Algiers	First OPEC summit conference endorses linking of energy talks to other development issues
	March 12-26 Lima	UN Industrial Development Organization (UNIDO) conference calls for increase in developing nations' share in world industrial production from 7 percent to 25 percent by year 2000

1975	Apr. 7-15	Preparatory meeting for energy producer-consumer dialogue fails to resolve conflict over OPEC proposal to broaden agenda to include other North-South issues
	May 13 Kansas City	Kissinger speech indicates U.S. willingness to discuss individual commodity arrangements on case-by-case basis
	Sept. 1-16	UN General Assembly Seventh Special Session, Kissinger speech proposes numerous specific measures to promote development
	Dec. 16-19 Paris	Conference on International Economic Cooperation (CIEC) initiates 27 nation "North-South Dialogue"
1976	January 1	U.S. becomes last major industrial nation to implement Generalized System of Preferences (GSP)
	May 3-28 Nairobi	UNCTAD IV
1977	May 30-June 2	CIEC final session agrees in principle on establishment of common fund for raw materials
	December 1 Geneva	UNCTAD Negotiating Conference on a Common Fund suspended after failure to resolve conflict on specifics of common fund financing and uses
	December	Brandt Commission established
1978	March Geneva	UNCTAD ministerial meeting on debt reaches agreement on generalized debt relief for poorest nations
1979	May Manila	UNCTAD V
1980		UN General Assembly Special Session on progress toward establishment of NIEO

References

Baldwin, R.E., and Murray, T. (1977), "MFN Tariff Reductions and LDC Benefits Under the GSP," *Economic Journal,* 87: 30-46.

Bhagwati, J.N. (1977), ed. *The New International Economic Order: The North-South Debate.* Cambridge, Massachusetts: MIT Press.

Bhagwati, J.N., and Srinivasan, T.N. (1977), "Trade and Development." Paper presented at the Wingspread Conference on International Economic Policy, July 28-30, 1977. Forthcoming in *International Economic Policy: Theory and Evidence,* eds. R. Dornbusch and J. Frenkel. Baltimore: John Hopkins University Press.

Branislav, G., and Ruggie, J.G. (1976), "On the Creation of a New International Economic Order: Issue Linkage and the Seventh Special Session of the UN General Assembly," *International Organization,* 30: 309-45.

Brunner, K. (1976), "The New International Economic Order: A Chapter in a Protracted Confrontation," *ORBIS, A Journal of World Affairs,* 20: 103-21.

Business Week (1978), February 27, p. 86.

Bywater, M. (1975), "The Lomé Convention," *European Community,* 184: 5-9.

Cohen, S.D. (1977). *The Making of United States International Economic Policy.* New York: Praeger.

Diaz-Alejandro, C.F. (1978), "Delinking North and South: Unshackled or Unhinged?" *Rich and Poor Nations in the World Economy* (1980s Project/Council on Foreign Relations). New York: McGraw-Hill.

Economist (1978), March 25, pp. 91-92.

Fishlow, A. (1978a), "A New International Economic Order: What Kind?" *Rich and Poor Nations in the World Economy* (1980s Project/Council on Foreign Relations). New York: McGraw-Hill.

Fishlow, A. (1978b), "Debt Remains a Problem," *Foreign Policy*, **30**: 133-43.

Hansen, R.D. (1977), "Major U.S. Options on North-South Relations: A Letter to President Carter," *The United States and World Development: Agenda 1977,* J.W. Sewell and the Staff of the Overseas Development Council. New York: Praeger.

IMF Survey, various issues.

Jankowitsch, O., and Sauvant, K.P. (1976), "The Evolution of the Non-Aligned Movement into a Pressure Group for the Establishment of the New International Economic Order." Paper presented at the Seventeenth Annual Convention of the International Studies Association, Toronto, February, 1976.

Johnson, H.G. (1977), "Commodities: Less Developed Countries' Demands and Developed Countries' Response," *The New International Economic Order: The North-South Debate,* ed. J.N. Bhagwati, Cambridge, Massachusetts: MIT Press.

Kenen, P. (1977), "Debt Relief as Development Assistance," *The New International Economic Order: The North-South Debate,* ed. J.N. Bhagwati. Cambridge, Massachusetts: MIT Press.

Krasner, S. (1977), "The New International Economic Order and the Quest for Power." Unpublished paper, Department of Political Science, U.C.L.A.

Kreinin, M.E., and Finger, J.M. (1976), "A Critical Survey of the New International Economic Order," *Journal of World Trade Law,* **10**: 493-512.

McCulloch, R. (1977), "Economic Policy in the United Nations: A New International Economic Order?" *International Organization, National Policy and Economic Development,* Carnegie-Rochester Conference Series on Public Policy, vol. 6, eds. K. Brunner and A.H. Meltzer. Amsterdam: North-Holland.

Meadows, D.H.; Meadows, D.L.; Randers, J.; and Behrens, W.W. (1972). *The Limits to Growth.* New York: Universe Books.

New York Times (1978), March 6.

Newsweek (1977), December 12, p. 70.

Nye, J.S. (1974), "UNCTAD: Poor Nations' Pressure Group," *The Anatomy of Influence,* R.W. Cox and H.K. Jacobson. New Haven: Yale University Press.

_____(1976), "Independence and Interdependence," *Foreign Policy,* **22**: 129-61.

Smith, T. (1977), "Changing Configurations of Power in North-South Relations Since 1945," *International Organization,* **31**: 1-27.

UN Chronicle, various issues.

UNCTAD (1975), "An Integrated Programme for Commodities: Specific Proposals for Decision and Action." Report by the Secretary-General of UNCTAD, TD/B/C.1/193. New York: United Nations, October 28, 1975.

United States-Japan Trade Council, Council Report, various issues.

Vernon, R. (1976), ed. *The Oil Crisis.* New York: W.W. Norton.

Wall, D. (1971), "Problems with Preferences," *International Affairs,* **47**: 87-99.

Wall Street Journal, various issues.

THE POLITICAL ECONOMY
OF THE
CONGRESSIONAL BUDGET OFFICE

David I. MEISELMAN
Virginia Polytechnic Institute and State University

and

Paul Craig ROBERTS
The Wall Street Journal
and
Hoover Institution, Stanford University

Introduction and Summary

This study describes and analyzes the operation of the Congressional Budget Office's activities under the Congressional Budget and Impoundment Control Act of 1974. It focuses on C.B.O.'s macroeconomic analysis, which provides the basis for the fiscal policy options that are presented to the Congress. The study finds that C.B.O.'s analysis and empirical studies are seriously flawed.

In the C.B.O. analysis there is demand without supply, inflation without money, interest rates without capital, output without inputs, employment without wage rates or a labor market, and investment without saving or any change in the capital stock. Expectations are assumed to be static, and consumption is assumed to depend only on current disposable income.

Fiscal policy is seen as affecting aggregate demand with no incentive or disincentive effects on supply. The study notes an anomaly in the C.B.O.'s treatment of money. After presenting evidence that only money matters, C.B.O. proceeds to rely on a Keynesian fiscal model with no money at all. There is no attempt to reconcile the two views.

The study concludes that the new budget process has institutionalized Keynesian fiscal policy rather than budget balance as the concept of budget control. Now, deficits are rationalized in terms of scientific economic policy prior to the appropriations process. This tends to loosen rather than tighten constraints on government expenditures. But the new concept of budget control has not changed incentives, and we doubt that the C.B.O. has the power to change the incentives faced by politicians and bureaucrats in a democracy.

The analytical error that may be more critical than those inherent in the C.B.O.'s macromodel is the economist's assumption that public policy serves the public interest rather than the private interests of the policymakers.

I. The Congressional Budget Act

The Congressional Budget and Impoundment Control Act of 1974 established: (*a*) a new congressional budget process; (*b*) Senate and House Committees on the Budget; (*c*) a Congressional Budget Office; and (*d*) a procedure providing congressional control over the impoundment of funds by the executive branch.

The Act was deemed necessary for several reasons. At a time when the federal "budget had become the nation's principal tool for determining governmental goals and economic policy, affecting nearly every facet of American society. . .the Congress lacked a comprehensive mechanism for establishing priorities among its goals and for determining economic policy through the budget process. . . .Budget actions never explicitly decided the size of the budget, whether it should be in surplus or deficit, and precisely by what amount."[1]

Past budget reforms had enhanced and centralized budget authority in the Executive Branch, while permitting increased fragmentation of spending authority within the Congress. The concentration of financial and policymaking authority in the Office of Management and Budget had no counterpart in the Congress. The increasing use of impoundments by the Executive Branch was seen by the Congress as a direct challenge to its constitutional power to establish spending priorities.

The Congress was disturbed by its lack of control over spending. "Uncontrollables," the fastest rising part of the budget, had reached 75 percent of the total. Backdoor spending, spending outside the regular appropriation process, was more than half of all spending. With its budget actions restricted to the authority to obligate funds, the Congress had no control over actual expenditures or outlays, "resulting in little direct relationship between congressional budget actions and actual expenditures in any given year."[2]

Thus, the Act resulted from Congress's desire (*a*) to explicitly relate its budget actions to its economic policy, (*b*) to restore its power to establish spending priorities, and (*c*) to gain control over spending. This is the official rationale for the Act, and, like many official rationales, it conceals the fact

---

[1] U.S. Congress, House, Committee on the Budget (1976, p. 1).

[2] Ibid., p. 2.

that different groups supported the Act in the expectation of achieving different and mutually exclusive results.[3]

A. *Outline and Timetable of the Congressional Budget Process*

The timetable with respect to the various stages of the new budget process is as follows:[4]

On or before:	Action to be completed:
November 10................	President submits current services budget.
15th day after Congress meets...	President submits his budget
March 15..................	Committees and joint committees submit reports to Budget Committees.
April 1....................	Congressional Budget Office submits report to Budget Committees.
April 15...................	Budget Committees report first concurrent resolution on the budget to their Houses.
May 15	Committees report bills and resolutions authorizing new budget authority.
May 15	Congress completes action on first concurrent resolution on the budget.
7th day after Labor Day	Congress completes action on bills and resolutions providing new budget authority and new spending authority.
September 15	Congress completes action on second required concurrent resolution on the budget.

---

[3] Ellwood and Thurber (1977).

[4] Public Law 93-344, Title III, Sec. 300.

September 25 . . . . .Congress completes action on reconciliation bill or resolution, or both, implementing second required concurrent resolution.

October 1 . . . . .Fiscal year begins.

The first budget resolution in any fiscal year sets targets. The second budget resolution establishes a floor for revenues and a ceiling on spending, both in the aggregate and for each major functional spending category.[5]

B. The Budget Committees

The House and Senate Budget Committees "are created to guide the Congress in the new tasks of setting national fiscal policy aggregates; that is, total spending, revenue, and debt levels."[6]

II. The Congressional Budget Office

The mission of the C.B.O. "is to provide the Congress with detailed budget information and studies of the budget impact of alternative policies"[7] so that Congress can carry out the budget process and consider the budget "in the context of the current and projected state of the national economy."[8] "The law makes clear that the C.B.O. is to have a nonpartisan, highly professional staff and that it is to provide a wide range of fiscal and budget information and analyses. C.B.O. does not make recommendations on policy matters but provides Congress with options and alternatives for its consideration."[9]

C.B.O. (*a*) provides periodic forecasts and analyses of economic trends and alternative fiscal policies; (*b*) keeps score of congressional action on individual authorization, appropriation, and revenue bills against the targets and ceilings in the concurrent budget resolutions; (*c*) develops five-year cost

---

[5]There are 19 major functional categories: national defense; international affairs; general science, space and technology; energy; natural resources and environment; commerce and housing credit; transportation; educational training, employment and social services; administration of justice; general purpose fiscal assistance; allowances; agriculture; community and regional development; health; income security; veterans benefits and services; general government; interest; undistributed offsetting receipts.

[6]U.S. Congress, House, Committee on the Budget (1976, p. 4).

[7]U.S. Congress (1976, p. 1).

[8]Ibid.

[9]Ibid.

estimates for implementing any public bill or resolution reported by congressional committees; (*d*) provides at the beginning of each fiscal year five-year projections on the costs of continuing current federal spending and taxation policies; (*e*) provides by April 1 of each year "a fiscal policy report which includes a discussion of alternative spending and revenue levels, levels of tax expenditures under existing law, and alternative allocations among major programs and functional categories, all in the light of major national needs and their effects on balanced growth and development of the United States";[10] and (*f*) provides additional studies. (See Appendix for statutory tasks and organizational chart, Figure 3, of C.B.O.)

A primary motive behind the formation of the C.B.O. was the Congress's desire to have its own source of budget information. The Congress's ability to work its own purposes was constrained by its dependence on information supplied by the Executive Branch.

III. Macroeconomics at the C.B.O.

This study focuses on C.B.O.'s analysis of macroeconomic conditions and forecasts and related public policy issues regarding economic stability and growth, unemployment and interest rates which attract major attention of the Congress and the public.

Although it is less than three years since C.B.O. published its first report, its publication list is already lengthy. As of May, 1978, the C.B.O. bibliography contained 166 titles, 144 separate studies, and 22 Congressional Budget

---

[10] Ibid., p. 2.

Scorekeeping Reports.[11] On the basis of an unsystematic sample, we estimate that these average 70 pages, or roughly a total of 12,000 pages.

There are several main categories of published studies and reports in addition to those dealing with macroeconomic conditions and policies. Much of the C.B.O.'s work and the majority of their published studies are devoted to other budgetary and public policy analyses and problems which abstract from stabilization issues. Forty-eight of the published studies are "Background Papers," which are detailed analyses of a wide range of topics; e.g., "New York City's Fiscal Problems: Its Origins, Potential Repercussions and Some Alternative Policy Responses," "Highway Assistance Programs: A Historical Perspective," and "Force Planning and Budgetary Implications of U.S. Withdrawal from Korea."

Thirty-seven of the published studies are "Budget Issue Papers" that cover topics such as "Catastrophic Health Insurance," "The Costs of Defense Manpower: Issues from 1977," and "Federal Prison Construction: Alternative Approaches." There are also 30 published Staff Working Papers and 11 Technical Analysis Papers that tend to be more technically and methodologically oriented than the other studies.

In addition to these published reports, there is extensive testimony by the C.B.O.'s Director before Congressional committees as well as various unpublished reports and communications, and unpublished studies such as the C.B.O. wage-price model.

Given the volume and the scope of the C.B.O. studies, we have limited this paper to an evaluation of the main elements in the C.B.O.'s analysis of

---

[11]The count was made from C.B.O. documents listing their publications, which the C.B.O. kindly made available. In a somewhat earlier bibliography covering publications through Feb., 1978, the C.B.O. made a subject area listing of the 136 studies which had been published up to that date. The following is a tabulation of the numbers of studies by subject area:

Agriculture	4
The Budget and Budget Projections	20
Budget Procedures	5
Defense	26
The Economy and Fiscal Policy	23
Education	7
Employment and Training	15
Energy	12
Federal Work Force and Government Administration	8
Foreign Affairs	9
Health	9
Housing	4
Income Assistance	14
International Economic Relations	9
Law Enforcement and Justice	2
State and Local Government	2
Tax Expenditures	6
Tax Receipts and Distribution	12
Transportation	6
Urban and Regional Development	3
TOTAL	196

The total of the 196 studies exceeds the number of studies (136) because some studies are included in more than one subject area.

budget aggregates and of stabilization problems and policies, in many respects the main and mandated business of the C.B.O. In the concluding section we offer some judgments concerning the impact of the C.B.O. and its outpouring of studies, reports, papers, analyses, and computer runs.

In the main, the C.B.O. analyses of stabilization prospects, problems, and policies are disappointing. The analyses ignore both the important and fundamental advances in economic science of recent years and the openness of the U.S. economy. Given the current state of economics, they can surely do much better. Instead, the C.B.O. analyses are largely derived from the relatively unsophisticated Keynesian models of the 1950s.

The C.B.O.'s treatment of money and monetary analysis are deficient. The C.B.O. has also simply ignored the questions raised by rational expectations theorists and others about the efficacy of discretionary fiscal policy and discretionary stabilization policy. In keeping with the focus on short-run stabilization, there is no long-run analysis worthy of the name. Even in the one study that claims to be an analysis of long-run issues, saving impairs economic performance and growth. Further, C.B.O. analyses generally ignore international trade and capital movements by assuming a closed economy.

The empirical and econometric work reported by C.B.O. consists mainly of estimates obtained from large-scale econometric models by adding additional numerical constraints to the many constraints found in the large-scale models. The results of these numerical exercises are used as the basis for C.B.O. analyses. Most of the C.B.O.'s empirical work is little more than curve fitting and casual empiricism. However, despite the emphasis on curve fitting, there is not a single statistic showing goodness of fit for the C.B.O. estimates or for those of the large-scale econometric models employed in the keystone multipliers study we survey below. C.B.O. does not report how well parameter estimates have fit past data. The presumption seems to be that the set of fitted values correctly project the future *without error*. But this presumption is never tested, because there are no comparisons of post-sample forecasts and actual events.

To be sure, much of C.B.O.'s output, especially their forecasts and their evaluations of the impact of fiscal policy on economic aggregates, is a response to Congressional mandates and inquiries. But we believe that these tasks, as well as the questions themselves, largely derive from presumptions that (*a*) compensatory fiscal and stabilization policy work; (*b*) valid, precise, and dependable answers are readily available; (*c*) economists can tell Senators and Congressmen about the implications of fiscal policy changes for prices, employment, gross national product, and the like, quarter by quarter, at least up to, and sometimes even beyond, the next election. The presumption that a valid and relatively precise analysis already exists and that only relatively minor additional efforts are required to yield a host of dependable answers biases the kinds of questions asked. The same presumptions also bias what are perceived to be policy problems, workable policy instruments, and attainable solutions. For example, if tax cuts are seen as affecting only aggregate demand, there is no point in considering any connections between taxes and aggregate supply, labor force participation, and the like.

We have had thirty years of experience with the Employment Act of 1946 and its presumption that the type of model used by C.B.O. is valid and that short-run stabilization goals for employment can be achieved by the use of fiscal instruments. These presumptions follow, in part, from belief in the analytical power of adding up GNP components, the ease of forecasting and fooling markets, the efficacy of fiscal policy, essentially static anticipations, and the general absence of supply and relative price considerations. The results have been inflation, big government and more intervention without much evidence that economic stability has been increased, or unemployment reduced, by policy action.

IV. The C.B.O.'s Stabilization Policy Model

The most explicit statement of C.B.O.'s macroeconomic model is found in a C.B.O. study, *The C.B.O. Multipliers Project: A Methodology for Analyzing the Effects of Alternative Economic Policies* (1977). As this study, itself, states, "the basic model presented there is in fact the one C.B.O. has used for nearly all its policy simulation work" (p. 15).[12]

Our reading of the various C.B.O. reports, especially those prepared by the C.B.O. Fiscal Policy Division and dealing with forecasts, the analysis of current economic conditions, and the implications of alternative stabilization policies, indicates that the C.B.O.'s own statement of the widespread use to which this basic model is put is substantially correct. This is why it is especially instructive to focus special attention on this one study.

---

[12]The same model was still in use at the time our paper was prepared and at the time of the Carnegie-Rochester Conference at which an earlier draft of this paper was presented. For example, as late as April, 1978, the C.B.O. (1978) Background Paper, *Understanding Fiscal Policy*, used these multipliers and the model of the multipliers project as central features in the analysis of fiscal policy. Citing the C.B.O. Multipliers Project study, the paper states:

> In the course of using a number of econometric models, the Congressional Budget Office has had occasion to develop its own sets of GNP multipliers for several different kinds of fiscal policy change. These multipliers are based on a careful analysis and comparison of five econometric models; they discount some of the more questionable elements of each model while still maintaining consistency in the treatment of different kinds of fiscal action. (pp. 15-16)

The paper then goes on to compare the effects of different policies based on "C.B.O.'s system of multipliers" (p. 16).

However, we should point out that, for all the shortcomings of this "basic model," some of which are described below, it is an improvement over the first models used by the C.B.O., which must have raised the doubts and suspicions of both monetarists and fiscalists. These earlier models generated rather novel and somewhat bizarre results, and parts of them appear to have been abandoned since. For example, in the first C.B.O. study, *Inflation and Unemployment: A Report on the Economy* (1975), faster growth of the money supply is seen as leading to somewhat lower, not higher, prices. In addition, although effectively *raising tax rates*, by not extending the temporary tax provisions of the Tax Reduction Act of 1975 scheduled to expire at the end of 1975, was analyzed as having *no* effect on prices, an additional *tax cut* of $15 billion was analyzed as causing prices to be somewhat *lower* than they would otherwise be. (See pp. xv, xvi).

The novelty and complexity of large econometric models and their estimating techniques mean that most of the analysis used to generate the computer output is unfamiliar to the typical Senator and Congressman, and to most members of their staffs. Thus, the results must be taken on faith by policymakers, if they are taken at all. This faith is frequently shaken because, although there are many common elements in these large-scale models, they frequently yield vastly different answers, much to the embarrassment of analysts who have access to more than one model, or who have to defend one set of results against another. Because of the complexity of the models, it is frequently difficult to know why these differences exist. Moreover, these differences tend to create a lack of confidence in models as well as in the analytical orientation that they reflect.

In the C.B.O.'s own words, "The Multipliers project is an attempt to understand and deal with the diversity of results that various models may produce" (1977b, p. ix). The various models that the C.B.O. examines are restricted to the five large-scale econometric models of Data Resources Incorporated (D.R.I.), Wharton, Chase Econometrics, MIT-Penn (MPS), and Fair. The presumption seems to be that large-scale econometric models are essentially the only kind of analysis useful for estimating the impacts of federal tax and expenditure policies. To avoid the problem of the diversity of answers, the C.B.O. makes its own estimates of a set of "key ratios," to be discussed below. These ratios appear to be the middle-of-the-range consensus of the five models. The C.B.O.'s study includes the calculation of at least 60 different "key ratio" values for each of these five models and the C.B.O.'s Basic Multipliers Model. In all cases the C.B.O. parameter values are bracketed by the other five. Neither the original models nor the C.B.O. "key ratios" are tested.

The C.B.O. exercises clearly intend to estimate parameter values; they are not intended to test any of the large-scale models or the C.B.O. "key ratios." Not every useful empirical exercise must include a rigorous test, but unless "key ratios" or other parameters are tested (or testable), there is no way to know whether there is any validity to the exercise, and whether the Congress is being supplied with good analysis.

Differences in "key ratios" are resolved by the C.B.O. "on a basis of reasonableness, other empirical studies, and, when necessary, simply averaging across models (1977b, p. x). The selected "key ratios" are called "a uniform set of procedures for calculating policy impacts" (p. ix). "Key ratios" and multipliers are presented on a quarterly seasonally adjusted basis for 10 quarters. Real variables, such as output and unemployment, are also derived from a two-equation wage-price model, which we discuss below.

In addition, the C.B.O. analysis asserts that "key ratios" and multipliers depend on initial conditions, which are likely to change from year to year. Therefore, "the analysis needs to be redone whenever there is a substantial change in initial conditions. C.B.O.'s tentative plan is to redo it once a year" (p. 2).

This raises the question of how to identify a substantial change, or how to systematically alter the "key ratios" on the basis of new information. There does not appear to be any tested basis for doing so, especially since the various interest, price, and substitution elasticities as well as the supply and labor market responses to changes in initial conditions are omitted from the analysis. Expectational considerations are omitted also.

The elasticities are a set of empirical presumptions about a limited range of nominal expenditure responses. C.B.O. claims, however, that the elasticities summarize a wide range of price and wealth responses as well as income-expenditure relationships and that they are reduced-form coefficients. C.B.O. never explains or makes explicit what price and wealth responses are being summarized or what structure generates the reduced-form. Whatever the partial responses may be, they, too, are omitted, so it is difficult to derive testable implications or to test the unspecified set of structural relations that constitute the overall model.

To derive the nine a, b, and c coefficients for the model, simulations of the fiscal policy in five full-scale models were used. According to the C.B.O., "Each econometric model simulation yields a specific set of values for the key components that together capture the total change in G.N.P. implied by that model. The G.N.P. multiplier is an algebraic function of the coefficients of the basic model, called 'key components' of the multiplier."[13] Then, C.B.O. derived quarterly values for each of the coefficients for the first through tenth quarters. Comparisons of some of these estimated coefficients are shown below.

The Basic Multipliers Model (1977b, p. 4) is

$$\Delta GNP\$(t) = \Delta C\$(t) + \Delta FI\$(t) + \Delta GG\$(t) + \Delta GE\$(t) + \Delta X\$(t), \quad (1)$$

$$\Delta C\$(t) \quad = a_{1t}\,(\Delta INC\$(t) + \Delta TR\$(t) - \Delta TP\$(t)),' \qquad (2)$$

$$\Delta INC\$(t) = b_{1t}\,\Delta GNP\$(t) + c_{1t}\,\Delta GE\$(t), \qquad (3)$$

$$\Delta TR\$(t) \quad = -b_{2t}\,\Delta GNP\$(t) - c_{2t}\,\Delta GE\$(t) + \Delta TRO\$(t), \qquad (4)$$

$$\Delta TP\$(t) \quad = b_{3t}\,\Delta INC\$(t) - c_{3t}\,\Delta GE\$(t) + \Delta TPO\$(t), \qquad (5)$$

$$\Delta FI\$(t) \quad = a_{2t}[\Delta GNP\$(t) - \Delta GE\$(t)],' \qquad (6)$$

$$\Delta X\$(t) \quad = a_{3t}\,\Delta GNP\$(t) + \Delta XO\$(t), \qquad (7)$$

where

$GNP\$$	=	Gross National Product,
$C\$$	=	Consumption,
$FI\$$	=	Fixed investment (business and residential),
$GG\$$	=	Federal government purchases except public employment,
$GE\$$	=	Public employment spending net of displacement, federal and state and local (displaced funds used for tax reduction or general state and local spending enter as TP$ or GG$),
$X\$$	=	Rest of GNP$: inventory investment, net exports, state and local spending other than public service employment,

---

[13]U.S. Congress, Congressional Budget Office (1977b, p. 5).

INC$	=	Wages and salaries and other labor income and nonwage income,
TR$	=	Federal transfer payments,
TP$	=	Federal personal tax revenues (including employee payroll taxes),
TRO$	=	Intercept, transfer payments,
TPO$	=	Intercept, personal tax revenues,
XO$	=	Intercept, other spending,
t	=	Time, in quarters.

All variables are in current dollars.

Note that the model has two main equations. There is a simple consumption function; current personal consumption expenditures per quarter is a linear function of disposable personal income. Fixed investment is a function of GNP less net public employment spending. The investment function is little more than a simple accelerator modified to exclude public employment expenditures from GNP. This equation implies that public employment expenditures reduce investment. The other equations are either identities, or equations that deal with the residuals, or predetermined variables, as in the case of federal government expenditures.

The model has a limited range of implications. It will not provide answers (implications) for many important questions. The model is mute about the effects of changes in relative prices or in the tax structure. (The same is generally true of the large-scale models.) For example, when the Multipliers Project tried to analyze the GNP implications of a change in the corporate profits tax, it correctly noted (p. 20), "The basic multipliers model does not include dividends, corporate cash flow, or the corporate tax rate as separate determinants of consumption and investment spending and, therefore, cannot account for the effect of change in corporate taxes on spending." (The same general problems also hold for the analysis of money.) To deal with these deficiencies, the study adds several other variables. But, it simply ignores the impact of a change in corporate profits taxes on the cost of capital or the effect of a differential tax cut on expenditure patterns or on relative rates of return.

The quarterly values of the marginal propensity to consume, a_1, in the Basic Multipliers Model are close to the average marginal propensity to consume out of current disposable income for the five large-scale econometric models. These are shown in Table 1, taken directly from the C.B.O. study (p. 6). Model 1 is from D.R.I.; Model 2, Wharton; Model 3, Chase; Model 4, MIT-Penn (MPS); and Model 5, Fair. The parameter values for the five models were derived by simulating a change in federal government expenditures, holding the path of unborrowed reserves constant. As the C.B.O. notes, "Selecting unborrowed reserve implies that both interest rates and the money supply rise moderately in response to an expansionary fiscal move" (p. 6). The C.B.O.'s study does not attempt to distinguish between the monetary effects of fiscal policy and the corresponding changes in prices, interest rates, and the like stemming from the change in the stock of money and, on the other hand, the purely fiscal policy effects of changes in government expenditures or taxes when the money stock is held constant.

TABLE 1

Quarterly Values of a_1

Quarter	Models					Basic Multipliers Model
	1	2	3	4	5	
1	0.41	0.26	0.55	0.25	0.68	0.35
2	0.63	0.26	0.47	0.37	0.80	0.45
3	0.68	0.28	0.56	0.44	0.95	0.51
4	0.71	0.30	0.65	0.51	0.97	0.55
5	0.73	0.39	0.68	0.58	1.02	0.60
6	0.73	0.49	0.67	0.62	0.96	0.62
7	0.73	0.69	0.69	0.65	0.97	0.67
8	0.71	0.83	0.70	0.70	0.98	0.70
9	0.71	0.75	0.70	0.72	0.95	0.71
10	0.71	0.67	0.70	0.76	0.90	0.71

The quarterly values of a_2 in Table 2 are copied from the C.B.O. paper's Table 4 (p. 10). These values are for a sustained shift in one of the disturbances, not a once-for-all increase in the level of, say, government expenditures in a given quarter followed by a decrease the subsequent quarter. Again, the C.B.O. "basic multipliers" are near the middle of the range of estimates.

TABLE 2

Quarterly Values of a_2

Quarter	Models					Basic Multipliers Model
	1	2	3	4	5	
1	0.02	0.07	0.03	0.04	0.08	0.06
2	0.03	0.12	0.05	0.10	0.14	0.11
3	0.04	0.18	0.07	0.14	0.17	0.17
4	0.05	0.21	0.09	0.16	0.21	0.19
5	0.06	0.22	0.08	0.18	0.22	0.20
6	0.06	0.23	0.06	0.18	0.25	0.20
7	0.05	0.23	0.04	0.18	0.24	0.19
8	0.05	0.22	0.03	0.17	0.24	0.18
9	0.03	0.16	0.01	0.16	0.24	0.16
10	0.03	0.06	-0.01	0.16	0.24	0.14

The seven equations are combined to yield the following multiplier expression for analyzing fiscal policy disturbances. C.B.O. (p. 12) summarizes the fiscal multiplier as follows:

THE FISCAL MULTIPLIER FORMULA

The seven equations listed in the basic multipliers model can be combined through simple algebra to yield the following multiplier expression for standard changes in fiscal policy:

$$\Delta GNP\$(t) = \left[\frac{1}{[1-(a_{1t}(b_{1t}(1-b_{3t}) - b_{2t}) + a_{2t} + {}_{3t})]} \right] \text{x}$$

$$[\Delta GG\$(t) + \Delta XO\$(t) + a_{1t} [\Delta TRO\$(t)$$

$$- \Delta TPO\$(t)] + [1 + a_{1t}(c_{1t}(1-b_{3t}) - c_{2t} + c_{3t})$$

$$-a_{2t}] \Delta GE\$(t)] . \tag{8}$$

The first expression on the right-hand side of the equation is the multiplier for changes in government purchases other than public employment programs. It depends on six of the parameters of the model, namely:

a_1, the ratio of a change in consumption to a change in disposable income

a_2, the ratio of a change in investment to a change in GNP

a_3, the ratio of a change in "other GNP" to a change in GNP

b_1, the fraction of a change in GNP going into wages and salaries and other labor income and nonwage income

b_2, the fraction of a change in GNP serving to reduce transfer payments

b_3, the fraction of a change in wages and salaries and other labor income and nonwage income going into personal tax payments

296

The GNP multiplier derived from the Basic Multipliers Model, which is shown in C.B.O. Table 6 (p. 14), is reproduced here as Table 3. Note that the implied balanced budget multipliers, the difference between the federal government expenditure multiplier and the federal tax multiplier, are always below unity. They range from 0.70 in quarter 1 up to 0.98 in quarter 6, and decline to 0.87 in quarter 12.

TABLE 3

Change in GNP Resulting from a Permanent Increment in Policy Instrument:
in Billions of Current Dollars
for Each Billion Dollar Permanent Increment

Quarter	Federal Government Purchases of Goods	Public Service Employment	Federal Taxes or Transfers (with Opposite Sign)
1	1.10	1.15	- 0.40
2	1.42	1.34	- 0.63
3	1.79	1.57	- 1.09
4	2.00	1.66	- 1.07
5	2.22	1.78	- 1.27
6	2.41	1.90	- 1.43
7	2.62	2.04	- 1.64
8	2.71	2.12	- 1.77
9	2.66	2.01	- 1.74
10	2.53	1.96	- 1.64
11	2.44	1.89	- 1.57
12	2.44	1.89	- 1.57

V. The C.B.O. Multipliers Model and Monetary Policy

Fiscal policy simulations discussed above assume constant paths of unborrowed reserves. The C.B.O. multipliers model does not ignore monetary policy. Monetary policy is identified as the path of "unborrowed" reserves. Because borrowed reserves have generally been small in recent years, the C.B.O.'s indicator of monetary policy is close to total reserves for recent observations. In other years, however, changes in borrowed reserves were important sources of change in the base and in the money supply, so parameters estimated using data for earlier periods may be inappropriate to the current period. In addition, unborrowed reserves may also be a poor proxy for the money stock because of changes in currency and the variability of the currency-deposit and of the currency-base ratios, thus making for additional instability in the relationship of unborrowed reserves to the monetary base and money. Also, changes in the money multiplier and money, result from reserve requirement changes. These

297

factors are an additional source of discrepancies between unborrowed reserves and money.

Because Concurrent Resolution 133 requiring the Federal Reserve to present money supply targets was adopted by the Congress over two years ago, it is surprising that the C.B.O. still uses the unborrowed reserve concept. (The Open Market Committee directives do not.) Although the Federal Reserve may have problems because its targets are inconsistent, the set of inconsistent targets is essentially made up of the money supply and interest rates; it excludes unborrowed reserves.

The five large-scale models have even more diverse responses to monetary policy than to fiscal policy. Table 4 shows the simulation results of a $1-billion step increase in unborrowed reserves on the Treasury Bill rate (in percentage points) and nominal GNP (in billions of dollars). Note the standard Keynesian results. Expansionary monetary policy lowers interest rates; the initial decline in rates is later moderated by the effect of rising income on the transactions demand for money. Four of the five models also show long lagged effects of changes in unborrowed reserves on GNP. Note also the very wide range of simulation results for both interest rates and nominal GNP. Chase, Model 3, shows almost no GNP impact of the change in unborrowed reserves; Wharton, Model 2, shows only a small change; the others appear to have substantially larger GNP changes. The C.B.O. makes no attempt to reconcile the differences.

TABLE 4

Changes in Three-Month Treasury Bill Rate and GNP$ in T-1
Resulting from a Step Increase of $1 Billion Reserves

Quarter	Model 1		Model 2		Model 3		Model 4		Model 5	
	Rate	GNP	Rate	GNP	Rate	GNP	Rate	GNP	Rate	GNP
1	-0.98	3.4	-0.60	0.3	-0.13	0.0	-0.6	0.5	-1.26	0.1
2	-1.06	5.4	-0.42	0.9	-0.13	2.5	-0.8	1.8	-1.24	3.7
3	-1.08	13.3	-0.45	1.9	-0.12	4.8	-0.8	4.2	-0.97	6.8
4	-1.05	19.8	-0.45	3.3	-0.12	4.9	-0.8	7.4	-0.97	10.0
5	-0.96	25.5	-0.44	5.0	-0.11	5.5	-0.7	11.4	-0.83	14.2
6	-0.83	30.0	-0.42	6.9	-0.09	4.2	-0.7	15.8	-0.65	16.4
7	-0.73	33.2	-0.39	9.4	-0.08	4.2	-0.6	20.9	-0.54	20.8
8	-0.61	34.8	-0.35	12.5	-0.08	4.3	-0.5	26.9	-0.33	24.9
9	-0.51	35.2	-0.33	13.7	-0.09	4.1	-0.5	33.6	-0.29	28.2
10	-0.45	34.2	-0.32	13.0	-0.10	3.7	-0.4	40.9	-0.17	31.3

In the C.B.O. treatment of monetary policy, unborrowed reserves is added as an additional variable in three of the seven equations of the C.B.O. basic multipliers model. This model is modified to include unborrowed reserves in three of the equations by simply adding unborrowed reserves as an additional variable. The three equations are the consumption function (equation 2), the fixed investment function (equation 6), and the residual "rest of GNP" (equation 7). The equations become

$$\Delta C\$(t) = a_{1t}(\Delta INC\$(t) + \Delta TR\$(t) - \Delta TP\$(t)) + d_{1t}\Delta RU\$(t), \qquad (2)'$$

$$\Delta FI\$(t) = a_{2t}\Delta GNP\$(t) + d_{2t}\Delta RU\$(t), \qquad (6)'$$

$$\Delta X\$(t) = a_{3t}\Delta GNP\$(t) + \Delta XO\$(t) + d_{3t}\Delta RU\$(t), \qquad (7)'$$

where $RU\$$ = unborrowed reserves.

The parameters d_1, d_2, and d_3 evaluate the impact of the change in unborrowed reserves on personal consumption expenditures, fixed investment expenditures, and "rest of GNP," respectively. The coefficients portray what is expected to happen to each of the three GNP components as a direct result of changes in unborrowed reserves. Analogous to the usual Keynesian formulation of specific income effects on particular classes of expenditures, there are assumed to be separate dependable relations between changes in unborrowed reserves and consumption, fixed investment, etc.

To derive the formal unborrowed reserves GNP multipliers, equations $(2)'$, $(6)'$, and $(7)'$ are substituted into the basic multipliers model, yielding

$$\Delta GNP\$(t) = \frac{[(d_1 + d_2 + d_3)\,\Delta RU\$(t)]}{[1 - (a_{1t}(b_{1t}(1 - b_{3t}) - b_{2t}) + a_{2t} + a_{3t})]} + [\text{Fiscal Multiplier}]$$

$$\times\ [\text{Fiscal Policy Variable}].$$

The denominator is the same as the denominator of a simple government purchases multiplier, and the numerator shows the total *direct* GNP increment stemming from a change in unborrowed reserves.

This approach permits the C.B.O. Basic Multipliers Model to include monetary policy without changing the format of the basic set of equations. Again, the model presumes that only the simple Keynesian framework and transmission mechanism are valid. It rules out the possibility that the dependable link is between the nominal stock of money, or even unborrowed reserves, and aggregate nominal GNP, and that relative prices largely determine resource allocation and the components of GNP. It rules out the alternative, and widely-held view that, for a given stock of money, changes in supplies of and demands for particular components of GNP change relative prices and resource allocation but leave aggregate nominal income fixed, so that changes in the demand for any class of expenditures tend to alter or crowd out some others. The link between nominal money and nominal GNP may be a dependable one even if the connections between money and any one specific component of GNP are weak. Indeed, the evidence would seem to be consistent with this alternative view.

The weak relationship between changes in the stock of money and any given class of expenditures can explain the unusual range of estimated values of d_1, d_2, and d_3 in the five large-scale models summarized in C.B.O.'s Table 8, reproduced as Table 5 here. C.B.O. simply takes the means of the five large-scale models as the appropriate estimate for its model.

The structure that generates these results is a standard Keynesian or Hicksian IS-LM model (p. 17). The supply and demand for money depend on income and the rate of interest. The rate of interest is determined when the quantity of money demanded equals the stock of money. Thus, the chain of causation goes from an increase in unborrowed reserves, the proxy for money, leading to lower interest rates, and thereby to more investment, and, by the multiplier process, to higher GNP. In turn, higher GNP increases the transactions demand for money, moderating the initial decline in interest rates. In this model more money, or more unborrowed reserves, cannot cause interest rates to rise above their initial level. There are no effects of inflation expectations on interest rates, no distinction between real and nominal interest rates, and no changes in real interest rates resulting from changes in the productivity of capital stemming from changes in capital-labor ratios.[14] It is distressing that, despite the overwhelming evidence supporting at least the general outline of the Fisherian distinction between real and nominal interest rates and the widespread acceptance of the general Fisherian analysis of the effects of inflation on interest rates, the C.B.O. continues to ignore the distinction.

Despite the C.B.O.'s flawed monetary analysis, the economy is very responsive to monetary policy in the C.B.O. model. According to their Table 9 (p. 20), shown below as Table 6, a $1-billion increase in unborrowed reserves leads to an increase in nominal GNP of close to $9 billion after 4 quarters, an increase in nominal GNP of close to $24 billion after 8 quarters, and $26 billion

---

[14]Meiselman (1976a).

TABLE 5

Quarterly Values of d_1, d_2, d_3, and b_1

Quarter/Parameter	d_1			d_2			d_3			b_1		
	Multipliers Model	Range Provided by Econometric Models		Multipliers Model	Range Provided by Econometric Models		Multipliers Model	Range Provided by Econometric Models		Multipliers Model	Range Provided by Econometric Models	
		Low	High		Low	High		Low	High		Low	High
1	0.17	0.03	0.74	0.33	0.00	1.18	0.00	-0.33	1.41	0.36	-0.96	0.68
2	0.82	1.06	2.81	1.11	0.87	2.84	0.15	-0.84	0.80	0.51	0.00	0.70
3	0.54	0.28	3.38	1.95	1.49	4.40	0.55	-0.43	1.31	0.53	0.05	0.70
4	1.05	0.55	4.48	2.73	1.43	6.00	0.87	-0.26	2.85	0.60	0.15	0.72
5	1.30	0.76	5.97	3.42	1.15	7.50	1.20	-0.24	4.02	0.62	0.24	0.74
6	1.70	1.01	6.76	4.18	1.15	9.23	1.26	-0.33	4.90	0.68	0.26	0.74
7	2.05	1.05	7.74	4.83	0.86	10.54	1.53	-0.12	5.47	0.70	0.26	0.76
8	2.38	1.04	8.98	5.56	0.62	12.11	1.79	0.03	5.83	0.70	0.26	0.77
9	2.64	1.20	9.67	6.01	0.37	12.95	2.17	0.07	6.46	0.71	0.28	0.78
10	2.85	1.25	10.48	6.43	0.32	13.42	2.26	0.04	6.26	0.73	0.29	0.78
11	3.00	...	...	6.60	...	...	2.45	...	...	0.73	...	...
12	3.00	...	...	6.60	...	...	2.45	...	...	0.73	...	...

after 12 quarters. These multipliers are *9 to 10 times greater* than the federal government expenditure multipliers and from *13 to 16 times greater* than the federal tax or transfer multipliers shown in Table 6. Given the far greater ease, neutrality, and reversibility of altering unborrowed reserves compared to varying federal government expenditures or taxes, it would seem that the C.B.O. estimates are, themselves, compelling arguments for the importance of monetary policy and for placing greater reliance on monetary management in stabilization policy, even given the discretionary stabilization policy the C.B.O. appears to favor. It also suggests that giving monetary policy a minor role in the C.B.O.'s forecasts, analyses, and policy evaluations has the effect of removing a central actor from the stabilization and inflation dramas.

TABLE 6

Changes in GNP Resulting from a Permanent Increment in Unborrowed Reserves:
in Billions of Current Dollars for Each Billion Dollar Permanent Increment

Quarter	Multiplier
1	1.00
2	2.86
3	5.12
4	8.77
5	12.10
6	16.17
7	20.29
8	23.80
9	24.83
10	24.88
11	26.15
12	26.15

Despite the sensitivity of GNP to changes in unborrowed reserves in the C.B.O. model, the model appears to understate the responsiveness of GNP to changes in unborrowed reserves. The reason for the understatement is that, as the C.B.O. itself states (p. 18), "A step increase in unborrowed reserves above a baseline path lowers the velocity of money relative to its baseline path." This holds true even three years after the expansion of unborrowed reserves.

In contrast, the evidence on the connections between money and GNP over many business cycles indicates that more money causes velocity to rise, not fall.[15] Thus, GNP is far more sensitive to monetary change than even the C.B.O. results indicate.

For a rough evaluation of the unborrowed reserves-GNP multiplier, consider that in December, 1977, M1, was $335 billion, 8.4 times as large as the

---

[15]Friedman and Schwartz (1963, pp. 676-86).

$39.9 billion reserves of all commercial banks. Income velocity of M1 was approximately 5.8. Thus, the ratio of reserves to GNP was 1:48.7. Because borrowed reserves were close to zero, close to the same figure also holds for the ratio of unborrowed reserves to GNP. This is somewhat more than double the C.B.O.'s unborrowed reserves-GNP multiplier of 23.80 after 8 quarters and almost twice the unborrowed reserves-GNP multiplier of 26.15 after 12 quarters.

The C.B.O. results reflect the decline of income velocity in the C.B.O. model. GNP is sensitive to unborrowed reserves. However, given the currency-deposit ratio, variations in which would be relatively minor over the short span considered in this exercise, the marginal income velocity of new unborrowed reserves would seem to be only half of the average. This is the strange and startling result noted by the C.B.O. in their study.

The inconsistency with the evidence does not seem to trouble the C.B.O., perhaps because of the absence of hypothesis testing already noted. Despite the evidence that, during the short spans of time characteristic of major business cycle phases, M and V generally tend to move together, the C.B.O. analyzes the economy using a model that denies this established result. If the C.B.O. had tested the interest rate and velocity implications of its model, the model would have been contradicted by the evidence and rejected. But no tests were run, and, as elsewhere, there was curve fitting by simulation with no analysis of goodness of fit.

VI. Real Output and Unemployment

The C.B.O. Multipliers Model is specified in nominal values. To separate output and price level effects of a change in nominal GNP, C.B.O. depends on a two-equation wage-price model that incorporates a number of constrained or assumed empirical relations. The model is presented in *A Simplified Wage-Price Model,* an unpublished but readily available paper.[16] The procedure consists of simultaneously estimating wages and prices, largely on the basis of a set of highly constrained and mechanical autoregressive relations. The study claims that the procedure yields a set of consistent and valid solutions for nominal GNP (from the Multipliers Project), wages, prices, real GNP, and unemployment.

The wage equation is

$$\dot{W}_t = a_o - a_1 \log U_t + \sum_{i=0}^{4} b_i \dot{P}_{t-i} ,$$

---

[16]U.S. Congress, Congressional Budget Office (1975c).

where $\dot{W}_t$ is the percent change in an average wage rate in year t, U_t is the overall civilian unemployment rate, in year t, and $\dot{P}_{t-i}$ is the percent change in the consumer price index in year $t-i$.

As the study notes,

> A lot of controversy has centered on the strength of the influence of past price changes on wage changes, measured in equation (1) by the sum of the b_i's. Rather than attempting to resolve this controversy, C.B.O. has made two alternative assumptions about the sum of the b_i's and used the results as two alternative forms of the model. One assumption–an 'accelerationist' variant–is that the sum is 1.0. The other assumption–a 'long-run Phillips curve' variant–is that the sum is 0.7. In neither variant are past price changes ignored, as was the case in much economic analysis of twenty years ago. The difference between the two is the difference between a 70 percent and a 100 percent reflection of past inflation in current wage settlements. (p. 2)

Since the only alternative values for the sum of the b_i's are assumed ones of 0.7 and 1.0, the solution is constrained by these assumptions. Apparently no attempt was made to generate an unconstrained estimate of the lagged relationship between wages and prices. Note also that these values are relevant only to long-run equilibrium solutions, not the short periods typically covered in C.B.O. analyses and in the Multipliers Project. Moreover, despite widespread evidence of major changes in the association between the inflation rate and unemployment rate since the 1950s (including the evidence that the traditional Phillips curve has a positive slope in recent years),[17] the C.B.O. procedure precludes these outcomes.

There is also no recognition in the C.B.O. wage-price study of the large and growing problems in the measurement and interpretation of unemployment statistics and potential GNP. More than usual measurement error may result from taking these data at face value.[18] The same considerations also raise serious questions about the immutability and dependability of Okun's law.

The price equation of the model relates annual price changes to this year's and last year's wage changes as well as to changes in the prices of foods and fuel. The price equation is

---

[17]Meiselman (1976b), Meiselman and Davis (1978), and Friedman (1977).

[18]Clarkson and Meiners (1979) and Perloff and Wachter (1979).

$$\dot{P}_t = c_0 + c_1 \dot{W}_t + c_2 \dot{W}_{t-1} + c_3 \dot{Fm}_t + c_4 \dot{Fu}_t \, ,$$

where $\dot{P}_t$ is the percent change in the consumer price index in year t, $\dot{W}_t$ and $\dot{W}_{t-1}$ are percent changes in an average wage rate in years t and t-1, and Fm_t and Fu_t are percent changes in wholesale farm prices (Fm) and wholesale fuel prices (Fu) in year t.

The price equation was also estimated subject to another constraint, i.e., that the two wage change coefficients, c_1 and c_2, sum to 0.9. Further, as the C.B.O. (1975c, p. 3) notes, the price equation "does not include any representation of cyclical changes in productivity, of order backlogs and capacity constraints, or of price controls. Detailed representation of these influences would greatly complicate the model."

Experiments are performed using dummy variables to capture the effect of imposing and removing price controls. The dummy variables for price controls are 1 for 1971 and 1972, 0 for 1973, and -1 for 1974. The solution is constrained by the C.B.O. assumption that imposing and removing price controls have equal and opposite effects. There is no evidence presented or cited for this presumption of fact. Productivity changes or capacity bottlenecks are seen as captured by the change in the logarithm of the unemployment rate. Productivity changes have no direct link to wages. There is also no justification given for singling out food and fuel prices for special treatment.

More constraints were added on the price coefficients of the wage equation and on the wage coefficients of the price equation. Still more constraints were added when the effect of lagged prices was estimated by "the Almon distributed-lag method with coefficients assumed to lie along a third-degree polynomial crossing the origin at the distant end" (p. 5). Another constraint takes the form of a correction for autocorrelated residuals in the price equation. The mechanical adjustment used to make the correction is no substitute for a missing variable or an incorrectly specified functional form that may be the cause of the autocorrelated residuals. The claims of the C.B.O. study that these constraints make the danger of simultaneous equations bias quite small (p. 5) are therefore questionable, especially since it is not at all clear that these constraints and mechanical corrections are correct or appropriate.

Because of these and other constraints and omissions, we have little confidence in the results. Further, other evidence[19] contradicts some of the constraints the C.B.O. imposes on the data. It may have been better, at least it would have been more candid, if numerical values had simply been explicitly

---

[19]Meiselman and Davis (1978) and Friedman (1977).

assigned to the parameters. Moreover, because many of the results are highly sensitive to small changes in the coefficients, for example, equations 3 and 4 (p. 7) which attempt to estimate the long-run relationship between inflation and unemployment, it is important that estimates be properly done.

Finally, we do not see any economics behind these numerical exercises. Surely, there is more to unemployment and inflation than inertia.

VII. The C.B.O.'s Economic Forecasts

Economic forecasts are a mandated task of the Congressional Budget Office. Not only are C.B.O. forecasts presented as part of the general concern about future events, but the forecasts are an important and integral part of C.B.O.'s analysis of the consequences of alternative public policies.

C.B.O. forecasts are presented in their semiannual reports devoted to analyses of current economic conditions. The reports appear early in the calendar year and at midyear. The first C.B.O. forecast is found in *Inflation and Unemployment: A Report on the Economy,* C.B.O.'s initial publication.[20] Since then, forecasts of periods up to two years ahead have been presented at intervals of approximately six months.

How good are the C.B.O. forecasts? To evaluate the C.B.O. forecasts, we have compared their accuracy with that of other widely cited forecasts analyzed in various studies by Stephen K. McNees of the Federal Reserve Bank of Boston. Because the C.B.O. has been in operation only a few years, it is not possible to do extensive comparative tests. However, several comparisons can be made. They indicate that C.B.O. forecasts are less accurate than other available forecasts.

First, consider the relative accuracy of C.B.O.'s first three forecasts made from mid-1975 to early 1976, covering 1976. The first forecast was published June 30, 1975,[21] the second on September 17, 1975.[22] The third forecast was published March 15, 1976,[23] two and a half months into 1976, a factor which did not improve the accuracy of the forecast relative to the earlier two. The C.B.O. forecasts and the range of forecasts assembled by McNees are presented in Table 6, which also includes the figures for the actual results. The specific high, median, and low forecasters are not identified, but the C.B.O.

---

[20]U.S. Congress, Congressional Budget Office (1975a).

[21]Ibid., p. 28.

[22]U.S. Congress, Congressional Budget Office (1975b, p. 34).

[23]U.S. Congress, Congressional Budget Office (1976, p. 20).

forecasts are drawn from forecasts made by five widely known forecasters, The Bureau of Economic Analysis of the U.S. Department of Commerce; Chase Econometrics Associates, Inc.; Data Resources, Inc.; Wharton Econometrics Forecasting Associates, Inc.; and the median forecast from the Economic Research survey by the American Statistical Association and the National Bureau of Economic Research. Three of the five, Chase, D.R.I., and Wharton, also provide three of the five large-scale models the C.B.O. used in their Multipliers Project. Because C.B.O. forecasts are presented as ranges without any statement about probabilities within the forecast range, we merely took the midpoint of the range as the point forecast for purposes of comparability.

TABLE 6

Forecast and Actual Changes, 1975_{IV}-1976_{IV}

Growth Rate (percentage points)	Five Forecasts*			C.B.O. (midpoint of range)			Actual
	High	Median	Low	6/30/75	9/17/75	3/15/76	
Real GNP	5.7	5.4	5.2	5.5	6.0	6.25	5.0
GNP Deflator	6.2	5.9	5.0	7.5	6.75	5.75	4.6
GNP	11.9	11.7	10.7	13.3	13.0	12.15	9.8
Unemployment Rate†	7.8	7.3	7.2	8.0	7.25	7.25	7.9
				Range			
Real GNP				5.0-6.0	5.0-7.0	5.5-7.0	5.0
GNP Deflator				6.5-8.5	6.0-7.5	5.0-6.5	4.6
GNP				12.6-14.0	11.5-14.5	11.5-12.8	9.8
Unemployment Rate†				7.8-8.2	6.9-7.6	7.0-7.5	7.9

*McNees (July/August, 1976, Table IX, p. 11).

†Level in final quarter.

Consider the C.B.O. September 17, 1975 forecast for changes in real GNP, the GNP deflator, and nominal GNP from fourth quarter, 1975, to fourth quarter, 1976, and for the fourth quarter, 1976 level of the unemployment rate. The March 15, 1976 forecast was almost a quarter into the forecast period, and the June 30, 1975 forecast was made earlier in the year than the other forecasts.

The C.B.O. forecasts do very poorly in these comparisons. For real GNP, the GNP deflator, and nominal GNP, the C.B.O. forecast has the largest error.

For the unemployment rate, the C.B.O.'s first forecast is best. The later forecasts are close to the median.

The forecast range is also shown in Table 6. The actual GNP deflator, nominal GNP, and the unemployment rate fall outside the range, and real GNP is at the end-point of the range. Simply taking the median of the otherwise available forecasts would be an improvement over the C.B.O.'s own forecasting effort.

The earlier June 30, 1975 forecast for real GNP was closer to the actual figure than the later two forecasts, but the other three forecast values involved greater forecast errors. The March 15, 1976 forecast values are somewhat closer to the actual figures for the GNP deflator and for nominal GNP, but even here they are worse than the poorest of the other forecasts. For real GNP, the forecasting error actually increased.

We also compared the same three C.B.O. forecasts for 1976 with eight forecasts surveyed in another McNees study.[24] The eight forecasts include those of the Council of Economic Advisers and seven private forecasters. These are the median forecasts of the survey by the American Statistical Association and the National Bureau of Economic Research and those issued by Chase Econometric Associates, Inc.; Data Resources, Inc.; the MAPCAST group at the General Electric Company; Irwin L. Kellner, of Manufacturers Hanover Trust; RSQE forecasting service at the University of Michigan; and Wharton Econometric Forecasting Associates, Inc.

The mean of the absolute errors made by the eight forecasters is shown in Table 7 for the growth rates of real GNP, nominal GNP, and the implicit GNP deflator, and for the change in the unemployment rate. Forecasting errors of each of the C.B.O. forecasts are also shown in Table 7. In Table 8, the errors of the three C.B.O. forecasts and the C.B.O.'s mean error for each variable are compared with the mean errors of the eight other forecasts. Again, it turns out that the C.B.O. forecasts are generally less accurate than other available forecasts.

In each of the three C.B.O. forecasts, there is at least one variable with a smaller forecast error. However, the specific variable differs each time. For example, the June 30, 1975 forecast for nominal GNP was more accurate than the mean forecast, but the September 17, 1975 forecast was more accurate for real GNP. The same is true for the accuracy of the March 15, 1975 forecasts for the GNP deflator and for the unemployment rate. Thus, there is no variable that C.B.O. consistently forecasts better than the eight forecasters. Overall, the C.B.O. forecasts for 1976 were poorer than the eight in the McNees tabulation,

---

[24]McNees (1977, Table 4, p. 7).

so there was nothing gained by using C.B.O. forecasts rather than those otherwise available.

TABLE 7

1976 Forecast Errors, Absolute Percent Error for Eight Forecasters and The C.B.O.

Rate of Growth of:	Eight Forecasters (Mean Absolute error)	C.B.O. Forecasts			
		6/30/75	9/17/75	3/15/76	Mean
Real GNP	0.4	1.3	0.2	0.6	0.70
GNP Deflator	0.9	2.0	1.2	0.5	1.23
Nominal GNP	0.7	0.1	1.8	1.3	1.07
Unemployment Rate*	0.2	0.3	0.25	0.175	0.24

*First Difference.

TABLE 8

C.B.O. Forecast Errors as a Percentage of the Mean Absolute Error of Eight Prominent Forecasters

Rate of Growth of:	C.B.O. Forecasts			
	6/30/75	9/17/75	3/15/76	Mean
Real GNP	325	50	150	175
GNP Deflator	222	133	56	137
Nominal GNP	14	257	186	153
Unemployment Rate*	150	125	88	120

*First Difference

VIII. The Short-Run in Perpetuity

The C.B.O. Multipliers Project emphasizes the short-run. The C.B.O.'s
view of the long-run is found in *Closing the Fiscal Policy Loop: A Long-Run
Analysis* (1977 a). This study combines the viewpoint of a 1930 stagnationist
with the computer technology of the 1970s. There are neither resource allocation nor efficiency problems, nor market solutions. There is no supply and no
production. Even economic growth is determined by aggregate demand and
aggregate demand management. Saving is a threat to growth. The model is
summarized in Figure 1, a model flow chart copied from the study (p. 8).

The report's analysis and statistical projections are generally similar to
those found in the Multipliers Study, and they share its general deficiencies
when applied to short-period analyses. These deficiencies and biases are

MODEL FLOW CHART

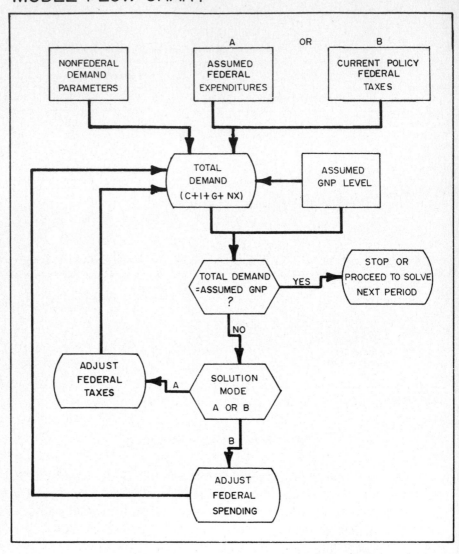

Figure 1

augmented when the Keynesian framework and the C.B.O.'s statistical procedures are applied to long-run analysis. Despite the title, however, there is no long-run in the C.B.O. study. The rigidities and information deficiencies that characterize the short-run and impair full and informed adjustments remain. The C.B.O. assumes that there is no lessening of rigidities and ignorance in the long-run.

The C.B.O.'s long-run analysis has demand without supply, inflation without money, interest rates without capital, output without inputs, employment without wage rates and a labor market, and investment without saving or any change in the capital stock. There are static expectations throughout; either nobody ever learns anything, or people just don't care enough to change their behavior. More than twenty years after the consumption analyses of Friedman and of Modigliani and Brumberg, analyses which have been validated by extensive tests and have been accepted by virtually all economists, consumption spending is taken to depend on current disposable income rather than on income received over a wider span of time. In addition, households only spend current income; they cannot or do not borrow. There is no consumer credit. Households have essentially no assets and no capital management decisions.

IX. Understanding Fiscal Policy

When this paper was presented at the Conference, representatives of the C.B.O. said that there had been changes in the C.B.O.'s fiscal policy views since the studies we examined were prepared. Specifically, they called attention to a new study *Understanding Fiscal Policy*, which was brought to our attention in unpublished form on March 23, 1978, when our own paper was in the final stages of preparation. It was alleged that we had ignored this study because it did not support the criticisms that we made of C.B.O.'s fiscal policy model.[25]

We had not ignored the study. We found it contained the main points we had criticized in the C.B.O.'s fiscal policy model. Since the study was unpublished and appeared late, we focused instead on published studies which C.B.O. acknowledged to be central. Now that C.B.O. representatives have said that *Understanding Fiscal Policy* is their current view, we discuss it more thoroughly.

As before, C.B.O. "compares effects of several different policies based on C.B.O.'s system of multipliers" (p. 16). Once again, C.B.O. concludes that increases in government purchases and public service employment programs

---

[25] A footnote to the discussion of the effectiveness of fiscal instruments states, "A somewhat similar discussion of fiscal instruments appears in an earlier C.B.O. report, *Temporary Measures to Stimulate Employment*, Sept., 1975" (p. 38).

are more effective in stimulating GNP and employment than are equivalent reductions in personal income tax rates. In C.B.O.'s words, "a permanent income tax cut is a relatively expensive way of reducing unemployment in terms of budget dollars (net or gross costs) per additional job" (p. 38). Dollar for dollar, C.B.O. finds that government purchases have the greatest impact on GNP (nominal and real), while "despite the displacement assumptions (50 percent), employment effects are largest for public employment; and these programs are estimated to be more effective in stimulating jobs per dollar than federal purchases or tax cuts.[26] Since tax rate reductions are considered to have the weakest impact on GNP and employment, they are considered to have the weakest impact on the price level (p. 17). Notice that these results imply no shift in the aggregate supply function. There is only movement along a given schedule, so, the less production and employment, the less inflation. This is true to the standard Keynesian model in which fiscal policy affects demand, and there are no incentive or disincentive effects that shift the supply schedule.

In response to critics who have pointed out that C.B.O. ignores the supply-side incentive and disincentive effects of fiscal policy, C.B.O. argues that

> among the least understood effects of fiscal policy are any influences on personal incentives to work or to save. Even at the theoretical level, there is no clear presumption that these effects run in one direction or another. (p. 7)

C.B.O. says that it is entirely an empirical question, and that the evidence is skimpy.[27] As an example, they cite a worker who may retire earlier (and thus work less) because a tax reduction lets him achieve his targeted level of income and wealth sooner. "Higher tax rates," says C.B.O., "could make one perfectly rational person work less and another perfectly rational person work more" (p. 7). Although the idea of a targeted level of income and wealth *irrespective of the cost of acquiring it* is foreign to the price-theoretical perspective of economic science, for the sake of argument, suppose that one person works less and another more in response to a tax rate reduction. It does not follow from this assumption that "even at the theoretical level there is no clear presumption that these effects run in one direction or another."

C.B.O. is arguing that the income effect of a tax rate reduction works counter to, and offsets, the substitution effect so that the net effect is ambiguous.

---

[26]The C.B.O. study makes strong claims for public service employment without defining what a job is. Some economists wonder if we attain full employment by redefining unemployment compensation as public service employment. Is a tax-supported job that does not produce marketable goods and services the same as a tax-generating job that does?

[27]They make no reference to Michael Boskin's work on the responsiveness of savings. (See Boskin, 1978).

C.B.O. has confused the income effect of a productivity change, which produces more real income in the aggregate, with the income effect of a relative price change that does not in itself produce more aggregate real income.[28] In aggregating the individual responses to a change in relative prices, C.B.O. appears to ignore the general equilibrium effects. In the absence of bizarre distributional effects, the income effects of the relative price change wash out, leaving only the substitution effects, which unambiguously increase work effort and savings. There can be no aggregate income effect from a relative price change unless the incentive effect raises real aggregate income.[29]

C.B.O.'s argument that people respond to tax rate reductions by working less (or reducing their savings rate) is directed against the effectiveness of incentives in shifting the aggregate supply function. But if people were to respond to tax cuts by working less, real GNP would fall, and it would mean that Keynesian fiscal policy could not be expansionary.

C.B.O.'s argument against the incentive effects of fiscal policy is contradicted by their exposition of the effects of expansionary fiscal moves, such as a tax cut:

> In most expansionary fiscal moves, a relatively small propor-
> tion of the increase in national income goes directly to the
> newly employed. A significant proportion goes into
> increasing profits, another significant proportion into
> *increasing average hours of those already employed.* (p. 45,
> italics added)

If workers respond by working less, these propositions are no longer correct.

Whatever the reason for the C.B.O.'s considerable confusion about this issue, the result is to misinform policymakers about the relative strength of personal income tax rate reduction as a tool of employment and economic growth policy.

C.B.O. apparently thinks that criticisms of the models for neglecting supply-side effects have been answered by making the models "sensitive to disturbances from the supply side," such as higher fuel and food prices. C.B.O. thinks of supply-side effects, not in terms of incentives, but in terms of episodic events having to do with the weather and the OPEC oil cartel.

---

[28] See Roberts (1978a).

[29] An income tax rate change is a relative price change. It changes the relative price of leisure in terms of foregone current income and the relative price of current consumption in terms of foregone future income. Therefore, it affects at the margin the choices between leisure and current income and between current consumption and future income.

The analysis of corporate and payroll tax changes and public service employment, like the analysis of personal income tax changes, neglects incentives. Payroll taxes affect costs and spending--not incentives to work and to hire. C.B.O. does not analyze the effect of a payroll tax by noting that it raises the price to the demander and lowers it to the supplier and thus affects the number employed. Instead, in the C.B.O. view, if the tax falls on employees, their spending is reduced, and this sets "in motion a chain of contractions in responding" (p. 5). On the other hand, if the tax falls on the employer it could be used to offset short-run changes in private spending:

> A temporary cut in an element of business costs can lead to temporary price discounts, which should stimulate buying while the temporary cut is in effect without any long-run impact on prices. A temporary increase should have the reverse effect. (p. 41)

The way payroll taxes affect employment is by causing higher interest rates:

> The higher prices that are set in response to an increase in employer payroll taxes, reduce the real value of wealth and cause higher interest rates, and thereby depress real output and employment. (p. 41)

That a payroll tax affects employment only through the interest rate, and not through take-home pay and the gross cost to the employer, is testimony to C.B.O.'s neglect of supply-side effects. This neglect is underlined by the fact that C.B.O. views a value-added tax as a cost and compares it dollar-for-dollar with a payroll tax (p. 41). C.B.O. overlooks the fact that a value-added tax, unlike a payroll tax, is neutral with respect to resource allocation and income distribution.

In C.B.O.'s fiscal analysis of March, 1978, corporate income tax rate changes continue to be a weak tool of fiscal policy. C.B.O. does not mention that a reduction in the corporate tax rate raises the after-tax rate of return to capital and increases the profitability of investment. Rather, the effect is modeled in terms of increased cash flow and higher stock prices, "with significant effects on personal wealth and hence on consumer spending" (p. 39).

On the other hand, investment tax credits and accelerated depreciation have powerful impacts, because they affect "the after-tax return on investment" (p. 39). C.B.O. does not explain why an income tax rate reduction (corporate and personal) does not affect the after-tax return on investment. That a reduction in corporate income tax rates has to affect the economy by affecting consumer spending through a wealth effect is another indication that supply-side effects on incentives are neglected.

C.B.O. believes that tax rate reductions have indirect effects that discourage investment. Since tax cuts increase spending (but not saving--See p. 7), the results are tight credit markets and higher interest rates which "make borrowing for new investment more expensive." The financing effects work contrary to the spending effects. On the other hand, a tax increase, which reduces the after-tax return to savings and investment, "has opposite effects, easing credit markets and encouraging spending" (p. 5). In other sections of the March, 1978 study, C.B.O. allows savings to increase in order to dampen the expansionary effects of tax rate reductions, but the savings remain idle and do not ease credit markets, lower interest rates, or encourage spending (p. 43).

As a final example of C.B.O.'s neglect of supply-side effects, consider C.B.O.'s inability to differentiate a tax rate reduction from a rebate of taxes on past incomes, which leave current and future relative prices unchanged. C.B.O. compares the 1964 tax rate reduction with the 1975-76 rebates in terms of the impact on disposable income and demand. C.B.O. ignores the fact that a rebate has no incentive effects, since, unlike a rate reduction, a rebate does not change the relative prices that govern the choices between additional current income and leisure and between additional future income and current consumption.

The same study states that "any discussion of the impact of fiscal policy is incomplete without an indication of what is assumed about the response of monetary authorities" (p. 23). The study reports results from a simulation showing that an increase in federal purchases that is accomodated by monetary policy is practically self-financing (i.e., no net deficit after reflows). The C.B.O. study then attacks the contention that permanent tax rate reduction under the Kemp-Roth bill would be self-financing, *but does not indicate C.B.O.'s assumption about the response of monetary authorities*. In Keynesian models, why is an accomodated spending increase self-financing, while an accomodated tax cut is not?

In its analysis of the budget "cost" (net deficit) of the Kemp-Roth bill, the C.B.O. calculates only the higher revenue resulting from the projected increase in spending. There is no calculation of increased revenue arising from an increase in aggregate supply or the tax revenues that result when lower marginal tax rates draw people from tax shelters and from the underground economy into the tax base. Neither is there any calculation of the increase in private savings as an offset to any net budget deficit.

315

There are other examples of deficiencies in the C.B.O.'s analysis that bias the C.B.O. conclusions. In the discussion of the expansionary spending effect of a personal income tax reduction, attention is also called to the restrictive effect of the higher federal deficit and higher interest rate (p. 1). In comparison, public service employment programs apparently do not have any restrictive deficit and interest rate effects. Even a program with a 100 percent displacement rate is favorably viewed:

> Even if displacement under a particular program is 100 percent, it would not be correct to conclude that the program has no economic effects. Federal grants used to support local programs increase the total financial resources of local governments (or other sponsors), and this increase will generally lead to some change in economic behavior. Even if local governments "displace" public service employment money, the federal funds provide resources that can be used to cut taxes or avoid tax increases or to undertake (or avoid cutting back) other spending programs. Moreover, if state and local governments were to let their budget surpluses merely increase, such increases would still serve to cancel any restrictive credit market effects that are caused by the expanded federal deficit. (p. 4)

When C.B.O.'s simulations show that public service employment causes higher prices than alternative employment policies (p. 17), the claim is advanced that "public service employment programs also can potentially cause less price pressure per job created than other fiscal instruments" (p. 46). Another example is that distributional issues are apparently only raised by personal income tax reductions (p. 39), and not by increases in government spending programs. In view of Alice Rivlin's statement that "the study is written for the informed citizen, not for the trained economist" (p. iii), more care should have been taken not to mislead an untrained layman.

Perhaps the most striking feature of *Understanding Fiscal Policy* is its brief discussion of monetary policy. (See pp. 21-23). The paper correctly notes that "the effects of a fiscal policy change depend a great deal on whether monetary authorities use their control over bank reserves to neutralize the impact of the fiscal policy on interest rates, to neutralize the impact of the policy on the money supply, or to follow some other strategy, such as supplying the same level of bank reserves they would have supplied in the absence of the policy." The paper then goes on to estimate "what difference the response of monetary authorities makes in the estimated effects of the $10 billion one-step increase in federal purchases."

Using only the MPS model, C.B.O. obtains the results shown in their Figure 4 (p. 22), which we have reproduced as Figure 2. The exercise shows the estimated impact of an increase in federal government purchases with three different monetary policy targets: (1) money supply unchanged; (2) bank reserves path unchanged, and (3) bill rate unchanged. (The paper has no corresponding estimates for tax cuts.) Our previous discussion shows that the results of simulating monetary change in the other large-scale models would not differ substantially from the results of the MPS model. The C.B.O. apparently thinks well enough of the MPS model to run these simulations and publish the results.

Taken at face value, the results indicate that there is complete long-run crowding out after 8 quarters. Thus, there is no such thing as pure fiscal action.[30] Only money matters! If increases (decreases) in government expenditures have any expansionary (contractionary) impact on output and employment, it is only when these are accompanied by money supply changes. As Figure 2 shows, a $10-billion sustained increase in federal purchases with money supply unchanged causes nominal GNP, which includes federal purchases, to increase a total of approximately $14 billion after 4 quarters, but this increase in GNP falls below $10 billion within 8 quarters and approaches a steady state increase of $7 billion after 11 and 12 quarters. This means that nonfederal expenditures, mainly private sector spending, *declines* by $3 billion. The price level rises, however, so the $3-billion decline understates the real effect. As shown in Figure 2, real GNP *falls* after 8 quarters.

The results are startling. After 12 quarters, for given money, the price level increases by 0.7 percent; *employment is unchanged,*[31] and real GNP is $2.0 billion lower. Private real GNP declines more than $2 billion because GNP also includes the federal purchases. If the real value of the $10 billion of spending falls by 0.7 percent after 12 quarters because of higher prices, the increase in real federal purchases after 12 quarters is $9.3 billion, and private real GNP declines by $11.3 billion, or $2.0 billion *more* than the increase in real government purchases. More government expenditure reduces the total size of the pie. This is crowding out with a vengeance! Is this a government expenditure multiplier or a divider? As expected, the results differ sharply when pegged bill rates are assumed and differ moderately when the monetary target is taken to be an unchanged bank reserves path.

---

[30]Roberts and Van Cott (1978) arrive at the same conclusion on the basis of theoretical considerations.

[31]Figure 2 shows employment changes at zero after 11 quarters; there is no reading for quarter 12.

The Monetary Response and the Impact of a $10 Billion Increase in Federal Purchases

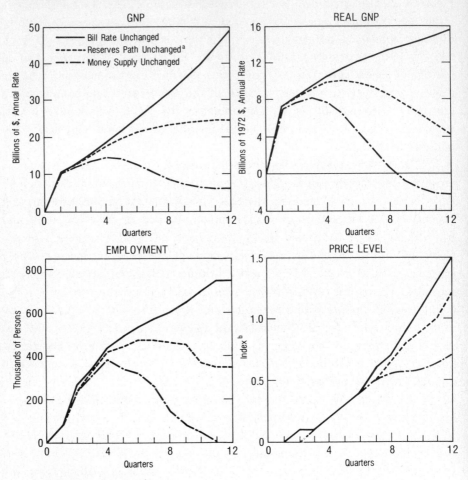

NOTE: Step changes begin in first quarter.

a Unborrowed reserves only.
b Records number of point changes in the index.

Figure 2

If these results are accepted, it means that the only point to fiscal policy is to affect the money stock. Since the money stock can be and typically is altered independently of fiscal action, it would seem that there is no basis for using fiscal policy for stabilization purposes. What remains is the pre-Keynesian use of tax and expenditure powers primarily to affect resource allocation and to finance government expenditures.

Taken at face value, these results imply that the C.B.O. fiscal policy multipliers have only temporary impact effects. Yet, after presenting these startling results, the paper continues as if it hadn't happened. There is little or no attempt to reconcile these results with the remainder of the paper or with other C.B.O. analyses and pronouncements.

X. Consequences of the Congressional Budget Act

Is the new budget process a success or failure? It would be convenient if we had some nice clean measures of success or failure and good empirical data, but as Ellwood and Thurber point out, "One cannot create measures to judge the success or failure of the new process until these terms are defined. The critical fact is that different groups supported the new process expecting it to achieve different results."[32] On the basis of personal experience while working on the staff of the House Budget Committee, one of the authors concludes that Ellwood and Thurber are correct to point out divergent expectations from different supporters of the Budget Act. Many Congressmen who were dissatisfied with the budget expressed concern that the budget was out of control, but control did not mean the same thing to all of them. Some were concerned by the growth of federal spending and the number and size of deficits. Others were concerned with the extent of back-door spending and the fact that less than half of the budget was subject to the appropriations process. For still others, the budget being out of control meant that it was an ex post result of an appropriations process that did not take into account its "fiscal" impact on the economy. For yet others, it meant that the appropriations process did not provide a mechanism for achieving their spending priorities. For economists outside, looking in through the window of their public choice theory, the Budget Act meant better tools with which to pursue the social welfare.

How, then, does one measure the success of a system that was supported by some in order to eliminate budget deficits and by others in order to set fiscal policy, particularly in a period when measures of unemployment and capacity utilization suggested the need for economic stimulus, i.e., deficits?

---

[32]Ellwood and Thurber (1977, p. 90).

Even if we picked a success indicator--say holding down the growth in federal spending and the deficit--in order to have a basis for looking at the empirical data and generating some numbers, we still face difficulties. First, the budget process may still be evolving as a result of unresolved differences among the participants over what it is.

Second, the deficit and spending figures may give conflicting indications. For example, the first budget to come out of the new process, the budget for FY 1976, had the largest deficit on record. But if the expenditure figure is adjusted to a full employment basis and put in constant dollars, there is a decline in the rate of increase in spending. Before concluding that the process was holding down spending below what it would otherwise have been and that the record deficit was the result of recession, one would have to consider whether the recession also resulted in a lack of new spending initiatives. The control problems are substantial.

Third, the budget may be determined by a process unrelated to the new procedures. For example, since no group wants another's power to dispense expenditure favors to grow relative to its own, if one group attempts to increase its relative position, the spending process can be deadlocked, and the growth of spending reduced, by another group's defense of its relative position.[33] We would have to have data over a longer period to separate the effects of the budget process.

The combined deficits for the three years since the new budget procedure has been in operation are three times the size of the deficit for the three years prior to the new process. While this suggests that the Budget Act has contributed to deficits, it is not conclusive evidence. Economists who can only interpret evidence found in statistical tables may have to wait some years before they can tender a tentative judgment whether the budget process affects spending, and even these data may not allow us to say whether the process is a success or failure.

There is a more interesting question than whether the budget process is a success or failure, and that question is: Do the new budget process and the C.B.O. really matter? To answer this question, economists can look to see if the new process caused any changes in incentives, constraints, or information.[34] Some who supported the new process clearly thought that it would. Some members of Congress thought that colleagues whom they regarded as "big

---

[33] During a time period that overlaps with the new budget process, Senator Edward M. Kennedy has been using the concept of "tax expenditures" to launch an attack on the powers of the tax-writing committees. "Tax breaks," he says, are equivalent to government grants and should be handled through the authorization and appropriation process and dispersed through the appropriate federal agency. The Senate Finance Committee's response was to block the energy taxes that could have financed Kennedy's national health program and welfare reform. See *Congressional Record* (Nov. 15, 1977, pp. S19034-35) and Senator Kennedy's press release of April 16, 1978.

[34] A discussion of incentives should not be confused with a discussion of motives.

spenders" had it too easy, because they could indirectly legislate big deficits by voting in favor of many separate bills. Fiscal conservatives believed that if "big spenders" had to vote on an aggregate outlay figure and the size of the deficit itself, there would be lower and firmer limits to spending. Fiscal conservatives thought of the budget process, not as a way to set fiscal policy, but as a way of putting the "big spenders" on the spot.[35]

Fiscal liberals, on the other hand, were attracted by the prospect of having deficits shed their political onus by being sanctioned prior to the appropriations process.[36] If the criteria for control were defined in terms of Keynesian demand management fiscal policy, deficits would then originate in the economic policy proposals of the experts in the C.B.O. and Budget Committees and would no longer be evidence that spending was "out of control" but, instead, "under control." They thereby redefined control.

Fiscal conservatives may have suffered from constituency "ethnocentricism" in thinking that "big spenders" would be voted out of office if they voted in favor of large deficits. They overlooked the fact that being "liberal" was not entirely a matter of a state of mind; in many instances it is a matter of rational self-interest among politicians whose districts or states provide opportunities to build spending constituencies.

It is difficult to conclude that the new budget process has changed the incentives that produced the "overspending" (deficits) and the perceived lack of expenditure control that led conservatives to support the new process. Rather than tightening the constraints and increasing the costs on the "big spenders," it would seem to have loosened spending constraints and reduced costs to Congress by institutionalizing the Keynesian rationale for deficits. The fiscal policy information supplied by the C.B.O. and the Budget Committee staffs does not conflict with the spending incentives that already exist.[37] Proposed deficits now emanate from a professional staff as scientific economic policy recommendations upon which the nation's level of employment and rate of economic growth depend. Fiscal conservatives would seem to be in a weakened

---

[35] Ellwood and Thurber (1977, p. 84) came to the same conclusion. They write, "Some members, mostly conservatives, felt if Congressmen and Senators were forced to vote on the deficit or surplus, the tendency for even larger deficits would be reversed. To this extent they saw the vote not as a way to exercise fiscal policy but as a means to limit spending."

[36] As Ellwood and Thurber (1977, p. 94) point out, "Both committees, but particularly the Senate Budget Committee, were willing and eager to use the new process to set fiscal policy."

[37] The argument may be made that other information supplied by the C.B.O., such as studies of specific spending proposals and the scorekeeping reports, work counter to the fiscal policy justification of deficits and serve to hold down spending. The problem with this argument is that neither the analysis of specific programs nor the scorekeeping process has anything to do with the determination of the overall level of outlays and the size of the deficit. The fact that some programs lose out in the competition for budget shares does not mean that total spending is reduced. The processes are unrelated. The scorekeeping process takes as givens the outlay and revenue figures set in the budget resolution. It does not hold down spending, but merely keeps the Congress informed of its progress toward the mark it set.

position, because their resistance to deficits can now be portrayed as an attack on the budget process and on scientifically derived stabilization policy.

Some academics also supported the new budget process as a result of their view that Congress could not achieve budgetary control on a year-by-year basis. They saw the budgetary process in terms of advanced budgeting, or forward planning, through which Congress would decide now what the budget should be for future years. But, given the short-run stabilization criteria of Keynesian fiscal policy, it is impossible to know today what deficits will be needed in future periods. The idea of achieving budgetary control through advanced budgeting means that fiscal policy would have to operate through tax policy. To try to operate fiscal policy through the outlay side would mean constantly undoing the forward planned outlays.

This may prove to be a problem for advanced budgeting. Assume a policy prescription for more stimulus. For given forward planned expenditures, more stimulus would require tax reductions, which is not the favored policy tool.

The C.B.O.'s analysis finds tax reduction to be a less effective policy tool for providing economic stimulus than increases in government expenditures. First, the C.B.O. believes that the GNP response to more government expenditures is greater, and the lags shorter, than it is to a corresponding dollar change in taxes. Government expenditure multipliers are systematically higher than tax multipliers. Second, the effects of government spending are taken to be more dependable for government expenditures because consumers may decide to save still more of the given tax cut. Third, the general presumption of underemployed resources and a persistent problem of insufficient aggregate demand implies little or no resource cost of more government.

In its analysis of the fiscal policy effects of changes in personal income tax rates, the C.B.O. ignores the incentive and disincentive effects of tax rate changes on aggregate supply, efficiency and resource allocation.[38] In the C.B.O.'s analysis, tax rate changes affect only current disposable income and spending. Thus, the C.B.O. cannot differentiate between a temporary tax rebate and a permanent reduction in personal income tax rates. One of the authors, while on the staff of the House Budget Committee, brought this to the attention of the C.B.O., and Members of the House Budget Committee officially raised the issue with Alice Rivlin, Director of the C.B.O. In her response, Dr. Rivlin acknowledged that the econometric models used to simulate policy alternatives do not include the relative price effects of changes in personal income tax rates. However, since C.B.O. believes that the performance of the economy is a function of spending levels,[39] not of production incentives, she expressed

---

[38]This is discussed in more detail by Roberts (1978a).

[39]See, for example, *Closing the Fiscal Policy Loop: A Long-Run Analysis*.

little concern over the neglect of the supply-side effects of fiscal policy. As she said in her March 11, 1977 letter to Representative Rousselot,

> In the range of policy options that we have been dealing with, I think the assumption that changes in marginal tax rates have no quantitatively significant effect on labor supply is quite plausible. . . .the models do tend to neglect the influence of tax rates and other incentives on aggregate supply and capital formation. But it is far from clear that these effects are quantitatively important, especially over one or two years.[40]

Some members of Congress claim to be interested in "tax reform" and in closing "loopholes" without compensating rate reductions. This would raise effective tax rates, and would redistribute the tax burden. To have fiscal stimulus provided by tax reductions is inconsistent with goals of income redistribution--unless the budget committees can gain sufficient power over the tax committees to specify the form of the tax reductions as well as the amount.

C.B.O.'s analysis and conclusions are not at odds with the activities of the majority of members of Congress, who continue to support new spending programs and growth in existing programs. There do not, then, seem to be any pressure points from which the participants in the process can change the fiscal policy content of the budget options.

Advocates of public service employment (PSE) now cite the C.B.O. estimates to document their case that tax reduction is a weak tool of employment policy. For example, Killingsworth and King state,

> There is some doubt that business tax cuts result in reductions in unemployment; the Congressional Budget Office estimating procedure assumes that they do not.[41]

They refer to the September, 1975, C.B.O. study, *Temporary Measures to Stimulate Employment,* done at the request of Senator Muskie, Chairman of

---

[40]For the correspondence, see *Congressional Record* (July 11, 1978, pp. H6473-74). C.B.O. has been under mounting pressure for their disregard of the supply-side effects of fiscal policy, and there is some hope that the C.B.O.'s future analyses will start to take supply factors into account. In a letter of June 2, 1978 to Representative Barber Conable, Ranking Minority Member of the Committee on Ways and Means, Dr. Rivlin said that C.B.O. is "unable to provide estimates of the long-run impact of tax cuts" and cannot "provide estimates of the impact of rate cuts in corporate income taxes." She went on to say that "C.B.O. is currently planning to undertake an in-depth study of the issue of the incentive effects of large tax cuts and the impact of reductions in business taxes. This will enable us to address these issues in greater detail in the future." (See *Congressional Record*, July 27, 1978, pp. H7445-46.)

[41]Killingsworth and King (1977, p. 21).

the Senate Budget Committee, which "implies that the gross cost per job created by a tax cut is about $25,000, and the gross cost for a PSE job is about $8,000" (p. 23). (As Meiselman indicates, the "cost" here is the assumed expense to the Treasury, not the cost to the public or the taxpayers.)[42]

C.B.O. assumes that corporate income tax rate reductions are an even weaker tool of employment policy. When asked by Representative Rousselot, a member of the Budget Committee, about C.B.O.'s use of an econometric model which reported declines in GNP in the event of a reduction in corporate income tax rates, Dr. Rivlin replied, "While we do not believe that corporate tax rate cuts reduce investment, it would not be surprising to find that tax cuts had only a minor expansionary effect."[43]

If, as Milton Friedman and some other economists believe, tax reductions deter spending increases, the C.B.O. analysis which asserts that tax reductions are relatively ineffective, weakens one possible constraint on spending increases.

Two other goals of the new budget process are to gain control over "backdoor" spending and to limit presidential impoundment power. It seems to us that since the existing incentives for Congress are not changed by the Act, whether the Congress uses the budget process to exercise control over "backdoor" spending will depend upon the extent to which the budget can accommodate everyone's spending priorities. If not, "backdoor" spending will continue to relieve the pressure.

The purpose of the impoundment control section of the Budget Act, of course, was to reduce presidential constraints on congressional spending. We predict that this section of the Act will be the most successful. Future Presidents will not have the opportunity, as did Nixon, of attempting to limit the growth of federal spending and the size of the deficit by supplementing the use of the veto with the refusal to spend funds appropriated by Congress. Thus, the effect of this section of the Budget Act will be toward more rather than less expenditures.

After writing all of this, we must admit that the analytical deficiencies, the biases, and information content of the C.B.O.'s model may be the wrong focus. C.B.O. does not have the power to change the incentives faced by politicians and bureaucrats in a democracy. To understand better how C.B.O. is constrained by the process, consider this question: What would happen if C.B.O. abandoned their Keynesian model? Would C.B.O. be ignored or would the new Congressional budget process be abandoned? Where does the more critical analytical error lie--in the C.B.O.'s macro model or in the economist's public policy model?

---

[42] Meiselman (1978).

[43] See *Congressional Record* (July 11, 1978, pp. H6473-74).

Is it correct to assume that public policymakers maximize their own interest by maximizing the public's welfare or that, alternatively, people who happen to have jobs in which they effectively make public policy maximize their own interests independently of the public's welfare or possibly even at the expense of the public's welfare? Is this an unexamined assumption–that people in the private sector maximize their own profits or utility, whereas people in government do not–reflecting a normative commitment to democracy and a dichotomy in the economist's assumption about behavior?

There is a growing literature that explains politicians as private entrepreneurs who are not wholly constrained by the interests of their constituents.[44] In such a framework, the privateness of public policy becomes an issue.

---

[44]See, for example, Roberts and Rabushka (1973), Roberts (1976, 1978b), Meckling (1976a, 1976b), Jensen and Meckling (1976), Wagner (1977). See also LePage (1977), who writes in *Realites*:

> Most economists act as if they have two different weights or measures by which they analyze the private economy and the public economy. It is assumed that individuals in the private economy are egocentric, guided by narrow self-interests, whose motives must be subject to a collective control embodying the general interests of society. On the other hand, in the public economy the state, a divine supermachine, reflects the interest of the collectivity. It is operated by officials who are motivated by affirmation and respect for the public interest. It is this fiction from which we must escape.

Appendix

Statutory Tasks Assigned to C.B.O.

Listed in the order in which they appear in the Congressional Budget Act of 1974 (PL 93-344). Citations are to the US Code and, in parenthesis, to section numbers of PL 93-344.

(1) In general, provide information to the two Budget Committees on all matters within their jurisdiction, *2 USC 602(a), (202(a))*.

(2) On request, provide information to the appropriating and taxing committees, *2 USC 602(b), (202(b))*.

(3) On request of any other committee, provide information compiled under 1) and 2) plus "to the extent practicable," additional information which may be requested, *2 USC 602(c) (1), (202(c) (1))*.

(4) On request of a Member, provide information compiled under 1) and 2) plus "to the extent available," additional information which may be requested, *2 USC 602(c) (2), (202(c) (2))*.

(5) Perform the duties and functions formerly performed by the Joint Committee on Reduction of Federal Expenditures, *2 USC 602(e), (202(e))*, *see also 31 USC 571*.

(6) Annually on or before April 1, furnish to the Budget Committees a report on fiscal policy for the next fiscal year, to include a discussion of alternative levels of revenues, budget authority, outlays and tax expenditures, plus alternative allocations among major programs and functional categories, all in the light of major national needs and the effect on "balanced growth and development of the United States," *2 USC 602(f) (1), (202(f) (1))*.

(7) From time to time, furnish the Budget Committees such further reports as "may be necessary or appropriate," *2 USC 602(f) (2), (202(f) (2))*.

(8) Develop and maintain filing, coding and indexing systems for all information obtained by C.B.O. from the Executive Branch or from other agencies of the Congress, *2 USC 603(b), (203(b))*.

(9)   With respect to each committee bill providing new budget authority, furnish to the reporting committee for its consideration: (a) a comparison of the bill to the most recent concurrent resolution on the budget, (b) a 5-year projection of outlays associated with the bill, and (c) the amount of new budget authority and resulting outlays provided by the bill for State and local governments, *31 USC 1329(a) (1), (308(a) (1))*.

(10) With respect to each committee bill providing new or increased tax expenditures, furnish to the reporting committee for its consideration: (a) a report on how the bill will affect the levels of tax expenditures most recently detailed in a concurrent resolution on the budget, and (b) a 5-year projection of the tax expenditures resulting from the bill, *31 USC 1329(a) (2), (308(a) (2))*.

(11) Periodically, issue a scorekeeping report on the results of Congressional actions compared to the most recently adopted concurrent resolution on the budget, plus status reports on all bills providing new budget authority or changing revenues or the public debt limit, plus up-to-date estimates of revenues and the public debt, *31 USC 1329(b), (308(b))*.

(12) Annually, "as soon as practicable after the beginning of each fiscal year," issue a 5-year projection of budget authority and outlays, revenues and tax expenditures, plus the projected surplus or deficit, year by year, *31 USC 1329(c), (308(c))*.

(13) Prepare "to the extent practicable," a 5-year cost estimate for carrying out any public bill or resolution reported by any committee (except the two appropriating committees), *31 USC 1353, (403)*.

(14) Jointly study with OMB, but separately report, on the feasibility and advisability of year-ahead budgeting and appropriating, the report to be made by February 24, 1977, *31 USC 1020 note, (502(c))*.

(15) Cooperate with the Comptroller General in the development of standard fiscal terminology, *31 USC 1152(a) (1), (801(a)), (Sec 202(a) (1) of the Legislative Reorganization Act of 1970)*.

(16) Cooperate with the Comptroller General in developing an inventory of fiscal information sources, providing assistance to Congress in obtaining information from those sources and furnishing, on request, assistance in appraising and analyzing information so obtained, *31 USC 1153(b), (801(a)), (Sec 203(b) of the Legislative Reorganization Act of 1970).*

(17) With the Comptroller General, establish a central file or files "of the data and information required to carry out the purposes of this title," *31 USC 1153(c), (801(a)), (Sec 203(c) of the Legislative Reorganization Act of 1970).*

(18) Cooperate with OMB in providing useful federal fiscal information to State and local governments, *31 USC 1153(d), (801(a)), (Sec 203(d) of the Legislative Reorganization Act of 1970).*

CONGRESSIONAL BUDGET OFFICE

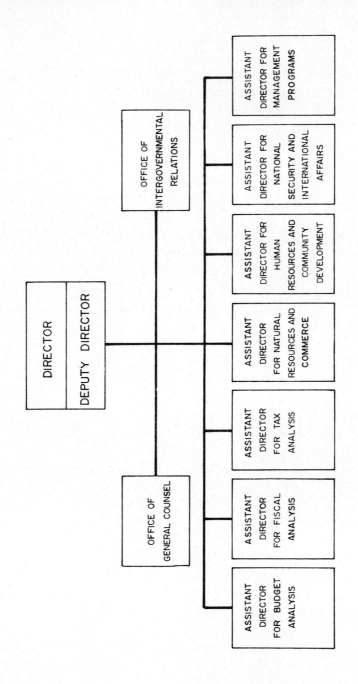

Figure 3

References

Boskin, M.J. (1978), "Taxing, Saving and the Rate of Interest," *Journal of Political Economy*, **86**: S3-S27.

Clarkson, K.W., and Meiners, R.E. (1979), "Institutional Changes, Reported Unemployment and Induced Institutional Changes," *Carnegie-Rochester Conference Series*, 10, eds. K. Brunner and A.H. Meltzer. Amsterdam: North-Holland.

Ellwood, J.W., and Thurber, J.A. (1977), "The Congressional Budget Process, Its Causes, Consequences, and Possible Success, *Legislative Reform and Public Policy*, eds. S. Welch and J. Peters. New York: Praeger.

Friedman, M. (1977), "Inflation and Unemployment" (Nobel Prize Lecture), *Journal of Political Economy*, **85**: 451-72.

Friedman, M., and Schwartz, A. (1963). *A Monetary History of the United States: 1867-1960*. Princeton, N.J.: Princeton University Press.

Jensen, M.C., and Meckling, W.H. (1976), "Theory of the Firm: Managerial Behavior, Agency Costs and Ownership Structure," *Journal of Financial Economics*, **3**: 305-60.

Kennedy, E.M. (1978), "Kennedy Criticizes Congressional Committee System for Abuses of Tax System." Press Release, April 16, 1978.

Killingsworth, C.C., and King, C.T. (1977), "Tax Cuts and Employment Policy," *Jobs Creation--What Works*, ed. R. Taggart. Olympus Press.

LePage, Henri (1977). *Realites*. November, 1977.

McNees, S.K. (1976), "The Forecasting Performance in the 1970s." Federal Reserve Bank of Boston. Updated and corrected version of "The Forecasting Performance in the Early 1970s." *New England Economic Review*, July-August: 29-40.

_____(1977), "An Assessment of the Council of Economic Advisers' Forecast of 1977," *New England Economic Review*, March-April: 3-7.

Meckling, W.H. (1976a), "Towards a Theory of Representative Government." Paper read at the Third Annual Conference on Analysis and Ideology, June, 1976, Interlaken, Switzerland.

_____(1976b), "Values and the Choice of the Model of the Individual in the Social Sciences," *Schweizerische Zeitschrift fur Volkswirtschaft and Statistik,* December, 1976.

Meiselman, D.I. (1976a), "Money, Factor Proportions, and Real Interest Rates." Testimony at Congressional Hearings, House, Committee on Banking, Currency and Housing, 94th Congress, 2nd Session, June 9, 1976.

_____(1976b), "More Inflation: More Unemployment," *Tax Review.* January, 1976. New York: The Tax Foundation.

_____(1978), "Welfare Reform and the Carter Public Service Employment Program: A Critique. University of Miami School of Law, Law and Economics Center Occasional Paper.

Meiselman, D.I., and Davis, R.R. (1978), "Unemployment and the Variability of Inflation." Paper read at meetings of the Western Economic Association, June, 1978, Hawaii. Mimeographed.

Perloff, J.M., and Wachter, M. (1979), "A Production Function--Nonaccelerating Inflation Approach to Potential Output: Is Measured Potential Output Too High?" *Carnegie-Rochester Conference Series,* 10, eds. K. Brunner and A.H. Meltzer. Amsterdam: North-Holland.

Public Law No. 93-344, Title III, Section 300.

Roberts, P.C. (1976), "The Political Economy of Bureaucratic Imperialism," *The Intercollegiate Review,* **12**: 3-11.

_____(1978a), "The Breakdown of the Keynesian Model," *The Public Interest,* No. 52: 20-33.

_____(1978b) "Idealism in Public Choice Theory," *Journal of Monetary Economics,* **4**: 603-15.

Roberts, P.C., and Rabushka, A. (1973), "A Diagrammatic Exposition of an Economic Theory of Imperialism," *Public Choice*, **14**: 101-107.

Roberts, P.C., and Van Cott, T.N. (1978), "Restrictive versus Permissive Money: Two IS-LM Views of Pure Fiscal Action," *Public Finance Quarterly*, **6**: 267-76.

U.S. Congress (1976). *The Congressional Budget Office: Responsibilities and Organization*. Washington, D.C.: U.S. Government Printing Office.

U.S. Congress, Congressional Budget Office (1975a). *Inflation and Unemployment: A Report on the Economy*. Washington, D.C.: U.S. Government Printing Office.

_____(1975b). *Recovery: How Fast and How Far?* Washington, D.C.: U.S. Government Printing Office.

_____(1975c). *A Simplified Wage-Price Model*. Washington, D.C.: U.S. Government Printing Office.

_____(1976). *Budget Options for Fiscal Year 1977: A Report to the Senate and House Committees on the Budget*. Washington, D.C.: U.S. Government Printing Office.

_____(1977a). *Closing the Fiscal Policy Loop: A Long-Run Analysis*. Technical Analysis Paper. Washington, D.C.: U.S. Government Printing Office.

_____(1977b). *The C.B.O. Multipliers Project: A Methodology for Analyzing the Effects of Alternative Economic Policies*. Technical Analysis Paper. Washington, D.C.: U.S. Government Printing Office.

_____(1978). *Understanding Fiscal Policy*. Washington, D.C.: U.S. Government Printing Office.

U.S. Congress, House, Committee on the Budget (1976). *The Congressional Budget and Impoundment Act of 1974: A General Explanation*. Washington, D.C.: U.S. Government Printing Office.

U.S. Congress, House (1977). *Congressional Record*. November 15, 1977.

_____(1978a). *Congressional Record*. July 11, 1978.

_____(1978b). *Congressional Record*. July 27, 1978.

Wagner, R.E. (1977), "Economic Manipulation for Political Profit: Macro-economic Consequences and Constititional Implications," *Kylos,* **30**: 395-410.

A COMMENT ON THE MEISELMAN AND ROBERTS PAPER

Frank DE LEEUW*

Bureau of Economic Analysis

The central contention of the Meiselman-Roberts paper is that the macro-economic analysis of the Congressional Budget Office (C.B.O.) is a calamity. To come to grips with this contention, I shall attempt to summarize and discuss what the paper has to say about five topics: (1) the nature and impact of C.B.O.; (2) how fiscal policies work; (3) how monetary policies work; (4) C.B.O. forecasts; and (5) miscellaneous assertions about C.B.O. I conclude that very little of the Meiselman-Roberts case withstands careful examination.

1. The Nature and Impact of C.B.O.

Summary. C.B.O. and the new budget process, according to this paper, have "institutionalized Keynesian fiscal policy rather than budget balance as the concept of budget control." "Proposed deficits," the paper claims, "now emanate from a professional staff as scientific economic policy recommendations upon which the nation's level of employment and rate of economic growth depend." Some statements in the paper suggest that the result has been increased support for a big and growing federal government. Toward the end of the paper, however, the view is advanced (based on a theory concerned with the shortcomings of representative government) that the new budget process and C.B.O. have not changed anything since they have not changed the incentives faced by Congressmen and other policymakers.

Comment. The germ of truth in these assertions, it seems to me, is that C.B.O.'s economic analysis has been based on the premise that discretionary fiscal policy is possible and can, if well designed, help to stabilize the economy. C.B.O. reports have on occasion discussed challenges to this view by monetarists and rational-expectations theorists,[1] but these opposing views have not been adopted in presentation of fiscal policy options.

What seems to me erroneous about the Meiselman-Roberts view is: (*a*) the implication that C.B.O. makes policy recommendations; and (*b*) the assumption that the C.B.O. framework of analysis always makes deficits look desirable. With respect to policy recommendations, the paper itself contains a quotation

---

*Views expressed in this comment are my own and do not necessarily represent those of the Bureau of Economic Analysis, where I am presently employed, or the Congressional Budget Office, where I was employed during 1975-77.

[1] See, for example, U.S. Congress, Congressional Budget Office (1978a, pp. 42-43) for a recent discussion of the rational-expectations view.

from a document summarizing C.B.O.'s responsibilities, stating that "'C.B.O. does not make recommendations on policy matters but provides Congress with options and alternatives for its consideration.'" Elsewhere, however, the paper seems to ignore this quotation. Making policy recommendations requires a set of goals (and weights attached to those goals) as well as a framework of analysis, and C.B.O. has not attempted to formulate its own goals for the economy.

With respect to deficits, even a policymaker equipped with a set of goals and accepting an analytical framework in which fiscal policy matters would not necessarily favor deficits or higher spending. If his goal, for example, were to bring actual GNP toward potential GNP, then his views about desirable fiscal policy changes would depend on an analysis of the outlook for GNP relative to potential under current policies (including an assumption about monetary policy). Certainly at times this process would lead to recommendation of budget balance or surplus rather than deficits.[2] The Meiselman-Roberts view is, I believe, far too heavily affected by the fact that during most of C.B.O.'s existence the economy has been in a relatively depressed state and expansionary policies have looked attractive to many policymakers.

It is important to keep in mind that fiscal policy analysis has been only a part of C.B.O.'s total output. Examination of even a small portion of the rest—for example, the analyses of energy and welfare reform proposals—will, I believe, quickly dispel the notion that C.B.O. has been an automatic friend of big government. Although Meiselman and Roberts do note the existence of this other output, they argue that "studies of specific spending proposals and the score-keeping reports" have no connection with "the determination of the overall level of outlays and the size of the deficit." This argument about the irrelevance of other C.B.O. activities to budget totals seems to assume that C.B.O.'s fiscal analysis leads to some unique (or narrowly circumscribed) path of the deficit, and that a deficit leads to a unique level of outlays. I have argued above that neither assumption is accurate.

Finally, it is hard for me to believe that even the authors take too seriously their argument that C.B.O. is irrelevant to the future of the budget and the federal government because it has not changed the incentives facing policymakers. The Meiselman-Roberts paper has not changed incentives facing policymakers either; do the authors conclude that it is similarly irrelevant to the future of the budget? The tone of the paper belies any such conclusion. The evident zeal of the authors to press their criticisms of C.B.O. suggests to me that they accept—as I do—the relevance of analytical frameworks, reports, and arguments to public policy outcomes.

---

[2] It would not in itself, furthermore, lead to any conclusion about the desirable size of government, which even in the simplest analytical framework is independent of the degree of fiscal stimulus or restraint.

2. How Fiscal Policies Work

Summary. The paper reviews four C.B.O. documents dealing with the impact of fiscal policy. The review of a technical paper entitled *The C.B.O. Multipliers Project* concludes that C.B.O. relies on a simple income-expenditure model in which GNP depends solely on exogenous categories of spending and on tax rates. In their review of an unpublished C.B.O. note on a two-equation wage-price model, Meiselman and Roberts conclude that the constraints imposed in estimating the model are inappropriate, and that they do not "see any economics behind these numerical exercises." The short discussion of the paper entitled *Closing the Fiscal Policy Loop: A Long-Run Analysis* is even more critical; I believe that the essence of the criticism is that the paper uses an income-expenditure framework to make long-run projections, where such a framework is even more misleading than in the short-run. Finally, the discussion of a C.B.O. paper entitled *Understanding Fiscal Policy* is particularly critical of C.B.O.'s treatment of the effects of after-tax wage rates on the supply of labor. C.B.O. is also alleged to be biased against the reduction of income taxes as compared to other forms of fiscal stimulus. Intertwined with these discussions of fiscal policy are discussions of monetary policy, to which I shall turn in the next section.

Comment. C.B.O.'s fiscal policy analysis has, I believe, been based on a "mainstream view" of macroeconomics. Oversimplifying somewhat, this view might be described as an IS-LM structure augmented by significant wealth effects, by linkages with the world economy, and by a wage-price adjustment process in which labor market tightness plays a major role. A permanent-income or life-cycle view of consumption and a steeply sloping or vertical long-run Phillips curve are important parts of the framework. So are time-lags in key relationships, in part reflecting the assumption of adaptive expectations in much market behavior.

Meiselman and Roberts attribute a different view to C.B.O., a much simpler income-expenditure framework characterized as "largely derived from the relatively unsophisticated Keynesian models of the 1950s." Much of their discussion of fiscal policy is occupied with criticisms of this simpler view. I agree with their criticisms of this view, but I believe they are seriously mistaken in attributing this view to C.B.O. The following paragraphs examine their case.

a. Fiscal policy multipliers. One important source of confusion is the authors' discussion of the "Multipliers Model" as if it were a structural model of the economy.[3] The model is a device for factoring fiscal policy multipliers

---

[3] Perhaps the multipliers document itself contributed to the confusion with the statement that "the basic model presented there is in fact the one C.B.O. has used for nearly all its policy simulation work." "Model" was not intended to mean "structural model" in that sentence, but perhaps it is easy to misinterpret it in that way. The sentence would have been clearer if it had said, "The policy multipliers presented there are in fact the ones. . ."

into various component ratios such as the ratio of the change in consumption to the change in disposable income, the ratio of the change in disposable income to the change in GNP, and so forth. As Meiselman and Roberts note, the model is essentially an algebraic device for comparing five different short-run models of the economy and for chosing sets of fiscal multipliers to use in analyzing changes in purchases of goods and services, personal income taxes, transfers, and certain types of grants. The purpose of the exercise was to develop an explicit and consistent way of responding to the continual flow of requests for policy simulations, rather than shifting from one model to another or relying exclusively on one model even in areas where it seemed implausible.

The parameters, or ratios, in the Multipliers Model are clearly reduced-form results of the five underlying models and have no unique structural interpretation. This is made clear at the outset, where it is stated (U.S. Congress, Congressional Budget Office, 1977b, p. 3) that each of the ratios

> summarizes a wide range of price and wealth responses as well as income-expenditures relationships incorporated in the full-scale models. For example, one of the coefficients in the simple model (a_2) is the ratio of a change in fixed investment to a change in GNP. The value of this ratio in a particular model is not simply a naive accelerator coefficient but rather reflects the net outcome of all the investment determinants in that model, including accelerator-type forces, cost of capital components, and a range of other influences (all as of early 1977). The ratio could be less than zero in a model with very strong "crowding-out" forces, or it could be greater than zero in a model with strong accelerator-type forces. The same is true of the other coefficients in the simple income-expenditure model. . . .The coefficients of the basic model are thus reduced-form rather than structural relationships.

Meiselman and Roberts, after acknowledging that the ratios are intended to be reduced-form relationships, go on to treat them as structural parameters. Thus, the ratio of the change in investment to the change in GNP is referred to as "little more than a simple accelerator modified to exclude public employment expenditures from GNP," and other ratios are also given a structural interpretation. Actually, the ratios in the study are the result of complete model simulations in which interest rates, relative prices, and other investment determinants change as well as total GNP. The investment-to-GNP ratio for each model is the result of the following steps: (1) simulate a $10-billion step change in government purchases starting in early 1977; (2) record the impact of this change on investment; (3) record the impact of this change on GNP less public employment spending; (4) calculate the ratio of (2) to (3), quarter by quarter. Clearly, such a ratio can be calculated for *any* model in which fiscal policy has some impact. Nothing follows from the existence of this ratio about the structure of behavior in any underlying model, and the ratio calculated this way need not (and, in this exercise, does not) lie anywhere close to the average ratio of actual investment to actual GNP.

I would fully agree with the Meiselman-Roberts criticism of the Multipliers Model if it were used as a structural model. It is not, however; the structure of economic behavior assumed in the Multipliers Project is some blend of the structures represented in the five underlying models. Speaking broadly, these structures reflect the mainstream view of macroeconomics described above, although each model has special features which depart from this view.

One indication that C.B.O. uses much more than a simple income-expenditure analytical framework is the range of factors considered in the discussions of economic developments in its semiannual reports on the economy. In the latest report, for example, (U.S. Congress, Congressional Budget Office, 1978a, pp. 15-20) the outlook for consumption is discussed not only in terms of disposable income, but also in terms of price expectations, consumer debt, interest rates, capital gains, and tax rates. Business fixed investment is discussed not only in terms of capacity utilization in the U.S., but also in terms of excess capacity in Europe and Japan; the prospective rate of return including the effect of historical-cost depreciation, uncertainty about prices, government regulations, and macroeconomic policy; the stock market; and prices of construction and equipment. There is far more in the C.B.O. view of how the economy works than a simple relation between consumption and disposable income with static expectations, or a naive accelerator coefficient.

b. Wages and prices. The two-equation price-wage model which the paper criticizes is also a "mainstream" model in which the rate of wage increase depends on unemployment and current and past price increases, while the rate of increase in prices depends on current and past wage increases and on two exogenous elements, farm prices and fuel prices. As the first sentence of the model description notes, it is essentially the framework used by Tobin, R.J. Gordon, and others in recent writings on inflation. The criticism that "we do not see any economics" in this two-equation model has, I believe, some justification if it refers to the difficulty of providing microeconomic foundations for aggregate price-wage behavior. It is hard for me to see that it has any special relevance to the Congressional Budget Office.

It is helpful to understand the purpose of this two-equation exercise. C.B.O.'s initial attempts to simulate policy changes gave price results which were hard to believe; as of mid-1975, simulations of expansionary policies improved productivity so much that they actually lowered prices in the short-run. C.B.O. reported these results (as Meiselman and Roberts note), and it also reported that the results were hard to believe (as Meiselman and Roberts fail to note).[4] The two-equation model was estimated so that C.B.O. would not be forced to rely on results of this sort in future reports.

c. *The budget and the economy.* Another technical paper, *Closing the Fiscal Policy Loop: A Long-Run Analysis* is harshly criticized but not explained apart from a flow diagram, which I would guess to be largely incomprehensible out of context. The study was intended to demonstrate the shortcomings of the standard method for making long-run budget projections, in which economic developments are allowed to affect the budget, but the budget is not allowed to have any effect on the economy. The paper introduced a simple and flexible two-way interaction between the budget and the economy to illustrate how the standard method could be misleading. There was no intention to construct a complete model of an economy. I believe the paper had some success in accomplishing its purpose.

I agree with Meiselman and Roberts, however, that the paper is a completely unsatisfactory framework for analyzing the economy in the long-run. The subtitle *A Long-Run Analysis* is surely inaccurate if it is taken to refer to the long-run of economic theory in which capital stocks and expectations adjust fully to equilibrium values. The detailed assertions about the model--that it assumes static expectations, that households have no assets and no capital management decisions, and so forth--do not seem to me justified if the model is viewed simply as a way of making a point about the budget and the economy; the criticisms do seem justified if the model is viewed as a complete model of the economy in the long-run.

There is a danger of overreliance on this model. Criticisms of it should be taken seriously. I wish that Meiselman and Roberts had explained and criticized the model more carefully, instead of relying largely on undocumented denunciation in this section of their paper.

d. *Understanding fiscal policy.* The paper finds what it believes to be a fundamental defect in the treatment of the supply of labor by C.B.O. (and by mainstream macroeconomists generally). In its discussion of the supply of labor,

---

[4] See U.S. Congress, Congressional Budget Office (1975, pp. 53-55, 67).

C.B.O. noted that the income and substitution effects of a change in after-tax wage rates work in opposite directions so that even at the theoretical level there is no clear presumption that an increase in the after-tax wage will increase or reduce the supply of labor. The Meiselman-Roberts paper, however, denies that this theoretical ambiguity exists and claims that at least at the aggregate level there is only a substitution effect. The argument seems to be that if there were an income effect—that is, if higher after-tax wage rates had any tendency to reduce willingness to work—then a tax cut could not expand GNP, as a majority of macroeconomists claim it does.

There are, I believe, two flaws in this argument. The first is that a change in incentives to work has its direct effect on *willingness* to work but not necessarily on actual hours worked. Its direct impact, in other words, is on the labor force and on potential GNP rather than on employment and on actual, realized GNP. Unless actual GNP is always equal to potential GNP, there is therefore no contradiction between the proposition that a tax cut expands GNP and the proposition that it does not change, or even that it reduces, willingness to work and hence potential GNP. In the long-run in a stable economy, there *is* a tendency for actual GNP to bear a fixed relation to potential GNP; accordingly, in the long-run a policy which reduces the supply of labor reduces growth. In a period of a few years, however, the equivalence of actual and potential GNP certainly does not hold.

The second flaw in the argument is perhaps more a matter of exposition than basic disagreement. Even in the long-run, if one believes that an increase in after-tax wage rates expands GNP, it does not follow that there is *no* income effect. It merely follows that the substitution effect is greater than the income effect.

In spite of this disagreement with the logic of the Meiselman-Roberts criticism, I agree with the point that the supply of labor and its responsiveness to after-tax wage rates deserves more attention from C.B.O. and from macro-economists generally. One reason is that proponents of large federal income tax cuts have been making strong assertions about this responsiveness, assertions which should be tested carefully. Another reason is that recent analyses of the Seattle and Denver income maintenance experiments have implied larger substitution effects (e.g., larger reductions in work effort in response to high tax rates) than earlier studies indicated. The weight of evidence as to the importance of labor supply responses, in other words, may be shifting, at least for one group of the population.

The argument that C.B.O. is biased against income tax reductions is marred by selective and misleading quotation. Thus, it is stated that *Understanding Fiscal Policy* calls attention "to the restrictive effect of the higher federal deficit and higher interest rate" in the case of an income tax cut, but not in the case of a public employment program. In actuality, the statement about income taxes uses a tax cut as one example of fiscal policy changes in general. The statement reads,

> When personal tax rates are reduced, to take one example, an immediate expansionary effect occurs when some of the increase in take-home pay is spent on goods and services. In contrast, a restrictive effect occurs when the higher federal deficit resulting from a tax cut leads to more federal borrowing and higher interest rates. Respending effects and financing effects are two of the forces unleashed by a reduction in tax rates. They are not the only two. (U.S. Congress, Congressional Budget Office, 1978b, p. 1)

Shortly afterwards the report states that

> any change in fiscal policy–a tax increase, a new spending program, a change in the provisions of an income support program--sets in motion a number of forces whose effects spread through the entire economy. (U.S. Congress, Congressional Budget Office, 1978b, p. 3)

It goes on to discuss these forces one by one, including financing effects. There is no singling out of an income tax with respect to restrictive effects.

To take another example, the paper states that "distributional issues are apparently only raised by personal income tax reductions. . .,and not by increases in government spending programs." In actuality, *Understanding Fiscal Policy* refers to distributional issues not only in connection with individual income tax but also in connection with other fiscal instruments. For example, in its discussion of transfer payments, the report notes that "decisions about transfer payments, like decisions about taxes, have special power to affect the incomes of particular groups--the retired, the unemployed, and veterans, among others" (U.S. Congress, Congressional Budget Office, 1978b, p. 43). In connection with public service employment, the paper notes that they can be targeted at "groups of workers whose average wages are relatively low" or "groups with especially high unemployment rates" (U.S. Congress, Congressional Budget Office, 1978b, pp. 45-46).

A third example of misstatement in this section of the paper is the assertion that C.B.O. is unable "to differentiate a tax rate reduction from a rebate of taxes on past incomes. . ." In actuality, *Understanding Fiscal Policy* does discuss the difference between a rebate and a permanent tax reduction, notes that a rebate can get out a lot of tax relief in a hurry, but then adds,

> there is widespread doubt, however, whether a rebate has nearly as much impact on the economy per dollar of costs (gross or net costs) as does the first year of the permanent cut in taxes. (U.S. Congress, Congressional Budget Office, 1978b, p. 38)

In summary, I recommend extreme skepticism about the section of the paper dealing with C.B.O.'s views on individual fiscal policy instruments.

3. How Monetary Policy Works

Summary. Monetary policy is discussed at two points in the paper. A review of the section of the Multipliers Report which compared the unborrowed reserve multipliers of five macroeconomic models sharply criticizes the use of unborrowed reserves as a measure of monetary policy. It notes that an average of the models' unborrowed reserve multipliers, which Meiselman and Roberts argue is below the true multiplier, implies that a dollar of additional unborrowed reserves has a much bigger effect on nominal GNP than a dollar of additional government purchases or personal tax reduction. The paper concludes that these estimates "are. . .compelling arguments for the importance of monetary policy and for placing greater reliance on monetary management in stabilization policy. . . ." Later, the paper reviews a C.B.O. discussion of the sensitivity of fiscal multipliers to what is assumed about monetary policy. The paper emphasizes one set of simulations cited by C.B.O. in which the real effects of a fiscal action, significant at first, fall to nearly zero by the end of three years if the path of the money supply is assumed to be unaltered by the fiscal action. This simulation is cited as "evidence that only money matters."

Comment. I agree with the authors that unborrowed reserves has serious defects as an indicator of monetary policy. The C.B.O. Multipliers Report, in fact, differentiated between fiscal policy multipliers, which it noted were frequently used by C.B.O. and the multipliers for unborrowed reserves, which, to my knowledge, have not been used.

343

Nevertheless, it seems to me that in performing fiscal policy simulations, unborrowed reserves may be a better monetary policy variable to hold to a fixed path than the money supply. The argument runs as follows: In simulations of fiscal policy, presumably it is desirable to make a realistic assumption about how monetary authorities will in fact react to a change in taxes or spending. One possibility would be to assume that the Federal Reserve will hold strictly to a target path of the money supply. Another assumption would be that the Federal Reserve will hold strictly to an interest-rate target path. I believe that the truth lies in between--that in the face of a fiscal policy move which alters the path of GNP, there will be some give in the path of money (perhaps taking the form of falling near the top or the bottom of the announced range of growth rates) and also some give in the path of interest rates. Neither a fixed money supply path nor a fixed interest rate path therefore seems to me the most likely response to a change in fiscal policy. What unborrowed reserves has in its favor is that its results (in the short-run) lie in between the results of holding to a fixed interest rate path and holding to a fixed money supply path. Better still would be a well-worked-out endogenous reaction function for the Federal Reserve, but it is very difficult to develop a convincing reaction function of this kind.

For describing monetary policy initiatives, as contrasted to monetary reactions to fiscal policy changes, unborrowed reserves has much less to recommend it. The discussion of this issue in the paper once again suffers from a confusion of reduced-form and structure. However, I agree with the paper's conclusions that unborrowed reserves is a poor indicator of monetary policy.

Unlike Meiselman and Roberts, I find only minor significance in the relative "bang for a buck" of unborrowed reserves or money on the one hand and fiscal policy instruments on the other. It has no necessary connection with how much of the variance in GNP is associated with monetary or fiscal policy changes; to take an extreme case, a policy instrument with a huge bang for a buck will account for none of the variance in GNP if it is never changed. "Bang for a buck" is one, but only one, element in calculating the relative advantage of using various policy instruments to achieve the same goal. On this score monetary policy rates high, since compared to fiscal policy instruments it has low resource costs per dollar and large macroeconomic effects per dollar. There are, however, other factors which I believe argue against exclusive reliance on monetary policy; they have to do with time-lags, uncertainty about the size of policy multipliers, and possible effects of the monetary-fiscal mix on aggregate savings, housing investment, and other variables.

With respect to the "evidence that only money matters,"[5] the paper misstates C.B.O.'s discussion. The chart reproduced in the paper (Figure 2), based on simulations of the MPS model, indicates that if the monetary response to a fiscal action is strict adherence to money supply targets, then the GNP and employment effects are minor by the third year. My view, argued above, is that the assumption of strict adherence to monetary targets is probably not realistic. Even if this assumption is made, however, zero effects during the third year are far different from no effects at all. The policy simulated is estimated, as the chart shows, to add 400,000 jobs after a year and only after that to decline gradually toward zero. This general time-contour–large effects shortly after implementation and zero effects later–could be a highly desirable feature of a discretionary policy instrument. Policymakers are often much more confident that they know the needs of the economy currently than that they know the needs of the economy in three years.

4. Forecasting

Summary. The paper presents three C.B.O. forecasts for the fourth quarter of 1976, made at three different dates. It concludes that the forecasts contain significant errors and that they were worse than averages of other forecasts.

Comment. I heartily endorse the conclusion that forecasts are subject to error. While the 1976 forecast errors do not seem to me seriously misleading, the general point is worth continuing emphasis because (1) there is often a tendency toward overconfidence on the part of forecasters and (2) there is often a tendency on the part of policymakers to minimize uncertainty, a factor very difficult to cope with intellectually in formulating policies.

Meiselman and Roberts's comparison of C.B.O. forecasts with other forecasts, however, suffers from some of the well-known pitfalls of forecast evaluation. First of all, while the dates of C.B.O.'s forecasts are given, the dates of the other forecasts are not. In fact, the dates of the other forecasts were close to the last of the three C.B.O. forecasts. The earlier C.B.O. forecasts should have been compared with what other forecasters were saying at earlier dates.

In the second place, the comparison of a single forecast with an average of other forecasts is a biased procedure. Each individual forecast can be worse than an average; for example, consider a set of two forecasts, one of which substantially overstates every variable and the other of which just as substantially understates every variable. Each individual forecast will be much worse than the

---

[5] It is interesting that the authors here use the term "evidence" to describe the results of large model simulations although elsewhere they complain that "there is no way to know whether there is any validity" to the results of such simulations.

average, but it does not follow that each individual forecast is worthless. Yet the Meiselman and Roberts paper, finding C.B.O.'s forecast worse than an average, concludes that "there was nothing gained by using C.B.O. forecasts." They should have compared C.B.O. forecasts with other individual forecasts rather than with an average.

More important than these points is the fact that the C.B.O. forecasts were *conditional* on the second concurrent budget resolution for fiscal 1976 and on current policy extrapolations of that budget. C.B.O. was saying, to oversimplify somewhat, "If fiscal policy follows the course Congress has enacted in its budget resolution, then this is our forecast for the economy." Since federal spending in fact fell some $11 billion below what Congress had enacted for fiscal 1976, and continued below current policy in subsequent quarters, the fact that actual GNP fell below the C.B.O. projection is no criticism of C.B.O.'s forecasting ability. The errors in budget targets and projections, of course, are an important problem for all forecasters. But in the projections reviewed in the Meiselman-Roberts paper, C.B.O. deliberately made no attempt to forecast the federal budget.

Finally, it should be noted that Meiselman and Roberts could easily have doubled the size of their sample by considering C.B.O. forecasts for 1977 as well as for 1976.

5. Other Assertions

Summary. This comment would be incomplete without reference to Meiselman and Roberts's many other assertions about C.B.O. In the second paragraph, for example, they assert that in C.B.O.'s economic analysis there is "demand without supply, inflation without money, interest rates without capital, outputs without inputs, employment without wage rates or a labor market," and a number of other transgressions. Other assertions, scattered through the paper, are too numerous to list. To cite just four: It is asserted that C.B.O. assumes a closed economy; that C.B.O. explains unemployment and inflation solely in terms of inertia (C.B.O.'s analysis is criticized by the statement that "Surely there is more to unemployment and inflation than inertia"); that monetary policy plays a "minor role in C.B.O.'s forecasts"; and that econometric models are presumed by C.B.O. to "project the future *without error.*"

Comment. A few of these assertions probably relate to points argued elsewhere in the paper. For example, the assertion that C.B.O.'s analysis contains "demand without supply" may well refer to the Multipliers Model considered as a structural model rather than a set of reduced-form ratios.

For most of the assertions, however, there is no supporting evidence and no relation to positions—valid or invalid—developed elsewhere in the paper. These unsupported assertions, as far as I can determine, are simply false.

6. Concluding Comment

Meiselman and Roberts missed an opportunity to write a useful paper. They could have examined critically what C.B.O.'s reports and testimony have had to say about recent inflation, about the interpretation of unemployment rates, about the slowing of productivity growth, and about policy options for alleviating these problems. They could have presented arguments and evidence for alternative views. The fact that they are dissenters from what was described earlier as the "mainstream view" of macroeconomics could have been an advantage in turning this task into an interesting and quite possible fruitful discussion.

I regret that they did not confront this task, but chose instead to write a polemic sorely deficient in logic and accuracy.

***

References

Meiselman, D.I., and Roberts, P.C. (1979), "The Political Economy of the Congressional Budget Office," *Carnegie-Rochester Conference Series*, **10**, eds. K. Brunner and A.H. Meltzer. Amsterdam: North-Holland.

U.S. Congress, Congressional Budget Office (1975). *Inflation and Unemployment: A Report on the Economy*. Washington, D.C.: U.S. Government Printing Office.

_____ (1977a). *Closing the Fiscal Loop: A Long-Run Analysis*. Washington, D.C.: U.S. Government Printing Office.

_____ (1977b). *The C.B.O. Multipliers Project: A Methodology for Analyzing the Effects of Alternative Economic Policies*. Washington, D.C.: U.S. Government Printing Office.

_____ (1978a). *Inflation and Growth: The Economic Policy Dilemma*. Washington, D.C.: U.S. Government Printing Office.

_____ (1978b). *Understanding Fiscal Policy*. Washington, D.C.: U.S. Government Printing Office.

THE RELATIONSHIP BETWEEN ECONOMICS AND POLITICS
A Response to Meiselman and Roberts

Marvin PHAUP*

Fiscal Analysis Division, Congressional Budget Office

The paper by Meiselman and Roberts expresses a prevalent view of the relationship between economists and politicians. This comment first summarizes and extends Meiselman and Roberts's conception of this relationship and then presents a different view which, I argue, is useful in indicating how economics could have a greater influence on political decisions and in explaining the behavior of policy analysts.

1. The Meiselman-Roberts View

Most of the Meiselman-Roberts paper is devoted to an evaluation of the economic content of studies prepared by C.B.O.'s Fiscal Analysis Division. If the caliber of analytic work done at C.B.O. is of any importance, it must be because policy analysis either does or could exert an influence on policy decisions. Meiselman and Roberts conclude, however, that because "C.B.O. does not have the power to change the incentives faced by politicians," the possibility that C.B.O. might "matter" is remote. Government-sponsored policy analysis exists principally to provide justification for policy decisions made on other grounds. Neither politicians nor their advisers have incentives to maximize the total good: politicians have no such incentives, because their greatest rewards arise from the service of rather narrow interests;[1] policy analysts also lack them, because they must win the favor of their politician employers. Even the advice provided by independent experts will not affect decisions. It will only be used if it suits a political purpose. Little social utility can be attached, therefore, to the attempt to provide scientific advice to politicians.[2] The advice will not be "scientific," or it will not be used, or it will be used improperly. Of course, the analyst has the option of presenting his advice directly to the electorate, which may then decide to change the incentive structure facing politicians. But within the closed, deterministic system envisioned by Meiselman and Roberts, one could not predict such an outcome because (*a*) analysts have no incentive to

---

*The views expressed are the author's and do not necessarily reflect either the views of other C.B.O. staff or the official position of the C.B.O. I am grateful to John W. Ellwood and Sandra Phaup for helpful comments.

[1] This proposition is developed more fully in Haveman (1976).

[2] The futility of policy analysis also arises in Roberts (1978). Tobin (1978) and Buchanan and Wagner (1978) are more hopeful.

provide such advice and (*b*) even if they did, it would make no difference because voter ignorance is not regarded as the cause of the present incentive structure. Thus, in the Meiselman-Roberts framework, political decisions are immune to the influence of science.

2. The Weber View

A different view of the relationship between science and politics may be found in Max Weber (1918a, 1918b) and in modern political science.[3] In this view, the distinctive features of science and politics stand in sharp contrast to each other. Both are worthy vocational callings, but they are governed by vastly different ethical imperatives.

The object of science is truth and knowledge; that of politics, power and action. Method is fundamental to science because it is precisely method that has led to scientific progress. It is a method peculiar to the aims of science. Value judgments must be avoided. Hypotheses must be clearly stated, logically developed, and, importantly, open to examination by other scientists. Other investigators must be able to replicate the tests of these hypotheses. By contrast, in politics, method is a matter of personal choice. Further, whereas scientists approach their work with a strong sense of uncertainty and tentativeness, politicians approach theirs with a confident interest in determining the "facts." Attitude toward the definiteness of knowledge may be the litmus test for distinguishing between the politician and the scientist.

As Eckstein (1967, pp. 148-49) puts it,

> . . .since choice is the essential business of politics--choices of ultimate goals that require moral commitments and of immediate means that cannot be purely technical since they may have to be selected upon inadequate technical knowledge and may pose moral problems of their own-- politicians need, and generally develop, passionate convictions and a sense of certainty, even personal infallibility. The social scientist's vocation, per contra, is morally silent and implants a zealous uncertainty, dispassion, and tentativity, and a deep sense of fallibility of all personal beliefs and labors.

---

[3]See Eckstein (1967) and Price (1965), especially Chapter 5, "The Spectrum from Truth to Power." The most incisive presentation of the Weber view that I have encountered is Hargrove (1975). Unfortunately neither Hargrove's comments nor Niskanen (1975) have been published. I am indebted to Erwin Hargrove for the references to Eckstein and Price.

The limits of scientific knowledge define the domains of both science and politics. Scientific knowledge is never sufficient to settle a social issue. But where science cannot decide, politics must. Nevertheless, there is evidence that politics cannot ignore firmly established scientific knowledge. Note, for example, the relatively free state of international trade among democratic states, the existence of policies directed toward increasing the rate of capital accumulation, the current movement toward deregulation of transportation. When scientists speak as a body, within the realm of their competence, the impact on public policy is palpable.

3. Two Implications of the Weber View

This view implies that an expanded body of scientific knowledge will further modify and prescribe the limits of politics in policy decisions. It is not by chance, but rather by virtue of its "hard science" qualities, that economics has dominated all other social sciences in their influence on public policy. Better science and greater economic knowledge is a promising course. But the future progress of science requires rejection of the notion that for science to have a bigger impact on politics, economists must adopt the ways of politicians. As Price observes (1965, p. 171),

> The union of the political and scientific estates. . .will not be improved if the two become like each other, but only if they respect each other's quite different needs and purposes.

Second, the view that scientists, even economists employed by the government, are more than hirelings suggests that policy organizations, like the C.B.O., will often behave in a manner that will seem "irrational" in the Meiselman-Roberts framework. The publication of the *Multipliers* report (Congressional Budget Office, 1977) is a good case in point. *Multipliers* sets out in reproducible detail the method by which C.B.O. converts five different estimates of fiscal impact into a single estimate of *the* effect of a contemplated budget change. Why would a maximizing apologist restrict his range of apologies by tying himself to a consistent method? Yet, this kind of openness is consistent with the view that analysts are scientists before they become government employees. They have specialized human capital as scientists. The market value of that capital is directly related to their standing with their scientific peers and hence to their adherence to the rules of scientific conduct. That is why an external evaluation of a policy analysis unit can be effective in counterbalancing the incentive structure described by Meiselman and Roberts.

351

Multipliers, however, is an illustration of one of the unsatisfactory solutions to the scientist-adviser dilemma created by the existence of multiple paradigms. The growth of scientific knowledge is aided by competition between alternative models of complex processes (and their developers). And this means that there is never a single state of the art model. *Multipliers* contains a restricted set of the universe of competing models. A different procedure would be to present policymakers with a set of alternative models as well as a set of alternative policies. My experience is that politicians are extremely annoyed by this multiple-model option. Given their attitudes toward the definiteness of knowledge, they view the "expert's" inability to choose between models as a sign of incompetence. Moreover, most scientists, when drawn into this competition either as participants or spectators, tend to become champions of one paradigm over another. Qualified witnesses are thus available who, when pressed, are willing to offer their judgment as to the superiority of one model. But, I know of no way by which economic science can maintain an essential distance from politics unless economists refuse, *qua economists*, to make such judgments.

References

Buchanan, J.M., and Wagner, R.E. (1978), "Dialogues Concerning Fiscal Religion," *Journal of Monetary Economics*, **4**: 627-36.

Eckstein, H. (1967), "Political Science and Public Policy," *Contemporary Political Science: Toward Empirical Theory*, ed. I. de Sola Pool. New York: McGraw-Hill.

Hargrove, E. (1975), Comments made to the American Economic Association Meeting, Panel on "How Can the Government's Need for Policy Research Be Better Met?" December, 1975, Dallas, Texas.

Haveman, R.H. (1976), "Policy Analysis and the Congress: An Economist's View," *Policy Analysis*, **2**: 235-50.

Meiselman, D.I., and Roberts, P.C. (1979), "The Political Economy of the Congressional Budget Office," *Carnegie-Rochester Conference Series*, **10**, eds. K. Brunner and A.H. Meltzer. Amsterdam: North-Holland.

Niskanen, W.A. (1975), "How Can Government Performance Be Improved by Policy Research?" Comments made to the American Economic Association Meeting, Panel on "How Can the Government's Need for Policy Research Be Better Met?" December, 1975, Dallas, Texas.

Price, D.K. (1965). *The Scientific Estate*. Cambridge, Mass.: Harvard University Press.

Roberts, P.C. (1978), "Idealism in Public Choice Theory," *Journal of Monetary Economics*, **4**: 603-15.

Tobin, J. (1978), "Comment from an Academic Scribbler," *Journal of Monetary Economics*, **4**: 617-25.

U.S. Congress, Congressional Budget Office (1977). *The C.B.O. Multipliers Project: A Methodology for Analyzing the Effects of Alternative Economic Policies*. Washington, D.C.: U.S. Government Printing Office.

Weber, M. (1918a), "Politics as a Vocation," *From Max Weber*, translators and eds. H.H. Gerth and C.W. Mills. New York: Oxford University Press.

_____(1918b), "Science as a Vocation," *From Max Weber*, translators and eds. H.H. Gerth and C.W. Mills. New York: Oxford University Press.

A COMMENT ON THE MEISELMAN AND ROBERTS PAPER

Alice M. RIVLIN
Congressional Budget Office

The Meiselman-Roberts paper is an attempt to evaluate the work of the Fiscal Analysis Division of the Congressional Budget Office (C.B.O.). The tasks performed by this division--largely preparing projections for the U.S. economy and estimating the impact of alternative fiscal policy proposals--are difficult. Consequently, C.B.O. is continually working to improve its analysis and welcomes responsible criticism. Unfortunately, very little constructive criticism can be found in this paper. Indeed, much of it is simply wrong. The fundamental problem with the Meiselman-Roberts analysis is that the authors misunderstand both the use and content of macroeconomic models and how C.B.O. analyzes issues concerning factor supply. In an attempt to reduce some of this misunderstanding, I will try to review C.B.O. procedures in those areas.

1. C.B.O.'s General Methodology

The new federal budget process requires that the Congress vote on the budget aggregates, both the broad functional categories and the overall spending ceiling and revenue floor.[1] The preparation of budget estimates begins with an economic projection and alternative projections for alternative policies. The budget process, then, requires both projections of economic activity and estimates of the incremental effect of alternative policies.

Although C.B.O. prepares fairly detailed economic and budget projections, C.B.O. has never assumed, as Meiselman and Roberts assert, that the various methodologies used can "project the future without error." Indeed, C.B.O.'s reports continually take note of uncertainty by such techniques as presenting economic forecasts in ranges, describing the sources of uncertainty in forecasts and estimates of the impact of alternative policies, and presenting views based on alternative methodologies.[2]

---

[1] "The Congressional Budget Act of 1974" (Public Law 93-344 § § 310(a) and 311(a)).

[2] See, for example, *The Economic Outlook* (U.S. Congress, Congressional Budget Office, 1978c). In this economic report, the GNP forecast generated from large macroeconomic models and other information was presented in ranges (p. 21), accompanied by a description of the major sources of uncertainty in the forecast (pp. 23-26). An alternative forecast, based on the St. Louis monetarist model, was also presented (p. 25). A section on measures to stimulate business investment described alternative theories and the wide divergence of empirical estimates, illustrated by simulations from three econometric models (pp. 31-35 and Appendix A).

In short, C.B.O. seeks the most defensible methods of analysis. As a result, C.B.O.'s analysis generally reflects the predominant view of informed economists. One outcome is that C.B.O.'s economic forecasts are usually similar to the consensus forecast, excepting for budget assumptions imposed on the C.B.O. projection.[3] It would be irresponsible for C.B.O. to present, as its best estimates, analysis based upon the views of a selected minority in the economics profession unless the superiority of that analysis could be demonstrated.

2. The Content and Use of Models

C.B.O. does make extensive use of a number of macroeconomic models.[4] It is recognized that these models have many shortcomings. But the Meiselman-Roberts characterization of C.B.O. analysis as "largely derived from unsophisticated Keynesian models of the 1950s" is not an accurate characterization either of these models or of C.B.O.'s use of them. Certainly, the commercial success of some of the large econometric models suggests that many others share my view.

Much of the misunderstanding evident in the Meiselman-Roberts paper appears to arise from a lack of familiarity with macroeconomic models and with C.B.O.'s use of them. It requires only a brief review of large econometric models to discover that they do not, as asserted by Meiselman and Roberts, "ignore the openness of the U.S. economy" or assume that consumption depends *only* on current disposable income. Also, contrary to Meiselman-Roberts, inflation is related to money growth in these models. A characteristic of many large macroeconomic models is that in the long run the price level is determined primarily by the money stock.

It is true, however, that large econometric models are relatively weak in terms of modeling supply-side effects. Much work is being done to improve this situation. C.B.O. is particularly concerned that this shortcoming limits the use of these models for long-run analysis. It is not evident, however, that this situation significantly distorts short-run analysis.

It is also true that the theory of rational expectations has not been incorporated into macroeconomic models. However, the Meiselman-Roberts statement that "Expectations are assumed to be static" is simply not true. Most models incorporate adaptive expectations--essentially distributed lags on

---

[3] Because the purpose of the forecast is to determine the outlook under a specified fiscal policy, budget assumptions may not be similar to the consensus.

[4] At this time, C.B.O. subscribes to three commercial models (Chase, DRI, and Wharton) and regularly examines the output of three others (MPS, Fair, and St. Louis). In addition, C.B.O.'s Fiscal Analysis Division has developed a few special-purpose models.

prices. Furthermore, it is not true that C.B.O. has "ignored" work on rational expectations, as indicated by Meiselman and Roberts.[5]

In addition to exhibiting confusion arising from unfamiliarity with the nature of econometric models, Meiselman and Roberts misunderstand the use of these models by C.B.O. C.B.O. does not use models in a slavish or mechanical way. Whether the purpose is forecasting or estimating the incremental impact of a policy change, the model results are tempered with judgment. As suggested earlier, this judgment is derived by studying evidence of all kinds. In some instances, the quantitative results of a model simulation conflict with the best available empirical evidence and, therefore, the results of the model are not used. In other circumstances, C.B.O. concludes that the models do not have the appropriate structure to deal with the problem at hand.[6]

3. C.B.O.'s Special-Purpose Models

The Multipliers Model. C.B.O. receives a large number of requests from members of the House and Senate for policy simulations. Some wish to see the results before policy changes are proposed. The Multipliers Model was developed as one means of responding to these requests. The model is based on "consensus" multipliers derived by comparing the responses of several large econometric models to fiscal policy shocks. The results of these exercises are summarized in a small number of equations in which the parameters represent a variety of ratios--the ratio of a change in consumption to the change in disposable income, the ratio of a change in investment to the change in GNP, and so on. The model is not a structural model, though the parameters are a "reduced form" summary result of the five structural models used in the original simulations. Thus the Multipliers Model provides C.B.O. with a cost-efficient and consistent way to respond to frequent requests for policy simulations.

Despite C.B.O.'s statements to the contrary, Meiselman and Roberts interpret the Multipliers Model as a structural model and thereby misunderstand its nature and application.[7] For example, Meiselman and Roberts give a structural interpretation to an equation expressing the change in fixed investment as a ratio of the change in GNP less the change in public employment spending (allowing for displacement); they suggest that the equation is "little more than a simple accelerator modified to exclude public employment

---

[5]For example, see *Inflation and Growth: The Economic Policy Dilemma* (U.S. Congress, Congressional Budget Office, 1978b, pp. 42-43).

[6]This was the judgment, for example, when C.B.O. was recently asked to simulate the impact of the integration of personal and corporate income taxes on macroeconomic models.

[7]*The C.B.O. Multipliers Project* (U.S. Congress, Congressional Budget Office, 1977, p. 3).

expenditures from GNP."[8] In fact, the equation reflects the structural complexity of the large models upon which it is based and is, therefore, much more than a simple accelerator. They go on to say that "the impact of a change in corporate profits taxes on the cost of capital or the effect of a differential tax cut on expenditure patterns or on relative rates of return are simply ignored." They leave the incorrect impression that, as a result of the structure of the Multipliers Model, C.B.O. ignores the impact of a change in corporate profit taxes. They neglect to state that C.B.O. has made it clear that the model has a limited purpose and is not intended to do simulations of corporate tax rate changes. Indeed, such simulations cannot be done on this model.[9] The fiscal policy changes that can be analyzed in this model are changes in purchases of goods and services, personal income taxes, transfers, and certain types of grants.

Since the Multipliers Model is not appropriate for the analysis of corporate tax rate changes, other tools are used for this purpose. For example, in a recent report, the macroeconomic impact of cutting the corporate tax rate was assessed by using simulations from three large econometric models.[10] In this way, the postwar record of the relationship between the cost of capital and investment activity was accounted for--not ignored--in the C.B.O. analysis.

Although C.B.O. has never used the Multipliers Model to analyze a change in monetary policy, the model does include summary ratios derived from the five large models, showing the effect of a change in unborrowed reserves on a few major components of GNP. Again, the reduced-form equations do not suggest a unique structure, though they do reflect the outcome of the structure contained in the five models. It appears that Meiselman and Roberts's main objection to the results of the model is that the money multiplier is not large enough. They attribute this to the fact that a step increase in unborrowed reserves above a baseline path lowers the velocity of money. They assert that C.B.O. ignores evidence that more money causes velocity to rise. "Despite the evidence that, during the short spans of time characteristic of major business cycle phases, M and V generally tend to move together, C.B.O. analyzes the economy using a model that denies this established result."

Even if it were true that M and V tend to move together over short periods of time, it does not follow that, other things being equal, V would not fall as a result of an increase in money supply. A tendency for M and V to move together may be explained by changes in expenditures and in the Federal

---

[8] They also incorrectly state that public employment expenditures reduce GNP.

[9] C.B.O. has been asked to investigate whether it is possible to develop "consensus" multipliers for corporate tax rate changes.

[10] *The Economic Outlook* (U.S. Congress, Congressional Budget Office, 1978c, pp. 47-49).

Reserve response to these changes over the cycle. Moreover, the "established result" that M and V move together is hardly a settled issue. A recent extensive empirical study of this issue (Gould, Miller, Nelson, Upton, 1978) concluded that analyses of postwar quarterly data are mixed. According to the study, "In general, there is a tendency for changes in velocity to offset changes in money" (pp. 245-46). Further, the study noted a disturbing sensitivity of the results to both changes in the time period and changes in the definition of money.

The Closing-the-Loop Model. The Meiselman-Roberts paper also criticizes C.B.O.'s "closing-the-loop" model. The model was developed by C.B.O. for a particular purpose. For years the federal government's long-run budget projections showed the budget moving into balance in outyears. But surpluses were rarely achieved, in part, because the economic assumptions and budget assumptions were not consistent. There was a clear need for improving budget projection methodology. The closing-the-loop analysis was designed to provide a simple framework for testing the consistency of GNP growth goals relative to fiscal policy projections under assumptions about the behavior of the nonfederal components of GNP, the composition of fiscal policy, and monetary policy.

The nature and application of this model also seem to be misunderstood by Meiselman and Roberts. The closing-the-loop model is not a structural or behavioral model of the economy, and Meiselman and Roberts are not accurate in asserting, for example, that the model has "no supply and no production" and that it is not suited for long-run analysis. The inherent flexibility of the closing-the-loop model does allow consideration of scenarios in which supply does respond to changes in fiscal policy or in which savings and investment rise together. More important, however, is the ability of this framework to highlight the assumptions and preconditions that would make such scenarios possible.

4. The Treatment of Aggregate Supply

Perhaps the most frequent assertion made by Meiselman and Roberts is that C.B.O. ignores issues of aggregate supply. The record does not support this claim.[11] It may be that the available econometric models do not handle supply-side effects as well as demand effects. But these large models are not devoid of supply-side effects; they include extensive treatments of supply--labor, physical capital, financial capital, and materials.[12] More important,

---

[11]The C.B.O.'s response to earlier criticism by Roberts--charging that C.B.O. uses models that ignore supply-side effects--was presented in earlier correspondence with Congressman Rousselot. C.B.O.'s views on this issue were recently amplified in a background paper, *An Analysis of the Roth-Kemp Tax Cut Proposal* (U.S. Congress, Congressional Budget Office, 1978a).

[12]U.S. Congress, Congressional Budget Office (1978a, Appendix).

when issues for which the big models are judged inappropriate are analyzed, C.B.O. turns to the available economic literature for evidence on which to base its conclusions. For example, the proposed Roth-Kemp tax cut is larger than previously enacted tax reductions; therefore, there is the possibility that non-linearities in actual adjustment processes--especially in factor supply response to changed incentives--would not be captured by large model simulations. Consequently, in its analysis of Roth-Kemp (ch. II), C.B.O. examined and summarized a large number of economic studies of the labor and savings response to changed marginal tax rates.[13] C.B.O. used this evidence to assess the likely supply impact of Roth-Kemp. Even then, C.B.O. was careful not to overstate its conclusion:

> One shortcoming of these empirical studies is that the Roth-Kemp tax reductions are themselves larger than previously experienced; these findings may therefore under-estimate the supply response. But even if there were a sharp increase in the total number of hours worked and in saving, it is not reasonable to assume that total productive capacity would increase quickly. Total demand can increase rapidly in response to tax cuts. But major capital projects take years to plan, design, finance, and put in place. Thus, even with a large labor and savings response, the Roth-Kemp tax reductions would risk widespread capacity shortages and an acceleration of inflation, because the increase in total demand is unlikely to be matched quickly by a corresponding increase in plant and equipment. (p. xiv)

The Meiselman-Roberts critique of C.B.O.'s treatment of aggregate supply results from an excessively casual reading of C.B.O. reports. Moreover, the Meiselman-Roberts critique is additionally flawed by their own economic analysis. A striking example is that the Meiselman-Roberts world is characterized by perpetual full employment.[14] Since they are abstracting from such problems as involuntary unemployment, the analytical simplicity of the Meiselman-Roberts world is appealing. Policymakers, however, cannot just assume problems away.

---

[13] This survey reviewed Michael Boskin's recent findings about the sensitivity of saving to variations in the real interest rate. Meiselman and Roberts criticize C.B.O. for not including reference to Boskin's study in *Understanding Fiscal Policy* (U.S. Congress, Congressional Budget Office, 1978d), even though this paper was published almost simultaneously with the Boskin paper.

[14] Involuntary unemployment can exist in their theoretical construct for only very short periods while workers remain ignorant of true labor market conditions.

The nature of the Meiselman-Roberts analytical framework heavily influences their critique of C.B.O.'s treatment of supply. For example, they write,

> C.B.O.'s argument that people respond to tax rate reductions by working less (or reducing their savings rate) is directed against the effectiveness of incentives in shifting the aggregate supply function. But if people were to respond to tax cuts by working less, real GNP would fall, and it would mean that Keynesian fiscal policy could not be expansionary.[15]

In the Meiselman-Roberts world where all resources are fully and productively employed, the conclusion that real GNP would fall is obvious. Even in a Keynesian model, expansionary fiscal policies do not increase output when there is full employment. Moreover, it is not appropriate to apply their analysis to a world in which involuntary unemployment exists. In such circumstances, a rise in total demand stimulated by the tax could result in higher employment and production, even if the income effect dominated the substitution effect. Meiselman and Roberts apparently believe that the question of the relative size of the income and substitution effects can be resolved by their choice of analytical framework without reference to the empirical evidence.

5. Conclusion

C.B.O.'s methodology for analyzing macroeconomic issues is to seek out the best evidence from a variety of sources. Economics is an imperfect science, and C.B.O. is constantly working to improve its models and procedures. To help in this endeavor, C.B.O. continually seeks out constructive criticism. For example, the Fiscal Analysis Division conducts periodic meetings with a group of outside advisors--drawn from a wide spectrum of economic thought--in order to obtain external evaluation of its forecasts and analyses. In addition, reports are reviewed by outside readers when possible prior to publication.

Unfortunately, the Meiselman-Roberts paper is not a useful critique of macroeconomics at C.B.O. It is flawed by fundamental errors in description and interpretation of C.B.O.'s work. As a result, it does little to help us in our efforts to provide the Congress with the best possible advice, and this outcome is most disappointing.

---

[15] In fact, the C.B.O. argument in question stated that people may respond by working less.

References

Gould, J.P., Miller, M.H., Nelson, C.R., and Upton, C.W. (1978), "The Stochastic Properties of Velocity and the Quantity Theory of Money," *Journal of Monetary Economics,* **4**: 229-48.

Meiselman, D.I., and Roberts, P.C. (1979), "The Political Economy of the Congressional Budget Office," *Carnegie-Rochester Conference Series,* **10**, eds. K. Brunner and A.H. Meltzer. Amsterdam: North-Holland.

"The Congressional Budget Act of 1974" (Public Law 93-344 § § 310(a) and 311(a).

U.S. Congress, Congressional Budget Office (1977). *The C.B.O. Multipliers Project: A Methodology for Analyzing the Effects of Alternative Economic Policies.* Washington, D.C.: U.S. Government Printing Office.

_____(1978a). *An Analysis of the Roth-Kemp Tax Cut Proposal.* Washington, D.C.: U.S. Government Printing Office.

_____(1978b). *Inflation and Growth: The Economic Policy Dilemma.* Washington, D.C.: U.S. Government Printing Office.

_____(1978c). *The Economic Outlook.* Washington, D.C.: U.S. Government Printing Office.

_____(1978d). *Understanding Fiscal Policy.* Washington, D.C.: U.S. Government Printing Office.